THE NATION
AND ITS CITY

THE NATION AND ITS CITY

Politics, "Corruption," and Progress in Washington, D.C., 1861–1902

Alan Lessoff

The Johns Hopkins University Press

Baltimore and London

© 1994 The Johns Hopkins University Press
All rights reserved
Printed in the United States of America
on acid-free paper

The Johns Hopkins University Press
2715 North Charles Street
Baltimore, Maryland 21218-4319
The Johns Hopkins Press Ltd., London

Library of Congress
Cataloging-in-Publication Data

Lessoff, Alan.
The nation and its city : politics, corruption,
and progress in Washington, D.C., 1861–1902 / Alan Lessoff.
p.   cm.
Includes bibliographical references (p.) and index.
ISBN 0-8018-4464-9 (alk. paper)
1. Washington (D.C.) — Politics and government — To 1878.
2. Washington (D.C.) — Politics and government — 1878–1967.
I. Title.
F198.L58   1994
975.3'03 — dc20   93-17513

A catalog record for this book is
available from the British Library.

Contents

Preface   *vii*

Acknowledgments   *xi*

Introduction   *1*

1

Washington and the Wartime Union   *15*

2

Improvers and Old Citizens   *44*

3

Energy and Engineering   *72*

4

The Origins of the District Commission   *101*

5

The District Commissioners and Congress   *130*

6

The Army Corps and Gilded Age Washington   *164*

7

An Unsectional Public   *199*

8

Promotional Government and Urban Planning   *233*

Conclusion   *268*

Note on Sources   *277*

Abbreviations   *283*

Notes   *285*

Index   *329*

Preface

L IKE SOME GOOD IDEAS, and many more bad ones, this book was born
in a bar. It was mid-September 1983, and Professor Ron Walters of
Johns Hopkins University, who had recently consented to serve as my
graduate advisor, offered to buy me a crabcake lunch at Frazier's, a local land-
mark in the Hampden section of Baltimore, in order to acquaint me better
with my new hometown.

As we ate, Ron and I discussed the condition of research in the areas of
American history that interested me most, political economy, cities, and social change. I reiterated my belief, which I had already foisted upon him in a
letter the previous summer, that historians were spending too much time
talking about how people adapted to the emergence of an urban, corporate,
industrial society, and not enough time talking about how people had built
the institutions and shaped the environments that composed this society.
I wanted to look at modern American life as something that people had
made, rather than as something that had happened to them, to study the
creation of cities as a human activity, rather than urbanization as an abstract
force.

Walters told me that my rambling letter had prompted him to hunt for a
specific episode that could highlight the question I raised. He recalled an
essay[1] that mentioned a controversy in Reconstruction Washington. A "ring"
of contractors and real estate developers had created a storm when they seized
control of the District government in order to implement a public works program of unprecedented speed, scale, and cost. If I was interested in what
people thought they were doing as they built the modern American city, what
could be more basic than a city's physical elements—asphalt, concrete, iron,
and brick? Perhaps I should look into who these people were, why they
wanted streets, water mains, and sewers so badly, and what bothered the
people who opposed them.

Professor Walters referred, of course, to the "District Improvement scandal," sparked by the Board of Public Works of 1871–74 and especially by its
flamboyant leader, Alexander R. Shepherd. I have now spent three times as
much time researching the "New Washington" that Shepherd helped set in
motion than the legendary so-called boss spent trying to implement it. I
quickly realized that the uproar surrounding Shepherd's furious drive to implement his "Comprehensive Plan of Improvements" was only the most dramatic episode in a story that went backwards and forwards. I could not un-

derstand the lively moments in that story, I decided, without understanding the quiet ones. What began as a master's essay thus swelled over years.

The resulting book is the only full-length study of Washington's municipal history written by someone who never lived in the capital and who has no special tie to it. Washington has engaged my attention not because it belongs to me but because its experience conveys important lessons about the American city and the American polity in general. What this study may lack in appreciation for subtleties evident to a Washingtonian I hope it gains through a removed perspective, which helped me to grasp that this city, which its residents are apt to consider unique, in fact reflects many national and international trends.

Originally, I became interested in Gilded Age efforts to "improve" Washington, to create a capital "worthy of the nation," because persons at the heart of that undertaking seemed very different from me, and yet they and their counterparts all across this country did an enormous amount to shape the American city as we now know it. I merely wanted to see the world through their eyes and to elucidate for the contemporary reader the perspective and methods of these people who left such a legacy.

The decade when I wrote this, however, witnessed the dissipation of the widespread hope, which I shared, that American cities might soon overcome their frustrating stagnation and begin to showcase admirable rather than distressing features of our society. It now seemed insufficient simply to recount what the creators of modern Washington had wanted to and did accomplish. I also had to examine why in Washington, as in every large American city, those who in the last century struggled successfully to provide impressive new public works and services at the same time failed to provide the political, institutional, and economic foundations that might have enabled these accomplishments to endure.

Like many recent writers on the American polity, I wondered if there was not a tendency deeply rooted in our history, governmental structure, and political culture to place obstacles in the way of efforts to pursue "public" goals in a "public-minded" fashion. This quality of American governance has seemed to manifest itself not only in city-building, but also in health care, education, housing, and indeed nearly every area of public concern where sound policy depends upon coordinating and balancing a wide variety of competing interests over a long period. This apprehension led me to look into what others have written about historical patterns of public sector/private sector relations in the United States. I came to believe that, despite Washington's unique function and economy, its political and civic leaders — like their counterparts at every level of government throughout the nineteenth century — operated within a political tradition and a governmental framework that equipped them to be more effective at spurring material progress than at harnessing it to serve public ends. In fact, public officials in America have often defined growth and material progress as ends in themselves, as if public goals were merely the sum of private ends — as if addition alone could make a nation. The creators of the modern urban environment at Washington and elsewhere built this dilemma into their cities, and we live with the consequences.

Like most historians, then, I admit that a current worry determined which features of the past I noticed most. I hope the reader finds this a case of enlightening, rather than debilitating, present-mindedness. It would be easy and comforting to distance ourselves from the intricate, often unsettling maneuvering through which the nation built itself a city by dismissing it as mere "corruption." The harder but truer and more useful lesson, I argue below, is that the drive to create a worthy Washington represented the natural unfolding of the politics of progress, as the Gilded Age understood it, and as in many ways, unfortunately, we still do.

Acknowledgments

FIRST OF ALL among those whose assistance I should acknowledge are the staffs of the libraries and archives where I carried out the bulk of my primary research: the National Archives, the Manuscript, Newspaper, and Current Periodicals divisions of the Library of Congress, the former Columbia Historical Society (now the Historical Society of Washington, D.C.), and the Washingtoniana Room of the District's Martin Luther King Memorial Library.

A research grant from the Everett McKinley Dirksen Congressional Leadership Research Center, Pekin, Illinois, enabled me to travel to view papers of three Senate leaders who had enormous influence over Washington's government and development: James McMillan's are at the Detroit Public Library; Francis G. Newlands's in the Manuscripts and Archives Division of the Yale University Library, which has granted permission to quote relevant passages; and the Iowa State Historical Department in Des Moines went to great trouble to make William B. Allison's papers available, despite being in the midst of a move to a new building and a midwestern winter storm. The Newberry Library in Chicago allowed me to use papers that shed light on the shadowy career of Orville E. Babcock. The Government Publications and Audio-Visual departments at Johns Hopkins University's library provided much help, as did the Dickinson College Library.

Without my doctoral advisor, Ronald G. Walters, I would never even have thought of this subject. While on a superficial level our interests have diverged since that late summer talk over crabcakes and beer, on a moral level, they grow ever closer, as I at last can see. Professor Louis Galambos, who often advises young scholars to develop their own point of view by "tunneling under" someone else's, offered constant, gracious encouragement, even though the theory I have tried to bore under is his. John Higham made several useful comments, the most memorable being that I should reflect carefully upon the cost of practicality in the Gilded Age. Colleagues who provided ideas and criticism included Kathryn Jacob, Stu McConnell, and Thomas Welskopp.

Washington's local historical community not only abided but abetted me. Howard Gillette of George Washington University read the manuscript twice and offered many practical comments on how to bring out my main points. Keith Melder of the Museum of American History supervised a semester spent as a Smithsonian Graduate Student Fellow. Steven Diner of George Mason

University took time at several stages to show me what I was thinking and where those thoughts came from. Others Washingtonians who helped include Ruth Ann and William Becker of George Washington University, Martin Gordon of the Office of History of the U.S. Army Corps of Engineers, Melissa McLoud of the National Building Museum, and Larry Baume and Elizabeth Miller, both formerly of the Columbia Historical Society.

Joseph Arnold of the University of Maryland, Baltimore County, provided a careful reading of an earlier version of chapter 6. Jessica Elfenbein did the same for chapter 7. Dr. Lothar Hönnighausen of the North American Program at the University of Bonn enabled me to test my major ideas in an essay (bits of which reappear here) for a volume that his program was publishing. Former colleagues at Dickinson College offered moral and practical support. The college subsidized many costs, especially towards the preparation of illustrations, as has my current employer, Texas A&M University-Corpus Christi. Dr. Robert J. Brugger of the Johns Hopkins University Press contemplated my offer to found a joint guano venture, the bats inhabiting the attic above where I wrote the final draft providing the necessary raw material. As we lacked capital, he was forced to revert to book editing, which he and copyeditor Anne Whitmore have performed with admirable sensitivity, frankness, and diligence. My colleague Robert Wooster rendered invaluable proofreading assistance.

Dan Gross and I were old friends already when this project began. As we became older friends, *he* also evolved into a Washingtonian — the capital being one city where adopted citizenship poses no bar to that status. My wife, Mineke Reinders, entered the picture several years after Washington's parks and streets, but of course occupies a larger place. She knows better than anyone what has driven me to revive such a parcel of long-dead rogues. Of her practical contributions, most visible is the artistic skill she applied to retouching some of the illustrations.

All errors of fact or judgment, as the disclaimer goes, belong to me alone.

THE NATION
AND ITS CITY

Introduction

There are many reasons why Washington should be considered a desirable place of residence, especially in winter, for persons of wealth and refinement. . . . but . . . we must arouse ourselves, remove nuisances, and contribute in every way to make our city attractive and pleasant. . . . It would prove the best investment our property holders could make. The wisest monarch of our age has set us a good example. . . . Napoleon is . . . improving and adorning Paris, and it is rapidly becoming the centre of fashion and interest for all Europe . . . , and immense expenditures enriching all classes are the natural consequence.

—"A Taxpayer for Thirty Years,"
National Intelligencer, November 5, 1862

IN MOST PARTS OF THE WORLD, cities emerged over centuries and bear the marks of many phases and aspects of their country's life. Large American cities typically were built for a few purposes during a single historical period; they filled niches in the continent-wide commercial and industrial network that sprang up with astonishing speed during the nineteenth century. The fact that our major cities grew almost exclusively as centers of exchange or production distinguishes the American urban experience from that of many other societies. In other societies, the metropolis serves as a focal point for political as well as economic power. The United States has produced national and regional metropolises—New York, Chicago, San Francisco, Houston—that have no formal position in our polity, that are not even capitals of their respective states. When we reflect upon these cities, we think first about the structure and career of American enterprise and only later about the growth and character of the American state.[1]

Washington, D.C., stands as the exception to this pattern. During the last third of the nineteenth century, the period covered by this study, it grew into a major city for political rather than economic reasons. Great capital cities such as Washington deserve close scrutiny, because in them, through encounters with a series of concrete, observable problems, a government displays its personality. The means a nation uses to ensure prosperity for its home city, the aesthetic standards it chooses to guide official embellishment, the measures it takes to safeguard the health, comfort, and safety of the capital's residents, and the strategies it adopts to resolve conflicts between na-

1

tional authorities and the local community all shed light on the character of politics and policy-making in a nation overall.

This thought gives rise to a guiding assumption of this book: Washington, despite its unique function and place in the nation, is immediately recognizable as an *American* city. Studying it might throw into relief the effect on all of urban America of factors other than the industrial transformations and commercial trends that predominate in our other cities. These factors, which include legal and administrative structures, political tendencies, economic traditions, and governmental practices, have deep roots in this country's history and political culture.

In the half-century after 1850, the federal government of the United States, like that of other Western capitalist countries, expanded in size, responsibility, and authority. As these governments grew larger and more powerful, capital cities inevitably grew in size and visibility. The special problems and possibilities of such cities invariably attracted much attention from governing regimes and the public. In large measure, the Gilded Age campaign to "improve" Washington was simply the American manifestation of an international movement.

Yet Washington's late-nineteenth-century experience also varied from the transnational trend, because of practices, institutions, notions, and sentiments that other countries did not exhibit to the same degree as the United States. By the turn of the century Washington had taken on many of the qualities and quirks familiar to twentieth-century urban Americans, because it was both the capital of an expanding Western state and an American city, designed, constructed, and managed by people of the same cast of mind as the creators of Chicago, Pittsburgh, and San Francisco, and indeed by some of the same individuals. Throughout the twists and turns of plot in the next eight chapters, I will draw attention to the curious interaction between the Western impulse towards capital-building and the American tradition of city-building that modern Washington represents.

I

A capital city illustrates not only the country's policy and politics but also its national self-image, at least the image that the current regime hopes to project. During the last third of the nineteenth century, one spectacular endeavor in capital-building, Georges Haussmann's rebuilding of Paris, towered in the thinking of promoters of national cities from Washington to Buenos Aires. While the value of Haussmann's legacy appears in retrospect to be mixed, contemporaries saw his work as an ingenious combination of the majestic with the prosaic, the practical with the symbolic. On one level, Haussmann was nothing but a gruff career bureaucrat and his program a mundane affair of streets and bridges, water and sewers, cemeteries and parks; but the designs that the Prefect of the Seine and his boss, Napoleon III, chose for their city also demonstrate a capacity for political poetry. Paris's new *grands boulevards* with their spectacular vistas probably served to explain Louis Napoleon's regime to the French people as well as any writing or speech. The capital's rebuilt streets embodied the relationship that the Second Empire sought to build between government and country.[2]

Foreigners who praised and imitated Haussmann were not usually well versed in recent French history and politics, even though these had nourished the impulse to reconstruct Paris. Nor did such observers think in a sophisticated way about the French tradition of *dirigisme*, the Saint-Simonian social theories, and the Napoleonic administrative practices that also shaped Baron Haussmann's approach to Paris's infrastructural needs. This ignorance left outsiders free to reinterpret the Parisian improvements as they would.

During the second half of the nineteenth century, capitals — and indeed many other cities — looked to Second Empire Paris for inspiration when planning ambitious public works and designing majestic public places. Cities throughout Europe and the Americas imported much of their face from France. Still, the particular methods adopted and message sent by the capital-building endeavors in each country reflected that country's own governmental practices and political culture. The Washington that emerged at the end of this decisive period of physical, economic, and political change reflected the mixture of assumptions, imperatives, and goals contained in the letter to the Washington *National Intelligencer* cited above. While the self-described "Taxpayer" thought the improvement program he recommended for the capital corresponded to what was going on in Paris at the time, his reasoning was as American as it was Haussmannic.

Like Napoleon III and his advisors, Americans who advocated a federal effort to transform Washington into a world-class capital believed that such a program would reinforce national identity and increase the legitimacy of the state. In 1859, *Harper's Monthly* reiterated what soon would become the improvers' slogan when it demanded a federal program "to render the seat of Government worthy of the nation." Such a program would provide "hope for the perpetuity of strong *Union*." A Washington with splendid streets, abundant water, and distinguished buildings, could furnish "a centre of attraction" to hold restless states — "the wildest comets that seek to fly off into new orbits."[3]

Disunion ensued, however. The terrible war that resulted convinced many Northern politicians that forceful measures were needed to strengthen the federal government's presence in and grip upon the country. Massive improvements to the District of Columbia might help the regime in Washington to loom larger and more continuously in the public mind. Moreover, embellishment of the capital might reassure loyal citizens that their sacrifices had not been in vain, that their cherished Union had emerged from the crisis with its authority intact and even enhanced.

In later years, patriotic observers remembered pre–Civil War Washington as having been as much a failure as the antebellum Union itself. In order to emphasize the magnitude of the physical change that Washington had undergone during the quarter-century after the war, Charles Burr Todd, a writer of guidebooks, noted in 1889, "Modern visitors can have no conception of the struggling, unkempt, provincial-like appearance of the city in 1861, when the defenders of the Union began pouring in for its protection." Todd accurately portrayed the disappointment expressed by thousands who came to Washington for the first time on account of the rebellion. Back in 1864, a talented Sacramento reporter named Noah Brooks, in an appraisal atypical only in its pithiness, had informed Californians that their distant capital was "so ill-kept, noisome, and stinking" that "the man on the moon would hold his nose going over it." Abraham Lincoln won praise for continuing two major improvements in spite of the war—the spectacular cast-iron dome of the Capitol and the innovative aqueduct that each day would carry twenty-five million gallons from the Great Falls of the Potomac twelve miles away. Lincoln's cabinet saw prosecution of these works as a symbolic way to reaffirm its commitment to the Union. Neither project, critics felt, compensated for Washington's undistinguished commercial buildings, "indifferent" hotels, and churches that *Harper's* said should "disgrace . . . a Western city of twenty thousand."[4]

Embarrassed patriots indignantly pointed to the Washington Monument, which for want of money had been abandoned half-finished in its scaffolding back in 1854. Also galling was the lack of proper sewerage for houses and public grounds. Washington's streets and avenues, undrained, ungraded, and unpaved, were the aspect of the city most vociferously deplored. The government did pave Pennsylvania Avenue with cobblestones before the war, but the wartime traffic ground the stones to rubble, making it impossible to drive on America's main street at more than walking speed. Even at its best, asserted Public Buildings Commissioner B. B. French, driving on Pennsylvania Avenue had been "like riding over a road covered laterally with corrugated roofing iron." The capital's "truly fearful" streets, Brooks wrote, "are seas or canals of mud, varying in depth from one to three feet." Their "geographical features" were "conglomerations of garbage, refuse, and trash."[5]

One might counter that most cities across the United States and around the world tolerated distressingly inadequate public works, services, and places at that time. Washington did not in fact lag terribly far behind its counterparts. Frustrated Unionists could not be satisfied with a respectable town of seventy thousand grown from nothing in six decades. Wartime critics measured the capital not against actual cities elsewhere but against what they felt was the city's—and the nation's—unfulfilled potential. A view of Civil War–era Washington from any height or angle was likely to wound national pride, because the most obvious aspect was not how much had been accomplished but how little had been finished of French engineer Pierre Charles L'Enfant's original plan, made in 1791–92.

Of the many grandiose city plans devised during the eighteenth century, L'Enfant's design was more ambitious than any of the others that were actually meant to be executed. The Frenchman's sketches embodied the aspirations of George Washington and his friends for the country they had founded. The city's famous street system — radiating 160-foot-wide avenues imposed on a grid of streets 90 to 130 feet wide — mirrors the first President's stated intention of establishing the seat of an empire as great as Rome. Baron Haussmann's improvements to Paris included broad streets, to project magnificence and power, but streets and avenues occupied only 26 percent of his Paris, as opposed to nearly 55 percent so dedicated in Washington. Dissatisfied with L'Enfant's management of the capital-building project, George Washington fired him in early 1792. Yet the President kept the Frenchman's surveys and drawings, which were also approved by the supposed proponent of limited government, Thomas Jefferson. The secretary of state worked with the new engineer, Andrew Ellicott, in preparing the official map published in October 1792.[6]

The hopeful patriotism of George Washington and his associates led them to compound the difficulties posed by their lavish planning. Washington and Alexander Hamilton schemed to finance public buildings and principal thoroughfares with the sale of city lots, assuming that a multitude would certainly rush to join the adventure. Despite the presence of Washington, Jefferson, and James Madison, the initial auction, on October 17, 1791, sold only thirty-five lots out of ten thousand and raised only $2,000. Blaming bad weather, the city commissioners tried again the next year, with similar results. With funds donated by neighboring states, the government pressed ahead anyway and managed to attract three thousand residents by the time the President and Congress arrived in 1800.[7]

The founders' intentions did not stop with making the seat of government impressive. Throughout history, the architecture and street designs of imperial capitals have conveyed a forbidding message, since they have often stressed the state over the people. Washington and his advisors exhibited a different spirit when they placed their city at the junction of a major river and a navigable tributary. They planned a canal to run through the city's heart, in front of the President's mansion and the Capitol. They intended the symbols and structures of commerce to stand alongside those of the state. This was in keeping with the American revolutionary belief that a state is most admirable when, rather than standing above and apart from the citizenry, it invites the public's presence and derives energy from a bustling populace.

Washington wanted his city to become "the emporium of the United States." He hoped to shift the center of trade and industry from northern ports to his native Potomac valley. This part of Washington's vision was stillborn. The federal district never developed trade beyond that of local use. The coal, flour, and lumber that came to the Potomac waterfront mostly stayed in the District after being processed. This pattern had been in place for many decades when Carroll D. Wright, one of the most accomplished statisticians of the last century, argued in an 1899 address to the Washington Academy of Sciences that George Washington's "dream" of commercial power had "not been realized" and probably never would be. In Wright's view, the "industry of government" drove Washington's economy. The Census Bureau, in its 1902 survey of American manufacturing, agreed: Washington supported only "neighborhood" industries, "not manufactures in a large sense."[8]

The stunted growth of commerce was accompanied by stagnation of the waterways that George Washington had imagined would become traders' thoroughfares. By the Civil War, more anxiety than wealth came from his beloved Potomac. Erosion from land clearance upstream encouraged the river to form disease-filled marshes along the city's front. The Washington Canal, which ran where Constitution Avenue now is, had degraded into a "fetid bayou," a Civil War–era journalist recalled, bearing "dead cats and all kinds of putridity and reeking with pestilential odors" so bad that people on Pennsylvania Avenue occasionally needed to hold their noses. Besieged by swamps and open sewers, Washingtonians ventured to question the wisdom of the Father of the Country, who had bequeathed to them not self-sustained prosperity but the threat of plague.[9]

Although the city's growth was steady, it was too slow for Alexandria County, the part of the original District of Columbia on the Virginia side of the Potomac. With the expectation that development aid would be more forthcoming from Virginia's legislature than from Congress, Alexandria won permission in 1846 to return to that Commonwealth. This left only sixty-nine of the one hundred square miles designated for the federal district by the Constitution. Alexandria's retrocession underscored the belief that the capital was languishing.[10]

On the eve of disunion, *Harper's* complained that "every wandering Englishman" took advantage of the capital's discreditable condition to demean the upstart republic. Over the previous half-century, foreigners wishing to ridicule Americans' pretenses to greatness had found "Washington expectancy" an easy target. The city had been "laughed at by foreigners, and even by natives," the English traveler Frances Trollope noted in 1830. Trollope, for her part, considered the L'Enfant Plan "beautiful" and saw "nothing in the least degree ridiculous" about its scale. On the contrary, she found the plan's gradual execution "a spectacle of high historic interest." More typical was the opinion of Portuguese envoy Abbé Corrêa da Serra, who, believing L'Enfant's sprawling street system more grandiose than grand, gave currency to one of the capital's uncomplimentary nicknames—"the City of Magnificent Distances." Charles Dickens, disgruntled by his first visit to the United States, which resulted in the acerbic *American Notes,* asserted that Washington "might with greater propriety be termed the City of Magnificent Intentions."

Dickens found "spacious avenues, that begin in nothing, and lead nowhere; streets, milelong, that only want houses, roads and inhabitants; public buildings that need but a public to be complete."[11]

II

Little wonder that the proud generation that saved the Union looked with shame upon its administrative and symbolic home. In 1870, Congress rebuked an effort by local businessmen to organize an international industrial fair, such as the Centennial Exposition eventually held in Philadelphia. The city's capitalists pledged $1.5 million for the show, but the legislature refused them the needed federal support. Nevada senator William Stewart, expressing the consensus of his colleagues, asserted that with money and effort, Washington "might be made a city, but let us have a city before we invite anybody to see it." As organizer of the California Syndicate of real estate investors, Stewart had an interest in boosting Washington. Yet the Nevadan suggested that the government would do better to subsidize a fair in Chicago or St. Louis. An international exhibit should "show off our grandeur, show off our power," Stewart concluded. "None of us are proud of this place."[12]

As the second half of the nineteenth century progressed, patriotic politicians and commentators came to look on their capital less sullenly. Washington's fortunes seemed to take a turn for the better, a circumstance that former detractors argued was a direct consequence of the long-term boost that the Union's victory had given to the power and prestige of the federal government. When trying to explain the many improvement movements of the postwar period, Charles Todd echoed a common judgment: "The principal reason why Washington has become a national capital in fact as well as in name, is because within her limits was fought the great contest which changed the American people from a confederacy to a nation." Todd suggested that prior to 1861 sectional jealousy had led Congress "to treat the city with indifference." Charles Moore, who in a variety of offices in the late nineteenth and early twentieth centuries organized federal efforts in the District, wrote that before the war, relations between the country and the city had been "like a mother eating her young." Northern victory gradually led to a healthier situation because "the national idea assert[ed] itself. Washington, which is always a reflection of the nation, felt the new impulse."[13]

By the 1890s, the national political establishment felt moved to display and celebrate its capital. When local businessmen launched an effort to secure what eventually became Chicago's Columbian Exposition of 1893, politicians did not dismiss the idea out of hand, as Senator Stewart had done twenty years before. The word around town had it that Chicago's victory over Washington and other contenders had resulted from the intrigues of Joseph Cannon and other powerful midwestern politicians, not from the capital's shortcomings. Nobody claimed that the federal city had lost because it was unfit to be seen.[14] Congress soon honored its residence by organizing a colorful celebration of the city's centennial, which took place December 12, 1900. President William McKinley captured the spirit of this celebration in an annual message. L'Enfant's plans, wrote McKinley, "have been wrought out with a constant progress and a signal success even beyond anything their framers could have foreseen. The people of the country are justly proud of the distinct beauty and government of the capital, and of the rare instruments of science and education which find here their natural home."[15]

District Commissioner Henry B. F. Macfarland was called upon to address the centennial reception at the President's Mansion on "Development of the District of Columbia during the Century 1800–1900." Macfarland, a former journalist and an articulate propagandist, reiterated what had by then emerged as the establishment version of Washington's history, a story of neglected duty followed by awakening and redemption. Like the statistician Wright, Macfarland felt that George Washington had been mistaken in providing for a commercial center but that subsequent events had justified nearly every other feature that Washington, L'Enfant, and their associates had planned. The first President, said Macfarland, had undertaken construction of his capital "with his customary energy, thoroughness, and patience." Afterwards, however, Congress had been unwilling and the local people unable to improve Washington City "as [its founder] doubtless intended should be done." "Washington's reputation for common sense did not save [his city] from being called a visionary scheme. For more than half a century home and foreign wits jested at it as it lay undeveloped, half village, half capital, through the neglect of the General Government." Macfarland argued: "It was not until the civil war had made the National Capital known to the whole country and endeared to two-thirds of it as never before, it was not until it had been contended for by the bravest armies ever arrayed in battle, that the national interest in it induced Congress to assume the nation's share of its government and its burden." The eventual result was that "the District of Columbia was saved from being, like the then unfinished Washington Monument, a disgrace rather than a credit to the great founder." Now, Macfarland concluded, "larger patriotism" required Congress to allocate additional money so that "the nation's city . . . shall be kept the most beautiful capital in the world."[16]

III

It might seem rude for the District commissioner to raise the subject of money at the stately centennial celebration, yet in insisting that Washington's future progress depended on regular, substantial federal subsidies to the capital's public works and services, Macfarland merely emphasized what local elites and their allies in national politics felt to be the lesson of forty years' experience. From the point of view of the capital's civic and business leaders, whether Washington would continue to project the grand face that it had attained by the turn of the century rested upon a set of fiscal and institutional arrangements that had emerged after a protracted, many-sided struggle over responsibility for and control of the District's governance and physical development. Since rumblings that these arrangements had become outmoded could frequently be heard in the Capitol, city officials such as Macfarland felt a constant need to cajole and berate the country's leaders not to abandon what local interests perceived to be an equitable division of responsibility. The standard version of Washington's history was in fact an argument for continuing the particular fiscal and governmental system that had evolved over the preceding four decades and that seemed to underpin the period's accomplishments. It was also an argument for continuing to define improvement in a way that conformed to the point of view and goals of that system's major backers.

Improvement, as most Gilded Age Washingtonians used the word, was an expensive undertaking with tangible goals. Improvement referred primarily to the institution of modern public works, services, and utilities and to their geographic extension throughout the city. The great city that had been realized, a New York congressman noted during the 1900 ceremonies, consisted of "beautiful streets and avenues," paved with asphalt, using techniques considered among the most innovative in the world. In contrast with thirty years before, the capital's streets, proclaimed *Frank Leslie's Monthly* in 1887, "surpass[ed] in some respects even those of Paris." The city and the Army Corps of Engineers by the mid-1890s had spent millions of dollars to cover 2.73 million square yards with the most modern asphalt, imported from Trinidad, Venezuela, and Switzerland. The only American city with more square yards of asphalt was Buffalo. The nation's taxpayers had pitched in approximately half the cost of this asphalt blanket.[17] Local and federal officials had spent many more millions on water supply, sewerage, bridges, parks, public buildings, and other components of a reputable city's infrastructure.

The postwar wave of nationalism, as Macfarland and other commentators noted, spurred interest in such projects. Realization of the contemplated improvements, however, was not simply a question of supplying tar, concrete, and steel. The remarkable physical transformation depended upon a thorough political reordering, upon the emergence of a durable working alliance that incorporated essential public and private interests and national and local institutions. The creation of Washington's modern infrastructure offers a useful study in the character of the American state because it was a matter of politics and governance as well as of architecture and engineering.

Washington's Gilded Age political history contains episodes filled with stormy conflict and dramatic change. The Radical Republican movement, dedicated to making the capital a showcase of black political participation and civil rights, briefly gained power, only to break apart on account of internal division and fierce opposition. During Washington's tumultuous territorial period, 1871–74, the legendary Alexander "Boss" Shepherd and his board of public works implemented a mammoth $18 million infrastructure program that transformed the capital's physical appearance and economic character but at the same time mired the city in scandals, financial confusion, and partisan squabbles. In the aftermath of the fall of Shepherd's regime, Congress, with the acquiescence of local business and civic elites, abolished self-government in Washington and provided that an appointed board of commissioners would rule the republic's capital, in exchange for a promise that the federal treasury would henceforth cover half of the District's annual budget.

Gilded Age Washington also saw institutions quietly evolve and alliances gradually consolidate. Congress elaborated procedures for exercising the authority and maintaining the fiscal commitments that it assumed under the permanent government act of 1878. The District of Columbia Commissioners, appointed by the President, oversaw construction of a municipal administration that had ragged edges but commanded respect from both residents and nationally known writers on urban affairs. The Army Corps of Engineers gained and then began to lose a position of enormous influence over the planning and management of Washington's public works. A movement of "downtown" businessmen and professionals created a formidable "commercial-civic" association, the Washington Board of Trade, which forged such strong links to the District commissioners and to relevant congressional committees that it became, for all intents and purposes, a quasi city council for the disenfranchised municipality.[18]

Through these upheavals and evolutions, the major players in the movement to create a worthy Washington invariably conceived and pursued improvement according to ideas and procedures that mixed the transnational, Western impulse towards state-oriented nationalism with a tradition of policy-making and political economy that, while it existed elsewhere, was distinctively strong in nineteenth-century America—the tradition of promotional governance.[19] The first concerted post–Civil War attempt to embellish Washington, Alexander Shepherd's "Comprehensive Plan of Improvements," entailed implementation of myriad works and services, all of which promised the capital not only splendor and dignity but also self-sustained prosperity driven by durable growth in the private sector. Shepherd's projects would accomplish their aims by complementing and facilitating—rather than channeling and directing—the activities of real estate developers and other entrepreneurs. The scenario envisioned by Shepherd and his "improver" faction of the local Republican party was reminiscent of the wave of "boosterism" or "Whiggism" that swept through state and municipal governments across the United States in the 1830s and 1840s. In the angry controversy that surrounded Shepherd's massive, frantic enterprise, friends and foes alike lost sight of the extent to which the improvers' territorial regime expanded upon rather than departed from the antebellum theory and practice of government in this country.

Like the spate of loans and land grants that Reconstruction Congresses gave to western railroads, the Comprehensive Plan represented the application to a national project of promotional ideas and methods long familiar at the regional and municipal levels. Shepherd's clique of well-connected businessmen-politicians adhered to the old assumption that the well-being of the city more or less corresponded to the visions and desires of its largest real estate and commercial interests. The national feelings that prompted the congressional Republicans and the Grant administration to encourage and assist the territorial regime were in some ways analogous to the sentiments that induced Louis Napoleon and other state-building politicians in Western Europe to undertake the embellishment of their capitals. Yet Reconstruction-era proponents of a worthy Washington pursued this apparently Haussmannic objective not with procedures and ideas borrowed from abroad but with a political economy that conformed readily to American law, history, governmental practice, and political culture.

The national-local governing alliance that emerged during the decades after Shepherd's downfall in June 1874 did not depart from his idea of how to render the capital functional, admirable, and prosperous; instead, they built upon it. By the end of the century, every group and institution that played a major role in policy-making for Washington adhered to a promotional strategy regarding public works and development. The only exception—a partial one—was the Army Corps of Engineers, whose institutional culture and standards of performance and behavior encouraged attitudes towards politics and the state that on occasion could make the engineer officers awkward participants in a promotional polity.

Fitfully before 1890 and steadily thereafter, an actor entered the local scene who in theory should have been able to advance a public-minded approach capable of balancing and moderating the promotional tendency. Local civic leaders and congressional policy-makers increasingly turned for advice and assistance to expert consultants in municipal engineering, public health, landscape architecture, and urban planning. These experts offered innovative techniques and a fresh, up-to-date style that, by making Washington appear cosmopolitan and dynamic, furthered the cause of a world-class capital.

We naturally look upon such new-style urban professionals as purveyors of a progressive outlook on public life and the modern city, and they might very well have nourished a vision of the worthy Washington that entailed moving the city in a direction different from the one it had taken over the past decades. Yet even the most influential and imaginative professional consultants had to accommodate themselves to the exigencies and perspective of the pre-existing political establishment that sponsored their activities. Urban professionals thus found themselves bound by a mode of politics and policy-making that they had intended to supersede and render obsolete. As is suggested by the last episode in our story, the famed 1902 "McMillan Plan" for reshaping Washington's parks and public places, these newcomers paid a price for cooperating closely with groups and institutions who remained firmly within the promotional tradition, while alienating those institutions, particularly the Army Corps, most given to a statist or public-minded notion of government's proper relation to the private sector.

So long as their position in Washington depended upon the capital's pre-existing governing structure, progressive-style innovators in municipal administration, public works, and similar fields were in effect compelled to give up their ability to start the new century by altering public-private relations in Washington and other American cities. They were precluded from setting Washington on an alternative course, one that calculated for the usefulness and humaneness of growth as well as its size and speed. Right at the start of this century, one of the oldest, most characteristic patterns in American political economy managed to weave itself into what seemed a totally innovative approach to municipal management—to Washington's eventual great cost. During the rest of this century, the tendency towards promotional governance inclined the American polity to surrender to and sometimes facilitate those economic and cultural forces that have caused our cities to fall apart.

In Washington's case, these confusing, often paralyzing inclinations were exacerbated by a tolerance, built into the local regime at its creation, of many of the most destructive and blatant forms of racial exclusion. The political role gained by local blacks during Reconstruction proved a volatile factor in conflicts that ensued between various groups of local whites. Previously antagonistic whites were able to reconcile in the late 1870s in large measure because the commission system, made permanent in 1878, was designed to leave blacks out of debates over development and indeed out of all debates over public works and services except those, like the segregated schools, that concerned blacks in the most narrow possible sense. Certain white leaders recognized that to deny participation to the poorest third of the population was both unjust and unwise. Such skeptics, however, could not attack Washington's racial politics without calling into question the city's entire institutional and political structure.

As the events culminating in the 1902 McMillan Plan will reveal, not even Washington's most ardent champions at the turn of the century claimed that the task of improvement was complete, that the nation's city already projected an ideal face. Even so, the capital's friends were satisfied that Washington had at last come to justify its founders' lofty dreams and that it provided the world with an example of the nation's special virtues—energy, confidence, and an undogmatic, progressive spirit. Sadly, Washington's system of governance, like that of other American cities, had at the same time come to harbor a mix of mutually exclusive imperatives and tendencies that would soon halt urban progress and later contribute to its reversal.

IV

Washington's Gilded Age experience has broad significance for our effort to understand the American urban polity precisely because Washington is unique. American thinking about the transformation of urban governance during the Gilded Age and Progressive era almost always interprets it as a "response to industrialism." This analysis begins with the observation that when the industrial revolution moved out of the countryside in the middle of the last century, when innovations in transport, distribution, and energy technology at last rendered it advantageous for factories to cluster in cities, the result was an economic, demographic, and geographic explosion that created unprecedented demands for services and infrastructure. To complicate matters, the system of municipal governance handed down from the period of mercantile dominance was genteel and unsystematic, no match at all for the troubles that threatened to overwhelm it. In large measure, therefore, the "politics of efficiency" that spread through late-nineteenth-century American cities — the desire for system, professionalism, and expertise that by 1900 had become central to progressive reform movements — constituted an understandable reaction to unimaginable new complexities in city life and the urban environment. It was a sophisticated, if ultimately flawed, attempt to wring a considered, orderly city out of impending chaos.[20] When considered from such a perspective, the movement to expand urban public works and services that spread through the United States towards the end of the last century had essentially the same origin and nature as parallel and simultaneous movements in Western Europe.

While the analysis just outlined sheds light on key aspects of the political transformation American cities experienced a century ago, it obscures or oversimplifies other key points. Its most vexing weakness is that it encourages the assumption that each phase and every difficulty of the American city in the last 150 years can in the end be traced to long-term developments or cyclical trends in industrial capitalism. Industrial and commercial change affected how Western cities looked and worked so quickly and fundamentally that urban scholars on both sides of the Atlantic often write as though industrialism were the only force shaping cities in this period and as though the dynamics of urban change worked more or less the same way wherever industrialism appeared. With notable exceptions,[21] American writers on urban polity give less careful attention to the influence on our cities of factors that existed prior to or independent of industrialism. By relying too heavily on this familiar framework, we preclude analysis of important features of our urban governance that resulted from historical, political, or cultural factors peculiar to or more predominant in the United States.

Industrialism had no direct effect on Gilded Age Washington. Nor, after the 1870s, did representative democracy, another factor American writers sometimes claim was decisive in shaping our urban environment. These considerations, taken in conjunction with Washington's unusual relationship with the American national state, mean that the typical interpretive framework simply cannot be applied to Washington.

Just as we cannot comprehend the Gilded Age movement to embellish Washington as merely one more manifestation of the Western movement towards capital-building, we likewise cannot portray this enterprise as another instance of American urban society responding to industrialism. Distinctive features of nineteenth-century American political economy—the ubiquity and strength of the promotional tendency being a primary but not the only example—molded the Washington that arose in the decades after the Civil War as much as did social and economic trends that were transnational. In discussions of Gilded Age urban development, questions pertaining to state structure, administrative practice, government-business relations, and so forth are often overshadowed by the spectacular growth of commerce and industry.[22] In Washington, these overshadowed but essential matters come to the fore.

Because Washington is simultaneously a city and a component of the national state, the tale of how it acquired modern public works, services, and administrative structures weaves together two stories we usually tell in separate places and from which we usually draw separate morals. Observers of the American city wonder why the very undertakings and practices that are supposed to bind residents together in an interdependent social entity seem themselves to have accelerated urban America's physical and social fragmentation. Why, despite a century of efforts to plan urban space and coordinate public works and services, do we still seem to build nothing but "giant urban wildernesses?"[23] At the same time, observers of the national polity wonder why Americans seem able to construct at best an "uneasy" state, distinguished, one political scientist writes, "by incoherence and fragmentation in governmental operations," a state barely capable of pursuing even the most pressing domestic goals in a consistent fashion over an extended period.[24]

Perhaps the impasse of our nation and the impasse of our cities spring from a common source, rather than separate ones, as we often assume. Perhaps the problem began in the aftermath of the Civil War, because the energetic generation that set out to build a great nation and fill it with "worthy" cities had no traditions to draw upon except those that ensured the enterprise would end in fragmentation.

1

Washington and the Wartime Union

Dignified work for the House of Representatives of a great Nation! To snub
poor, modest me, just because I dared to speak well of Andrew Johnson.
— Diary of Public Buildings Commissioner Benjamin French,
February 24, 1867

MANY OF THE THOUSANDS used opera glasses to follow the moving
cables and turning pulleys. The "considerable" crowd gathered on
the Capitol grounds was impressed by the skill of the workmen,
who maneuvered on the scaffolding at the "dizzy height" of three hundred
feet. At twenty-five after noon, the workers raised a Union flag, which "spread
gayly in the breeze." To the east, below the building, thirty-five artillery guns
fired, one for each state, including the Confederate ones then out of the
Union. The guns were answered by those in the ring of forts protecting the
city. The artillery salute continued for two hours. By the end of the day on
December 2, 1863, Thomas Crawford's nineteen-foot statue of Freedom, polished and preserved with an acid wash, stood atop the new Capitol dome.[1]

While Freedom rose over Washington, news spread of General Grant's victory at Chattanooga. No officials made speeches that day. The army captain
in charge was under orders to limit the ceremony that accompanied the raising, perhaps for fear of rebel interference. Still, the government intended the
event to be meaningful. "If people see the Capitol going on," Lincoln reportedly said, "it is a sign we intend the Union shall go on." The *New York Tribune*
remarked upon the meaning of erecting such a statue in the midst of such a
war. Horace Greeley's paper hoped that the statue would not prove "a mock-
ing memorial of fading traditions." Until then, the *Tribune* wrote, Americans
had "been but timorous wooers" of Freedom.[2]

Freedom faced east over the Capitol's main entrance. Before her were the
dirt streets and brick rowhouses of Capitol Hill. The section's major thoroughfares, East Pennsylvania, Maryland, and North Carolina avenues and
East Capitol Street, sputtered out after about ten blocks. Following a barely
occupied stretch were the municipal almshouse and the congressional cemetery. These stood on the Eastern Branch, also called the Anacostia River, the
original boundary of L'Enfant's Federal City. The District of Columbia also
included the hills across the Anacostia, occupied, except for the Government

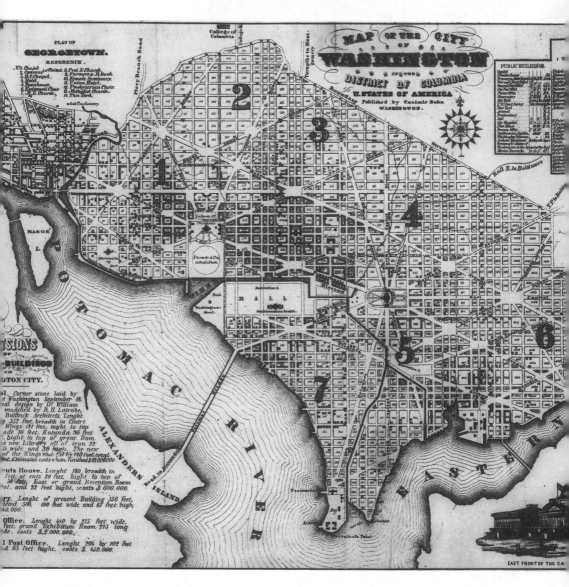

Washington City and Georgetown, 1861. The limited area covered by the filled blocks shows how slowly development overtook the uncompleted L'Enfant street system. Courtesy the Geography and Map Division, Library of Congress.

Hospital for the Insane and the settlement of Uniontown, by small farms, no different from those in neighboring Maryland. In 1867, across the Anacostia at Barry Farm, the Freedmen's Bureau helped organize a historic settlement of former slaves, whose progress Freedom might have been pleased to see.[3]

L'Enfant imagined healthy, picturesque Capitol Hill as an important residential and commercial quarter, with grand houses along avenues radiating from the Capitol and busy docks lining the Eastern Branch. Contrary to these expectations, the most prosperous early settlements radiated from the President's House and the executive departments in northwest Washington. Business flourished on both sides of west Pennsylvania Avenue. The busiest docks remained in the prerevolutionary port of Georgetown, to the west, and later arose along the Washington Channel of the Potomac, in the southwest. Freedom's back was turned upon the nation's city.

Had Freedom been sensible to mockery, she might have been glad that she faced away from Washington. Rather than being a physical incarnation of the country's ideals, the capital of the Republic in the Civil War era was a target for humorists. From the Capitol, wrote Mark Twain, one could look down into the "muddy low marsh" on which most of the city was built. By the river in the distance rose what looked like "a factory chimney with the top broken off" — the abandoned Washington Monument, which Twain speculated might be finished by the time the hero was "the Great-Great Grandfather of his country." Twain imagined that Washington's ghost sometimes sat on the decaying scaffolding enjoying the nation's "unappeasable gratitude." North of the monument stood the President's House, "a fine white barn, with wide unhandsome grounds," inside which "dreariness, flimsiness, bad taste reduced to mathematical completeness." From there back to the Capitol ran Pennsylvania Avenue, walled by "mean, and cheap, and dingy" stores and hotels. Walking was impeded by the "deep and all-pervading" mud and slush. A visitor during the spring thaw would "wonder at the shortsightedness of the city fathers," who had not thought to dilute the muddy streets "and use them for canals."[4]

High-minded champions of freedom also deplored Washington. Horace Greeley warned that it was no place for a young man to pursue a career: "The rents are high, the food is bad, the dust is disgusting, the mud is deep, and the morals are deplorable." The city appeared to the young Henry Adams to be a "rude colony" camped in a forest. The government buildings that towered over the "scattered" wooden houses and the "sloughs for roads" were "like white Greek temples in the abandoned gravel pits of a deserted Syrian city." In Adams's acerbic view, the Washington of his youth indeed epitomized a nation that was "a sentiment, but not much more."[5]

I

The Twains of America made a profession of pricking the country's pretensions. The Greeleys and Adamses preferred chastising America for its shortcomings. Had either set preferred the amiable profession of booster, they would have pointed out that in December 1863, the forces of improvement were camped on every available piece of ground in the District of Columbia,

Table 1.1 Population of the District of Columbia

Year	Total	Percentage of Increase	White	Black	Percentage Black
1840	43,712		30,657	13,055 (4,694 slave)	29.9
1850	51,687	18.2	37,941	13,746 (3,687 slave)	26.6
1860	75,080	45.3	60,793	14,317 (3,185 slave)	19.1
1870	131,700	75.4	88,278	43,422	33.0
1880	177,624	34.9	118,006	59,618	33.6
1890	230,392	29.7	154,695	75,697	32.9
1900	278,718	21.0	191,532	86,702	31.1
1910	331,069	18.8	236,128	94,446	28.5

Sources: Carroll D. Wright, "The Economic Development of the District of Columbia," *Proceedings of the Washington Academy of Sciences* 1 (Dec. 1889): 185–87; Constance M. Green, *Washington: Capital City, 1879–1950* (Princeton: Princeton University Press, 1962), p. 89.

if they were not in Tennessee with Ulysses S. Grant. The war to save the Union increased the capital's importance as an administrative center. The federal government in 1865 was far from the pervasive construction that arose during the Second World War. Yet never again would it be the distant, half-legitimate, half-ignored state of the antebellum period.

Along with the troops defending Washington came clerical workers to organize and provision them. The District of Columbia's population was 75,000 in 1860. By 1864, approximately 155,000 people lived in the District.[6] Many went home after the Union victory, but the census at decade's end still showed over 130,000, a 75 percent increase. The majority of the decade's permanent increase came from former slaves seeking refuge during the war or work afterwards (see table 1.1). Much of the increase, however, was the result of a permanent 183 percent rise between 1860 and 1870 in the number of federal workers employed in Washington. Their numbers would double again in the next decade. Before the war only 6 percent of all federal jobs (including postmasterships) were in Washington. For the rest of the nineteenth century this figure would be between 12 and 13 percent (see table 1.2). Whereas the mean proportion of federal employees in Washington for the period 1831–61 was 5.7 percent, the mean from 1871 until the present has been 12.25 percent. In no decade since the Civil War has this figure been below 10 percent or above 14.3 percent. This illustrates the extent to which the war indeed proved a turning point in relations between capital and nation.[7]

Twain was exploiting prejudice when he characterized the typical aspirant to federal employment as a helpless child thrown upon "good and motherly"

Table 1.2 Paid Civilian Employment in the Federal Government

| Year | Countrywide | | In District of Columbia | | |
	Total	Percentage of Increase	Total	Percentage of Increase	Percentage of Total
1841	18,038		1,014		5.6
1851	26,274	45.7	1,533	51.2	5.8
1861	36,672	39.6	2,199	43.4	6.0
1871	51,020	39.1	6,222	182.9	12.2
1881	100,020	96.0	13,124	110.9	13.1
1891	157,442	57.4	20,834	58.7	13.2
1901	239,476	52.1	28,044	34.6	11.7
1911	395,905	65.3	39,782	41.9	10.0

Sources: U.S. Bureau of the Census, *Historical Statistics of the United States: Colonial Times to 1957* (Washington, D.C.: Government Printing Office, 1960), p. 710.

Washington — "doesn't know anything, and does not want to go into the bother of learning something, and has no money, and no employment, and can't earn a living."[8] On the contrary, government clerks had steady work habits, families, conventional tastes, in short were upright folks. The Civil War and other events that made for more federal workers would eventually translate into improved municipal amenities and public works and a flourishing local economy centered around real estate, retail trades, and services. As the national government gained authority and importance, the fortunes of the national city would rise as well (see table 1.3). Washington would become more "worthy of the nation" as the country developed a national state.

Despite these prospects and the bustle and excitement of wartime, the crowd that watched Freedom's unveiling needed such symbolic acts of commitment to sustain their faith. In December 1863, Union victory was uncertain, though the cause seemed to be prospering. The grinding war, with its endless carnage and destruction, was proof that the federal republic had been flawed. No one could predict how much more effort and sacrifice would be needed to bring about the "new birth of freedom" that Lincoln had called for at Gettysburg that November.

Like the Union, the federal district had begun with great expectations that had not been fulfilled. L'Enfant and George Washington laid out the capital's streets and squares on a scale to accommodate millions of people and reflect the wealth and power of a continental empire. Perhaps, as a leading Republican told Congress in 1862, the war would make Washington City and Georgetown "great metropolitan cities" and spark the unprecedented investment and growth needed for the nation's city to live up to its founders' grand vision. The press claimed that Washington's property values rose 70 percent between 1860 and 1866, the fastest increase east of the Rocky Mountains.[9]

Table 1.3 Estimated Market Value of Taxable Real and Personal
Property in District of Columbia, in Dollars

Year	Estimated Value	Per Capita	U.S. per Capita
1850	14,018,874	271	308
1860	41,084,945	547	514
1870	126,873,618[a]	963[a]	780[a]
1880	220,000,000[b]	1,239[b]	870[b]
1890	198,643,618	862	975
1900	540,814,589	1,940	1,083
1912[c]	767,316,951	2,293	1,836

Sources: U.S. Bureau of the Census, *Reports on Wealth, Debt, and Taxation,*
1904, pp. 42–44, 49; 1913, vol. 1, pp. 24–26; Wright, "Economic
Development," pp. 186–87.
[a] Value in greenbacks
[b] Census provides only combined figures of taxable and exempt property.
[c] Census report published in 1913 gave most recent figures rather than those
at turn of the decade, as previous reports had done.

Still, no one in 1863 could say what needed to be done to make the capital
live up to its potential, or even how a "worthy" Washington should look and
feel. The entrepreneurs and engineers who, by their leadership and effort,
would stamp the new metropolis with their character had not yet emerged.

Twain's "memorial chimney" stood on the original bank of the Potomac
River. When George Washington chose the site, the river had been relatively
healthful and navigable close to shore. L'Enfant imagined here a pleasant
place from which to watch river traffic. For decades, as farmers developed
land upriver, silt built up downriver, forming marshes. The resultant Potomac
Flats composed what local physicians assumed to be the city's leading source
of disease. The vicinity of the Flats acquired—and retains today—the name
"Foggy Bottom." Successive Presidents feared that malaria might enter the
executive mansion from these swamps.[10]

Between the monument and the Capitol lay the Mall, planned by L'Enfant
as a majestic park. In 1850, President Fillmore retained Andrew Jackson
Downing, the romantic landscape architect, to develop what many regarded
as a "mere cow pasture" into a "national park . . . planted in a thorough
manner." Downing began to lay out the Smithsonian grounds with curving
walks and drives, in the "natural style of Landscape Gardening," which the
architect hoped would soften L'Enfant's "straight lines and broad avenues."
Although the 1902 McMillan Plan obliterated Downing's work, for which
Beaux-Arts architects expressed contempt, it helped inspire Frederick Law
Olmsted's romantic plan for the Capitol grounds, carried out in the 1870s
and early 1880s, much of which work survives.[11]

Downing perished in a steamboat fire in 1852, his work in Washington barely begun. The Mall remained "broken, confused, and unsatisfactory," in Olmsted's words, "a standing reproach against the system of government." Downing had planned a military review ground in the area between the monument and the President's House, then known as the White Lot but now called the Ellipse. In the 1860s, mud and stagnant water covered the area. Immediately after the war, the city sought federal permission and aid to fill in this marsh with material dredged from the adjacent Washington Canal. Congress balked at what proponents claimed was a "comparatively trifling" $60,000 expense and delayed the project several times, despite anxiety over the health of the President's family.[12]

L'Enfant's ideas seemed to have been lost. One could not walk from the President's House to the Capitol without going through the business part of the city. The Mall was divided into eight distinct grounds in varying states of languor. A "comprehensive scheme," Olmsted pointed out, was impossible, because the grounds came under the jurisdiction of "a dozen independent committees of Congress assisted by nearly as many heads of bureaus and other officials." Railroads began to encroach on the Mall in 1855 when, during the recess of a skeptical Congress, the Alexandria and Washington Railroad, with the connivance of the city government, built tracks along First Street at the foot of Capitol Hill. In 1872, the Pennsylvania Railroad flexed its political muscle to acquire a free grant of a route across the Mall along Sixth Street, "blasting all the possibilities of a National Park," as a disappointed Congressman James Garfield noted in his diary. Sections of the Mall grew gloomy and threatening; the papers reported gruesome crimes there. At a hearing in 1890 on one of many proposals to remove the railroad tracks, a vice-president of the Pennsylvania Railroad defended the Sixth Street station. Millions used the railroad, he testified, but he had never seen more than a thousand people in the park.[13]*

Southwest Washington was isolated from the rest of the city and became known as the Island. Geographically, the Mall and all south of it were a sort of island. The region was cut off by the Washington Canal, which ran along the north side of the Mall and then turned south below Capitol Hill towards the Eastern Branch. No feature of the L'Enfant Plan proved so troublesome as the scheme to bring trade to the center of the city by running a canal straight through it. The canal's sluggish waters collected and preserved pollution from at least three sources: runoff from the city's streets and sewers; garbage blown or thrown in, including dead animals and an occasional illegitimate baby; and Tiber Creek, which flowed into the Mall from the northeast immediately below the Capitol. The Tiber, once Goose Creek, acquired its name in a fit of imperial inspiration that predated L'Enfant. It accumulated

---

* The Pennsylvania acquired rights to a route between Baltimore and Washington through the purchase of an unsuccessful Maryland company, the Baltimore and Potomac Railroad. Federal documents usually refer to the Pennsylvania's Washington line by the title of the subsidiary, but I have stayed with the parent company's name, for the sake of clarity.

rubbish and sewage as it meandered along. Complaining that "this always filthy, sluggish stream performs the functions of *night carts* for about one-third of the city," the superintendent of the Botanical Garden managed to convince Congress to build an arch over portions of the Tiber. While affording slight relief to the nation's flowers, this expedient would not have lessened the amount of waste water converging on central Washington. General Richard Delafield, former chief of engineers, calculated in 1870 that 340 water closets and 78 urinals from government offices alone discharged into the canal.[14]

The "Great Ditch" also proved a loser for all who dared sink money into it. A private company, chartered in 1802 to contruct the canal, needed a lottery before it could begin digging in 1812. Private enterprise failed to make the project work, so in 1831, the city acquired the canal and attempted to integrate it into the Chesapeake and Ohio Canal. The city, however, failed to clear all the low bridges that impeded traffic or to find an effective means to prevent silting, which inhibited C & O business from venturing below Georgetown. Even so, the ever-hopeful Washington City floated a loan in the Netherlands in order to subsidize its canal projects. By 1836, the capital was over a year in arrears on this debt, in addition to having an alarming deficit in its current account. On the Senate floor, rumors circulated that foreign agents had come to demand their money: "There is danger," one member cried, "that this city may be sold to the Dutch." In 1836 and 1837, Congress bailed out its bankrupt city and in 1849 and 1851 appropriated funds to clean the Washington Canal, to little avail.[15]

The canal and the decrepit coal and lumber yards that clung to its banks had a deleterious effect on the vicinity. The area south of Pennsylvania Avenue, now called the Federal Triangle, was a notorious slum. Around 13th and D streets, three blocks from the Treasury, was a red light district that came to be called "Hooker's Division," after General Joseph Hooker, who vainly tried to confine local prostitution there during the war. The area was also known as Murder Bay. Drunken brawls spilled out of dives and bawdy houses and earned the quarter its nickname. Sadly, Murder Bay was one of the few places available for residence to penniless former slaves, who squatted there in "overwhelming" numbers. In March 1866, Major A. C. Richards, the police superintendent, reported that in Murder Bay, freedmen's families "crowded into mere apologies for shanties" with little light or air and no protection from the weather. Within fifty square yards, Richards counted one hundred families of three to five persons, living in "stifling and sickening" rooms often as small as eight square feet.[16]

Twain was not alone in disparaging Pennsylvania Avenue. Its three-story brick buildings contained, a local historian writes, "saloons, boarding-houses, restaurants, the offices of newspapers, patent attorneys and solicitors, dealers in second-hand clothing, and pawnshops." During the war, officers promenaded Pennsylvania Avenue with courtesans met in the more upscale

"A dirty, stinking, filthy ditch," the Washington Canal as it looked during construction of the new Capitol dome, c. 1861. Courtesy the Still Picture Branch, National Archives.

establishments at 13th and D. Unlike in Baltimore or New York, the great boulevard of Washington featured no fine stores. Saks and Company came to Pennsylvania Avenue at Market Place only in 1876. The Boston Dry Goods Store, a Chelsea, Massachusetts, firm that grew into Woodward and Lothrop, established a branch on Pennsylvania Avenue in 1880. This firm later built a department store in the elegant late-century style at 11th and F.[17]

The cobblestone pavement of Pennsylvania Avenue that army wagons had ground into rubble during the war badly needed repairing. Congress hesitated to do what the city council felt was "simple justice" and pay the cost of a new pavement. One House opponent grumbled that the government already over the years had expended $422,693 on Pennsylvania Avenue, "enough for the people of the United States to have spent on one avenue in this city." The city of Washington, he said, should be "making its own streets." Proposals to split the cost of repaving with adjacent property owners failed until late 1870, even though some congressmen worried that such delay threatened the government's claim to the country's main boulevard.[18]

Pennsylvania Avenue was one of the few streets in Washington that evidenced a serious attempt at improvement. No other thoroughfare was graded

Pennsylvania Avenue, looking southeast from the Treasury building during a carnival celebrating the avenue's repaving with wooden blocks, February 1871. Courtesy the Still Picture Branch, National Archives.

or paved for more than a few blocks. The expense of improving 160-foot-wide avenues and 100-foot-wide streets daunted officials, but the mud and dust led to more grumbling against L'Enfant. "The blunder of the plan," one resident wrote to the *National Intelligencer,* "is seen to be prodigious." The streets, "almost universally too wide," formed "a great Sahara of dirt."[19]

Pennsylvania Avenue ran on low ground that straddled the city's watershed. In the absence of sophisticated drainage, central Washington was subject to flooding. In Jefferson's time, the avenue contended on both sides with bogs and swamps, which that knowledgeable gardener attempted to restrain with rows of poplar trees. After a flash flood or a heavy spring tide, the officials of the young republic sometimes had to use the packet boat from Georgetown to the Washington Navy Yard for routine communication.[20]

Over succeeding decades, a jumble of brick and wooden sewers displaced the problem into neighboring basements or onto the Mall. The intent had been to drain the city into the canal and then into the river, but the tides of the obstinate Potomac kept pushing the sewage back. Sewer mains ran uphill in places or across underground streams. Pipes were laid at the wrong depth in muddy ground without proper backing. In October 1866, the 14th Street sewer collapsed, suddenly causing the street to sink. A horse fell into a hole that the *National Intelligencer* said was big enough to hold a railroad car. The collapse, said the paper, demonstrated the folly of the city council's "short-sighted policy" of running sewers every which way without expert advice. "No one sewer should be laid until a *system* of sewerage is adopted." Even if the city could afford such a system, implementing it would be complicated by the fact that no record existed of the location of sewers built before 1856.[21]

The $3.3 million Washington Aqueduct was opened in December 1863. Engineers knew that the introduction of running water would make the problem of sewerage more pressing, yet they did not imagine that a daily capacity of 25–31 million gallons would prove less than the "good supply of water" that Congress had vowed to provide.[22] Officials were at a loss to explain their inability to supply water above the first floor of houses on Capitol Hill. Incapacity occurred in all elevated areas, despite a daily supply of nearly 160 gallons per capita, about the largest in the country. The city water registrar blamed public fountains, the Navy Yard, and the Government Printing Office. At first, government engineers also thought federal buildings were the problem, but they eventually demonstrated that they used only ten percent of the daily supply and that water use was nearly as great in the night, when the government offices were closed, as in the day. It was obvious, federal engineers charged, that water was short because residents were profligate. Congress debated whether to instruct the police to conduct house-to-house searches for running faucets. Frustrated at not being able to take a bath after 6 a.m., former Public Buildings Commissioner Benjamin French wrote in his diary that the Aqueduct was "a d—nd humbug and nothing shorter." The water supply, which Mayor Richard Wallach took as a sign of "the great nation we have become" when it was new, had become a source of "great anxiety" within a decade.[23]

In the 1860s, Washington did not meet expectations. Little worked as intended. E. L. Godkin's *Nation* in 1871 depicted the capital as "a struggling, shabby, dirty little third-rate Southern town magnificent only in its distances." Dairymen drove herds through the city. Pigs roamed streets poking at rubbish. Farm animals conspired against L'Enfant. "Whenever we appropriate money to set up a shade tree, there comes along a cow, or a horse, or a goat, and tears it down again the next day," complained Vermont senator George Edmunds, adding, "and then we appropriate again."[24]

II

Reality was bound to appear desultory measured against L'Enfant's imagination. Yet George Washington's city did not come out badly when measured against the condition of other contemporary cities. The Washington Aqueduct, for example, posed problems, but they were not more vexing than the difficulties New York's engineers had with the Croton Aqueduct. New Yorkers complained of high rates and low pressure well into the twentieth century. Congress committed Washington to a public water supply decades before cities such as New Orleans, Buffalo, and San Francisco quit trying to make private sources suffice. London at the time had eight "thoroughly entrenched," quarrelsome water companies. The proportion of American cities with privately owned water supplies actually increased between 1875 and 1890, a consequence of reluctance on the part of local governments across the country to incur new debts in the aftermath of the financial crash of 1873. Certain features of the Washington Aqueduct fascinated engineers from America and Europe, for example the bridge over Rock Creek and especially the one at the Cabin John ravine. A tourist attraction, the Cabin John Bridge, 220 feet high and 105 feet wide, was for decades the largest stone arch in the world.[25]

The District was at least stumbling toward turning the canal and the Tiber Creek into the basis of a sewer system. As a leading historian of the subject makes clear, no city in the United States constructed adequate sewerage in conjunction with its water supply; all introduced "large volumes of water into systems designed to accommodate much smaller amounts." At mid-century, New York also had a poorly mapped jumble of ill-constructed brick sewers that fouled rivers at any number of points. Water mains and gas lines ran through the sewers. In 1865, the New York State legislature, with the acquiescence of Boss Tweed, passed a sewerage act, to enable the city to integrate its 195 miles of waste tunnels into a system. New York then began using vitrified pipe for new sewers, but converting existing brick to piping took decades. Not until the late 1870s did American cities embark on massive sewer construction, stimulated by the growing influence of municipal engineers and public health experts and by the sewer gas theories of Colonel George Waring. If anything, Washington stood slightly ahead of the national trend. The capital certainly outperformed nearby Baltimore, which in 1906 became the last major American city to embark upon municipal sewerage.[26]

One puzzle for engineers was how to coordinate sewerage and water supply along populated waterways. Drainage from towns upstream polluted the Potomac aqueduct more and more, but Washington's water compared favorably to that drawn by Philadelphia from the Schuylkill. At least the federal district was not fouling its own drinking water: Ellis Chesbrough's legendary ten-foot street raisings in the late 1850s drained central Chicago's streets but increased the mingling of sewage, dumped into the Chicago River, with water the city drew from Lake Michigan. To give Chicago an uncontaminated supply, Chesbrough designed a water tunnel that ran two miles into the lake. Such constructions were objects of interest but only abated, rather than solved, Chicago's problems. In the 1890s, engineers managed the still greater feats of building a four-mile tunnel into the lake and reversing the Chicago River's flow, so that the city's sewage would find its way south to the Mississippi.[27]

The width of Washington's streets made paving them an especially daunting prospect, but paving universally posed problems of technology and expense. Though durable and easily drained, cobblestone collected garbage and hindered traffic and thus was not a sufficient improvement over dirt. Contemporary methods for preparing asphalt still yielded a surface that was too soft in hot weather and too brittle in cold. Horses were thought to slip easily on such pavings in the rain. Officials often viewed as charlatans or con men promoters of asphalt or of concrete, which was still more brittle. European cities, such as Berlin and Paris, were installing stone block pavements made of granite, flagstone, or Belgian trap blocks. Though noisy, these were durable and easily cleaned, and they provided horses with sure footing. Yet their tremendous cost confined them to the busiest boulevards and squares. Elsewhere, cities covered roads with gravel or macadam. The latter consisted of fragments of stone pressed together and loosely cemented with a mortar of fine particles. Macadam was slightly more expensive than gravel and about that much tougher. The desire for quiet, attractive pavings for central city streets led to the idea of using wooden blocks, which were also easy to clean, easy on horses, and readily available. The tendency of dead wood that lay on the ground to rot led entrepreneurs to promote a variety of preservative processes, none of which worked.[28]

By 1865, New York had decided that stone blocks were the best solution. To meet the expense, the metropolis changed its taxing procedures. Half the cost would come from street railroads or from the city's general fund and half would be assessed against adjacent property, except in well-traveled business streets, where the city could assume the entire cost. In New York's slums, the inability or unwillingness of landlords to pay special taxes, combined with the poor's lack of political influence, delayed pavements, yet this system proved more viable than the customary procedure of assessing abutting property for the whole cost.[29]

Most cities made extensive use of some system of special assessments, even though it complicated immensely the politics of street paving, as well as of sewerage. In France, resistance to them exacerbated the financial difficulties of the Second Empire's infrastructure program and contributed to the mighty Haussmann's downfall. In democratic America, many cities, including Washington, could not as yet order street work except upon petition of local property owners. In places, this request had to be unanimous. Adjacent property owners were free to choose gravel or cobblestone, if they wished to save money or discourage traffic. Where, as in New York, city councils could order work done under special assessment, conflicting property and contracting interests presented a political minefield, as well as opportunities for graft. Little wonder that in 1880, when the Census Bureau first studied the matter, more than half the urban streets in the United States were unpaved, and the most common pavings were gravel and macadam. In 1890, when nearly 70 percent of Washington's streets and alleys were paved, this was true of less than 15 percent of streets in Cleveland, Atlanta, and Kansas City.[30]

Nor was Washington as backward as it appeared when it came to acquisition and development of public parks. Park advocates demanded that the Mall be cleared of railroads and systematically landscaped. They also called for Rock Creek Valley to be purchased for parkland. The advocates cited as precedents Druid Hill Park in Baltimore and—the most famous American example—Frederick Law Olmsted's Central Park. Olmsted's difficulties, political and economic, in implementing his plans are nearly as famous as the design itself. After Olmsted, Central Park endured the less-sensitive management of Tammany Hall, which meant a hodgepodge of modifications in Olmsted's plan, as well as uncollected litter, unrepaired benches and walks, and neglected trees, shrubs, and lawns.[31] New York, Chicago, Cleveland, and Philadelphia also had to contend with railroads that bisected major parks or isolated the city from its waterfront.

Patriots wanted Washington to compare favorably with capitals abroad. Advances made during this period by the French, Germans, and British in beautification, land use control, sanitation, and municipal services were considerable and much discussed, but the Europeans' accomplishments were easier to envy from a distance than after close inspection. Behind their elegant facades, the national capitals experienced some of the most severe housing and public health problems in Western Europe. By the 1880s, London and Berlin were falling conspicuously behind provincial cities in Britain and Germany in providing basic services and regulating development. Fragmented authority and the mutual suspicions of national and local officials sapped the vitality of those capitals' administrative and environmental reform movements. The financing of Baron Haussmann's Paris projects, the most vivid model of capital building then available to Americans, was often insecure and even fraudulent. Legal, financial, and political considerations compelled Haussmann to adopt methods of cutting streets through residential districts that had the effect of exacerbating crowding in tuberculosis-ridden central quarters. This in turn gave credibility to plans to tear down historic sections. While government in the Paris region was more unified than in most large European or American cities, the conflicts of authority that did exist perpetuated the trend towards an urban area divided into an overbuilt, expensive central city surrounded by ill-built, underserviced suburban slums.[32]

Wherever cities grew, so did their problems. When Edo acquired the name Tokyo in 1868, the imperial city of six hundred thousand may have been more sanitary than contemporary cities in the West. Yet only samurai were allowed running water in their homes and waste disposal depended on vigorous night soil and rubbish collection, rather than water closets and sewers. Drainage ditches cut through Tokyo's streets and carried waste water into rivers and moats. The city's unpaved streets were "like paddy fields on rainy days and turned into accompanying clouds of dust in dry periods."[33]

Washington sometimes hurt itself by basing policies on an exaggerated fear that it was falling behind other cities. An example was the favorable terms given to the "foreign," that is out-of-town, investors who during the Civil War constructed the Washington and Georgetown Railroad, the W & G, the capital's first horsecar line. In March 1862, Pennsylvania's Thaddeus Stevens played upon anxiety about the capital's condition in order to push through Congress a charter for a tramway company that was dominated by Philadelphians and organized by lobbyist Henry D. Cooke, banker Jay Cooke's brother. The House put aside a competing concern among Washington businessmen about out-of-state corporations when Stevens argued that if the bickering of rival local contestants for the franchise continued to delay construction, as it had for a decade already, "we shall never get a railroad here." The charter, granted for an indefinite period, exacted no fees for the franchise, although the company was required to pave between its tracks. Such loose charters were certainly common, but better models were available.[34]

In operation by late 1862, the W & G started at the Navy Yard and ran across the District along Pennsylvania Avenue. Despite a mandated 5¢-per-ride or 6-for-25¢ fare, the line returned an average dividend during its first two decades of 7.5 percent, on stock watered as much as four times. A group of local businessmen and Republican officeholders secured a charter two years later for the Metropolitan Railroad, whose downtown route ran along F Street and went out New Hampshire Avenue to what is now DuPont Circle. The Metropolitan also built lines on 7th and 14th streets, but it proved inconsistently profitable, largely because the W & G had pre-empted the best route.

Congress, a concerned senator asserted, had permitted Washington to be shut out of a profitable enterprise by "speculators from abroad,"* while Boston was successfully demanding bonuses in exchange for streetcar franchises. The justification given for allowing this to happen was the need to remedy the city's developmental backwardness. Yet in larger American cities, such as Philadelphia, Boston, and St. Louis, use of horsecars began to affect urban

---

* A temporary situation, as it turned out, since the Washington and Georgetown later fell into local hands.

transit on a wide scale only after 1856. In the United States, most tramway lines were laid after the Civil War. For the innovation to spread through the great cities of Europe took an additional decade.[35]

Such progress notwithstanding, leading District policy-makers and prominent residents were certain that the national city was dangerously backwards in this area and disgracefully run-down in many others. The conviction, inspired by the Union's great crisis, that the republic's capital must be transformed into an inspiring, worthy showcase perhaps predisposed both local and national patriots to downplay Washington's accomplishments and magnify its shortcomings. The national city's anxiety was deeply felt, however misplaced and whatever its cause.

III

The Civil War raised new hopes and opportunities, but it also nurtured a hazard in the form of efforts to remove the capital to a western city, such as St. Louis. Relocation was never likely, though it inspired ardent petitions by state legislatures from Indiana to Kansas. Proponents admitted that many found it a foolish project. Congress's authorization in early 1871 of the massive State, War, and Navy Building at Pennsylvania and 17th was a setback for those who would have moved the capital. Nevertheless, District businessmen worried over a proposal backed by influential editors such as Horace Greeley and Joseph Medill of the *Chicago Tribune*. Washington had "served the purposes" of a small country confined "to a narrow strip of Atlantic shore," wrote L. U. Reavis, a St. Louis pamphleteer, but the growing dominance of the Mississippi Valley rendered the capital on the eastern seaboard "a place of no great interest in common with the great wealth, industry, and progress of the American nation." Congressman John A. Logan, the powerful Illinois radical, tried to make the plan amenable to northern opinion by recalling Washington's vulnerable position during the rebellion. Subject to "hostile legislation of neighboring states," the present capital was "an unsafe and unfit place for Congress." Others made the strong, though contradictory argument that relocation might have a unifying effect on the war-torn nation, since Washington symbolized to southerners a government they had abandoned and that had defeated them.[36]

Observers with a consciously northern point of view asserted that Washington had stagnated because southern "ways, tastes, and enthusiasms" had enervated business and civic leaders. The capital would not prosper, they claimed, until local government was dominated by Yankee-style entrepreneurs who had the energy for boosterism and did not sniff at risk and hard work. As one proponent of aggressive improvements argued, Washington had for too long "been a Southernized city, little intent upon things of general value, and immethodical and slovenly as to its police, sanitary, and scientific regulations." This notion that Washington needed to break with its southern past and reorient itself towards the North both culturally and economically became a theme in local political battles throughout Reconstruction.[37]

Residents countered that their lack of drive was not to blame. Rather, a complicated, antiquated municipal structure was "prejudicial to the interests of the United States, as well as the people of the District." Since the retrocession of Alexandria in 1846, the sixty-nine-square-mile federal district consisted of three jurisdictions—the municipal corporations of Washington and Georgetown and the County of Washington. The two cities had mayor–city council governments, with bicameral legislatures consisting of a board of aldermen and a common council. The county included all land outside the cities, extending from the Potomac west of Georgetown to the heights across the Anacostia. An old Maryland institution called a Levy Court governed it. Of the court's nine members, who were appointed by the President, four came from the cities, which were then supposed to contribute substantially to the county budget, a duty performed grudgingly.[38]

Divided authority meant that the cities' policy regarding vital waterways and highways was uncoordinated and that their control was inadequate. Major roads through the county were still in the hands of old-fashioned turnpike companies, "petrified abusers," in Alexander Shepherd's view. The county surveyor found other country roads a "great perplexity." "Carelessly surveyed," they were laid out more "to accommodate individuals and to follow boundaries no matter where they run, than for the accommodation of the public." The cities did attempt to cooperate on waterfront improvements, but they lacked sufficient funds to implement a thorough program.[39]

Blocked from working together, Washington and Georgetown pursued prosperity individually. After the memories of failed canal promotions faded, the municipal corporations tried their luck with railroads. In 1853, Georgetown succumbed to door-to-door lobbying by the Maryland-chartered Metropolitan Railroad (not the streetcar company), which promised to give the old port a direct connection to Cleveland and make it a "splendid mart of commerce" for the goods of western Maryland and southern Pennsylvania. The town voted to subscribe $250,000, a sum equivalent to perhaps 10 percent of the town's wealth. Two years later, Georgetown mayor Henry Addison vetoed the bill to issue bonds for the subscription. When the Georgetown council overrode him, Addison refused to sign the bonds. He accused the Maryland state legislature of an "unreasonable and selfish act" in trying to assure that Georgetown's capital would be spent in Maryland first. Friendly senators presciently warned District residents that this railroad would prove a myth. No trains ever arrived in Georgetown.[40]

Washington City resisted the temptation to invest in the Metropolitan, but it was caught in the claws of an institution dearer to Maryland than the Chesapeake hard-shell crab. Between 1835 and 1872, the Baltimore and Ohio Railroad monopolized long-distance service to the District. The railroad exploited this position to acquire, without having "paid a single dollar for the use of

any public street or private property," the right to build its station on New
Jersey Avenue near C Street, two blocks from the Capitol. The railroad also
managed to "usurp" until 1910 the rights of way on Delaware Avenue and
other streets in northeast Washington, along which it stored cars and built
freight sidings. Residents from North Capitol Street eastward complained that
the B & O choked their neighborhoods and that the movement of trains
along the street grades was an annoyance and a danger.[41]

The Baltimore riots of 1861 strengthened the belief that the B & O was "a
powerful, if not objectionable monopoly." Its route between New York and
Washington required transfers in three places, the most important being Baltimore itself. On April 19, 1861, pro-Southern mobs attacked Northern troops
as they transferred between stations in Baltimore. Ben Butler's cannons soon
arrived on Federal Hill, near Camden Station, to intimidate the mobs and
protect Washington's "notoriously inconvenient and inadequate" route
north. The War Department urged the B & O to link itself to the Northern
Central, which would give the capital an alternate connection through Har-
risburg, to double its tracks, to facilitate the Baltimore transfer, and to request
Maryland to lower its taxes on through freight, which contributed to wartime
inflation in the District. In February 1862, John Work Garrett, the B & O's
president, responded that these proposals were not war measures but a ruse
to get the railroad to set up "a means of commercial rivalry with our Maryland lines." Garrett opposed all schemes to "isolate the city of Baltimore."
Instead, the company proposed to move troops across Baltimore by harbor
ferry, rather than by horse-drawn cars. In return, Garrett asked congressional
help in repairing the B & O's western lines, damaged by Confederate raids.[42]

Washington residents wondered whether Garrett cared more for his country or his railroad. To its credit, the B & O did agree a short time later to push
ahead with Washington's alternate connection. In exchange for completing
this "new and arduous enterprise" motivated by "patriotic considerations,"
the B & O demanded in 1866 that Washington City grant it certain "indispensible privileges." In particular, Garrett wanted to build the "Y" connecting its
northern and western branches off Delaware Avenue at H Street, four blocks
north of Massachusetts Avenue. The Columbia Institution for the Deaf (now
Gallaudet College) was to be sandwiched between two lines running at street
grade. The northeast's problems would double. Despite its preference for a
"Y" north of the city line, the municipality gave in, after Garrett threatened
that the B & O might confine the new line entirely to Maryland. "The capital
of the nation," commented the *National Intelligencer,* "is at the iron feet of
Mr. John Garrett."[43] Little wonder that Washington was willing to concede
the Mall in order to invite competition from Tom Scott's Pennsylvania
Railroad.

The outdated division of the federal district into Washington City, Washington County, and Georgetown hampered everything. There were divisions
within the three jurisdictions also, which hindered comprehensive policies.

In 1858 the Supreme Court settled a dispute between Washington and the federal government by ruling that the city corporation could regulate most street grades. The city was now legally free to take advantage of a grading plan developed by a former city surveyor. The venerable ward system, however, stood in the way. Four ward commissioners supervised improvements in the city's seven wards. Each ward had a small fund, based upon local taxes, to pay for a limited amount of grading and graveling. Money could not be transferred between wards, although in certain circumstances the city could assume a ward's debts. Ward funds sufficed to build the odd sewer and to flatten mounds or fill in ruts over sections of dirt streets. For more complicated projects, including all pavements, the city council had to vote a special assessment, upon petition of a majority of property owners. In this way, the city built extensive brick sidewalks. On the other hand, by the start of the Civil War, Washington's municipal government had managed to install cobblestone pavements over a total of twenty city blocks.[44]

During the war, the city moved to centralize and enhance its power over public works. It pressed Congress for charter amendments that would enable it to order improvements without a property owners' petition. Congress obliged in 1864 with a bill drawn up by Shepherd, at the time president of the Common Council. This bill provided a taste of the young leader's resourcefulness. Buried beneath an avalanche of resolutions and preambles extolling the measure's significance was a provision that Washington, whose debts were a constant bother for Congress, could charge improvements entirely to the general fund.[45]

Before the municipality could abuse this freedom, Congress repealed the provision, in February 1865, and instead gave the city council unrestricted authority to order special assessments. The council jumped at the chance to order sewerage, grading, and paving downtown from D to I streets. These improvements remained largely theoretical. Until it collected special taxes for a particular project, the city could pay contractors only in certificates of indebtedness, which banks would redeem only at severe discounts. Resistance by property owners to the new taxes thus discouraged contractors from pursuing their tasks with vigor. Taxpayers charged that "heavy, severe, and unequal" assessments favored real estate speculators over homeowners. Owners on streets slated for main sewers were especially annoyed, as the crudely written law forced them to pay for large pipes that drained other wards. The resisters won encouragement from famous politicians. Maine senator W. P. Fessenden called the taxes "all very well for a rich man" but "oppressive beyond measure" to the poor. Maryland's Reverdy Johnson said that a similar system in Baltimore was resulting in forced property sales. Iowa's Senator Grimes reported that people in Washington were taking up collections to pay the sewer taxes of the most hard-pressed residents. Even under the radical regime of Mayor Sayles J. Bowen, who was elected in 1868 with the support of prodevelopment businessmen, improvements merely sputtered along. The

Bowen administration managed to get 223 squares graded but only ten paved before it was destroyed by Reconstruction racial politics.[46]

In 1870, the District and Congress did settle one exasperating issue. Congress authorized the city to narrow and "park"—to plant grass and trees along the side or down the middle of—all but the most important thoroughfares. In 1865, the municipality, with backing from the Interior Department and the Army Corps of Engineers, had asked authority to rid itself of "inordinately wide" streets, but admirers of L'Enfant had delayed the proposition for three sessions of Congress, out of fear that street narrowing would wreck the plan's symmetry. Matthew G. Emery, Bowen's successor and Washington's last elected mayor until the 1970s, had no opportunity to implement the street narrowing law. On February 21, 1871, the same day the business community sponsored a carnival to celebrate the completion of Pennsylvania Avenue's wood block pavement, President Grant signed legislation to consolidate the old jurisdictions under one government.[47]

This record of frustration seemed to fulfill the famous gloomy predictions of New Jersey senator Samuel Southard, who in 1835 had admonished that it would be *"utterly impossible"* for the city to solve its problems "unaided by congressional legislation."[48] During the 1860s, officials reiterated the argument that the capital would never progress without continuous and systematic federal involvement. At the end of Buchanan's administration, Interior Secretary Jacob Thompson wrote that, although the past was "full of evidence of the generosity of Congress to this District," the city suffered from "the want of any definite rule or settled policy" regarding the country's responsibilities toward it. Likewise, John P. Usher, Lincoln's Interior Secretary, argued that, while the government should not take upon itself the "exclusive management" of Washington's streets and sewers, it ought to work out with the city an arrangement for sharing tasks. As for how that might be done, one common notion, outlined in an 1867 memorial from the District's wealthiest taxpayers, was that the United States should provide "for the improvements of the avenues and the public squares, and the city corporations for the streets." Yet no procedure on even such a basic matter had ever been endorsed in legislation.[49]

Under the Constitution, Congress has "exclusive" legislative powers in the federal district. From Senator Southard's day onward, respected members tried to persuade colleagues to stop appropriating for Washington ad hoc and to devise a strategy for the city that would encompass both methodical administrative oversight and predictable federal expenditures. Such arguments had not hit the mark. "Why should we undertake to make all these works for Washington more than for any other city?" asked Senator Solon Borland of Arkansas during the debate over the Washington Aqueduct in 1852. Kentucky's J. Proctor Knott, a member of the House District Committee, expressed the sentiments of legislators who delayed the repaving of Pennsylvania Avenue from 1864 to 1870: "Let us go home and tell our constituents that there is plenty of money in the Treasury for the brawney-armed, able-bodied negro man and the wealthy property owner on the main thoroughfare in the nation's capital." No one benefited from Washington's "splendid public edifices," Knott claimed, except the "hungry flock of small retainers who hover like vultures above this capital to prey on governmental garbage." Should local citizens complain of the Avenue's width? It was "not an inch wider than when the present owners purchased their property upon it." Knott was tired of those who regarded Washington as "the pride of the Republic, if not the glory of the entire universe."[50]

IV

Despite the hostility of Knott and others like him, the postwar surge of enthusiasm for nationalistic endeavors inspired Congress actively to pursue a "settled policy" that would facilitate the embellishment of Washington. While the anticipated program of "comprehensive" improvements appeared to necessitate reorganization of the capital's local government, the federal government already had a bureau able to coordinate its end of things—the Public Buildings Office. Significantly, the Commissioner of Public Buildings and Grounds, as this bureau's head was known, tended to be well-connected, familiar among both residents and politicians, and able to focus the interest of Congress on matters pertaining to Washington, despite the distraction of more exciting or pressing business.

The commissioner's wide duties made him aware of both national and local interests and gave him influence in both camps. During the 1860s, the Public Buildings Office, loosely controlled by the Interior Department, oversaw the Capitol police, the government-owned gaslights and telegraph wires, and most bridges, parks, and squares. The commissioner managed a variety of buildings, including the President's mansion, the Patent Office, and the Capitol, where he had his office. Benjamin B. French, commissioner during the Pierce administration and again from 1861 to 1867, remembered the President's traditional New Year's receptions as his "most irksome" task. French sought to stop "petty depredation" by White House tourists, who cut souvenirs from wallpaper and curtains. On one occasion, French's duties included mediating a dispute between a tearful Mary Todd Lincoln and her husband, who indignantly scolded his wife for $6,700 in cost overruns on the mansion's furnishing account. Lincoln vowed to pay the bill himself.[51]

Commissioner French was even better connected than most who held this post. Born in New Hampshire in 1800, he came to Washington in 1833 as a Democratic office holder and rose to be clerk of the House of Representatives. A resident of Capitol Hill, with a house on the site of the present Library of Congress, he became involved in local clubs and was influential as Grand Master of the District's Masons. He spent eleven years on the Washington City Council, serving two terms each as president of the Common Council and Board of Aldermen. After a flirtation with Know-Nothingism that led to his dismissal by Pierce, French emerged in the late 1850s as president of Washington's Republican association. This resulted in his election as chief marshal of Lincoln's inaugural and his appointment to the administration.[52]

French's business activities were as varied as his political ones. Through his friendship with Amos Kendall, the Jacksonian politician, French became president of Washington's Magnetic Telegraph Company when Congress in 1847 converted the line it had built for Samuel F. B. Morse to a private operation. French was active in many local enterprises, for example the East Capitol Building Association. In addition, he provided local backing for several of the Washington ventures of the Cookes, the era's leading Republican bankers.[53]

By the time French regained his old post in 1861, the bureau had already begun to draw up plans for improved federal-local cooperation. In March 1860, Buchanan's commissioner, Dr. John B. Blake, who was also prominent in Washington business and party politics, had sent Congress a list of local projects that he thought merited federal expenditures. Blake reiterated the need for "some definite understanding as to the improvements to be respectively made by the Government and the City."[54] French took up this theme energetically. Although he did not argue this explicitly, French appears to have assumed that the Public Buildings Office, which had been mainly a management office for the federal establishment, would expand into the umbrella agency that would coordinate any more active national policy regarding the city.

By long custom, the commissioner handled arrangements and accounts with the city government for work near federal property or on streets of national significance. Before the war, Blake used this role to win appropriations for grading Missouri Avenue and B Street where they adjoined the Mall. During the war, French employed the same rationale to push Congress into funding more widespread public works. French and his allies in the city government made sure to present each new project to Congress in terms of its direct benefit to the country. It was necessary to grade Virginia and Georgia avenues, for example, because these roads led to the Navy Yard. Proposed improvements to New York and Maryland avenues would benefit the military. French pressed for completion of the Capitol dome in order to indicate "the sincerity of the expressed belief" in the Union. The bureau worked with Washington's city surveyor to replan drainage, gas lines, and streets in the blocks around Lafayette Square and promoted these plans on the grounds that existing conditions around the executive departments rendered doing business with the government unpleasant. Congress responded in 1864 by providing French with blanket authority to reimburse the city for work that benefited the government. However, Congress then delayed making appropriations under this provision when estimates quickly rose into the hundreds of thousands.[55]

French put his office at the service of out-of-town businessmen who wished to invest in Washington. In January 1865, French suggested to Thaddeus Stevens, House chairman of Ways and Means, that Congress give $10,500 to open East Capitol Street to 11th Street East and to begin to lay out there the park that French proposed to call Lincoln Square. To persuade Stevens, the commissioner enclosed correspondence from a Philadelphia firm that was already building in the vicinity and that promised to erect two hundred to three hundred houses affordable to government clerks. The President's assassination four months later gave the project patriotic as well as entrepreneurial purposes. Authorized during the next congressional session, Lincoln Square is now the heart of Capitol Hill.[56]

On the subject of paving, the bureau entered negotiations with Boston entrepreneur Samuel Nicolson, who had a patent on a form of wood pavement. In 1864, French reported that "Nicolson wood" might prove an affordable way to repave Pennsylvania Avenue. According to Nicolson, his wood pavements were successful in St. Louis, Milwaukee, and Chicago. They lasted three times as long as other materials and were so strong that they might "be safely constructed over quicksand." His method, Nicolson argued, provided a "pleasant foothold" for animals, leading to "*saving in horse flesh.*" The Army Corps of Engineers also proved receptive to such arguments. The laying of wood blocks on Pennsylvania Avenue in 1871 represented the height of prestige for wood paving.[57]

In sum, the Public Buildings Office was assembling the elements of an improvement plan that Congress might be prepared to back. In early 1866, the House District Committee consulted Washington's mayor regarding financial relations between the District and the government. After a lengthy debate, the panel approved French's "repayments," and by July the House had appropriated nearly $80,000. The committee also conferred with federal and city officials regarding the canal, hospitals, and sanitary conditions in general. Finally, the legislators asked French to provide estimates for grading and paving the full distance of avenues such as Massachusetts, Vermont, and Rhode Island with different materials, including Belgian stone and Nicolson wood blocks. The commissioner used the occasion to prepare a table on the size and potential cost of paving all major thoroughfares.[58]

A year later, however, Congress ousted French by abolishing his office. The only government job he could find in his remaining years was a minor clerkship in the Treasury Department, from which he was also fired, a few months before his death in 1870, despite a family friendship with the secretary, George Boutwell. The commissioner's plans for the city sat on the shelf. Why would Congress, seemingly on the verge of at last settling upon a development strategy for the federal district, suddenly attack the federal officer with the most experience, knowledge, and contacts in the local community? The answer has much to do with rivalries and passions brought to the surface by Congress's battle with President Andrew Johnson over Reconstruction.

Although widely liked, Benjamin French was a spoilsman who never

earned a reputation for rectitude. In the mid-nineteenth century, petty ve-
nality did not disqualify one for office, but it gave one's enemies an angle of
attack. When Lincoln appointed him, French boasted to his brother of the
position's perquisites. He could get his ne'er-do-well son, Ben, a $1,000 mes-
sengership. He could receive "splendid bouquets" daily from the Botanical
Garden. "Honest Old Abe . . . calls me 'French' and always tells me a story."
Best of all, "a bath house is coming that, in all probability, never would have
come had not 'The Commissioner of Public Buildings' owned these prem-
ises." [59] In 1863, French became entangled in a jurisdictional dispute with his
ostensible superior, J. P. Usher, the secretary of the interior. French believed
"Jackass Puny" Usher to be as fit for the cabinet "as I am for Pope." Yet the
secretary knew he could worry French by threatening "to mouse" in the bureau's dispersal accounts for the Capitol extension and the Patent Office. [60] One
suspects that an audit would have revealed that the commissioner was using
government labor and supplies on his own property.

French survived as commissioner into the Johnson administration. He remembered the Tennessee politician fondly from when they both were Democrats, and so supported him, despite misgivings over the President's intransigence regarding Reconstruction. By 1866, even half-hearted approval of
Johnson was controversial. Whispering thus continued about the propriety
of the Public Buildings commissioner. Johnson contemplated firing him but
refrained. The grateful French, who used to recite celebratory poems at Ma-
sonic occasions, wrote verses in praise of the President:

Where Jackson stood now doth another stand —
The favored ruler of our favored land.
With heart as pure and patriotism as great,
A second Andrew steers the ship of state, . . .

When this doggerel found its way into newspapers, Republican radicals
smelled Johnsonian blood. Ohio's Robert Schenck had French's verses read
into the *Congressional Globe*. To the House's "jollification," Schenck, in as fa-
cetious a tone as he could strike, introduced a resolution that Public Buildings
funds not be used to compensate the "poet-laureate of the Administration."
The commissioner's supporters countered with his earlier anti-secession
verse. Schenck, "a miserable, sneaking poltroon" (in French's objective opinion), publicly impugned French's honesty and competence and advocated a
measure to abolish the Public Buildings Office. The legislation passed, on
March 2, 1867, the same day as the famed Tenure of Office Act. Congress,
forced on "the spur of the moment" to find someone to do French's work,
voted to replace the civilian commissioner with an officer from the Army
Corps of Engineers, thus moving the bureau from Interior to the War Department. French confided to his brother how much he regretted losing his gardener, an employee of the Capitol. [61]

Even though Congress acted precipitously in moving the Public Buildings Office to the War Department, some legislators sympathetic to Washington's needs argued that the change was fortuitous. The prestigious and trusted Army Corps, it was hoped, would prove a more effective advocate for the District. Lost, however, were historical knowledge of Washington's relations with the government and the wide circle of acquaintances in the business community that Blake and French had. At the moment when Congress appeared ready to accept a vigorous federal role in developing the capital, the legislature severely disrupted the agency potentially most capable of directing the impending national efforts and moderating local demands. French anticipated the mixed feelings District residents later developed regarding the Army Corps when he privately praised the new "Officer in Charge of Public Buildings and Grounds," Major Nathaniel Michler, as talented and a "free man," and yet worried that Washington would suffer because his replacement, unaware of Congress's "niggardly" record, presented his ambitious schemes in such an "ornamental" fashion that they would not survive the appropriations gauntlet. The Corps did succeed in securing $297,000 in "repayments" to the city in April 1868.[62] Even so, the absence of a civilian umbrella organization capable of mediating between contending interests contributed to the bitterness and confusion that accompanied Shepherd's Comprehensive Plan a few years later.

V

Reconstruction politics, which derailed the Public Buildings Office, on surface had little relation to the creation of an admirable, attractive Washington. In a larger sense, however, the great issues of the Civil War era were about the disposition of the national government, so they could not but affect the capital, which geographically and culturally stood on the border of the contending regions.

From the start of the war, in 1861, the Union government based its treatment of Washington's inhabitants on the assumption that the pro-Southern feeling might become a menace. The Metropolitan Police were nationalized. At one point, about three hundred District residents were in the Old Capitol Prison for proved or suspected disloyalty. Federal courts attempted to seize $7 million from large property owners who sided with the rebellion, among whom was former Washington mayor Walter Lenox. The Army occupied the estate of the District's wealthiest man, the Democratic banker William Wilson Corcoran, whose extended family included leading rebels. Rather than compromise himself, Corcoran went to France for the duration. There he added to his famous art collection, while his gallery in Washington served as a military clothing depot. Corcoran's considerable philanthrophy never offset bitterness caused by rumors that while in Europe he had negotiated Confederate war loans. Upon his death at age ninety in 1888, one obituary's description read, "Known as a sympathizer with treason and rebellion, . . . quite genial and kindly in his selfish and prejudiced way."[63]

When Washington mayor James G. Berret, a Breckinridge Democrat, refused to take the loyalty oath, he was imprisoned for a month at Fort Lafayette, New York, until he resigned and was replaced by an unconditional Unionist, Richard Wallach. Yet, secessionist sentiment in Washington did not present the problems that certain federal authorities expected. Even though the commander of the National Rifles joined the Confederacy, most local militiamen stayed loyal and permitted themselves to be organized into trustworthy units in time for Lincoln's inauguration. By the end of 1861, more than 6,500 District men were in the Union forces, while the number who joined the Confederate Army may have been as low as five hundred.[64]

Early in the war, congressional Republicans came to view the compensated emancipation of the capital's 3,200 slaves, enacted in April 1862, as part of an "inevitable sequence" of legislation that would gradually put the country's most vexing problem to rest. From that point forward, Congress tried out every important Reconstruction civil rights measure in the District before extending it across the South. For Washington, the result was a series of bills, municipal charter amendments, and local ordinances that by 1870 protected black civil rights and political participation. Reconstruction in the capital collapsed shortly thereafter, and integration broke down in the 1880s.[65] Antidiscrimination laws were dead letters by the turn of the century, but they were never officially repudiated. This may or may not have given Washington's blacks an advantage over their counterparts in the Southern states, where the Jim Crow system enjoyed government sponsorship.

Although most white Washingtonians stayed with the North, few condoned congressional solicitude for blacks. In April 1862, the revamped, pro-Union Washington City Council sent an emphatic joint resolution to the Capitol protesting that "unqualified abolition of slavery" would turn the national city into "an asylum for free negroes — a population undesirable in every American community." Before the war, Washington had already had nearly three times as many free blacks as slaves, so Congress was not proposing such an unprecedented innovation. Tens of thousands of "contraband" slaves, most destitute and illiterate, indeed began to crowd into the capital from the surrounding slave states. For a time, Unionist mayor Wallach refused to cooperate with Army efforts to relieve these "idle, dissolute, and reckless" people. In barely polite terms, Wallach suggested to the local provost marshal that the government that freed the slaves should care for them.[66]

Soon after the war, Congress began seriously to debate black voting rights. The District's two cities held referenda. The result was 6,591 to 35 against black suffrage in Washington City and 712 to 1 against in Georgetown. Congress proceeded to ignore the citizens' expressed wishes and in January 1867 overrode a presidential veto of a District equal suffrage bill, largely because

Johnson's spirited veto message challenged Congress's right to give Washington's blacks the vote.[67]

A local radical party emerged to fight in the 1868 mayoral election. Its candidate, Sayles J. Bowen, was born in Cayuga County, New York, in 1813 and had come to Washington in 1845 as a protégé of James Buchanan. In 1848, Bowen was fired from his post in the Treasury Department for supporting the Free Soilers. The New Yorker then became active in local business and politics. Despite a suspicious personality, Bowen made friends among prominent Washingtonians, such as Benjamin French. By 1856, Bowen was a Republican. While a Metropolitan Police commissioner early in the war, Bowen made allegations regarding disloyalty in the capital that embittered fellow residents. He became city postmaster in 1863; during the tenure of office fight that led to Johnson's impeachment, Bowen continued to deliver the War Department's mail to Edwin Stanton, the fired secretary. This record and his deeply felt support for black education and civil rights made him an ideal radical leader. Congressional radicals such as Henry Wilson, Ben Butler, and George Julian rallied newly enfranchised black voters to Bowen's side.[68]

District businessmen and their friends in Congress at first treated civil rights as a distraction that could only delay adoption of a District improvement program. During the equal suffrage debate, former Senate District chairman Lot Morrill, who in 1862 had managed the emancipation bill's passage, and Nevada's William Stewart, a moderate who acted as a spokesman for the capital's real estate interests, pushed an alternative measure to replace the municipal corporations with an appointed commission. This would achieve the business community's aim of a consolidated government, and it would render suffrage agitation irrelevant. Republican developers, however, led by Shepherd and Crosby Noyes, now partners in the *Evening Star,* soon began to suggest that business support for the radicals might be Washington's key to the U.S. Treasury. The *Star* asserted that Bowen's "influence," would not induce Congress "to pave our streets with pearl or otherwise New Jerusalemize the city at National expense." Still, the paper, which had opposed black suffrage until it was an accomplished fact, publicized Bowen's promises that a city administration "in accord with the great majority in Congress," would ensure "liberal appropriations." Bowen's election, argued the *Star,* would demonstrate "that we have at last consented to consider our business interests and respect the authority that controls us."[69]

The alliance of some businessmen with the radicals made the difference in the June 1868 election. Hostile white voters suppressed their distaste for associating with blacks and turned out in record numbers. Bowen won by only 83 votes out of 18,257 cast. Blacks won a single seat on both the Board of Aldermen and the Common Council, a representation that increased to eight in the two houses the next year. A dispute over the council results precipitated street fighting that left a white man dead. Election commissioners certified the election of Bowen and of a conservative council, but the city registrar, a radical from New England, refused to enter the result, on the grounds that the ballots of certain white soldiers in a ward that went conservative should be disallowed. For five days, Mayor Wallach refused to surrender his office. Finally, the new mayor had a locksmith break open the door to his chamber. Alternative councils organized and called for each others' resignations. After two weeks, Congress cut the Gordian knot by legislating the Republicans into office.[70]

In his inaugural address, Bowen promised to reform the city contract system and to pursue public works. Divisions among his supporters inhibited him, and the mayor's irascible temperament exacerbated these quarrels. Rumors circulated of a "Bowen Ring" that supposedly exploited blacks to compensate for disappearing white support. Allegedly, the mayor used tight public works funds to bring into the city unemployed blacks, who were set to work digging grass out of gutters with penknives.[71]

Bowen's friends in national politics began to back away. The anticipated federal assistance to the mayor's public works program did not materialize, which undermined the business community's motive for tolerating radicalism. Shepherd emerged as chairman of a so-called reform committee. Matthew G. Emery, a New Hampshire–born mason and architect, was the reform candidate for mayor in 1870. Except for the radical *Chronicle,* the press turned entirely against Mayor Bowen. More important, the anti-Bowen Republicans were able to convince some blacks to vote for a bipartisan coalition that brought together the Republicans' improvement faction and the local Democrats. Unsuccessfully, radical orators urged blacks to stay behind "your friend and the friend of our country." Of six blacks elected to the Common Council in June 1870, four supported Emery. Bowen lost by nearly 4,000 out of 17,000 votes. Although Bowen stayed active in Republican politics, he never again held a responsible office.[72]

Bowen's radicals wanted Washington to be a leader in emancipation, suffrage, and desegregation. Shepherd's improvers sought to make the national city a prospering innovator in public services, utilities, and sanitation. The founders of the Republican party in the 1850s imagined that the increase of liberty and the pursuit of national and personal wealth were complementary goals. As anti-slavery writer Richard Hildreth explained, liberty encouraged "that *spirit of industry* essential to the increase of public wealth." One of the reasons that Reconstruction became such a tragedy was that growth and liberty proved less complementary than the early Republicans had hoped. Political circumstances in the South and throughout the country increasingly placed Republicans who adhered most to an economic vision of progress in competition with those factions whose emphasis was more on rights and equality. Over and over, when the battle over race and civil rights became too heated, "modernizers" disentangled themselves from radicals in order to save their special programs. Shepherd's "Regular Republicans" argued that they better represented party principles than the Bowen group did. This had not been true once, but it was becoming so.[73]

Elected alderman in 1870, Shepherd continued to lead a group of real estate developers, bankers, and contractors who sought to replace the municipal governments of Washington City and Georgetown. This group designed the "territorial" government, to facilitate improvement schemes at the expense of the promotion of equal participation and civil rights. From atop the Capitol, Freedom continued to watch over the national city, but people below pursued other ends.

2

Improvers and
Old Citizens

Of all the drivel, stuttered or printed, none is surely quite so puerile as [the charge that] the effort to elect a republican Territorial Legislature and Delegate to Congress is in the interest of some mischievous and terrible "ring." This stupid stuff . . . is the familiar old hunker cry against improvements . . . , maligning the motives of those who show some public spirit. . . . These hunkers . . . pertinaciously resist every effort to lift the city out of the mud and make it what it should be as the capital of the nation. If anyone is daring enough to undertake to improve the condition of affairs, instantly the whole puddle is vocal with croaks of "ring!" "ring!" "ring!"

—*Evening Star*, April 6, 1871

A NY DISCUSSION of public works in Gilded Age Washington must assess the career of Alexander Robey Shepherd, the dominant figure in the territorial government of 1871–74. Operating first from the strategic post of vice president of the Board of Public Works and later from the office of territorial governor, Shepherd set in motion an amazing array of physical, economic, and political changes. Of equal importance, Shepherd's vast infrastructure program, the Comprehensive Plan of Improvements, affected the local business community's identity and direction so much that for the next generation, commercial and civic leaders defined the brief territorial period as the starting point of their own endeavors. As the Washington Board of Trade, the "commercial-civic" organization that would come to embody the city to residents and outsiders, thus eulogized Shepherd in 1902: "His greatest public service to the Republic was that rendered by him as the founder of the New Washington which is now developing in realization of his plans."[1]

Washingtonians tend to fill the story of Shepherd's "refounding" of their city with far more ambiguity than they impute to George Washington's original founding. They remember the more recent of these figures not as a stoic paragon but as a divisive, impetuous, flawed man. While he was in office, Shepherd's belligerent character and brash methods inspired either fervent admiration or vehement hostility. Supporters hailed him as a Napoleon of sewer pipe and pavement. Enemies insisted that Shepherd had put together a "ring" of coarse politicians and grasping contractors more reckless and sinister than the recently deposed Tweed Ring of New York. Defenders and detractors agreed on little except that the city was undergoing massive transformation and that the man most responsible was, for better or worse, "Boss" Shepherd.

By June 1874, argument over Shepherd's style of government and his massive public works program had grown so stormy that Senate friends stole out of the chamber to avoid having their votes recorded on President Grant's controversial nomination of the governor to a caretaker commission that was about to supersede his discredited Territory. Senate colleagues dissented adamantly when Senator Simon Cameron, himself reputed to be a formidable boss, defended the Washington leader as "the master spirit who had courage, intelligence, and vigor enough to combine the intellect of this town in favor of its prosperity." Cameron's insistence that within thirty years, "the much-abused Governor Shepherd will be almost canonized in this District," elicited head-shaking skepticism from his fellow senators.[2] Peers should have known better than to doubt this shrewd operator's judgments about public sentiment.

Still under forty when he was ousted, Shepherd never held another office. Bankrupt by 1880, the ex-governor left his home to spend the rest of his life running silver mines in Mexico. Yet on a return visit to Washington in 1887, residents, with "hearty good will," erected a reviewing stand for him south of the Treasury Building, from which he watched an "imposing" parade in his honor.[3] Local historians built Shepherd into a hero and legend. After his death, businessmen established a fund for a statue. In a 1909 ceremony to dedicate this likeness of the person who, next to Washington himself, ranked as the city's "chief benefactor," District Commissioner Macfarland remarked, "The fabric which has been building on the Shepherd foundation has now reached noble proportions." For the next seventy years, the "Boss" stood before the District Building on Pennsylvania Avenue, his right hand holding blueprints and his left hand open behind his back, presumably ready for a handout. Public bewilderment about the capital's most renowned chief executive was thereby "eternally preserved in bronze."[4]

Shepherd and other principals in the "District Ring" controversy were so colorful and their conduct in office so imperious that the Territory's supporters and critics easily slipped into circular arguments over character and motives. Contemporaries spent considerable energy on an irresolvable debate over whether Shepherd and his associates were primarily interested in ameliorating Washington or in lining their pockets. The Territory's enemies assumed that they could discredit the regime's concrete achievements by showing that Shepherd had meanwhile enabled an "improvement ring" to profit at the public's expense. Likewise, Shepherd's defenders imagined they could vindicate their idol by demonstrating that he had refrained from directly manipulating his position for his own avaricious ends. By the turn of the century, knowledgeable observers had come to agree with statistician Carroll D.

Wright, who noted in 1899 that, although Shepherd's Board of Public Works had often acted injudiciously, "there was no corruption . . . by which the members profited." Still, Wright's conclusion that this official served the public "patriotically and honestly" has rarely been accepted without doubt.[5] Shepherd received the acclaim his partisans sought but not the vindication they imagined would accompany recognition of the scale of his exploits and legacy.

No definitive assessment of the territorial period has ever emerged. Perhaps this is because Shepherd's idea of a New Washington raised questions about policy-making and political economy that are difficult in their own right and that the disputes over personality and motive have only muddled further. What assumptions and aims were built into the territorial program? From where did Shepherd derive his views regarding the relation of public works to progress? What were these ideas' consequences?

Shepherd and his allies embody that strand in Reconstruction Republicanism which had come to emphasize progress in physical and economic development at the expense of political and ethical progress, the other pillar of the original Republican vision. For this reason, I label the Shepherd faction "improvers" or "improver Republicans." Shepherd's Comprehensive Plan of Improvements was firmly within the venerable "promotional" tradition that historically had guided state-sponsored development programs on every level of government in this country. Like most Americans, especially those on the make, Washington's improvers accepted it as a matter of course that a town's welfare corresponded to the interests of its strategic enterprises. Shepherd and his associates, therefore, steered the municipality and the relevant federal bureaus into partnerships with dynamic entrepreneurs, who of course regularly turned out to be the territorial leadership's allies and friends.

Investigators tried and failed to uncover brazen forms of official corruption — kickbacks, embezzlement, and the like. On the other hand, a complicated, legally dubious network of personal connections, conflicts of interest, and indirect benefits did dominate territorial Washington. Still, this does not mean that the improvers simply exploited Washington's pent-up demand for public works. The outlook and prior experience of the contractors, real estate men, and Republican activists who contrived the Comprehensive Plan and ran the Territory encouraged them to equate their own group advantage and the public good. The old either/or question about the Shepherd group's motives is hopelessly inadequate, because it presumes a distinction that did not exist in the improvers' mental world.

The promotional model of state-sponsored development was widely accepted in Reconstruction Washington. Indeed, no major party in the dispute felt the impulse to articulate a competing scenario. The opposition by residents to the territorial regime was led by self-described "old citizens," who took that label because they felt that their links to prewar Washington made them natural leaders of a once-stable community that had lost cohesion and balance in the upheavals of war. The old citizens looked upon improvers as unscrupulous, uncouth upstarts. Eventually, a strategic group of out-of-towners, "reform" journalists from publications with national influence, took the old citizens' side. Crusading editors from New York, projecting their recent experience with the Tweed Ring onto the Washington situation, undertook to help purge the capital of "President Grant's Washington Tammany."[6] The combined activities of resident opponents and out-of-town editors finally derailed Shepherd in June 1874. Yet, in the long run, Shepherd's vision of Washington would prevail and his reputation would revive, even among many who were fierce antagonists at the time. This was because, despite the improvers' insistence that the old citizens were "puddle-croaking" obstructionists, Shepherd's opponents valued "improvement" nearly as much as his allies and defined "progress" in virtually the same way, though they would have preferred a government that pursued these goals at a more measured pace and in a less high-handed manner.

Perhaps what confused Washington's citizens and outside commentators is that Shepherd and his allies achieved the handsome capital that post–Civil War nationalists envisioned but accomplished their purpose by taking to an uproarious extreme methods that most Americans found appropriate if used with discretion. Reconstruction nationalists insisted that an infusion of the aggressive "Northern" spirit into Washington's business community might allow the federal district at last to become an embodiment of national greatness. Yet few were prepared to face the full reality of the program thus recommended—a program that ultimately incorporated the country's ruling political party and the federal government itself in a system of business-government cooperation similar to what had built the mighty North.

I

Although he was over six feet tall, "an Apollo in form," Alexander Shepherd had not, by the end of the war, reached heroic proportions. He was a recognizable type—the "clear-headed, energetic young man." Like many nineteenth-century businessmen, Shepherd enjoyed depicting himself as self-made, though his background was not especially humble. His father was a lumber merchant in southwest Washington. Born in 1835, Alexander attended preparatory school briefly, until age fourteen when his father died. Far from being cast, fatherless, upon the world, he was apprenticed to Canadian-born John W. Thompson, the largest plumbing and gas contractor in the District. In the 1850s, plumbing was an innovative, booming business. By late in that decade, the ambitious apprentice had become a partner. Soon thereafter, Thompson retired from the firm to manage his diverse investments in banking and utilities. Shepherd made his brother a partner in the

Alexander R. Shepherd in later years.
Courtesy the Washingtoniana
Division, District of Columbia
Public Library.

plumbing business he had inherited and planned to expand. By 1865, Shepherd Brothers' remodeled plant consisted of five shops for gas-fitting, plumbing, brass finishing, carpentry, and blacksmithing.[7]

Shepherd took a ninety-day enlistment in the Union's District Volunteers, right after the attack on Fort Sumter. Mustered out before the Battle of Bull Run, the young contractor involved himself in Washington's Republican politics and won three terms on the Common Council. At this time, the war was fueling rapid change in the composition and outlook of Washington's commercial and political elites. Shepherd emerged as the leader of a dynamic new faction. This up-and-coming group included bankers, subdividers, contractors, engineers, public officials, and persons who were a little of each. Shepherd's group had highly visible ties to the national Republican party and was committed to a nationalist, but also promotional view of the capital's function and problems.

In 1864 and 1865, Shepherd and John Thompson helped establish the Metropolitan Railroad Company, the District's second tramway. Another incorporator was Lewis Clephane, one-time business manager of the abolitionist *National Era,* a founder of the *National Republican,* and later Lincoln's collector of internal revenue. Another investor was Samuel P. Brown, a former Maine state representative whose associates included Hannibal Hamlin and other powerful New England Republicans. Brown made a fortune supplying coal and lumber to the navy, which inspired the ever-practical Lincoln to bring him to Washington as a navy agent. Brown quickly began to invest in a variety of local undertakings, the most memorable being a substantial tract beyond the old city boundary that later became the suburb Mount Pleasant.[8]

About the same time, Shepherd became friendly with Adolph Cluss. Born in 1825, the son of an architect in Württemberg, Cluss grew interested in socialist ideas while a construction engineer on the Mainz-Mannheim railroad. He became acquainted with Marx and Engels, with whom he corresponded for years. Cluss was obliged to flee Germany after the failed revolution of 1848. He found work at the Washington Navy Yard and settled in the American capital. By the 1860s, Cluss had developed an extensive architectural practice that included important work for the city government. In addition to the still-popular Eastern Market, Cluss designed the innovative Wallach and Franklin schools, which won prizes at international exhibitions in Vienna, Paris, and Philadelphia.[9]

Cluss's work for the city influenced council member Shepherd's views on municipal improvements. The architect's residential practice brought him into association with contractor Shepherd, who was by now engaged in large-scale speculation in real estate west of the White House and between what are now Farragut Square and Dupont Circle. In 1872, Cluss completed three fancy houses — total cost in excess of $150,000 — on K Street north of Farragut Square. Two were for himself and Shepherd. The third mansion on "Shepherd Row" was for another associate, Hallet Kilbourn.[10]

A native of Rochester, New York, Kilbourn had a peripatetic career until, while practicing law in Indiana, he served as a Lincoln elector. This led to a federal clerkship. Kilbourn stayed in Washington to become a real estate broker and free-lance investor.[11] He identified himself with the Washington interests of the Cookes, the Republican bankers. Later, he and a close associate, a New York–born contractor named John O. Evans, would be found at the center of the deplorable scandal that resulted from Henry D. Cooke's abuse of his leadership of the finance committee of the Freedman's Savings Bank. Others on that committee were William S. Huntington, cashier of the Cooke's First National Bank of Washington, Lewis Clephane, and Moses Kelly, a former Department of the Interior clerk become cashier of the National Metropolitan Bank. During the months when the Territory's infrastructure program was taking shape, these six men, along with another Washington businessman and a Philadelphia investor, put together a "ring," as Kilbourn termed it in an 1871 letter to Huntington, to "try and control the entire lot of asphalt pavements" in Washington. The group contributed officers to a set of interlocking enterprises, the largest and most noteworthy of which was the Metropolis (sometimes Metropolitan) Paving Company.[12]

When Kilbourn's letter became public during an 1874 congressional investigation, opponents trumpeted it as proof that the territorial movement constituted a ring, in the popular sense of a premeditated, coordinated conspiracy. Yet Kilbourn's paving ring was the only entity brought to light during the investigation that contained enough collusion to transcend ordinary cronyism. Kilbourn's letter probably conveyed an overblown impression of his alliance. He had a taste for flamboyance that alternately annoyed and amused his friends. Although most of the interlocking paving companies were formed in late 1870 and early 1871, when the individuals who incorporated them were simultaneously agitating for the territorial bill, Kilbourn had not, as enemies assumed, concocted the scheme simply to exploit a government sure to be dominated by friends. The spate of new companies was equally a result of Congress's having provided Washington with its first general incorporation act. Businessmen could only then give legal status to informal relations that had existed for some time. As Clephane, the former abolitionist publisher, explained, "We were all associated together in business operations and in friendly relations and we thought it best" to pool capital, patent rights, and contracts.[13]

During the postwar years, Shepherd also had become intrigued by experimental smooth pavements. The future Board of Public Works head invested in the Portland Cement Company. Kilbourn and his associates offered Shepherd a place in the Metropolis Company, but Shepherd, who by then anticipated his role in the pending Territory, was taking steps to distance himself from District paving interests.[14]

Of the improver group, Henry D. Cooke in particular built a reputation as "one of the very best men of the community . . . active, noble spirited, generous," in the words of diarist and sometime business partner B. B. French. Born in 1825, youngest of the Cooke brothers, Henry was educated at Transylvania University in Kentucky. While he tried shipping and law, Henry's main activity before the war was journalism. After stints as a foreign correspondent and an assistant consul in Chile, Henry Cooke purchased the *Ohio State Journal,* which he made an organ for Salmon B. Chase. Jay Cooke distrusted his brother's business sense but brought Henry into the family banking firm at the start of the war because of his connections; one purpose of the Cookes' First National Bank of Washington was to make loans to politicians. The head of the family, Eleutheros Cooke, wrote to Jay, "H.D.'s plan in getting Chase into the Cabinet & Sherman into the Senate is accomplished, and . . . now is the time for making money, by honest contacts out of the govt. . . . If H.D. don't avail himself of the hard earned favor of the Admn, he deserves poverty." Within a decade, Henry became the District's second wealthiest person (after W. W. Corcoran). His Georgetown mansion—furnished "in Oriental splendor," according to a society columnist, with silk, satin, and ebony—saw some of the Grant era's most extravagant political receptions.[15]

Henry Cooke's most direct business link to Shepherd came through their joint sponsorship of the Washington Market Company, an enterprise which illustrates how this pair straddled the worlds of business and politics. In 1869, a circle of New England investors—prominent among them William E. Chandler, the influential Republican national secretary—presented Congress with a plan for a private company to rebuild and assume operation of the dilapidated Center Market, which the municipality maintained between 7th and 9th streets south of Pennsylvania Avenue. To head off the resentment local businessmen often felt towards "foreign" corporations' activity in key enterprises, the New Englanders invited Cooke and Shepherd into the company. The involvement of these local notables did much to assuage misgivings in the city and to smooth the charter bill's passage through Congress.[16]

The Chandler group's market was housed in an ornate building designed by Adolph Cluss (Cluss's Market Hall was demolished in 1931 to make room for the National Archives). The operation would go on to win nationwide praise as a model municipal market, evidence that not all political companies are badly run. Yet, at the same time, the company had to defend itself against periodic legal and legislative attacks on its charter. Critics based their assaults in large measure on the firm's propensity for manipulating connections to rid itself of responsibilities specified in its corporate charter. The most flagrant instance occurred in March 1873. Cooke, at that time territorial governor, arranged with former mayor Emery, company president, to lower the company's annual contribution to the city's poor fund from $25,000, stipulated by charter as rental for the site, to $7,500. In return, the company signed over to Washington use of a portion of Market Square—land already owned by the United States—for a city hall that was never built.

Two of Shepherd's most important friends were Alfred Mullett, who as supervising architect of the treasury oversaw construction of most federal buildings across the country, and Major Orville E. Babcock, U. S. Grant's personal secretary and officer in charge of public buildings and grounds. Babcock's role in the Santo Domingo and Whiskey Ring affairs made him a symbol of Republican corruption, although his work in the District earned grudging respect (as we shall see in chapter 6). Mullett was a *bête noire* of the anti-Grant crowd, despite mugwumpish credentials: English-born and European-trained. To Charles A. Dana's *New York Sun,* Mullett was "the most arrogant, pretentious, and preposterous little humbug in the United States." Henry Adams, reflecting the architectural tastes of the educated elite, haughtily dismissed Mullett's best-known production, the massive State, War, and Navy Building (now known as the Old Executive Office Building), Mullett's "architectural infant asylum."

The architectural profession carried on a feud with the supervising architect and did much to foster public hostility toward him. The feud arose from the straightforward approach that Mullett took to his bureau's pork barrel function. Under pressure from Congress to churn out post offices and courthouses quickly and cheaply from coast to coast, Mullett encouraged the draughtsmen under him to repeat variations of a few basic designs. Besides filling the nation with unimaginative public buildings that made no pretense of relating to their sites, this practice undermined the profession's drive to persuade the government to commission licensed architects for all its work. So much bitterness ensued that for years Mullett refused to join the American Institute of Architects, a group he dismissed as "a bunch of unprincipled men."[17]

By moving in such circles, Shepherd came into frequent contact with President Grant, who reportedly drew the younger man into his informal "kitchen cabinet." By all accounts, Shepherd impressed the modest, stolid Civil War hero, who admired engaging, assertive characters. The naive Grant, quipped the *New York Tribune*, "doubtless believes that Mr. Shepherd is a good fellow."[18]

To some District residents, the improver group was an emerging civic elite that breathed new life into Washington business. Kilbourn, in a Republican campaign oration, called his friends, "energetic and enterprising young men, who had their fortunes yet to make and who prospered as the community prospered."[19] The improvers associated with certain charities, for example the YMCA. Their preference for the Washington Club on New York Avenue near the Treasury led the lavish building to acquire the nickname, "Ring Club House," even though the club's officers included James Berret, the deposed Civil War mayor, and Richard T. Merrick, who would act as counsel for local opponents of the Territory during congressional hearings.[20] It is impossible, and of limited interest, to determine whether this clique constituted a ring in the sense of clandestine collusion. That contemporaries on both sides saw the Shepherd group as a ring is relevant, however, because the idea played a large role in District politics throughout the 1870s. In any case, the Republican improvers used their array of strategic connections to take the initiative from Washington's "old citizens" in the debate over governmental structure and development policy that broke out right after the war.

II

Every major proposal during the 1860s to reorganize Washington called for transferring major powers from elected municipal officials to federal appointees. This sentiment for rolling back home rule arose to some extent from the perception of a need for better coordination of federal and municipal public works and services. Yet it is inconceivable that national politicians or local civic and commercial elites would have seriously entertained restricting local self-government but for the battle over black suffrage. Various interests saw reorganization as a device for containing the radicals' civil rights program.

Although they accepted emancipation, most old-line Washingtonians found black suffrage obnoxious. This attitude goes far in explaining why banker George W. Riggs and other prominent residents at first favored Senator Lot Morrill's plan for an appointed District commission. Riggs, of the opinion that "the majority of the voters here are incapable of self-government," enlisted assistance from his former partner, W. W. Corcoran, and from Henry Cooke, with whom Riggs had had business dealings. While Morrill pressed his bill in late 1866 and early 1867, Riggs organized public meetings and circulated petitions. The aftermath of the Civil War was an unpropitious time for such a blatant attack on democracy. Reams of counter-petitions arrived in the Capitol berating a "spasmodic" Congress for even considering the "degrading" commission proposal.* Leaders of the District bar from both parties (including two future commissioners) combined on an anti-commission memorial. Morrill spoke for many colleagues when he labeled the incumbent District government "outrageous" and insisted that the management and funding of the District would never be adequate until controlled by Congress itself. Yet at this point, neither party was convinced that, as Indiana Democrat Thomas Hendricks argued, it was necessary "to have one extreme or the other."[21]

In October 1867, Shepherd told a businessmen's meeting that business interests were not being protected under the current municipal system, because "low politicians have the management in their hands." Washington City, Georgetown, and Washington County should have consolidated government, he declared, with public works controlled by an engineer appointed by the Department of the Interior or another federal department. The following January, a public meeting appointed a committee of notables, including Shepherd, Clephane, Henry Cooke, and Riggs, to develop a plan for a "single local government." At the same time that Bowen's mayoralty was agitating Washington, this committee was meeting to consider various government plans featuring different combinations of appointed and elected officials.[22]

White civic leaders gradually reached a consensus in favor of a territorial administration, wherein the President would appoint executive officers and residents would elect one or both houses of the legislature. This compromise met Congress's demand for a system that would bring "the capital of the country under the more direct control and supervision of Congress and the national executive," while at the same time permitting moderate Republicans to evade radical charges that they were "departing from republican principles" in order to distance themselves from black suffrage. In early 1870, a bipartisan committee of prominent residents emerged to lobby for the District's being made a territory. This panel included three future members of the Board of Public Works—Shepherd, Samuel P. Brown, and Colonel James A. Magruder, a commission merchant and former army engineer whom Grant had named collector of customs for Georgetown. In addition to Hallett Kilbourn, the territorial committee also included four businessmen later active in the fight against Shepherd.[23]

By late 1870, when a territorial bill finally reached the floor of Congress, the plan featured a governor and an eleven-member council, both appointed by the President. Voters would elect the lower house of the new territorial legislature, the twenty-two-member House of Delegates, as well as a nonvoting delegate to Congress. One respected New England Republican, Hannibal

---

*Most of the anti-Morrill petitioners had the presence of mind to strike *spasmodic* from their forms, though not so thoroughly that the recipients could not read the original.

Hamlin, managed the Senate version of the bill; another, George Edmunds, defended it as an acceptable means "to make a decent city, with decent ornamentation, paid for by the public expense." Still, in January 1871, radical Republican senators such as Charles Sumner, Oliver Morton, and Henry Wilson, appalled by the civil rights implications of the measure, tried to have it recommitted, missing by only one vote. The coalition that defeated the recommital motion anticipated the emerging consensus against Radical Reconstruction. Combining with Democrats to save the bill were influential Republicans ranging from Roscoe Conkling and John Sherman to Carl Schurz and Lyman Trumbull.[24]

A few House radicals insisted that District reorganization was a trick being played by enemies of black suffrage. Most, however, accepted the word of the Republican District Committee chairman, who called the plan "simple, harmonious, economical." The House objected most strenuously to a Senate plan similar to one that the German government later used to regulate its financial relations with the city of Berlin. In effect, the District would have gained the power to levy property taxes against the federal government. The House killed this idea and nearly did the same with a provision authorizing the District to assess the value of federal holdings. The purpose of this clause was to shame Congress into making annual appropriations commensurate to its holdings. Congress postponed once again fixing a rule regarding the nation's fiscal responsiblity to the capital. This time delay proved costly.[25]

The District reorganization act signed by Grant in February 1871 also established a Board of Public Works, consisting of the governor and four additional members appointed by the President. The board was to have "entire control of and make all ordinances" concerning Washington's public works. Not part of the original scheme, the board showed up only at the bill's final stages. While no one knows who added the clause to establish this panel, the proposal itself had hardly been kept secret: Senator Hamlin called special attention to it when explaining late revisions on the floor.[26] Given that William Tweed's analogous agency in New York was just then gaining infamy, it is surprising that no one in Washington or in Congress raised questions about what proved to be the Territory's most notorious feature.

One cause of inattention to detail in the territorial proposal was that, at the moment of success, the coalition that had pushed it through Congress broke apart. The old citizens, who had been cooperating with the improvers, now launched a series of vituperative assaults on them. The Shepherd circle suddenly were dubbed a gang of "reckless" interlopers leading the city to "bankruptcy and ruin." As participants understood it, the "property-holding interest," with roots in prewar Washington, had grown wary and resentful of the improver Republicans. A year earlier, B. B. French had noted that longtime residents feared their views were being ignored by those "who, as citizens, are in their swaddling clothes." Shepherd's allies countered that their critics were in fact anti-improvement agitators, "rich people content with existing circumstances," tax-evading "croakers" who fought "progress and manifest destiny."[27]

The improvers had accumulated such momentum in the city and so many friends in the national Republican party that they were certain to dominate both the elected and appointed portions of the incoming regime. Taking comfort where they could, some old-line Washington businessmen expressed relief when Grant passed over Shepherd and chose Cooke as the first governor. Erstwhile partners imagined that the banker was more restrained than his associates and would moderate their lofty ambitions. Until investigations into the Panic of 1873 revealed the dubious expedients into which Cooke's financial tangles led him, many argued that the District's troubles would be mitigated if only the governor would assert himself. "Why is the Governor like a gentle lamb?" asked the anti-Territory *Patriot.* "Because he is led by A. Shepherd."[28]

The President's other appointments merely fueled the controversy. District Democrats charged that they had been shut out of the territorial council in favor of a motley gaggle of "darkies" (including Frederick Douglass), Yankee interlopers, and Germans with unsound opinions.[29] The initial Board of Public Works consisted of Cooke, Brown, Magruder, Mullett, and Shepherd. The young plumber was quickly installed in the unmandated post of vice president. This gave Shepherd—and through him the administration—control of all patronage and contracts related to local public works, which irked the opposition further.

In April's inaugural territorial election, opponents failed to win back anything lost through the President's prerogatives. Democrats took only seven of the twenty-one House of Delegates seats. For congressional delegate, District Republicans nominated a fervent partisan, Norton Chipman, a lawyer from Iowa. An army solicitor during the war, Chipman had gained renown for his part in the prosecution of Major Henry Wirz, the Confederate officer held responsible for the mistreatment of federal prisoners of war at Andersonville. Besides his law practice, Chipman held highly visible posts in the Grand Army of the Republic (G.A.R.). Frederick Douglass's *New National Era* asserted that the Democratic candidate, Richard Merrick, a lawyer from a prominent Maryland family, was a racist and urged District blacks to vote for the G.A.R. activist. The *Star* proclaimed the practical advantages of a delegate "in harmony" with the national administration. Chipman won by four thousand out of twenty-six thousand votes.[30]

As promised, the territorial government proceeded with alacrity. Shepherd wrestled control of public works from the old municipal corporation weeks before it expired on June 1. By the third week of June, the Board of Public Works submitted its Comprehensive Plan of Improvements. This promised to make a modern city of paved streets lined with trees, lighted by gas, and drained by sewers. Of the estimated cost of $6,578,397, only one-third would be assessed against adjacent property. The remaining $4 million would come from bonds that Governor Cooke would float through contacts in New York and Europe. Opponents warned that the board's "hot haste" spelled trouble, but the warning was to no avail. The legislature approved the plan within two weeks.[31]

The Board of Public Works immediately discarded as nothing but a "general guide" the program it had just rammed through the legislature. This freed territorial leaders to decide priorities and devise procedures at their discretion. Shepherd made a show of appointing an advisory board, consisting of public buildings officer Babcock, General Meigs, the designer of the Washington Aqueduct, General A. A. Humphreys, the chief of engineers, and park planner Frederick Law Olmsted. There is no evidence that this committee of experts performed a single concrete task. Shepherd and board engineer Mullett themselves put together an entire municipal engineering department in a matter of weeks. By midsummer, the Board of Public Works had hired dozens of engineers, surveyors, bookkeepers, inspectors, clerks, and laborers. August found Shepherd contracting for improvements in every section of the District, but especially downtown and in wealthier residential neighborhoods that the board identified as particularly inviting to potential investors.[32]

Meanwhile, the Territory's critics had trouble even finding a forum in the press. After demise of the *National Intelligencer* in 1869, the paper most active in Washington civic affairs was the *Evening Star*, which since 1867 had been owned in part by none other than Shepherd. Other powerful dailies were the Radicals' *Chronicle* and the *National Republican*, whose editor owned $2,500 in Metropolis Paving stock, among other improver-related investments. The *Republican*'s managing editor was Shepherd's younger brother, Arthur. In late 1870, the *Patriot* appeared, a Democratic effort to break the Republican press monopoly. The *Patriot*, whose strident partisanship lent credence to the improvers' dismissal of criticism as political rubbish, denounced the "unscrupulous designs" of "the Ring into whose hands the President has sought to deliver over the city." Ironically, this paper collapsed soon after embarrassing revelations that its financial backers included New York's William M. Tweed.[33]

Thwarted in the press, old citizens turned to the courts. A "taxpayers" group secured an injunction against the $4 million loan. On August 18, about one hundred "gentlemen" met to establish the Citizens Association to prosecute the lawsuit and other anti-improver measures. Cooke and Shepherd outsmarted the association by calling a referendum on the loan, which effectively negated the injunction. The legislature arranged for pro-loan tickets to be marked "For Special Improvements," while anti-loan tickets were marked "Against Special Improvements." Such distortions flabbergasted opponents, who vainly tried to explain that they indeed favored improvements, provided that plans were "mapped out and shown to us." Alienated white Democrats largely boycotted the November 21st poll—white registration was down by five thousand. The bond issue carried, 12,748 to 1,202. The Citizens Association resurfaced intermittently, under several names and forms, until it finally brought down the territorial government three years later.[34]

The Board of Public Works began as many contracts as the late season allowed. When bad weather came, streets throughout the District were torn up and impassable. Winter did not cool the tempers of the factions, nor did Christmas encourage them to charity. The *Patriot* maintained that only "speculators, contractors, communists, plunderers, and newspapers" supported the Board of Public Works. Shepherd's *Star* insisted that "chronic fault finders and professional grumblers" ran the opposition, "the same old crowd of obstructionists."[35]

III

A comparison of the background, occupation, and wealth of the antagonists over the territorial government justifies their self-images as "old citizens" and "Northerners." Shepherd's supporters were young entrepreneurs, overly infused with the "Northern" spirit of the Gilded Age, even if they were not all of Northern origin. Almost all Republicans, they proudly proclaimed their ties to the party of Union and progress. Although some key anti-Shepherd spokesmen were Republican, the Citizens Association's efforts tended to fuse with those of local Democrats, who had obvious reasons for attacking the Shepherd group. The quarrel over the Comprehensive Plan reflected discord within Washington's business community as well as ordinary partisan jousting.

As a guide to the anti-territorial group, studying the officers of the original Citizens Association of 1871 makes sense. They included the earliest, most persistent agitators, with the exception of the attorney Merrick and the banker Corcoran. (Corcoran happened to be abroad during the summer of 1871. Had his enormous wealth been averaged in with that of the other members of the Association, it would have made them appear even richer than they were.) The principal improver organization was the territorial government itself. Researched for this study were high officers of the Territory, members of the Board of Public Works, board employees visible in the dispute, officers of the legislature, an individual delegate whose relations with Shepherd came under strong attack, and contractors and other District businessmen identified as especially close to the government.[36]

"Old citizens" were found to be not substantially older than their rivals—a median age of fifty as opposed to forty-five years. What surprises is how mature Shepherd's "young" men were: of the twenty-five whose ages were found, only eleven were under forty, although the younger men did include some of the most influential—Shepherd, Kilbourn, J. O. Evans, and Mullett. Seventy-one percent of the Citizens Association members were born in the District or a neighboring state, while this is true of only 26 percent of their rivals. Sixty percent of Shepherd's group had Northern backgrounds, while

Table 2.1 Characteristics of Factions in the Washington Improvement Controversy, 1871–74

	Improvers			Citizens		
		N	%		N	%
Mean age	41.4	25		48.45	20	
Median age	45	25		50	25	
Birthplace						
		27	99.9		21	100.0
District of Columbia		4	14.8		8	38.1
Maryland, Virginia, Delaware		3	11.1		7	33.3
Northeast[a]		12	44.4		4	19.0
Ohio[b]		4	14.8		1	4.8
All other U.S.		0	0.0		0	0.0
Abroad[c]		4	14.8		1	4.8
Persistence in City Directory						
1860		13	35.1		34	75.0
1871		37	100.0		32	100.0
1885		22	59.5		24	75.0
Area of Residence						
		37	100.0		32	100.1
Northwest		27	73.0		27	84.4
Georgetown		6	16.2		3	9.4
All other sections		4	10.8		2	6.3
Occupation, 1871						
		36	100.1		31	100.0
Banking, insurance, corporate management		5	13.9		4	12.9
Engineering, architecture		3	8.3		0	0.0
Government		5	13.9		4	12.9
Law, claims agency		6	16.7		9	29.0
Real estate, building supply, contracting		11	30.6		7	22.6
Wholesale and retail sales		5	13.9		7	22.6
All other		1	2.8		0	0.0
Assessed Real Property, 1871						
Number holding property		28	75.7		31	96.9
Number above $5,000		22	59.5		27	84.3
Aggregate[d]	$1,242,410			$2,663,940		
Mean[d]	44,372			91,860		
Median[d]	23,487			36,590		

Sources: City directories, contemporary accounts, local histories, and biographical dictionaries. See also note 36.
[a] Includes Maine, Massachusetts, New Hampshire, Vermont, Pennsylvania, New York, and New Jersey; no other states were represented.
[b] Only Midwestern state represented.
[c] Includes Canada, Ireland, England, and Germany.
[d] Of those holding property, not of entire group.

only five of twenty-one association members whose birthplaces were discovered came from the North. However, excluding three "old citizens" born in neighboring Virginia, not a single member of either group was born in the South.

When opposition spokesmen claimed to represent "taxpayers," they were not joking. The Citizens Executive Committee held an aggregate of $2.7 million — 3.3 percent of the District's 1871 assessment, from under 0.03 percent of the population.[37] This was more than twice the aggregate property of the "speculators" linked to the Board of Public Works. In the late nineteenth century, one could buy a decent building lot for $500 and build a comfortable balloon frame house starting at $1,000. Of thirty-two association members traced, twenty-nine owned some real estate and twenty-seven owned more than $5,000 worth. The anti-Shepherd group claimed to speak for "every poor man, who by honest industry has secured a house for his wife and children," but nearly all its leaders had more real estate than they could use themselves.[38] The improvers were hardly poor, either. Fifty-nine percent owned at least $5,000 worth, and the median among those on the territorial side who held property was over $23,000. Shepherd, who in 1871 held property worth $267,578, was the only partisan of the Territory assessed at over $200,000. On the other side, this was true of Riggs, Columbus Alexander, and William B. Todd.

When explaining themselves to a House District Committee investigation in 1872, the Citizens Association stressed their roots in the community, their wealth, and their social position. Witness after witness related that he had been born in or near Washington, came from a prominent area family, headed an important bank or prosperous firm, and held real estate assessed at over $100,000. John B. Blake, president of the National Metropolitan Bank and former Public Buildings commissioner, under Buchanan, had lived in the District for more than sixty years. Blake's father had been mayor of Washington in 1814 when the British burned it. Corcoran's father had been mayor of Georgetown, as had the grandfather of Walter S. Cox, a Harvard-educated lawyer. Charles E. Edmonston, for decades one of Washington's leading contractors, had built the Adams and Hay Houses on Lafayette Square and the McLean House on McPherson Square. Patent attorney Columbus Alexander, who emerged as leader of the anti-territorial movement, came from the family after whom Alexandria was named.[39]

Shepherd and Clephane were both born in Washington, but neither had so prominent a background. Board treasurer James Magruder, brother of an antebellum Washington mayor, was the only territorial partisan who qualified as an old citizen as the term was generally used. Henry Willard, Shepherd's successor as the board's vice president, had been a local business leader since he and a brother had in 1847 taken over what became the famous Willard Hotel, but he was not a central character in the improver movement, and in any case, the Willards were Vermont Puritans. As the *Patriot* put it, improvers did not represent the community's "substance" as much as the old citizens did, and they appeared to have a less "solid stake" in the city.[40]

In effect, the old citizens were stamping the Territory a carpetbagger government and casting themselves as redeemers, a sensible strategy for such a movement in a North-South border region city in 1871. However demagogic, the carpetbagger charge had the merit of plausibility. Of thirty-seven men linked to the improver circle, perhaps fourteen came to Washington between the late 1850s and 1870 to occupy a federal office or for some other political reason. Of the thirty-two identified officers of the original Citizens Association, this was true for probably no more than six.

Frederick Douglass's *New National Era* turned this carpetbagger charge on its head. Black Washingtonians had an interest in helping improvers, who stood for "a new era in American civilization," supplant the city's prewar elite, "a people who could do nothing for themselves, or who were satisfied with things as they were." The old citizens, Douglass charged, had risen on the backs of blacks, the "foundation of whatever wealth was here at the end of the dark age of slavery." Douglass's claim that anti-territorial leaders were "wards of slavery" was literally true in several instances. Alexander received $4,818 compensation for fifteen slaves under the 1862 District Emancipation Act. Riggs received $788.40 for two people's freedom. John Blake asked $525.60 for a Henry Peterson but was awarded only $290. In sharp contrast, no key figure on the improver side received compensation under the 1862 act, although Shepherd's family may have owned slaves at some earlier point.[41]

While old citizens were more likely than improvers to have held slaves, Douglass was incorrect to imply that Shepherd's enemies did not merit consideration because they were merely reactionary Bourbon Democrats. Corcoran seems to have been the only prominent anti-improver with significant ties to the Confederacy. The anti-Shepherd movement certainly leaned towards the Democrats, but the presence in its ranks of men such as Thomas J. Durant countered the charge that the old citizens were merely a front for the party out of power. Durant, a Pennsylvania native who migrated to New Orleans as a teenager and became a successful lawyer, joined that city's Free State movement soon after the Union occupied it in April 1862. Among the most radical Unionists during Louisiana's military government, Durant probably supplied the evidence on alleged failings of Lincoln's Louisiana reconstruction that appeared in the fateful Wade-Davis Manifesto of 1864. After fleeing New Orleans during anti-radical riots in 1866, Durant established himself in Washington. As Grant-era Republicans such as Shepherd distanced the party from radicalism, Durant became very disaffected. He would later drift towards the Greenback party, a cause he shared with Ben Butler, an old friend.[42]

Another disaffected Republican who actively fought Shepherd was attorney Albert G. Riddle. Once a Free Soiler, Riddle spoke in favor of District emancipation during his single term as an Ohio Republican congressman in 1861–63. Riddle's opposition to the territorial government is consistent with the profile of well-educated, well-to-do Republicans who drifted towards the Liberal movement during the Grant years and later tended towards mugwumpery.[43]

A final example of an impeccable Unionist who agitated against Shepherd was Albert Grant, a Maine native and one-time builder in Milwaukee. Captain in a Wisconsin regiment during the war, Grant's health was permanently damaged by a harrowing experience as a prisoner of war in Georgia. Even so, he was later able to found an extensive architectural and development business in Washington. Political principles loomed large in the anti-improver stands of Durant and Riddle. Grant's involved the less lofty motive of direct commercial rivalry. He had invested mainly on Capitol Hill in east Washington; the territorial clique favored development in the northwest. Shepherd's allies taunted that Grant, who indeed made painful blunders around this time, was a bad businessman. The Captain retorted that the board boosted *its* entrepreneurs over other, equally progressive men.[44]

Nearly two-thirds of the improver group were not in the 1860 city directory. Three-quarters of the old citizens were already in business in the capital on the eve of the war, an impressive level of continuity during such a turbulent time. Still, because the war gave many their first occasion to visit Washington, it may be unfair to measure commitment to the community by looking backward. The way to determine whether backers of the Territory were really interlopers may be to see how many thought enough of the town to stay on after their government fell.

Seventy-five percent of the members of the Citizens Association were still active in the national city in 1885, a decade after the Shepherd controversy ended, despite the death of some leaders, such as Blake and Riggs. Numerous association members had moved up in the hierarchy of occupation and wealth, advancing from retail or building supply firms or managerial positions in corporations to running insurance companies or living off real estate. By 1889, Charles Edmonston, Michael Talty, and Walter Cox had joined the ranks of $100,000 property holders. Cox was now a justice of the District Supreme Court. He wrote the District Law Code, passed by Congress in 1901. After a long term as city attorney, Albert Riddle also became a leader in the Washington bar, as well as a writer of short stories and biographies.[45]

Just under sixty percent of the territorial group were still in Washington in 1885. Some key improvers, such as delegate Chipman, destined to become a federal judge in California, had indeed left the District abruptly enough after this episode to qualify as interlopers. Yet the improvers' lower degree of persistence seems to result as much from the Grim Reaper as from other causes. At least seven members of the territorial group had died since 1875, meaning that over 70 percent of those living had remained in the District. Henry Cooke was fifty-five, but worn out by years of difficulties stemming from the 1873 Panic, when he died in February 1881. Later that year, John O. Evans was killed by pneumonia at age forty-four. Letting bygones be bygones, the city's new Democratic newspaper, the *Post,* in its obituary, passed over Evans's role in the District improvement scandal (which Democrats had made much of for campaign purposes in 1876) to focus on recent endeavors of this "good citizen."[46]

Like the old citizens, the improvers who stayed became leaders in their occupations. From their ranks emerged bank presidents, insurance executives, and real estate developers. The architectural concerns of Cluss and Mullett prospered. Cluss won important federal commissions, including the Smithsonian's current Arts and Industries Building, begun in 1877, and the interior of the Patent Office, begun in 1878. In 1883, Cluss's firm designed Washington's first apartment building, the Portland.[47] Former abolitionist publisher Lewis Clephane remained president of the Virginia Brick Company. The only hitch in the subsequent career of suburban developer Samuel Brown was his indictment, eventually quashed, in the Star Route cases of 1881.[48]

Hallet Kilbourn remained a flamboyant character on the local scene until personal troubles brought him to a sad end. In 1876, Kilbourn's links to the Republican Cooke family came under scrutiny by the Democratic-held House of Representatives. When Kilbourn refused to open private books at a committee hearing, the House imprisoned him for six weeks. While friends sent the prisoner luxurious dinners twice daily in a hack, Kilbourn appeared a champion of civil liberties in the harangues of House Republicans. After a legal maneuver released him, Kilbourn filed a suit that helped establish limits to congressional subpoenas. By the mid-1880s, Kilbourn had purchased a former theatrical advertiser called the *Critic,* which he ran for a few years as an afternoon rival of the *Evening Star.* Later his mind deteriorated. When in 1902, a year before his death, Kilbourn's daughters went to court to have him declared legally insane, the *Star,* "pained to hear of his clouded and distressed condition," recalled his "kindly, genial nature."[49]

For the most part, the improvers, if not already rooted in the community, were probably trying to become so. The insults and partisan bombast of the territorial dispute depicted a town in revolution. Yet the Shepherd group sought mainly to gain entry into the capital's commercial and social elite and to redirect the emphasis of local enterprise. They struggled more to co-opt than to supplant the old citizens, whose capital and social prestige were, after all, valuable resources, even if they did seem short on entrepreneurial gumption. Other factors came into play later, when out-of-town papers and the national parties inserted themselves in the conflict. Within Washington's business community, however, the "District Ring" quarrel was originally provoked by differing backgrounds, attitudes, mores, and partisan allegiances, not by intractible conflicts of class or interest.

IV

Shepherd's big-thinking, eager friends assumed that their critics were stick-in-the-muds and snobs. "Some grew sour because others were doing what they ought to have done," Shepherd's attorney told Congress. Others "grew jealous because a mechanic has brains." To old-line business and civic leaders, the improvers were arrogant, unbalanced, and imprudent. The Board of Public Works was "drunk with sudden power," attorney Merrick argued, "dazzled, deluded."[50]

Old citizens claimed that, unlike their rootless, shifty opponents, they conducted affairs according to the straightforward ethics that had prevailed in the virtuous days when they were young. One may doubt whether wealthy political bankers such as Corcoran or Riggs ever embodied old-fashioned republican moderation and simplicity. Nevertheless, the citizens insisted that they had joined together to defend "conservative" mores and methods. Indeed, they spoke of the truculent Shepherd and the ostentatious Cooke as though appalled and offended by their behavior. Observers suspected that Washington's upper class was splitting into factions, with self-satisfied old timers scorning newcomers, who for their part were embracing the extravagant style of the Gilded Age.[51] Such differences in etiquette and deportment extended to business, where for a time they obscured overlapping aims and interests.

Established businessmen recoiled from "notoriously unscrupulous and dishonest" characters, such as furniture dealer John W. McKnight. While a member of the House of Delegates, McKnight received more than $16,000 to furnish District offices, including the Legislative Hall. McKnight was a relatively minor example of an indifference towards conflict of interest regulations that distressed many besides the city's entrenched propertied elite. The territorial legislature wrote into its act authorizing the Comprehensive Plan, "No member of the Council or the House of Delegates, or person holding any office of trust or profit under the District of Columbia shall be pecuniarily interested, either directly or indirectly, in any such contract. . . ." Shepherd made a token effort to comply with this stricture, but his plumbing and roofing enterprises continued to sell to contractors dealing with the city and to other federal agencies. Shepherd received more than $6,000 on a $4,000 estimate for supplying water and gas fixtures to the contractor renovating the District offices. In 1872, Public Buildings officer Babcock paid Shepherd, then board vice president, nearly $35,000 to install copper roofing on the White House.[52]

Territorial officials made no effort to divest themselves of property in neighborhoods slated for improvement. In fact, Governor Cooke invested an additional $25,000 in a real estate pool set up by Kilbourn. The contracting interests of the territorial circle were so numerous and intertwined that any work they did in Washington inevitably involved a conflict of interest. By

1874, firms run by three key members of Kilbourn's paving ring, J. O. Evans, Clephane, and Lewis Filbert of Philadelphia, had received at least $1.76 million from the Board of Public Works.[53]

This suspicious web of connections heightened the old citizens' apprehensions concerning the regime's plan to finance the Comprehensive Plan in one shot, through bonds floated on the New York and European exchanges, rather than gradually, through pay-as-you-go appropriations written into the city's annual budget. Pay-as-you-go was obviously a tedious way to finance a comprehensive public works program, but by forcing officials to return frequently to the legislature for money, it subjected improvement projects to ongoing public scrutiny. Opponent and former congressman Albert Riddle warned that, once the proposed bonds won approval, the Shepherd group would have gained, for who knew how long, "the complete power and control over appropriations for the public works of this District."[54]

Some speakers at "taxpayers meetings" proclaimed that the old-fashioned pay-as-you-go policy was preferable to public works bonds across the board. Just as often, citizens' spokesmen implied that they were against the Territory's loan plan first because they were anxious that a ring would misappropriate the money, and only second because they believed improvement bonds and other techniques of modern public finance to be suspect by definition. This is interesting, given our cities' custom of funding improvements through levies on adjacent property and given the popularity among American urban taxpayers of what historian Terrence McDonald calls "no-growth" sentiment, which means that politicians can expect flak simply for daring to propose deficit financing of capital projects. In the lead-up to the 1872 congressional investigation, one memorial from citizens who did "not believe that energy and enterprise consist in borrowing money" asked that Congress compel the District to pay for improvements "in a way more immediate and less complex." However, a larger anti-Shepherd petition insisted, "We are in favor of judicious improvements and liberal expenditures to meet them." Old citizens seemed willing to contemplate public borrowing, provided it was for a cautious program managed by officials they could abide.[55]

"No-growth" sentiment played a relatively weak part in the territorial dispute for several reasons. The years between the war and the 1873 Panic saw a unusual burst of enthusiasm for deficit financing in cities across the country; for a brief period, the true-blue American tax resister let his guard down. Moreover, the territorial format, by constraining popular participation, rendered the capital's municipal government less vulnerable to that intense pressure from ordinary taxpayers that McDonald sees as having forced San Francisco authorities into a no-growth posture. The quarrel over the Comprehensive Plan played itself out within a segment of the community that would derive immediate, tangible benefits from a capital program, that could most easily bear the cost, and that had direct experience of the decisive role of real estate in the District's economy. While some citizens were immovable on the question of public borrowing, others were merely distrustful, with concerns that a restrained, *well-behaved* politician might have assuaged.

The improvers were too strident and impatient to manipulate subtle differences among their foes. The Shepherd group scorned no-growth and anything that looked like it, and ridiculed pay-as-you-go as a pig-headed way to waste money. "Shepherd believed in debt, as all progressive businessmen do," remarked a well-informed historian from early in this century. "Sound enough in the principle," Shepherd's "application struck careful men as imprudent if not reckless." The *Patriot* in September 1871 asserted that the Board's "ill-digested, incoherent, and blundering scheme" would lead to $25 million in debts in four years. Actually, it took only three years.[56]

A publicly financed, large-scale public works program was a sound investment for Washington taxpayers, Shepherd's *Star* explained, because the infusion of cash would "give new life to our languishing business interests" and because improvements themselves would "return to our citizens manifold in the increased valuation of property." In official documents, congressional hearings, and the press, territorial leaders asserted repeatedly that their program was meant to spur a healthy cycle of property inflation, which improvers felt would have the dual effect of making existing owners wealthier and attracting new capital from the outside. In 1872, Shepherd testified, "A system of general improvements like this will enhance not only my property, but the property of every man who owns a foot of land in this District." The statement of James M. Latta, Kilbourn's real estate partner, at the same House hearing epitomized the outlook of the board's friends. Latta presented the committee a report, prepared by his firm, which claimed that a recent jump in values was owing "largely to the fact that persons of wealth from all sections of the country are purchasing residence sites, and making investments here." The faster the District implemented the Comprehensive Plan, "the more rapidly will capital seek investment in our midst." Latta then cited a number of recent transactions in support of his case. He was especially pleased with purchases made by a Philadelphian, who was "only one of not less than twenty-five gentlemen reputed to be worth all the way from $500,000 to two or three or four millions" who were investing in Washington. Rich investors were interested "because the streets were put in good condition, and it looked as though we were going to make a handsome city."[57]

"A city of varied and especially refined attractions," the *Star* argued, would draw "people of culture, wealth, and leisure."[58] Rich outsiders would bring capital devoted to residential development, utilities, and the upper end of the retail trade. These enterprises, to be sure, happened to be where the improvers had concentrated their private interests, but such a focus was consistent with advice Shepherd was receiving from widely respected quarters regarding the proper long-run relationship between infrastructure and development in a "worthy" national city. The capital's unique purpose may have set limits to commerce and manufacturing, yet its ornamental, service, and residential functions presented adequate opportunities for those indispensable agents of material progress, "energetic and enterprising young men," if only government would take the lead by enlivening the languid business environment and creating, through well-placed public works, an inviting field for investment. Bond issues and improvement taxes were a shrewd move, the *Star* asserted:

> Why not, if it will make you twelve times as prosperous—wake you up, improve your thoroughfares, multiply your railroad and steamship lines, give all your mechanics and laborers work at good wages, increase your population and means of living comfortably, stimulate trade, educate your children, and send you bowling along on the path of progress?[59]

The anti-territorial group never questioned the idea that property inflation was a harbinger of "steady and healthy prosperity." The *Patriot* noted that a vigorous building industry suggested "progress," because it meant that "families of wealth, education, and refinement" were moving to Washington.[60] Citizens urged caution but offered no alternative. They agreed with Shepherd's booster-like scenario in outline, if not in detail.

V

The Shepherd government was harassed with charges of bossism and "Tweedism." While one might in fairness call Shepherd strong names, the use of "Boss Shepherd" has encouraged misinterpretations of the territorial group's dynamics and objectives. In contrast to the great bosses of other large cities, none of the Territory's leaders was a career politician who had worked his way through the ranks of a local political organization. Shepherd relied upon connections with the Republican Party and the presidential administration, and he energetically used Board of Public Works patronage to control the elected House of Delegates, but he made little attempt to build a durable political machine whose presence might be felt at the precinct level. Public works contracts were the point of the Shepherd regime, not a sideshow or a currency in which the tangible favors that were the glue of machines could be distributed.

District businessmen contrived the District's territorial government to facilitate their vision of how Washington should develop. Those who ran the regime were either entrepreneurs or businessmen/politicians who believed that government should cooperate with business. The territorial movement is an example of how Gilded Age businessmen pursued objectives that led them into politics, not of how machine politicians ran infrastructure programs.

Outsiders viewed Shepherd's loose administrative style, the ad hoc way he threw together the Board of Public Works, and especially the multilayered connections among the contractors, craftsmen, and capitalists who coalesced around the board as evidence that Washington had been taken over by a "base, sordid, and unscrupulous class who go into politics for what they can steal."[61] In fact, the improvers were injecting into the management of Washington's public works methods and principles that then prevailed in most businesses and in most governmental enterprises that had promotion of business as their goal.

While highly structured, systematized corporate organizations were becoming commonplace in enterprises of national scope, such as railroads, on the city level enterprises were still characterized by partnerships and entrepreneurial firms. This was especially true in the sectors where the improvers were most heavily engaged. Corporate-style organization and management did not affect contracting and real estate development on a large scale until well into this century. Traditions of entrepreneurship and shifting partnerships remain strong in these businesses today. To construct a market, a row of houses, or a commercial district, Gilded Age entrepreneurs would throw together partnerships exactly like Kilbourn's asphalt ring. As Clephane implied with regard to the Metropolis Paving Company and its relatives, associations of local businessmen understood the value of general incorporation laws in providing legal protection to joint endeavors. Despite the surface formality that incorporation gave these undertakings, they remained essentially informal and shifting in character.[62]

Moreover, no city in this country or elsewhere had yet managed to set up a public works department that approached the level of complexity and professionalism required for the orderly execution of an infrastructure program on the scale of Shepherd's Comprehensive Plan. The specialized engineers, architects, accountants, and civil servants needed to staff such a department had only begun to appear.[63] It was natural for the Shepherd group to borrow standards and practices from the private sector in their pursuit of public goals; no models or precedents existed to guide them in another direction.

Likewise, it was understandable that the improvers should base their program on the developers' view of Washington's needs, formed during their years in the business. Everything in their experience and mental world suggested that their personal interests and inclinations were coincident with the public's wants and well-being. Mid-nineteenth-century businessmen often felt at liberty to apply private standards and practices to their forays into public affairs. Twain and Warner parodied this arrogance in *The Gilded Age*, yet Samuel Clemens's own failed ventures suggest that the humorist was not immune to the period's idealization of entrepreneurial zeal. In the aftermath of the Civil War—during which the Union's commercial and industrial might had, after all, proved a decisive advantage—the belief spread that ambitious young businessmen were more than simply the bringers of economic prosperity. They were heroes. Upon them rested the country's political and social well-being, so their rules governed all.

A writer on Victorian London's public works notes that even among "important and honorable businessmen" of the British capital, "the notion of conflict of interest, of the sharp distinction between public and private, was only meagerly developed." This distinction was even harder to impress upon men imbued with a culture that glorified the entrepreneur. Shepherd defended embattled associates in terms of what they offered as entrepreneurs: J. O. Evans was "one of the best businessmen I ever knew;" Kilbourn was "a responsible man [who] had a good reputation as a businessman." Henry Cooke, a well-traveled, sophisticated person, when questioned about real estate investments made while he was governor, dismissed the problem of conflict of interest. He implied, rather, that his business sense was also public spirit, a sign of his "unbounded faith in the future of Washington and in its growth."[64]

Congressman Robert Roosevelt, previously a member of the genteel Committee of Seventy that had fought the Tweed Ring, tried to convince Henry R. Searle, a politically connected architect who renovated the Territory's offices, that it was not a "proper arrangement" for the building's contractors to buy piping and fixtures from Shepherd Brothers, Washington's largest plumbing firm. Searle stood by Shepherd: "I think any man holding office under the government who is connected with a business firm, has a right to sell to anybody but the government, even if the article goes into a government building." To Searle it was "the usual way of doing business."[65]

Circumstances conspired to fix the Shepherd group's self-image as "citizens of energy and public spirit" upon whom had devolved great responsibility. The country appeared to ratify their scheme. Congress instituted the territorial system, the executive gave the improvers control of it, and the judiciary sanctioned their actions. The dominant Republican party identified itself with the improvers, as did a significant number in the minority Democratic party. Branches of the army and the treasury placed themselves at the group's disposal. Who could blame Shepherd and his friends for thinking that America had turned to them to stop Washington from drifting "into a chronic, hopeless state of seediness, unthrift, and permanent decay?" Criticism of them was surely "the clamor of do-nothings on the one side and malignants on the other."[66]

The gentlemanly old citizens, with their money made, could afford to frown upon such indecent boasting. They convinced themselves that in their day business had been virtuous and dignified. The cruder practices of the present were signs that the country had lost its moral compass, which they were being called upon to restore.[67]

VI

In casting about for terms adequate to convey the vision and courage of their hero, Shepherd's admirers in Washington and around the United States likened him to the giant of nineteenth-century city-building, Baron Haussmann. Comparisons with the mighty Prefect of the Seine were both natural and misleading. An explication of differences between Haussmann's reign and Shepherd's illustrates lessons regarding the role of business in the American polity, the role of the state in development, and the limits of nationalist thought and action during the Civil War and Reconstruction, periods commonly viewed as the height of state-centered nationalism in nineteenth-century America.

Haussmann's rebuilding of Paris was the most spectacular of a multitude of infrastructure projects undertaken by the Second Empire. The French government directed energy not only at the capital but also at provincial cities and the countryside. Napoleon III and Haussmann forged alliances with private investors and worked to foster new enterprises. Yet their underlying purpose was to increase the wealth, power, and majesty of the French state. As a young man, Louis Napoleon had written that France needed public works because they "destroyed the spirit of localism" that for centuries had fostered paralyzing internal strife. An infrastructural network bound a nation together. According to the Saint-Simonian ideas that influenced the imperial program, the state ought to promote business, but the resultant economic growth was to facilitate ends desired by the authorities. Louis Napoleon's advisors intended to fuse private interests to the state, to create a productive alliance that would produce rapid, tangible benefits for the regime and French society.[68]

Such "neo-mercantilism," wrote a pioneering historian of nationalism, "was motivated by nationalist sentiment as well as by economic reasoning." Nationalist writers on political economy, such as the German thinker Friedrich List, held that state sponsorship and supervision of commerce was essential to building a vigorous country. List's case for reorganizing the German economy according to the principle of nationality throws the relationship between state and nation in nineteenth-century America into sharp relief. The economist began forming his views on protective tariffs, unhampered internal trade, infrastructure, and so forth during the 1820s and 1830s, which he spent as a political exile in the United States. List imagined that Americans, with their "sound common sense," already employed his ideas in "actual life." The United States was rapidly becoming "a great nation" through "a return to that long-exploded mercantile system which had clearly been refuted by theory."[69]

The German exile clearly misapprehended the national state's potential for managing development in the United States of his time. Although List took note of the anti-centrist nature of the Jacksonian movement, he imagined that setbacks experienced during those years by the "American System" of Jackson's rival, the "eminent and clearsighted" Henry Clay, were merely strategic retreats. Soon, List predicted, the American system would "raise its head and again make new progress."[70] As it turned out, the vehement anti-centrism espoused by the Jacksonians proved more reflective of the public's basic attitudes and impulses than did Clay's nationalistic program. Mechanisms by which the federal government could exert economic power — protective tariffs, internal improvements, control of banking and currency, a strong navy — suffered debilitating popular attacks throughout the second quarter of the nineteenth century precisely because they were instruments of centralization. An enthusiastic sense of national pride and purpose lay behind mid-nineteenth-century development efforts in the United States, but in this version of nationalism, local government loomed larger than the national state.[71] Until several decades after the Civil War, most Americans wanted the locus of government involvement in the economy to be states and municipalities, not the federal government.

Moreover, while antebellum state-level economic activity was indeed meant to add to a state's progress and prosperity, not even the states seriously attempted to control business and direct it to governmental purposes. Charters, stock and bond purchases, land grants, and the like were primarily *promotional,* self-executing devices, not participatory, regulatory systems requiring the expansive, self-conscious administrative apparatus that would nurture a Baron Haussmann. In the United States, enterprises fostered by economic legislation were to sustain themselves. Carter Goodrich, in a highly regarded study, observed "a general tendency to leave initiative and the responsibility of management mainly to the private elements of the combination, even in cases in which the greater part of the funds came from public sources." At mid-century, while the tradition of governing by notions of "moral economy" still affected policy in places, government interacted with the private sector primarily as a promoter, a prime mover rather than shaper of society. Municipal and state governments were a complement of enterprise, as much as the reverse. Government served as an expression of "collective entrepreneurship," in historian Carl Abbott's phrase. The Napoleonic vision of bureaucratic partnership and state majesty was alien in the United States. Goodrich concluded, "That local governments had the authority to take these promotive measures, and that smaller communities were willing to incur such heavy charges for them, are facts that differentiate the American experience from that of most countries. What they suggest and illustrate is the importance of the 'booster' spirit in American economic development."[72]

The Civil War induced some Northern leaders to abandon the old hesitancy about concentrated power and to work towards "a strong and self-contained national state," in the words of Morton Keller, another noted historian of American political economy. Other wartime or Reconstruction measures — for example, banking reform and the Fourteenth Amendment — created broader, more durable links between the people and the nation-state. Still, as Keller writes, Alexander Shepherd's Washington program was "the most visible expression of America's rejuvenated post-war nationalism."[73] While Shepherd's Comprehensive Plan of Improvement was indeed a national cause, in its first postwar attempt to create a city "worthy of the nation," the government merely raised to the federal level those techniques of promotional government that states and cities had refined earlier and practiced most often.

The Civil War briefly gave the American national state a degree of prestige and power that it had not previously known. Even after that great triumph, the country's leaders could think about their capital's problems and prospects only within the framework of promotional governance. The Grant administration, the Republican leadership of Congress, and most other federal advocates of a worthy Washington did not define their task as strengthening the apparatus of the state and improving its ability to induce enterprise to serve its ends. Instead, they worked to foster a "Northern" atmosphere in the national city conducive to the fortune-seeking of "energetic and enterprising young men." Even if politicians and federal officials could have imagined acting in a Haussmannic fashion, they lacked the necessary legal precedents and administrative and fiscal structures for such an undertaking. The country was thus inclined by the weight of its history to reject administrative planning and control of Washington's development and to turn the project over to self-confident and self-interested entrepreneurs. What List called the Americans' "instinct of what was necessary for the nation" entailed procedures and principles quite different from the economic nationalism he professed to see in this country. Washington's territorial movement is another example of how basic political and institutional realities in the United States made it impossible to pursue a national goal in a nationalist fashion.

Eventually, the improvers' regime, like Reconstruction itself, collapsed under the weight of its own politics. Events would then force the federal government to assume the controlling position that it had previously avoided. The destruction of Shepherd's Territory would begin a trend towards more thorough administrative relations between the nation and its city. Even so, largely as a consequence of the territorial period, the customary promotional emphasis of American government became entrenched in the District's political economy and civic identity, and it persisted past the turn of the century.

3

Energy and Engineering

Governor Shepherd was a law unto himself. . . . The law of necessity was the
only law which he respected.

—Henry L. West, District Commissioner,
to the Beacon Society of Boston

I

ALEXANDER SHEPHERD charged that his enemies had created a self-
fulfilling prophecy by contriving cost-inflating delays in execution of
the Comprehensive Plan of Improvements. In early 1872, the old citizens convinced the House District Committee to hold hearings into the workings of the eight-month-old Territory. "Expert" witnesses sought to discredit
the Comprehensive Plan, but pro-Territory federal officials such as Babcock,
Mullett, and Professor Joseph Henry, the Secretary of the Smithsonian Institution, gave effective responses to technical and health concerns that opposition experts raised. Opposition attorneys failed to produce sensational reve-
lations—like the ones that brought down the board two years later.

With no conclusive evidence, the House committee's report could only
meekly suggest that "more work of improvement was undertaken at once
than was wise." The hearing's only visible result was an ineffectual ceiling on
the District's authority to create debt. Shepherd and Cooke had exploited
political connections to ensure a weak outcome to the hearings. Their associate in the Washington Market project, Republican national secretary
William E. Chandler, represented the city during the House investigation.
Two Democrats, including New York's Robert Roosevelt, did submit a minority report warning that the regime's bullying tactics afforded "a startling
example of the improper use of power."[1]

The investigation's failure left the old citizens in disarray. Shepherd used
this clear field to produce works on an astonishing scale. In just over two
years, the Board of Public Works constructed 120 miles of sewers, 30 miles
of water mains, 39 miles of gas lines, and 208 miles of sidewalks. It graded
and paved 150 miles of roads. Many streets were narrowed and "parked"—
planted—down the middle or along the sides. The board planted tens of
thousands of trees. The government also engaged in a public building program that included, among other projects, two new markets and six new

schools. Only four school buildings had existed in the entire District before the improvements.[2]

Local newspapers proudly reprinted accounts of the "New Washington" from out-of-town papers, whose correspondents marveled at the "vast public operations." Frederick Douglass's *New National Era* commented, "There is probably no city in the world in which such wonderful changes have been wrought during a single year."[3] Skeptics and critics also acknowledged the scale of Shepherd's activities. House Appropriations chairman James Garfield felt "a good deal in doubt" about certain board requests for federal funds. Still, Garfield believed that the Territory's "vast" accomplishments had "greatly bettered the condition of the city." The Baltimore *Sun,* so persistent a foe that Shepherd later sued the paper for libel, conceded, "The District has something to show for all the money which has been expended. . . . the city has been beautified and embellished."[4] This far-flung praise confirmed the improvers in their sense of mission — and in their high-handed manner. Soon, even people well-disposed to them worried that District officials were out of control and would listen to no one.

The Board of Public Works took only weak measures to reassure anxious homeowners, who feared, as builder Charles Edmonston explained, that "in some cases the improvement will amount to more than the property is worth," so that "the property holder may be obliged to sell to raise that amount." Shepherd and Cooke reiterated their views on the shared benefits of property-value inflation and pointed out that their practice of assessing adjacent property only one-third the cost of improvements was better than the old system of assessing the whole cost. Critics countered that improvements were so rapid and costly that advantages from the reformed special tax system were wiped out for all except speculators. Anti-government groups charged the regime with plotting "to force small holders of property to ruinous sacrifice," in order to make land available to real estate pools. Although critics offered no concrete evidence to support their dire predictions, homeowners understandably refused to wait until events justified their fears. Resentment over special assessments quickly translated into resistance and coalesced in lawsuits. At the abolition of the Territory in 1874, about $3.8 million in improvement taxes remained uncollected. Disputes arising from Shepherd-era improvement taxes remained a live political and legal issue for a decade and were not entirely settled until the 1890s.[5]

Changes in street grades meant that homeowners would need new stairs, rebuilt plumbing, and underpinning for foundations. Shepherd at first brusquely rebuffed homeowners seeking compensation; he cited court rulings indicating that cities were not responsible for damages to property adjacent to street improvements. But Shepherd and Cooke soon realized that, while lawful, this stance was hardly politic. The board eventually secured authority to compensate for damages, though the process was never effective.

In late 1872, the Territory embarrassed itself politically when two senators who lived on Massachusetts Avenue, Vermont's George Edmunds and Delaware's Thomas Bayard, returned from a recess to find their homes on ledges ten feet above the regraded street. The hole in front of Bayard's house "went down and down until the gulf seemed almost bottomless." The senators submitted bills totaling $5,500 for rebuilding steps and reconnecting pipes, but they ended up settling for having their special taxes canceled.[6]

Likewise, Shepherd did little to appease shopkeepers who worried that torn-up streets would paralyze business. Nor was he effective at mollifying inconvenienced pedestrians, such as the minister's wife who fell into waist-deep mud at a construction site on her way to church. Columnist Emily E. Briggs promised to praise Shepherd in her "Olivia" articles if he would stop dismissing charges of favoritism towards the northwest: "Your most bitter opponents are my neighbors on Capitol Hill. They say you have ignored us altogether."[7]

Shepherd dealt with big interests as brusquely as he did aggrieved individuals. The Alexandria and Washington Railroad ran along First Street below Capitol Hill. In November 1872, the Board of Public Works notified the railroad that those streets were to be rebuilt and it should remove its track forthwith. The company ignored the request, which was, as a local historian noted, in line with "current railroad practice in dealing with local authorities." After waiting ten days, Shepherd "organized a gang of men and tore up the track." He later asserted, "I did that without authority of law, but it was the right thing to do, and the nuisance would not otherwise have been removed."[8]

Most residents applauded the board's defeat of the railroad, but another coup reportedly prompted Shepherd to ask police for protection from a possible lynch mob. The board wanted to replace the dilapidated Northern Liberty Market on Mount Vernon Square with two better-located facilities, but stallholders refused to transfer to the temporary sheds the government had prepared for them four blocks away. In September 1872, when stallholders were threatening to obtain an injunction against the demolition, Shepherd invited the only available judge to dinner at his country house. That same evening, at 8 P.M. on a Wednesday, a gang sent by territorial authorities arrived to tear down the wretched old hall. Stallkeepers were still at work inside. In the ensuing confusion, two people were killed, a well-known butcher and a boy who was hunting rats with his dog. Afraid that Shepherd might be attacked if he went home alone from his evening at the Washington Club, friends put together a guard of local blacks. "Darkies were always very good to me," recalled the District's most prominent Republican. A crowd a half-mile long followed the butcher's funeral, and Shepherd remained under threat for a time. To the end, he defended his "sudden and heroic measures." In 1896, Congress debated compensation for the stallholders. Shepherd wrote to support the claim: "The property and business of these stall holders were necessarily sacrificed to the public good." He did not discuss whether avoiding "delay" and "long litigation" was worth two lives.[9]

The flamboyant improvers caught the attention of the national press. At first, the country's distinguished newspapers praised the territorial movement. In July 1871, the *New York Tribune* called the Board of Public Works' street and sewerage program amazing and declared, "It augurs well for the new generation of Washingtonians — mostly importations of the War like Governor Cooke and Delegate Chipman — that they comprehend the fact that Washington is a rich city, able to help itself." When an opponent wrote to object that the program was a "comprehensive swindle," the New York paper responded dismissively that Washington's grumblers were "unused to the novel experience of paying" for needed public expenditures.[10]

Within a year, the New York press had turned against the Territory. To Whitelaw Reid, Horace Greeley's successor as editor of the *Tribune,* the Territory became "nothing but an organization of swindling rings," a "system of profligacy and plunder." To Charles A. Dana's *New York Sun,* the Board of Public Works was "Boss Tweed outdone" and Shepherd, one of "so many dregs [brought] to the surface" by "Grantism," demonstrated "audacity, low breeding, and desire for meretricious display." The editors became so unrelenting that Shepherd attempted to prosecute Reid and Dana for criminal libel.[11] The continued support of the only exception among the big New York dailies, the *New York Times,* underscores how, during the Gilded Age, "reform" crusades against "bossism" were often indistinguishable from partisan maneuvering. In 1871, the Republican *Times* had taken the lead in exposing the Democratic Tweed Ring's misdeeds. The *Tribune,* although a Republican paper, was at odds with the Grant administration.

Unlike the local opposition, the New York newspapers knew how to back up their charges with evidence. In April 1873, the *Tribune* provided details of $15 million in debts incurred by the "bankrupt and irresponsible" Board of Public Works. The paper demonstrated that the board's estimate sheets, accounts, and vouchers did not reflect actual costs and expenditures, that millions were spent without appropriation, and that the federal government was being overcharged for work done to its property. "Frightful" special assessments were labeled inflated and illegal. "If the board collects eighty percent of the whole amount it will be very fortunate," wrote a correspondent, understating his case. The board hid this deficit, the paper reported, by canceling future contracts and covering old debts with new appropriations. The District appeared to be siphoning funds to the board from other departments; three-quarters of the school fund seemed to have disappeared, and Washington delayed the pay of teachers, police, and firemen. Shepherd wrote to refute the *Tribune*'s "gross misrepresentations." His letter contained "some truth and considerable equivocation," the paper remarked. "The fact remains that the business of the board has been managed with singular recklessness."[12]

That the District faced a financial mess became evident to others besides bulldog reporters. In March 1873, the board began to issue certificates of indebtedness to contractors, an abandonment of the cash-only policy that Shepherd and Cooke had maintained was essential if the Comprehensive Plan were to be affordable. Long experience had taught that such certificates swiftly depreciated, causing contractors to inflate their prices. That spring, despite challenges to existing special assessments, the District legislature authorized a further $2.1 million in "sewer certificates." This measure placed a flat surcharge on real estate and thus flouted the $\frac{1}{3}$-$\frac{2}{3}$ principle that supposedly made improvement taxes palatable in the first place.[13] In June 1873, even Shepherd's *Star* admitted that "rigid economy" had "become a necessity."

Throughout the summer, rumors spread that the District was having difficulty meeting loan payments to New York banks. In September, when the collapse of Jay Cooke and Company forced Henry Cooke to resign the governorship and attend to the family's business, city employees who had not received salaries in months overwhelmed his successor, Shepherd, with pleas that they finally be paid. While downplaying Washington's plight to the Joint Investigating Committee of 1874, Shepherd sent the opposite message to George F. Baker, the great New York banker who had absorbed remnants of Jay Cooke's financial operations. The city, Shepherd wrote Baker, desperately needed short-term credits to cover payroll and other current expenses. Shepherd secured the essential credits from Baker with liens on improvement taxes, which, when revealed, merely heightened outrage about the special assessments.[14]

The New York press made Washington's political and financial predicament known throughout the country. This created a dilemma for the national Republican party, already hard-pressed to explain many other accusations swirling around the Grant administration. Some congressional Republicans felt honor-bound to stand by the Washington branch of their party, but the stunning revival of the Democrats so soon after their electoral disaster in 1872 undermined the will of most Republicans. Democrats were hardly free from the taint of corruption. Regardless, their strategy for the pivotal congressional election of 1874 was to play the scandals plaguing Grant's presidency for all they were worth. In a desperate effort to preserve the party's loosening grip on Congress, Republican leaders found themselves under pressure to renounce Shepherd, Babcock, and similar presidential sidekicks.

II

By early 1874, more and more Republicans were insisting that the party demonstrate commitment to reform by moving against the Shepherd circle. Party members from the hotly contested Midwest voiced this sentiment most strongly. Even members of the Stalwart faction, such as Senators Logan of Illinois and Morton of Indiana, were concerned about "prolific" discussion of the Washington controversy in their section. A state party official wrote Iowa senator William B. Allison that the Shepherd group's links to the administration warranted vigorous congressional investigation: "There's a world of rottenness there that should be exposed *no matter who it hits*. My own impression is that parties higher in authority than even the beneficiaries of the French Arms Steal will be found lurking beneath wooden pavements and concrete streets."[15]

The District's financial plight, the country's concern, and the prospect of a friendlier hearing in Congress reinvigorated the anti-Shepherd movement, which formulated a new series of formal charges against the improver regime. To avoid a repeat of the House District Committee's questionable performance in 1872, Congress set up a bipartisan select committee, chaired by Allison. These legislators conducted a laborious inquiry for four months and produced three thousand pages of documents and testimony.

The committee determined that the chief cause of Washington's current plight was cost overruns that Governor Shepherd had authorized when he was vice president of the Board of Public Works. For his part, Shepherd blamed the city's apparent bankruptcy on the September 1873 panic: "The financial crisis came on . . . and the payment of taxes has been deferred. . . . if the assessments were in such a shape that the money on them could be collected, the board of public works would not be short over $1,000,000 or $1,500,000." This defense was implausible, as Washington's fiscal crisis preceded the panic by six months. More to the point, even had the embattled improvement taxes survived legal challenges intact, they would barely have begun to cover the liabilities incurred by the Board of Public Works between 1871 and the crash. Allison's committee estimated the District's total debt to be $21–24 million. The 1871 Comprehensive Plan promised expenditures of $6,578,397. Shepherd's own figures reveal that, in its brief life, the Board of Public Works spent $18,872,566. Panic or no, Shepherd would eventually have had to account for spending $12 million more than he initially projected.[16]

Shepherd had provoked the cost overruns, his critics argued, through his assertion of authority to make unilateral changes in published plans. In 1871, when he first sought approval for the Comprehensive Plan, the territorial leader promised that he would not burden property through "the introduction of wood or other expensive pavements." In the preliminary schedule Shepherd submitted to the territorial legislature, only 7th and 14th streets were to be wood. In its first year alone, the Board of Public Works authorized 34.3 miles of wooden streets. In 1872, 1.1 million of the 1.9 million square yards of pavements contracted were wood or concrete. The changes were expedient, the board explained, because patents for strengthening concrete and preserving wood had been perfected. Cobblestone was primitive and macadam dusty. Now that alternatives were practical, they should be used. When asked about these unilateral acts during the 1872 hearings, Shepherd had insisted, "We do not suppose that if the schedule calls for laying a cobble-stone pavement in a street, and we think that the needs of the city and the wishes of the people require a Belgian pavement, a wood pavement, or a concrete pavement, we have not the power to make the change." [17] This led the sympathetic House committee to admonish that the board seemed "somewhat intoxicated with the spirit of improvement." The less friendly 1874 panel concluded that, while minor modifications were allowable, routine, widespread departures violated both District and federal law. Whatever the advantages of new paving techniques, wrote the *Tribune,* Shepherd gave taxpayers "no voice in determining what improvements should be made, or how much money should be spent on streets." [18]

A "vicious" system for awarding contracts multiplied overruns. Shepherd contended, with justification, that open bidding for contracts led to straw bids and shoddy work. In an effort to render bidding unnecessary, Shepherd and Mullett developed a table of standard prices for each type of project. In theory, Shepherd had a sound case for his "board rates." The problem began when Shepherd let favored contractors suggest what was reasonable, so that the board would have paid too much even if it had stuck to its lists. The high fixed prices invited brokerage in contracts. A widespread practice in the construction business, such "contract jobbing" relieved builders of the hassles associated with seeking government work, but it undermined the municipality's ability to keep control of its own program. The 1874 inquiry revealed contract jobbers to have included newspaper men and government employees with personal connections to members of the territorial legislature. [19]

One instance of jobbery uncovered by the congressional investigators could have ended the career of a future U.S. President. A Chicago wooden paving firm, DeGolyer and McClelland, set up a $97,000 fund to hire "lobbyists" for District business. Most of the money disappeared into the hands of confidence men who used vague claims of influence to engage the company's agent in fanciful intrigues. DeGolyer and McClelland's agent did pay $15,000 to an Ohio congressman, Richard Parsons, to make the company's case to Shepherd in a more public manner. Though lobbying by congressmen was often deplored, many legislators regarded it as an acceptable part of their private law practice. When Parsons had to leave Washington for an extended period, he offered $5,000 to his perpetually strapped congressional colleague, James Garfield, to finish the business. As House Appropriations Committee chairman, Garfield was obviously a difficult person for Shepherd to refuse. After several meetings, some private and some open, Shepherd awarded 150,000 square yards of paving at $3.50 per square yard to the Chicago firm, locations to be determined later. The company's costs amounted to $1.50–$1.75 per square yard. [20]

A recent biographer of Garfield writes that the future President was lucky all details of this transaction did not become public at once, as he was "trapped in a clear case of influence peddling." Supporters at home wanted an explanation. The fees, wrote one, "at a distance look as though they might be disproportionate to the value of the legal services rendered." Already damaged by his role in the Credit Mobilier uproar, Garfield fumbled: "The fact of my being a member of Congress does not disable me from the legitimate practice of law." The congressman's stature carried him through, although as late as 1879, the unfriendly Ohio newspapers insisted that the affair made Garfield an unfit candidate for Speaker of the House.[21]

The high board rates that attracted the contract jobbers themselves became minimums. Shepherd and his colleagues routinely extended or amended contracts, often verbally, changing specifications, prices, even work locations at will. Favored contractors received double payments for certain work. For example, the board would pay for hauling dirt away from a street whose grade was lowered and then would buy back the same dirt, which the city owned all along, when the contractor dumped it on a street to be raised. The city marked unfinished projects "final" and paid as though they were complete. Later, the contractor might receive additional payment when the project really was finished. These practices caused still more anger against special taxes, since it was impossible to calculate even whether the board was charging property for work indeed done near it.

This time, the Territory's local opposition managed to document the favoritism shown to Shepherd's network of business associates. Perhaps 20 percent of the total monies spent on the Comprehensive Plan went to members of the improver circle. In addition to controlling disproportionate shares of paving and sewerage contracts, insiders sold supplies and services to other contractors. Board treasurer James Magruder made sure to expedite insiders' bills, and, when possible, to pay them in cash. Less-favored contractors had to accept certificates of indebtedness, which they then had no choice but to cash at severe discounts, often at banks with ties to the government's friends.[22]

Magruder's bookkeeping came to epitomize the loose methods of the board. The treasurer kept no record of which contractors received cash and which certificates, so the District had no idea of its debt. The 1874 congressional investigation concluded: "The checks he has issued do not correspond with the several amounts reported by him to have been paid; so that there is, as he himself concedes, no way of ascertaining whether his accounts are correct." A year later, Treasury Department auditors also threw up their hands. While "apparently regular on their face," Magruder's accounts, they found, would not tally, "nor have any data been found which will explain these discrepancies." To estimate what improvements had cost, the auditors had to reconstruct expenditures street by street.[23]

Many cities besides Washington experienced angry controversies over extravagant spending around the time of the 1873 panic. With New York's recent Tweed scandal a vivid memory, dissenting officials and aggrieved taxpayers in other cities understandably leaned towards blaming "Tweedism" for what had gone wrong with any administration. Although nowhere near as brazenly greedy as Tweed's, Shepherd's methods with vouchers, contracts, and claims were so strikingly similar to those of New York's Public Works commissioner that a story circulated that Shepherd had once traveled to New York to study with the master. The two officials indignantly denied this rumor.[24]

The only member of the Territory's inner circle who developed serious misgivings about these practices was architect Adolph Cluss. After he replaced Mullett as board engineer in late 1872, he began to worry that comparisons between Shepherd and Tweed had merit. Shepherd's secretive manner of conducting business struck Cluss as reminiscent of "the Jesuits in Rome," a group even more nefarious than the Tweed Ring, in the old anticlerical German socialist's mind. Testifying during the 1874 inquiry, Cluss could recall only eight regular board meetings between October 1872 and January 1874. The longest had lasted an hour and a half. The investigating committee concluded that Shepherd had "exercised the powers of the Board . . . as though no one else were associated with him." Decisions made by Shepherd were often recorded as having been made upon "consultation" with the others, as though they were formal acts of the entire board.[25]

The disenchantment of Shepherd's friend and neighbor, Cluss, gave the Territory's enemies the break they had long sought. Congress engaged a former member of Ohio's Board of Public Works to examine bills against the federal government submitted by the Board of Public Works and certified by Major Babcock's Public Buildings Office. Cluss agreed to testify to corroborate those damaging audits. In the process, he detailed various stratagems that the board's inspectors and engineers had employed to maximize the portion of the program chargeable to the United States. The engineer also revealed that measurements used to calculate costs were quite often "arbitrary assumptions," as contractors were allowed to begin work before engineers had even made a plat of a street. The Public Buildings Office, a bureau administered by the War Department, cooperated in these maneuvers. In addition, Babcock had assured congressional committees of the completeness and accuracy of bills used as a basis for reimbursements, when he should have known otherwise.[26]

Cluss's appearance gave the lengthy hearings a dramatic end. The architect said that he testified against old friends to save his professional reputation. He admitted signing incorrect measurements sent him by subordinates. He claimed he had acquiesced in the board's haphazard procedures because he could do little else. Journalists reported that the halting English of the "unfortunate" German immigrant left him at a disadvantage against the withering cross-examination of Nevada's Senator Stewart, a friend of the board and a shrewd lawyer, and against the badgering of Shepherd's attorneys. Cluss had been in Washington for twenty-five years, so one should treat skeptically this touch of newspaper melodrama. The questioning was indeed intimidating, but Shepherd came out the worse.[27]

Cluss's testimony was the second-to-last nail in the Territory's coffin. The Board of Public Works provided the final one itself. While New York newspapers hailed Cluss as an "honest citizen and a faithful officer," Shepherd die-hards in Washington raged against him as an "ill-balanced" traitor, "disemboweled by his own signature." The remaining board members resolved that because Cluss was a perjurer, they could not "recognize him as a fit officer to have charge of the engineering department." The board asked the President to sack this apostate. Grant complied, a move that backfired on the friends he had hoped to assist. The President's "extraordinary" interference with the ongoing congressional investigation, wrote the Baltimore *Sun*, underscored Cluss's "very damaging testimony." Two weeks later, on June 16, 1874, the committee's report appeared. The territorial system was labeled a failure.[28]

Some thoughtful commentators felt that the failure lay in the way Shepherd fused arrogance with incompetence. E. L. Godkin's *Nation* denigrated the territorial program on the grounds that the intelligence behind it seemed inadequate. Instead of systematic public works methodically pursued, Godkin asserted, the Comprehensive Plan had manifested the ill-considered whims of an autodidactic petty bourgeois who had overreached himself. The magazine believed that "a very audacious and knavish gang" had indeed victimized Washington but that the troubles of the Board of Public Works were "merely . . . what we must expect to find in every department of Government so long as a show of activity and energy is preferred to technical knowledge and administrative experience." The mugwumpish *Nation* labeled Shepherd a man "of large ideas and great personal ambition, who had never been known to cheat or steal" but was ignorant of the principles of administration and too presumptuous "to select a competent engineer in whom he was himself willing to trust." The magazine concluded, "However good [Shepherd's] ideas might have been, he had not the least notion of the conditions of their successful execution."[29]

The improvers' experiences in real estate, contracting, and local finance did influence them to pursue their public works in an ad hoc, disorderly manner, easily labeled "reckless mismanagement" or "ring rule," yet Godkin's implication that Shepherd did not base the projects on expert advice was a misapprehension, albeit one that the territorial leader encouraged with characteristic bluster. At the 1872 hearings, Shepherd raised eyebrows by asserting that his experience in the plumbing business and his "reading" afforded him sufficient technical knowledge to manage a large city's streets and sewers. "You have no practical experience?" he was asked. "All that I have is practical," the head improver disdainfully replied.[30]

The 1874 investigation deplored how the Board of Public Works had launched improvements "which were to extend over almost every street and avenue" without adequate "preliminary organization of the various details of the engineering work," including "plats, plans, and estimates." For instance, although the local population had doubled, the board undertook no systematic revision of the official street grade book adopted twenty years before.[31] The blame for this lies as much with Mullett, the European-trained architect, as with Shepherd, the self-taught plumber. Shepherd worked with Mullett when sketching out procedures for executing improvements.

The board also worked closely with Major Babcock, the official directly responsible for federal relations with the District on public works matters. At the time, politicians of both parties believed Babcock to be a competent civil engineer, if something of an adventurer. Both Congress and the federal departments counted on Babcock to supervise the Board of Public Works and to provide an accurate account of its activities.

Godkin's argument that Shepherd did not rely on adequate expertise was hindsight; the designated officials had sanctioned all the board's actions. The problem was not that Shepherd neglected experts, but that the experts made available to him by the federal government encouraged him to do what he did. The reasons for this (in addition to ambition, greed, and so forth) were political, organizational, and intellectual. Partisan and factional considerations would in any case have inclined Babcock to put at Shepherd's disposal the bureau that was supposed to restrain him. Even had the Major acted against character and followed the book with regard to the Board of Public Works, he would have found it difficult, since there was no book. After abolishing the civilian Public Buildings Office in 1867, Congress had simply transferred the work to the Army Corps, without providing much guidance regarding policies or procedures. The Corps had an impressive record in constructing large single works, such as the Washington Aqueduct, but it had no experience with the administrative and political difficulties of building and maintaining a variety of urban services all at the same time. Nor did anyone else. The municipal engineering profession was still in its infancy, and public works departments in all American and most foreign cities were at that point organized in a rudimentary fashion.

No integrated infrastructure program on the scale envisioned for Washington had yet been attempted in the United States. In Europe as well, only tentative progress had been made in managing large-scale urban public works programs. The most acclaimed recent enterprise, Haussmann's rebuilding of Paris, looked smooth only from a distance. Haussmann chose his staff members because they had happened to impress him at some point, but they often had little relevant experience. The baron's autocratic methods exacerbated harm done by ill-considered measures that caused social disruption on a scale not seen in American cities until the urban renewal programs of the 1950s. A respected history of Haussmann's Paris asserts that, "in a state less authoritarian than the Second Empire," the baron's leadership "would have become a political issue much earlier." That the Prefect endured for twenty years was more a tribute to his popularity with Louis Napoleon than with Parisians.[32]

The absence of adequate models for organization or procedure encouraged federal officers responsible for supervising the Board of Public Works instead to join in its "reckless" improvisations. Godkin suggested that Shepherd ruined an admirably ambitious program because, as a self-educated *nouveau riche,* he could not appreciate the intricacies of public works management. Authorities in the field did not know much more than he.

III

Two days after the 1874 investigative report was made, Congress passed legislation abolishing the Territory. The bill provided for a temporary, appointed three-member commission, until Congress could decide what to try next with the national city. That choice depended on what they decided had been wrong with the Territory. Encouraging the improvers to pursue a promotional approach to building a worthy national city had conformed with well-established political and administrative traditions. Washington would move in a new direction if politicians saw the turmoil and confusion of the Shepherd regime as evidence that the promotional approach was at heart bad policy, that such a confounding of public and private interests created as many problems as it solved. On the other hand, as was more likely, considering how deeply promotional attitudes and procedures were rooted in our governance and political culture, Congress might decide that the kinds of works undertaken by the Board of Public Works were worth doing but needed to be done by more circumspect and less venal officials.

Gradually, it dawned on the old citizens, Congress, the federal establishment, and the press that, while they might have found the improvers' character and methods unsettling, the goals and actual programs of the movement fit in well with their notion of what kind of city Washington should become. This realization rendered inevitable the rehabilitation of the reputations of those who had concocted the Comprehensive Plan. As rancor from the dispute faded, even the most hostile old citizens began to find virtue where once they had seen iniquity. Some old antagonists even found themselves agreeing in retrospect with one of the improvers' disturbing contentions — that Washington in the early 1870s had needed Shepherd's impetuous, imperious energy to jolt it onto the path to prosperity. In 1899, James Berret, the deposed Civil War mayor of Washington, recalled Shepherd as "a man of great energy, liberal views, and full of enthusiasm," who had precipitated a necessary crisis. Old-line residents had mistakenly opposed the Comprehensive Plan, Berret explained, because it was "upon scale so large as to startle the whole community. A great many of us thought that we were to be sold out."[33]

While Shepherd ran his government in an aggressive, autocratic fashion, the projects he elected to pursue were not randomly selected. The District improvers used their brief hegemony to thrust upon Washington's hesitant citizens a number of measures that respected observers, particularly Army Engineers intrigued with building a worthy capital, had long considered necessary but that had been repeatedly delayed by the muddled condition of the national city's politics and finances before 1871. The Army Corps's collected recommendations, which Shepherd wrote into his Comprehensive Plan of Improvements and meant to implement come hell or high water, did not constitute a unified "city plan" as we understand the term, since such plans did not yet exist. Yet, taken together, these proposals did offer a vision of a functional, admirable, and prosperous Washington that appealed to post–Civil War nationalists, as well as to politically minded entrepreneurs such as the improvers.

Perhaps the best example of how the Corps's examinations of Washington's needs influenced the Shepherd program is the Corps's four-year discussion of the design and paving of central Washington's streets. In 1867, the year the military acquired the Public Buildings Office, Major Nathaniel Michler, the officer in charge, urged the government to do more to complete L'Enfant's street plan. Michler argued that the United States should commence work right away on prominent avenues and squares. Beyond questions of justice, convenience, and health, the engineer argued, symbolic considerations demanded that the nation carefully regulate the design of and the materials used in the capital's thoroughfares, and play a major role in their construction and maintenance. Paving, Michler argued, signified "civilization and traffic." A healthy patriotism had led the Romans to pave city streets "in the same elaborate and solid manner" as their highways, even though highways had more obvious military and economic purposes.[34]

In keeping with this outlook, Michler's office backed a controversial proposal to narrow and "park" L'Enfant's broad thoroughfares. Parking, proponents claimed, would serve the dual purpose of making roadways more pleasant and of lowering costs enough to render citywide paving feasible. General Meigs, builder of the Washington Aqueduct and the Capitol extension, sent Michler a report that endorsed parking for Washington and underscored the patriotic value of a capital's streets. While traveling through Europe, Meigs had taken cross-sections of Unter-den-Linden in Berlin and the Champs Elysées in Paris, boulevards that Meigs found simultaneously magnificent, pleasant, and practical. Great European capitals, the general argued, spent lavishly on ornamental roads that interspersed paved sidewalks and carriageways with rows of parking and gravel rides and promenades. Michler later modified Meigs's ideas so that parking could be either close to houses or in a strip down the avenue's center, both forms that are familiar to present-day Washingtonians.[35] Congress authorized street-narrowing in 1870, but the municipal corporation made no progress with it before giving way to the Board of Public Works.

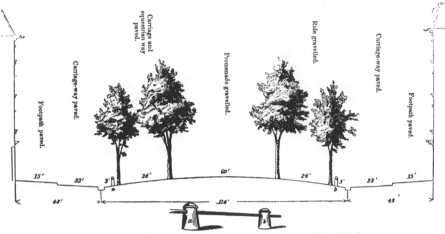

a and b represent lines of stone posts about 15 feet apart, connected by iron rods about 1¼ inch.

Sketch showing Plan for the Improvement of Streets and Avenues in the City OF WASHINGTON.

During 1867 and 1868, Gen. Montgomery C. Meigs and Maj. Nathaniel Michler prepared these drawings, which used Berlin's Unter-den-Linden (*top*) and Paris's Champs Elysées (*bottom*) as models for narrowing and "parking" L'Enfant's "inordinately wide" streets. From contemporary Corps of Engineers reports reprinted in Frederick Gutheim, consultant, *Worthy of the Nation* (Washington, D.C.: Smithsonian Institution Press, 1977); courtesy the Smithsonian Institution Press.

The old citizens took the extent and grandeur of the board's street improvements as prima facie evidence of mismanagement and corruption, especially as Shepherd, upon taking office, had submitted a less-lavish scheme. To abandon those lawfully adopted plans was an exercise of arbitrary power. Shepherd did not choose his plans arbitrarily, however; they had been elaborated over the preceding four years by respected military engineers. In fact, the Board of Public Works, following Meigs's suggestions, had decided that what it termed the "monotony" of the L'Enfant Plan should be broken, by trimming the streets' "imperial widths" and transforming the surplus space into a "vast garden." This system, the board argued, would give the capital "a leading feature, of rare beauty." By 1888, the "parking commission," which survived the fall of Shepherd, had planted 64,920 trees. Residents came to criticize some aspects of street-narrowing but grew to admire the scheme.[36]

The choice of materials for paving Washington's streets supposedly offered more evidence of "ring" perfidy. Many old citizens believed that wood, concrete, and asphalt could not make good pavements, and they insisted that the Board of Public Works favored these materials in order to funnel profits to its cronies. Citizens agreed that stone and Belgian block were legitimate pavings, but they added that Shepherd had completely abandoned his 1871 promise to confine such expensive materials "to a few of the principal avenues of communication." Wood, concrete, and asphalt dominated the paving program, finally accounting for more than two million square yards, about eighty miles of roadway. In addition, the Territory built twenty-five miles of luxurious stone pavements.[37]

The subsequent fate of the pavements built by the board appeared to support the criticism. In 1875, Lieutenant Richard L. Hoxie, municipal engineer under the interim commission that superseded the Territory, reported "disastrous" decay of wood pavements. The Board of Health found fungus growing on Pennsylvania Avenue. Garbage mixed into the wood, which then "decomposed so rapidly as to give rise to a mass of dangerous putrefaction." Wood treated with expensive patent preservatives appeared to rot faster than untreated materials. Over the next decade, the major part of the city's paving budget went towards replacing wood pavements. Engineers estimated that Shepherd's experiments with wood blocks ended in a clear loss of $4 million.[38]

Shepherd ought to have known that the value of wooden streets was in doubt, enemies said, because other cities had already had bitter experiences with them. In the Great Chicago Fire of 1871, wooden streets burned and spread the destruction. There were unanticipated maintenance problems. By 1873, Cluss was admitting that an effective preservative for wood pavements had not been found, which did "not augur well for their duration," although he encouraged seeking new treatments. On the other hand, Captain Albert Grant, whom the anti-Shepherd movement presented as an expert on paving, testified that wood was "the best pavement" if "properly laid."[39]

Shepherd's private secretary remembered his saying that wood pavements were his biggest regret but that army engineers had advised their use. "It was an experiment in other cities," Shepherd told the secretary, "and we did not know that there was anything in the soil here that would rot it out."[40] Shepherd recalled that Babcock, Meigs, and General Humphreys, the chief of engineers, all had recommended wood pavements for Washington. While on the commission to pave Pennsylvania Avenue in 1870, Michler had visited Boston, New York, and Philadelphia and returned a recommendation for wood, which he called "delightful, easy, and not noisy." When the Pennsylvania Avenue paving rotted in the mid-1870s, critics blamed Shepherd and forgot that the avenue had been built by a special commission before the Territory came into being. "Black muck" remained in Washington streets as evidence of a failed experiment pursued too zealously.[41]

The board's concrete roads gave the new commission and Lieutenant Hoxie nearly as much trouble as the wood ones. Adolph Cluss had advised that smooth pavements, like concrete and asphalt, were sanitary, provided good footing for horses, and would prove a lasting innovation. With Shepherd's links to Kilbourn's asphalt clique, he did not even need encouragement from his engineer. Shepherd paid premiums to contractors from New York, Brooklyn, and Philadelphia to install experimental mixtures of concrete, coal-tar, and natural asphalt, using processes such as the "C. E. Evans" and "Scharf" patents. The Kilbourn group controlled the latter, but even so it received enthusiastic attention in Washington. When a demonstration pavement, laid by John O. Evans in front of Corcoran's exclusive Arlington Hotel, elicited the fascination that Americans typically give a technological marvel, Riggs and Corcoran petitioned Shepherd to hire Evans to pave the streets of Lafayette Square. Delighted by the old citizens' praise, Shepherd contracted for as much smooth pavement as the market could deliver. "Every man who came here and was responsible and who wanted to lay a concrete pavement had all the work he could do," he recalled.[42]

Shepherd squandered the credit he earned for promoting this useful innovation by pushing it too hard. The Board of Public Works expected contractors to develop a durable product and still work quickly. Evans complained that Shepherd's restlessness added to the normal problems that attend new technologies. "We were very much hurried; the work was commenced late, I think in October, and the first work was necessarily slow," Evans testified. "It was not the proper time, but they were anxious to have the street covered with something, and we did not succeed at first in getting first-class material." Pressure from the District for quick results sparked quarrels among Evans's partners over proper methods for mixing, binding, and laying their product.[43]

Military engineers were slower than Shepherd and Cluss to recognize the potential of smooth pavement. In his 1867 survey, Meigs had treated European experiments with asphalt skeptically. He had suggested that stone blocks might prove more suitable for Washington, because of the accessibility of nearby quarries.[44] Later, the Corps of Engineers' work in Washington would earn international acclaim as a conclusive demonstration that asphalt was viable. The army's achievement consisted in working out the bugs in the process. Hoxie and his colleagues realized that the concrete and "artificial" asphalt pavings favored by Shepherd were only deceptively cheaper than pavings constructed chiefly from sand and imported natural asphalt. Shepherd's mixtures cost $2–$3 per square yard, while a natural asphalt road cost up to $4.50 per square yard. The cheaper mixture, however, tended to form "a solid mass" with its foundation, multiplying maintenance expenses: when the pavement crumbled, cracked, or wore away, the entire road needed replacing. In 1876, the engineers finally settled the question in favor of imported Trinidadian asphalt by laying competing mixtures on different parts of Pennsylvania Avenue.[45]

IV

The street designs and paving materials favored by Shepherd were meant to render the capital's thoroughfares majestic and attractive, on top of being practical, and thereby to promote Washington as a governmental and service center and an inviting field for real estate investors. The same purposes determined where street improvements were made. The Board of Public Works preferred to embellish streets near federal buildings, through downtown retail districts, and in wealthier residential quarters rather than improve access to wharves, warehouses, and freight yards. The territorial regime made no serious effort to assist the potential factory district in Foggy Bottom near Rock Creek. This tendency implied acceptance of an idea that commentators such as the Army Engineers had articulated every so often but that had previously encountered indifference or hostility among Washingtonians—that the community should abandon the old dream of an independent commercial or industrial base. Instead, the argument went, local civic leaders should put energy and resources into creating a first-rate residential and service center for the government. While this ambition did not offer the capital's commercial elite the immense wealth and power of their counterparts in New York or Chicago, it did promise healthy prosperity and partial immunity to business cycles.

The Territory produced meticulous reports and splendid discourses on Washington's industrial promise and on the utter necessity of fostering trade and manufacturing that did more than supply the local market. "We must cut loose from exclusive dependence on Government contracts and expenditures," urged one such document.[46] Grand talk, but serious businessmen speak with money, not words. In both public and private affairs, the improvers focused almost exclusively on ventures that exploited Washington's potential as a residential and service city. The Shepherd regime paid scant attention to extraregional industry or trade. Territorial leaders worked hardest at laying the foundations for a national, not a commercial city.

Shepherd's sewerage program demonstrates even more clearly than his street improvements how the Comprehensive Plan nudged local enterprise into activities in line with this understanding of the city's role. The plan of the board's drainage system distressed old-line Washingtonians because it clearly anticipated a diminished role for intercity trade. In this, also, Shepherd followed advice from acquaintances in the Army Corps who felt that hopes for an autonomous economic base should be downplayed when this interfered with Washington's ornamental, political, and residential destiny.

The problems of storm drainage, waste disposal, and surface pollution grew along with the city. By the end of the war, both local and national officials were adamant that piecemeal sewer construction must end. Adolph Cluss and others who studied the problem for the municipality or Congress sensed that sewer mains would eventually have to be extended far down the Potomac. Some hoped that tides in front of the city were strong enough that, for a few decades, the District could get away with outlets built deep into the Potomac in front of Washington, thereby postponing the necessity for long pipes and costly pumps.[47]

How far downriver to construct major outlets was a problem for the future. Observers argued that Washington's most immediate drainage problem was the Washington Canal, which degraded to a "more filthy, pestilent condition" as greater amounts of foulness meandered into it each year.[48] The notion surfaced that the city ought simply to arch the canal and thereby acknowledge that the effort to combine transport with drainage had failed miserably. More typical proposals, however, continued to envision saving the canal by deepening it, forcing water to flow quickly through it, or building interceptors alongside it. Washington had invested too much effort and heartache in the canal to abandon the conceit that the waterway could pay.

The stink of organic chemistry pervaded the nearby Smithsonian Institution. The museum's renowned secretary, Professor Joseph Henry, trained to regard decomposition unromantically, had long held the opinion that the canal was "merely an open sewer" and should be abolished. In 1868, the Smithsonian asked General Richard Delafield, former chief of engineers, to report bluntly on the waterway's effects on Washington's sanitation. Delafield reviewed the canal's dubious history and concluded that the Father of Our Country had made a mistake. A barge route through the center of this political, not industrial, city was unnecessary. A "vast fermenting vat" in the heart of a national capital in the late nineteenth century was barbaric, Delafield said. The venerable engineer concluded that the government should turn the canal into a drainage tunnel for Washington's marshy lowlands. If downtown wholesalers wanted transport, then "a railroad over the same ground . . . would better subserve the public welfare."[49]

Delafield's report caused an uproar, not because it gave advance sanction to the idea of allowing the Pennsylvania Railroad to run tracks onto the Mall but because it thoroughly debunked the virtue of the canal. Washington's canal engineer inundated Congress with petitions from lumber and coal dealers south of Pennsylvania Avenue. Delafield's proposal, the official wrote, was "too absurd to be dwelt upon." Sewage would stagnate in an arched tun-

nel; pent-up "sewer gas" would spread more disease than at present. With
the canal properly dredged, barges "laden" with coal from western Maryland might bring three times the coal trade of Baltimore to downtown Washington. Mayors Wallach and Bowen equivocated. Arguments disrupted public meetings. A writer in the *Chronicle* remembered fondly when "sloops,
schooners, longboats innumerable and even a steamboat" reached wharves
as far uptown as 12th Street. Another writer admitted that there might be
sanitary sense in covering the canal but why destroy "a work so valuable in
a commercial point of view."[50] In July 1870, Congress turned the problem
over to a federal/local commission, which also failed to achieve consensus.
The panel sanctioned dredging as an interim measure. Michler noted that
troublesome marshes near the President's House could be reclaimed with the
dredged soil. Winning the bid for the dredging contract was J. H. Teemyer
and Company, a three-man partnership that included John O. Evans.[51]

The Board of Public Works superseded the Canal Commission in May
1871. While Teemyer's work continued, Babcock, Mullett, and Henry
struggled to convince a skeptical Shepherd that, as Mullett wrote, the waterway's "value for commercial purposes is a myth" and dredging it "insanity."
Mullett insisted that the fish, coal, lumber, and building supply warehouses
along the canal should be forced to the riverfront, that they degraded downtown Washington and fueled the Murder Bay slums south of Pennsylvania
Avenue. Mullett calculated that filling the canal would add over 200,000
square feet to the Mall and would give the District an additional 425,000
square feet of downtown real estate worth at least $1 per square foot. Only "a
few petty officials connected with its management" want to save the canal,
Mullett concluded. The canal's enemies enlisted congressmen, who threatened to block funds for Mall improvements unless the waterway was abandoned. In August 1871, the Board of Public Works resolved to fill the canal
starting at 3rd Street, northwest, and to replace it with sewers. This meant
that the $40,000–$50,000 already due Teemyer and Company for dredging
was a total loss. Mullett pointed out that if the board hired new contractors
to do the filling, it would have to buy out Teemyer and Evans's dredging
contract or face a lawsuit. The board assigned the contractors to fill what they
had just dredged.[52]

The citizens, crying foul, claimed that the board had no authority to destroy the canal and that the extended Teemyer contract was a payoff to a
Shepherd sidekick. At the 1872 House hearings, however, Michler, Meigs, and
Humphreys were the only significant officials who did not wholeheartedly
endorse the board's decision. Babcock testified that the canal's squalor fright-
ened ladies from the Mall and that filling it would drive slum-dwellers from
the vicinity. William Smith, superintendent of the Botanical Garden, recalled
that Andrew Jackson had found the canal, "a dirty, stinking, filthy ditch."
William Wise, canal commissioner in the 1850s, related that the "privy-box"
had never earned more than $6,000 per year, had been navigable three years

in the previous forty, and made lumber only fifty cents per cord cheaper than it was at the Potomac wharves. The District's Board of Health estimated that, in addition to assorted garbage, ten thousand tons of excrement entered the canal annually. The House investigative committee concluded that even if the Board of Public Works had lacked authority to destroy the waterway, it had done the right thing.[53]

The canal was filled in. With the canal gone, the big water issue at last became how to pipe it in when clean and how to carry it away when dirty; Shepherd's destruction of the canal marked the true beginning of Washington's sewerage system. Filling the canal solved problems that were as much political as technical. On the other hand, the political struggle over the canal had unfortunate side effects. After disposing of the waterway, the Board of Public Works hurried to spread sewers as extensively as time and money permitted. Rather than risk politically hazardous delays in order to determine the optimal points at which waste could enter the Potomac, Shepherd simply used the fact that drainage and waste had long flowed through the canal and Tiber Creek. The board established the B Street sewer along the canal route and made it one of the city's main outlets (the others being lines that ran south to the Anacostia and into the Potomac along Rock Creek). Each had serious shortcomings, but the B Street system created the most severe headaches for Shepherd's successors.

To carry wastes from the B Street sewer across the Potomac marshes and into the river, the board built a cheap open channel at 17th Street near the State, War, and Navy Building. Because this ill-constructed outlet met the river below the level of high tide, it could not drain adequately. "The failure to discharge the sewage into the deep water of the Potomac River," Lieutenant Hoxie wrote, multiplied water pollution near Washington and exacerbated the "poisonous influence" of the Potomac Flats. Each day, the river retarded the flow of sewage 1.5 miles up the B Street sewer along the Mall and 2 miles up the old, now-arched Tiber Creek. The fact that the B Street main ran level and at places even slightly uphill across the District's low-lying watershed multiplied troubles at the outlet. Sluggish flow resulted in accumulations of raw sewage three feet deep and several thousand feet long. The fears Meigs had voiced when testifying against filling the canal became reality. A freshet in the Potomac or exceptional rains easily "gorged" downtown streets, dumping "the contents of privies" into basements of restaurants, hotels, and houses. At least five times between 1875 and 1889, main sewers burst, flooding central Washington. In the worst floods, three feet of water might cover the Botanical Garden.[54]

After an 1889 flood, Congress engaged the acclaimed sanitary engineer Rudolph Hering to lead an expert commission in replanning the city's sewers. "Apparently no consideration was given to ultimate requirements," by the Board of Public Works, the consultants wrote. The Hering panel repeated a complaint that had arisen as soon as the board fell. A District health official

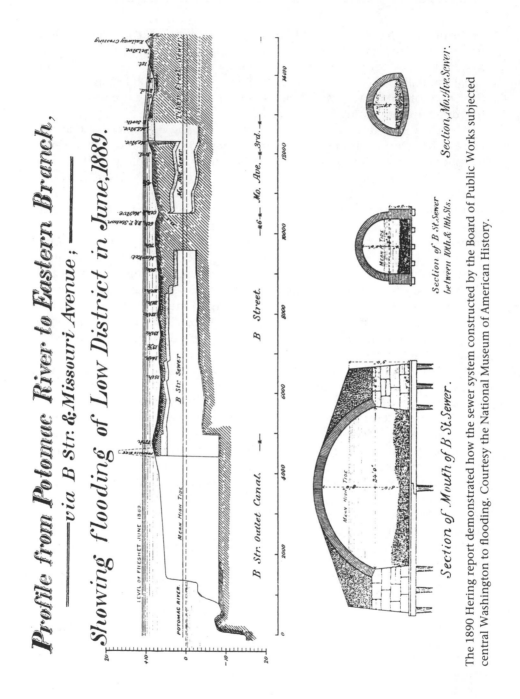

The 1890 Hering report demonstrated how the sewer system constructed by the Board of Public Works subjected central Washington to flooding. Courtesy the National Museum of American History.

During the 1889 flood in downtown Washington, punt boats appeared on Pennsylvania Avenue, northwest, near Market Square. Courtesy the Still Picture Branch, National Archives.

explained to Congress that by undertaking too grand a system all at once, Shepherd had bequeathed Washington the "confusion of hurriedness." Lieutenant Hoxie tried to examine why important sewers had inadequate diameters but could find "no record of any report submitted with [the board's sewerage] plans" nor "the data and formulae used in the computation of the dimensions." For the next decade, engineers kept finding piping that was too small, built poorly and of the wrong materials, badly aligned, ill-ventilated, and so weakly sealed that tree roots in the pipes became a major nuisance.[55]

By expanding upon pre-existing drainage patterns, the board willy-nilly committed the District to a "combined" sewer system, where storm drainage and home wastes ran through the same pipes. Homes and businesses had discharged solid wastes into Washington's sewers for many years already; the territorial legislature had sanctioned the connection of water closets to public pipes in 1871. Engineers and public health experts across the country were still debating the merits of combined systems against those of the "separate system," in which storm drainage and home wastes were kept apart from each other. As was the case in other large cities, Washington acquired through inertia a form of waste disposal that may have worsened the country's long-run environmental problems; some writers believe that the separate system permitted better control of river pollution. In 1878, Hoxie noted the loss of the opportunity to consider the separate system, but conceded, "The system being already established, it is hardly worth while to discuss its advantages and appropriateness now."[56]

Until the Hering report of 1890, however, experts disagreed as to how pressing all these concerns regarding Washington's drainage were and how difficult they would be to obviate in the short run. In 1878, the District commissioners summarized current thinking when they reported to a Senate committee that a project to pump sewage far from the waterfront might not be necessary "within the life of the present generation": "All of the conditions of health will have been sufficiently observed when the discharge takes place in deep running water and the flats of the city are filled so as to the prevent lodgement of fecal matters upon grounds which are exposed during the intervals of low tide."[57]

Given such attitudes and the aggressive nature of the Board of Public Works, it is little wonder that the board opted to put the canal out of its misery and end the mental muddle it was causing. Washington needed some system of sewerage, however inadequate. Once a system existed, there would be time to perfect it. The B Street sewer perpetuated flooding in central Washington and increased health hazards posed by the Potomac Flats. Shepherd, Cooke, and Babcock, however, constituted half of the Potomac River Commission of 1872, which conceived the idea of reclaiming the Potomac Flats. One goal of the river commission's plan was to have the sewerage outlets that the Territory was then constructing moved farther from the waterfront. Far from being unaware of shortcomings in his expedients, Shepherd helped write the report that pointed the city towards an eventual solution.[58]

V

Washington's distinguished historian Constance M. Green interpreted the territorial years in light of a tacit agreement among District businessmen to redirect the local economy towards real estate and services.[59] According to Green, such a reorientation served the city's long-run interests, but old-line civic and commercial leaders were too conservative and indecisive to implement it. For this reason, she suggests, Washington did need a period in the grip of a bold character, provided he had technical expertise to go along with his determination — that is to say, Shepherd with a master's in engineering. In *Washington: Village and Capital,* Green asserts, "Arbitrary power vested in a strong-willed but essentially honest man might have had few unhappy consequences had Shepherd had an engineer's training." This view falls short on two counts. First, Shepherd was not "ignorant of the technical problems involved." His Board of Public Works used engineers and other advisors who enjoyed respect outside the improvers' circle. Second, Shepherd's arbitrary tendencies caused much mischief. Chronic abuse of power was a greater defect in the territorial regime than many factors cited by other critics — the presumption of self-made men, the crassness of political operators, the greed of contractors on the make. The territorial leaders' contempt for public accountability, in combination with the shortcomings of the promotional approach to development, render Shepherd's legacy most dubious.[60]

A weak point in Green's analysis is the assumption that well-educated, cultivated public works experts formulate disinterested, apolitical proposals. Interest, prejudice, or expediency presumably enter the calculation only when initiative passes from engineers to politicians or businessmen. Yet Shepherd's associates included civil engineers who agreed on political and ideological grounds with the impulsive "readiness to improvise" that Green and others have deplored. Technicians as well trained as anyone at the time cooperated with Shepherd's rash "insistence upon trying to complete a vast program within the span of three years." Babcock, Mullett, and the rest shared a state of mind that saw Washington as being at a desperate impasse that required an episode of despotism.

To the District improvers, as their supporters insisted in numerous pamphlets, speeches, and articles, the threat of capital removal, however remote, was a "terrible scare." Authoritarian measures were needed, they felt, because "among the arguments used to accomplish this foolish transportation [was] the incapacity of Washington to make its own improvements." Despite "fiendish" assaults from "hump-dog, skulking soreheads," "far-sighted and public-spirited citizens" pressed forward. As an admirer wrote, the Board of Public Works dared "to strike without fear or favor, and hit whoever stands in its way; the way would never be cleared if it did not." Supporters saw Shepherd as a man on horseback who, for the general good, was "compelled in numerous instances to defy the laws and public sentiment."[61]

Shepherd relished this role. He told the House that he was tired of circumstances and people who obstructed "enterprise and progress." Now was the time for action. The Board of Public Works existed "for something or nothing," Shepherd asserted, and "if for anything, it was [created] to devise and carry out, as rapidly as possible, some system of improvements." Such an obsessive determination on the part of a city official to "get things done" despite political complication can turn into a moral obtuseness that ultimately harms the city.[62] The way Shepherd cast aside statutory responsibilities and took advantage of political allies, especially newly enfranchised local blacks, was, if not criminal, at least brutally single-minded. Shepherd himself may have refrained from actions that in the late nineteenth century would have been defined as corrupt, but he cared little whether others crossed that line, if it advanced the cause.

No member of the territorial government was ever indicted for an action related to the Comprehensive Plan.[63] Congress did hold hearings into an outlandish cloak-and-dagger episode that reinforced suspicions of criminality. On April 24, 1874, thieves burgled the office safe of Richard Harrington, the territorial secretary and an assistant district attorney. Tipped off beforehand, witnesses (including the chief of police, Major A. C. Richards, and Shepherd's brother Thomas) trailed one burglar as he brought the stolen account books of John Evans to the house of Columbus Alexander, leader of the citizens. The thief tried to call Alexander to the door but, having failed, left the books on the porch, at which point he was arrested. Others of the burglars were soon caught. One was Michael Hayes, a professional safe-cracker. It emerged that the burglary was commissioned not by Shepherd's enemies, as it first appeared, but by Hiram Whitely and Ichabod Nettleship, the chief and assistant head of the U.S. Secret Service. Whitely knew Hayes and the other thugs because they had been agents, of a dubious sort, in the Ku Klux Klan investigations. Harrington apparently arranged for his own safe to be robbed to embarrass the Territory's opposition.[64]

A trial of Harrington and Whitely and of other alleged conspirators connected to the Secret Service ended in a hung jury in late 1874. Treasury secretary Benjamin Bristow, a controversial crusader against corruption and the cabinet officer in charge of the Secret Service, wanted to know who was at the bottom of the intrigue. Harrington had met Cooke, Shepherd, and Evans at the Washington Club after 3 A.M. on the night of the break-in. "It is needless to ask why," remarked the *New York Sun,* but no other evidence implicated the main improvers. Attention shifted to Babcock, who was being embarrassed by the evidence regarding overcharges against the government that was appearing during the simultaneous congressional investigation. Babcock had many contacts in the Secret Service and had demonstrated a taste for skullduggery in the Santo Domingo affair and the Whiskey Ring. The Treasury Department prosecuted Babcock in 1876 for his supposed role in the safe burglary, but the beleaguered engineer was acquitted. The true story has never emerged.[65]

Although a less bizarre incident, the improvers' part in wrecking the Freedman's Savings Bank, chartered by Congress in 1865 as a charitable institution, was more revealing. After their personal affairs took a turn for the worse in the early 1870s, Henry Cooke and his partner William Huntington began to exploit their control of the bank's finance committee. The pair turned the institution into a dump for Jay Cooke and Company's bad debts and also used it to promote Washington ventures such as the Metropolis Paving Company. Cooke's entanglements with the Freedman's Bank became infamous because of the Seneca Sandstone swindle, in which the banker convinced Kilbourn and Evans to act as covers for Cooke's disposal on the bank of worthless bonds for quarries along the Potomac that Cooke had mismanaged. Trustees who fought such dubious transactions were contradicted by finance committee members such as Moses Kelly. In addition to being part of Kilbourn's asphalt ring, Kelly was cashier of the National Metropolitan Bank, which invested in District certificates of indebtedness, which the Territory's favored contractors were allowed to use as collateral for Freedman's Bank loans. Kelly was also commissioner of the District's Sinking Fund. At different points during the Territory's history, Cooke, Clephane, Freedman's Bank actuary and territorial councillor D. L. Eaton, and Street Superintendent George W. Balloch (once distributing officer of the Freedmen's Bureau) each held offices with the District as well as with the Freedman's Bank and also had contracting or real estate interests in the city which benefited from Freedman's Bank funds.[66]

In July 1873, when the Board of Public Works lacked cash to pay contractors, the Freedman's Bank paid John Evans $9,000, using Magruder's promise of reimbursement as security. After the Bank folded, federal inspectors found that contractor J. V. W. Vandenburg, another former Freedmen's Bureau employee, owed over $160,000 including interest, much of this well overdue. Investigators learned that Vandenburg had split profits from District contracts with Freedman's Bank actuary Eaton in exchange for Eaton's arrangement of financing. When Vandenburg fell behind on payments, the Freedman's Bank continued to fund him on Shepherd's personal urging. Many of Vandenburg's loans were not for personal debts but for disguised territorial debts of the Board of Public Works, debts which Shepherd promised to pay as soon as he received a congressional appropriation. According to testimony, Shepherd once promised to repay the Freedman's Bank on Vandenburg's account on Monday if the bank would give Vandenburg cash for his payroll on Saturday. "Vandenburg's accounts are approved, but look what a crowd," said Shepherd, pointing to contractors in his office to press claims. Shepherd then put off the bank's representative for weeks. He scolded the official, "If you do business in that kind of loose way, then you are a damned fool."[67]

VI

In the three decades after Shepherd's fall in 1874, no enduring critique of the territorial movement emerged, because the city grew accustomed to Shepherd's legacy, while misgivings regarding his scruples faded. As the century progressed, Washingtonians and outside observers grew more ambivalent even than the congressmen on the 1874 investigation who applauded the improvers' accomplishments but "condemn[ed] the methods by which this sudden and rapid transition was secured." The 1874 report depicted the Territory as "wanting sufficient safeguards against maladministration." It berated Babcock and Shepherd for misleading Congress into "improper allowances." Yet panel members still expressed contradictory views regarding the motives, vision, and talent of the Board of Public Works and particularly of its leader. Allen Thurman, the investigation's ranking Democrat, later told the Senate that while the special panel had agreed unanimously that the Territory must go, members had differed strenuously "as to the guilt or innocence of individuals." The investigators decided to avoid allegations against Shepherd or the others in their report, so as not to "excite passion on the floor" and jeopardize the effort to abolish the regime quickly.[68]

The bipartisan committee's unwillingness to repudiate Shepherd wholesale gratified his family and friends, who saw the investigation as the beginning of their hero's vindication. Cynical editors blamed partisan politics for the reluctance of congressional Republicans to concede that Shepherd was a rogue, but thoughts expressed privately by Republicans on the joint panel suggest that sentiment, as well as political advantage, accounted for the committee's less-than-sweeping conclusions, which did pave the way for the rehabilitation of Shepherd's image. Senator Allison, the panel's chairman, confided in a letter to another Iowan living in Washington that he was "sorry that Governor Shepherd was temporarily sacrificed, as he has done so much for the city. He can afford to wait, however, as no stain is cast upon his honor or integrity by the investigating committee." The Iowan showed the letter to Clephane and Shepherd, who broke a promise and gave it to the press. Midwest Republicans reproached Allison for defending "Saint Shepherd." His letter lent verity to Democratic muttering that the committee only appeared impartial. Forced into a statement, Allison conceded that the letter reflected his views and that he had been unwise to write them down. Meanwhile, former Iowan and District congressional delegate Norton Chipman remarked privately to Allison, "Even men who do not like him personally and who criticize much of his public work appreciate his wonderful ability and have faith in his integrity."[69]

In February 1875, Democrat Thurman maintained to the Senate that those who did not think the report brought disgrace on the deposed governor had "not looked into [it] with their glasses on." Thurman insisted that the Shepherd government had been "utterly bankrupt and had proved itself totally inefficient and ill-suited to rule over this people." The Ohio senator was disputing Pennsylvania's Simon Cameron, who asserted that he had "no patience" with those who criticized Washington's former leader. Because of the Board of Public Works, said Cameron, "this city will go on and prosper and every year become more beautiful." He predicted, "A man who has showed himself so superior in the ability required for the post to which he was called will not have to wait very long before he is appreciated."[70]

Thurman's analysis of the Territory's flaws has merit, but Cameron's remarks were prescient. When the bankrupt Shepherd left for Mexico in spring 1880, friends organized a grand send-off, highlighted by the reading of testimonial letters from prominent politicians. A year later, a newspaper noted that in his native city, Shepherd's name had "become a household synonym for public benefaction." By century's end, Washington's people, friends and foes, had indeed absolved Shepherd. Residents, national politicians, and federal officials interpreted his rule as a necessary turning point in the national city's progress. "Had not Mr. Shepherd been a 'boss' and just the kind of a 'boss' he was," a journalist wrote in 1898, "Washington would today be a city of mud and dust."[71]

In Mexico, Shepherd brought his legendary energy and determination to bear on Chihuahua's Batolpilas silver mines, which he made a success. He had anticipated using his earnings to re-establish himself in his home. Mexico was "practical banishment," he wrote to a friend, "but the prospects are such that four years will be sufficient to repair my shattered fortunes." As years became decades, Shepherd's wife, Mary, related that the former governor was often nostalgic, especially as "among ugly stones and rocks," few "appreciative souls" could admire his "first class work." After Shepherd's death in 1902, his daughter recalled, "How infinitely greater and harder has been his achievement in this hidden corner of a foreign land."[72]

Some of the edge was taken off Shepherd's exile when the sort of observers who had disparaged him most while in office exonerated him in retrospect. In 1885, the Johns Hopkins Political Science Department, then considered the most advanced in the country, published an account that adulated characteristics of Shepherd that E. L. Godkin had deplored: "Of indomitable perseverance and more than ordinary executive ability; naturally a leader of men—this man brought many of the most rare and valuable qualifications of success to the office which he held as the real dictator of the District government." Even in accounts as strongly influenced by progressive political morality as those of Fine Arts Commission chairman Charles Moore, Shepherd appeared a "practical idealist." Shepherd ruled "with a ruthless hand," and "of course there was corruption in connection with such hasty work," Moore concluded, but "the result was amply worth the cost."[73]

Richard Merrick, attorney for the resident opposition, in his argument to the 1874 joint investigation, pointed out that most of the Territory's public works "had long been projected and in some measure initiated in execution, before the present authorities came into power." The Board of Public Works had no irreplaceable "genius or originality," Merrick felt, as "similar things were being done in other cities throughout the land." The trend towards improved public works could not have bypassed the capital. Merrick's point was that Washington's situation, which improvers believed demanded a Lesser Napoleon, was not so desperate as that.[74]

Shepherd might have endured longer and accomplished more had he exhibited patience and tolerance. Eventually, Shepherd might even have persuaded wealthy old citizens to limit their attacks, if not to submit to his leadership. After all, his notion of Washington's future did not exclude the old citizens, though it modified their role. After the Territory's fall in 1874, the Baltimore *Sun* suggested that Congress and the city's residents would have accepted bonds up to $10 million had the board indicated that it would spend the money in "a moderate and guarded manner, without attempting to complete the work of years in as many weeks or months." This sum, spent methodically, might have gone as far as the $18 million Shepherd spent in his blaze of energy and engineering.[75]

Because of the force of the promotional tradition, public works implemented in a systematic fashion probably would not have differed much from those built hastily by the Board of Public Works. Yet one effect of Shepherd's rashness may have been that he discredited all at once the kind of mentality in the local business community that refused to let go of the Washington Canal. Without the irrevocable break with old dreams embodied in acts such as the canal's destruction, the capital's business community might have retained indefinitely ambitions that diverged from the city's role of serving the federal government. The Board of Public Works thus gave physical embodiment to the spreading idea that Washington was, and above all ought to be, the nation's city.

Such a reorientation of local enterprise was also probably inevitable. Nevertheless, it matters that the territorial regime pursued it in a burst. The drama surrounding Shepherd's public works program had a psychological effect on the city's elites that reinforced the concrete and economic changes that the works themselves brought to the city. Memories of the territorial period became crucial to the community's understanding of itself. The result was an unusual example of the "full urban community" about which social theorist Max Weber wrote. Weber believed that city culture reaches a high expression when prominent citizens manifest a common historical identity, a shared sense of purpose. In Washington, commerce would never be that shared purpose, as it had been for cities elsewhere in the West for a millennium. Even so, in the course of the improvement period the capital's dominant groups began to acquire the elaborate civic identity and strong sense of direction that outside observers during the early years of Reconstruction had felt the city sorely wanted. In a sociological sense, Shepherd was a kind of second founder—after George Washington—because his successors believed that the "New Washington" had been conceived and set in motion by the legendary Boss Shepherd.[76]

The brief territorial period represents a turning point for the capital's governance and political economy. In the aftermath of the District improvement controversy, federal and local interests consolidated and institutionalized the changes of these years. The results of the period became so thoroughly incorporated into the institutions and alliances that later ran Washington that they appeared natural. An alternative past or path for the city came to seem unimaginable.

4

The Origins of the District Commission

The present form of government by Commissioners . . . is a despotism in a republic, and an anomaly in American institutions, against which we utter our solemn protest. . . .

— In Opposition

The businessmen of our city and all those who have the greatest stake in its welfare and prosperity prefer the present form of government by Commissioners, to any that has ever been tried here. . . .

— In Support

— Memorials to the Joint Select Committee
to Frame a Government for the District of Columbia, autumn 1876

PRESIDENT GRANT's unswerving loyalty to subordinates—a "maxim of military honor" that the former general believed in wholeheartedly— complicated the delicate political task confronting those congressional Republicans who hoped to limit the usefulness of the District improvement controversy to the Democrats in the pending fall campaign. Whatever they thought of Shepherd personally, most leading Republicans agreed that Congress had to appear serious about reforming Washington. Still, within the party, Shepherd retained vocal, unapologetic defenders, who would make a fuss if Congress took any move that could be interpreted as a repudiation of him.

Rather than take the politic route and consign Shepherd to the background until tempers cooled, the steadfast Grant decided to vindicate his young friend right away. Five days after Congress abolished the Territory, President Grant nominated the deposed governor to the caretaker commission created under the Allison committee's interim government act. What hostile newspapers termed Grant's "vulgar petulance" placed Senate Republican leaders in a spot. They could not confirm Washington's "boss" to the commission to clean up after his own regime, yet they could not cast a vote against a figure still a hero among party regulars. Grant's announcement of the nomination came the evening Congress was to adjourn, so the Senate had to act immediately. Recriminations among Republicans frustrated by their President's political indiscretion resulted in a "stormy and exciting" closing night for the august chamber. In the end, though, only a handful of friends stood by Shepherd. Most recognized that while they might admire the man, the good of the party required sacrificing him. After postponing adjournment so that members could recite and then quarrel over testimony from the recent inquiry, the Senate rejected Shepherd 36 to 6. A number of Republicans left the chamber to avoid declaring themselves.[1]

The administration's attempt to uphold loyalties despite controversy undercut the Allison committee's work. It encouraged the notion that the interim commission was part of a plot to perpetuate the District improvers' influence. While Shepherd never would acquire a clandestine authority over his successors, as House Democrats were to charge over the next few years, his spirit did hang over the national city.[2] Events soon revealed that the country could distance itself from neither Shepherd's program nor his debts. Congress and the commissioners found that they were bound by assumptions and commitments left over from the territorial period. In the end, for reasons of policy, politics, and self-interest, Congress and the provisional authorities were inclined toward perpetuating the legacy and building upon the achievements of the Board of Public Works. Two key goals that had eluded the improvers while in power were achieved after their fall: acceptance by the United States of responsibility for a large, predictable portion of the cost of the capital's public works and services, and creation of a form of municipal administration that enabled local enterprise to work smoothly with relevant national interests and agencies over a long period.

Before the war, individuals from both parties had occasionally expressed support for systematic federal financing of Washington's public works; yet even at the height of Reconstruction, the number of congressmen committed to this principle remained insufficient to implement it. The failure of the Republican-dominated Congress to spell out in advance its financial stake in Shepherd's program did much to provoke the confusion and chicanery of the territorial years. Even the doubters in Congress came to realize that it would be highly expedient to define a position once and for all. Consequently, despite Democrats' purported determination to root out the legacy of Reconstruction nationalism, a bipartisan coalition gradually formed behind the notion, written into the 1878 District bill, that the United States would from then on cover 50 percent of the city's annual budget.

If Congress was to pay half of Washington's bills, it needed increased oversight of municipal affairs. While Congress would inevitably have demanded a large stake in the municipality that superseded the Territory, it was not prescribed that the system of appointed commissioners, begun in 1874 as an emergency measure, would continue indefinitely, that the Republic's capital would lose home rule altogether. Like the half-and-half budget arrangement, the permanent District of Columbia commission resulted from a specific mix of precedents, attitudes, and circumstances. The writers of the 1878 act, which made the commission system permanent, based this strange measure on their soberly considered understanding of Washington's history, character, and purpose. Short-term political opportunities and needs also contributed to the end of District home rule. Key to the political equation was the fading Republican commitment to civil rights for Washington's blacks. Republicans in Congress, reflecting the party's weakened position and changed priorities, knowingly handed enemies of black suffrage a substantial symbolic victory. By disengaging Washington's material progress from its civil rights, proponents of a worthy national city rendered federal underwriting of this goal palatable to skeptical Democrats.

As for resident reaction to the bartering away of their franchise, most old citizens considered abolition of local elections an acceptable trade-off in order to achieve "destruction" of the despised black vote. The Shepherd faction, which had always emphasized material over political improvement, was so pleased by Congress's offer to split municipal expenses that self-government seemed a small concession. What seems in retrospect a distasteful measure that patently violates the country's principles appeared to strategic local and national interests of the time to be a natural step to which all could assent without serious reservations.

To understand when and how the American polity acquired the traits that distinguish it from countries with comparable social and economic systems, we must pay close attention to the events and circumstances that gradually shaped the structure, orientation, and emphases of our governmental institutions. The creation and early development of the District of Columbia commission offer an illustrative example. We sometimes mistakenly look upon Reconstruction experiments in state-building as episodes that are of merely academic interest in the present. In important areas, the collapse of Reconstruction and the resurgence of an anti-centrist Democratic party did lead to reversal of the trend towards greater authority and visibility for the national state. Even so, it would be wrong to believe that in the Gilded Age nationalism and state activism were made to retreat to lines held in Jacksonian times, that upheavals of the 1860s and 1870s had no durable legacy for politics and policy in the United States, and that state formation in this country remained at a standstill until new social and economic challenges revived the trend in the Progressive era. The capital's development provides an example of how the tentative, often incoherent governmental ventures of those decades and the bitter struggles they provoked formed the environment and fixed the assumptions that would guide and constrain the American polity in subsequent periods.[3]

I

Grant nominated Shepherd mainly as a personal gesture. Anticipating defeat, the administration had already prepared acceptable alternatives. Agree-

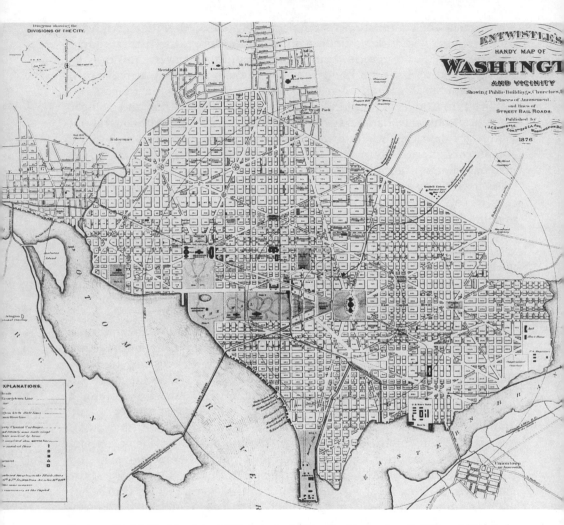

Post-territorial Washington, 1876, by which time the Pennsylvania Railroad bisected the Mall. Suburban subdivisions appear above Boundary Street (along perimeter of city, *upper left*) and in Anacostia (Uniontown, *lower right*). Courtesy the Geography and Map Division, Library of Congress.

ing to serve were William O. Dennison, former U.S. postmaster general and governor of Ohio, and former congressmen Henry T. Blow of Missouri and John H. Ketcham of New York. The administration apparently assured these respected but out-of-office Republicans that their tour in charge of the viper's nest could be finished in six months. In its June report, Allison's joint investigative committee refused to rule out a return to home rule in early 1875. The investigators pleaded only that Congress take "sufficient time to prepare a proper system." A new special panel was designated to work through the summer on a permanent government bill. Congress, underestimating the trouble to follow, intended to pass this measure during the next session.[4]

In the first week of July 1874, the District commissioners met at length with Senator Thurman, the ranking Democrat on the investigating committee, who was to explain Congress's intentions. Thurman and the commissioners thought that they had reached an understanding as to the interim government's mandate, but they were mistaken. The caretaker commissioners found city offices in such a state of confusion that they had no choice but to solicit help from former territorial officials, who of course guided them in a direction at odds with Thurman's notion of what had been decided. The commissioners reappointed several key territorial officials and received advice on reorganizing the District from Henry Willard, the last vice president of the Board of Public Works, and from Shepherd himself.[5]

One matter on which Congress and the ousted improvers agreed was the need to consolidate and eliminate offices, even if that meant sacrificing services for the time being. While creating new offices to address their special objectives, Shepherd and his colleagues had undertaken no review of the public roster that had accumulated over seventy years under the defunct municipal corporations, largely because the Republican party wanted to keep the patronage. The Territory was thus a proliferation on top of an accretion. In their first months, the temporary commissioners cut the District's employment rolls from 371 to 133 employees, not including teachers, police, and firemen. Congress legislated a 20 percent reduction, exempting teachers and firemen, whose salaries Shepherd had on occasion commandeered to keep public works going. Policemen had their salaries reduced to 1871 levels. The city's payroll was cut by half.[6]

A more urgent matter than retrenchment was how to handle the clutter of projects and contracts bequeathed by the Board of Public Works. Therefore, the most important official to present his views during July 1874, the temporary commission's first month in office, was Lieutenant Richard L. Hoxie, who had charge of the revamped engineering department. Born in New York in 1844, Hoxie grew up in Iowa and studied at Iowa State University and in Italy before attending West Point. A model of the cultivated Victorian engineer, Hoxie could read French, Spanish, Greek, and Latin and possessed an impressive knowledge of international writing on public works technology. Clever and fashionable, he became a protégé of commanding general William T. Sherman. Hoxie's influence would soon be strengthened by his marriage to Vinnie Ream, the sculptor who became a celebrity in political circles when Lincoln chose her to model him for what proved to be the first statue of the martyred President in the Capitol. After Grant fired Adolph Cluss in retaliation for the German's testimony to the Allison committee in June 1874, the President named Hoxie, a West Point acquaintance of Grant's son, to Cluss's place. When the Board of Public Works was abolished a few days later, Allison and his colleagues requested that an army officer supervise public works under the interim government, so the President nominated the dashing lieutenant to be municipal engineer.[7]

The appointment generated no controversy at the time. Soon, a group of House Democrats developed relentless "personal hostility" to the thirty-year-old engineer, whom they insisted on depicting as a boy, unfit for responsibility. This vendetta grew from the friendship, which proved lifelong, that Hoxie had struck up with Shepherd. In July, an Iowan living in the capital wrote Allison that Hoxie was "a free man," but a month later another friend of the Senator declared, "Hoxie the engineer is Shepherd as far as he can be."[8] We saw earlier that Hoxie was critical on technical grounds of much of Shepherd's work, yet, like most Corps officers assigned to the capital, the lieutenant understood and sympathized with the Comprehensive Plan and admired the boldness and energy, though not the lack of meticulousness, of its devisor.

Friendship and shared vision inclined Hoxie to take a broad view of how much of Shepherd's work now to continue. In addition, Congress's mandate to the commissioners, as Thurman had conveyed it in his meetings with the board, unwittingly endorsed a broad view on both legal and technical grounds. The legislature directed the commissioners to complete public works already in progress, to ensure "protection or preservation of improvements existing or commenced, and not finished." The caretakers were also to decide which Board of Public Works contracts remained "legal obligations" and which could be annulled without giving the contractor grounds for court action. Thurman stressed that Washington must not leave streets and sewers in a "dangerous condition," though the caretakers were to cancel as many projects as feasible. Hoxie persuaded his superiors that they needed to interpret their authority more broadly if they were to fulfill their instructions.[9]

Behind this disagreement lay serious confusion as to how many projects could be brought to a satisfactory stage under street and sewer contracts already in effect. Where major streets were incomplete, the senators believed, Hoxie could reactivate suspended contracts. Where pavements were in disrepair, he could enforce provisions that made contractors responsible for maintaining pavements for up to three years. Such expedients would allow Hoxie to wind down the street program without incurring new debts for Washington. Hoxie insisted that the senators grossly underestimated what could be achieved without large-scale rewriting of Shepherd's paving contracts. Thurman and Allison also thought that the Board of Public Works had already worked out details of sewerage plans and had let contracts adequate to finish main features of its new system. Hoxie found that sizes and materials specified in Shepherd's sewerage contracts were inadequate. To make matters worse, sewers that had been certified as complete by the Board of Public Works were already breaking down because of "bad workmanship and defective plan" or "unfit" and "worthless" materials. The sewer system could not be rendered functional without extensive readvertising and rewriting of contracts.[10]

Legal headaches compounded engineering concerns. During the joint investigation, most contractors had stopped work, waiting to see how Congress would compensate them for the depreciated certificates of indebtedness that Shepherd and Magruder had handed out after the Board of Public Works ran out of cash. At the start of July 1874, "dormant" projects suddenly recommenced "without authority or direction." The contractors needed to establish claims to the 3.65 percent bonds, or "3.65s," that Congress authorized to replace the shaky territorial paper. The new bonds paid lower interest than territorial certificates, but as they were issued by the U.S. Treasury and guaranteed by Congress, their prices were stable and close to par. Motivated by legal rather than engineering considerations, contractors began "working at random, without plans or supervisions." Competent contractors eagerly finished minor streets, while major thoroughfares crumbled or rotted, the relevant contractor having either disappeared or tied up the job in court.[11]

Hoxie adopted a straightfoward but controversial solution to this predicament. Instead of sticking with outmoded territorial contracts, the engineer negotiated with contractors (including several connected with Kilbourn's notorious asphalt "ring") to exchange claims against the Board of Public Works for new contracts that transferred them to projects Hoxie deemed more essential. Hoxie promised to continue paying Shepherd's generous board rates, if businessmen conformed to tighter regulations and specifications. Such expedients left the engineer free to concentrate resources on major unfinished features of the Shepherd program, even where no enforceable contract survived from the Territory. Hoxie's action, however, rankled residents and politicians who desired that the caretaker government stop improvements, beyond a few heldover contracts, and find ways to reduce the territorial debt.[12]

Remnants of the anti-Shepherd movement organized a "taxpayers" group, to demand repudiation of every public works contract with less than airtight documentation. Columbus Alexander, victim of the safe burglary conspiracy, and his new allies, Sayles Bowen and Adolph Cluss, accused Hoxie of validating claims "unjust in their character towards the District, if not really fraudulent."[13] The commissioners, however, ruled that which projects would continue "was in large measure, if not wholly, an engineering question," so they deferred to Hoxie. The taxpayers group then appealed to the first and second comptrollers of the currency, key Treasury officials who had been designated a special board of audit under the temporary government act. The taxpayers group demanded wholesale annulment of questionable Shepherd-era contracts. The comptrollers refused. The Board of Public Works might have been "improvident," they ruled, but this "did not necessarily constitute a badge of fraud in the contracts." Even poorly documented or oral agreements made by Shepherd were "clearly within the power conferred upon the board of public works."[14]

After failing to prevent Hoxie from reactivating and rewriting disputed contracts, his opponents maneuvered to stop him from paying contractors with the coveted 3.65 bonds. By calling into question the District's handling of federally backed bonds, the taxpayers raised a volatile issue, the repercussions of which extended beyond Washington.

In his first eighteen months as District engineer, Hoxie moved ahead with public works worth around $3.5 million. During this period, he spent $369,625.07 for repairs to wooden pavements alone. The District budget contained only $50,000 cash per year for street repairs. Clearly needing another means of payment, the lieutenant listed rewritten and readvertised contracts as "payable in 3.65 bonds," alongside territorial contracts renewed without revision and thus indisputably eligible for these special securities. Hoxie argued that to use 3.65s for revised contracts made sense, since the new agreements rationalized the confusion of the old and thereby facilitated his assigned task of finishing uncompleted work. To justify his position, Hoxie gave the press lists of defaulting wooden pavement contractors that ran to two-and-one-half columns. How, he asked, could he fulfill his duty to ensure the preservation of territorial improvements without reassigning these contracts?[15] Alexander's taxpayers group countered that the District could use 3.65s only to cover obligations "in strict compliance with the law in every respect." Alexander insisted that all Shepherd's extended or oral contracts were fraudulent, so any revised contract based on an such agreements had no validity. Alexander also asserted that whenever Hoxie reassigned a project, it was technically new and had to be paid in cash, that a rewritten or readvertised contract could not be paid in bonds, even if the contract concerned a street or sewer unfinished by Shepherd.[16]

Large property holders had reason to fear Hoxie's liberal use of the 3.65s. As long as debts arising from the Comprehensive Plan stayed in the form of dubious Board of Public Works paper, a legal challenge might overturn them. Federally guaranteed 3.65s were about as assailable as Gibraltar. Even worse, while Congress guaranteed the bonds' interest and principal, it had not exactly pronounced that the U.S. Treasury would provide any money toward this debt. Given the country's spotty record in financial dealings with its capital, Alexander and his allies could not dismiss the possibility that Congress, which had total legal authority to repudiate any responsibility for what Shepherd had wrought, might decide to welch on what residents saw as the country's fair share of the expense. The last thing residents wanted at that point was an army engineer from Iowa running up the city debt further when Congress had not promised to assume a substantial share of the existing debt. On the other hand, in early July 1874, Shepherd asserted to the new commissioners that Congress "thoroughly understood and purposed" that 3.65s could serve as a device to move forward public works despite uncertainties.[17] By accepting the argument that it was legitimate to use 3.65s on rewritten contracts, the caretakers in effect took over the massive infrastructure program many felt they had been hired to close out.

To the frustration of the taxpayers group, the U.S. Treasury endorsed all of Hoxie's expedients. Congress had assigned final say over Washington's finances to R. W. Tayler and J. M. Brodhead, the comptrollers who composed the special board of audit. Their acquiescence in Hoxie's loose interpretation of his legal authority seemed out of character for a department with a reputation for interpreting regulations literally and sternly. Yet, like the commissioners, the comptrollers faced vexing dilemmas whose most feasible solutions forced them, in effect, to ratify contested Board of Public Works actions and perpetuate its controversial program.

Whether to allow the District engineer to use 3.65s on rewritten territorial contracts, while a significant matter, was only one aspect of the immense, perplexing task, which Congress handed to the Treasury Department, of sorting out the Territory's finances. The Shepherd regime had left behind eight distinct categories of certificates, claims, and floating debts, which needed to be inspected and converted into bonds. Board treasurer Magruder's books were so choatic that Treasury accountants needed to reconstruct every project from scratch, street by street. Still pressed by regular duties, the comptrollers were unable to review more than a few territorial accounts personally. They depended on an inadequate staff composed of temporary clerks as well as regular Treasury accountants. These considerations led Brodhead and Tayler to conclude that "rigid adherence to forms and rules" would delay completion of the special audit too long and cause injustice to the city and its legitimate creditors. Accordingly, the comptrollers instructed their staff not to require formal representation of contractors' claims against the Board of Public Works and to disallow only those of Hoxie's 3.65 accounts that were clearly "new contracts for new work," a ruling conducive to the continuation of the public works.[18]

The 1874 investigating committee had hoped to limit the total issue of the 3.65s to around $8.3 million. Few in Congress objected when, in late 1874, the comptrollers estimated that 3.65s might amount to $10 million. Even so, throughout 1875, the comptrollers continued to accept accounts payable in bonds submitted by the District engineer. By December 1875, the Treasury had issued $12 million in 3.65s. A few months later, the total of District 3.65s in circulation had risen to $13.7 million, and the Board of Audit had certificates pending for hundreds of thousands more.[19]

As 3.65 circulation mounted out of control, the comptrollers and the commissioners grew nervous, expecting accusations of mismanagement. In the months before the meeting of the new Congress, which would feature a Democratic majority in the House for the first time since the Civil War, the commissioners became particular about recording details of relevant discussions with the Treasury. Some contractors had defaulted on maintenance clauses in their contracts, the commissioners' minutes claim, so the District was forced to hire new people in their place. The new contractors would be paid in 3.65 bonds, which would be redeemed as soon as possible with money recovered from defaulters. In assenting to the issuance of bonds to pay for a Pennsylvania Avenue project that would surpass by seventy cents per yard the Board of Public Work's own hefty estimate, comptroller Tayler argued that, with the commissioners admittedly "under obligations to repave the streets and recover costs from the contractors, he thought it a clear duty to lay a pavement which could be relied upon."[20] Since neither the commissioners nor the comptrollers could have have believed that they would recover more than a fraction of disputed costs from defaulting contractors, they were probably establishing a defense. These harried officials would need every explanation they could muster in the months ahead.

II

When Congress reassembled in December 1875, House Democrats launched the expected assault. The interim government "had not the shadow of a power" to add $5.5 million to Washington's debt, charged Samuel Randall, the new House Appropriations chairman. Randall, known as "Brakeman" on account of his tight-fistedness, reported adversely on a bill to pay a pending interest installment on the 3.65s, saying that, by picking up the interest, Congress merely enabled city officials "to go on in their extravagance to that extent in work upon the streets."[21]

The Republican strategy for taking the Washington uproar out of the national arena had backfired. Senate Republicans expressed dismay that their reform regime had managed to mire itself in the Shepherd scandals. "To criticize friends" was "unpleasant," asserted Henry Dawes of Massachusetts, but the caretakers had acted upon "a most wide and alarming construction of a statute enacted by us, for the effect of which we are responsible to the country." City officials, Dawes continued, "say that the only limit in carrying out this plan (a general plan . . . embracing the whole city of Washington from limit to limit on either side) is their own discretion, and that they could issue these bonds in payment of the contracts. As this bill stands there is no inhibition upon them or the board of audit." Allison lamented that the interim government had "totally misapprehended" its assignment. He had never intended, he claimed, that the interim government go forward with the "numberless contracts then floating about this city." On the other hand, John Sherman, perhaps the most important Republican senator, defended fellow Ohioan Dennison and the other caretakers. Sherman blamed the inexperienced Allison for putting men of "high repute" in a bind, since the Iowan's temporary government act had been vague regarding how 3.65s were to be used. For Allison now to accuse the commissioners of "undue exercise of power" was hypocritical and risky. "So far as the bondholder or the man who has purchased is concerned, he holds the security of the United States," Sherman explained. "Though not in name a Government bond, [the 3.65] is in fact a Government bond."[22]

This point, made by one of Congress's most respected voices on financial matters, hit home if no other did. While Hoxie was using some 3.65s to settle with contractors, the commissioners and the comptrollers had to employ another chunk of them to redeem millions in unstable territorial paper that had found its way to bankers. Upon taking office, the interim officials discovered that Wall Street institutions such as the First National Bank of New York, the National Bank of Commerce, and Morton, Bliss, and Company had underwritten much of Washington's new infrastructure. They had accepted notes from Cooke and Shepherd that lacked both a well-defined legal basis and proper security. Still, the financiers now insisted that the District and federal governments protect their investment.[23] The knowledgeable Sherman was calling colleagues' attention to the unpleasant fact that the improvers' manipulations had probably obliged Congress, whether it wanted to or not, to guarantee Washington's financial health for the foreseeable future.

Some legislators had worried all along that the Comprehensive Plan's wobbly finances might provoke a crisis that would compel federal assumption of the District's debt. This was why, during the 1872 hearings, the House District Committee had scolded Seligman and Company, the international bank, for giving German investors the impression that Congress rather than the territorial legislature had authorized the initial $4 million improvement loan of 1871.[24] Despite such warnings, Cooke and Shepherd had dealt with their escalating money problems by *increasing* the amount of District securities floated in New York. The pair circumvented a weak $10 million debt ceiling imposed in 1872 by informing bankers that new securities were not really city debts at all, but liens on uncollected (and probably uncollectable) special improvement taxes. Not until June 1874 did Shepherd give up on this transparent legalism. With the Territory on the ropes, Governor Shepherd informed Allison that few of Washington's securities had "proper provision." Shepherd urged that bonds be issued to replace insecure certificates. These bonds, he wrote, should "be under the authority of the Treasury Dept and at such rate of interest as will by public advertisement bring par in currency." Since outright assumption was politically unthinkable, Allison maintained in public the stance that the new bonds would not be United States debts, even though the Treasury would issue them and Congress would appropriate the interest. Allison's hedging back in 1874 had in fact set up the mess from which he now tried to distance himself.[25]

Throughout early 1876, the Democratic House majority loudly and deliberately questioned the country's commitment to Washington securities. This prompted Frederick Winston of New York's Mutual Life Insurance Company, a major subscriber of Civil War bonds, to admonish appropriations chairman Randall: "This company holds for permanent investment over a Million Dollars of the 3.65 District of Columbia bonds . . . which are guaranteed by the United States. We suppose that the honor and the interest of the Government will lead them to take measures to meet with like promptitude the payment of the interest on these Bonds, as on all other obligations."[26]

The connection Senator Sherman had perceived between Washington's governmental impasse and the thornier problem of the national debt now became abundantly clear to other legislators. Rather than risk election-year charges of repudiation, House Democrats retreated from Randall's hard line and voted to continue paying installments on the 3.65 interest. Missouri Democrat Aylett Buckner, the House District Committee chairman, conceded that there was "not any possibility of the Government escaping" from the 3.65 trap. The bonds' opponents extracted concessions. Issuing of 3.65s must stop immediately, not at the $15 million ceiling requested by the commissioners. Congress wrote into subsequent legislation concerning the bonds a proviso disclaiming federal responsibility for the principal, although how the city alone would fund them remained a mystery. Further, officials who would "knowingly increase, or aid or abet in increasing" the District debt were threatened with ten years in federal prison.[27]

Still seeking political benefit from the Washington morass, House Democrats initiated the third full-scale investigation of the city in five years. What the press cynically dubbed the "annual congressional inquiry" discovered that former territorial officials, including Shepherd's brother, Arthur, had acted as claims agents for contractors. More significant was testimony that employees of the special board of audit had taken advantage of the overworked comptrollers' inattention by soliciting kickbacks in exchange for expediting dubious accounts. The most scrutinized clerk, however, had received his place through the influence of two Kentucky Democrats, which undercut the inquiry's partisan utility. District chairman Buckner nevertheless went ahead and submitted a condemnatory majority report suitable for use as a campaign document. The testimony itself gave more credence to the minority report, which argued that the comptrollers and commissioners had acted in good faith, according to a reasonable interpretation of their duties. Hoxie made a coherent defense of his view that contract revisions were the only viable response to the "very tangled and confused mess" left by the Board of Public Works. The persistent Buckner forwarded the evidence he had collected to the solicitor general, who replied that any course other than that in fact adopted by the provisional authorities would have been "an inadmissable act of folly" that would have paralyzed the city. The only result of these hearings was abolition of the special board of audit, which the exasperated comptrollers had requested anyway.[28]

Despite mounting evidence exonerating the interim officials, Democrats stood by their claim that Washington's temporary commission had consisted of "tools and instruments of Shepherd and his corrupt crew." Republicans countered that their rivals were deliberately misrepresenting the situation because they felt "a necessity for a Republican Tweed." [29] Even as these charges flew back and forth, some Democratic leaders showed signs that the main lesson they would take away from the dispute was that public works in the national city were a governmental problem as much as a party issue. They realized that contradictory, uncertain responsibilities, as much as partisan loyalties, had prompted the commissioners' decision to proceed with the Shepherd program and the comptrollers' acquiescence to covering added costs with federally backed bonds.

Returned to positions of responsibility after a fifteen-year interval, the Democrats encountered vividly how the lingering question of the country's role in the capital could create turmoil. Democratic administrations in the 1850s had constructed the Washington Aqueduct, but from the Civil War through the territorial period, Republicans had dominated the pursuit of a worthy national city. In the decade after 1865, Democrats were at best skeptical of public works projects in the federal district. Democratic indifference towards Washington, like Republican enthusiasm, reflected the parties' competing stances on the great issues of the immediate postwar years. Shepherd's Republican improvers had framed their case in terms of the Union's grandeur, presence, and authority—partisan concepts during Reconstruction. As Reconstruction collapsed, the opposition returned to power, expressing aversion for "that contemptible word *Nation*—a word which no good Democrat uses," as a Kentucky senator phrased it. What use had such people for a majestic, wealthy capital? [30]

In the mid-1870s, however, a group of congressional Democrats began to support federal involvement with Washington. At least in this one instance, otherwise impeccable party members were willing to carry on a nationalist Reconstruction initiative. Although Republicans would remain the primary backers, there would now always be a circle of important Democrats, including many from the party's Southern stronghold, who would be willing to defy the anti-centrist impulse widespread in their party in order to play a positive role in the District. This new willingness to participate in embellishing the capital may have been part of a gradual revival of American patriotism in the postwar South. But this was the first postwar Congress in which the Democrats had a majority in either house, so the key factor was probably the desire to be effective, now that they had at last regained accountable positions. Events kept suggesting that a workable settlement of the dilemma of District government would have to include sweeping guarantees by Congress regarding Washington's finances, administration, and economic growth. If ambitious Democrats hoped to become responsible legislative leaders, they had no choice but to cooperate with more forthrightly national-minded Republicans in bringing stability to the national city.

III

The country's entanglements with Washington's debts meant that Congress was certain to give itself a large voice in the capital's next permanent government. Even so, the specific arrangement finally adopted — preservation of the commission format, federal control of Washington's budget, and total abolition of the local franchise — was not predestined. The 1874 Allison committee asserted that its provisional board should be viewed as an emergency measure, possibly but not necessarily a precursor to the next regime. Congress planned to have the new system in place within a year, but circumstances stretched the debate over four years. During this time, political interests and expediencies intersected with deeply rooted attitudes towards governance and policy-making to produce a formidable coalition in favor of perpetuating the odd spectacle of appointed rule in the Republic's capital.

The run-of-the-mill politicians who had conceived and implemented an appointed commission for the District were imbued with the political attitudes of their time. The District commission was not an early version of the commission system that came into vogue during the Progressive years of the early twentieth century. Progressive thinkers and politicians, with their stress on coordination, efficiency, and expertise, had a natural affinity for schemes such as this, but progressive-type arguments would have been lost on most Gilded Age politicians and citizens. The Gilded Age public still harbored the Jacksonian suspicion that streamlined, professional government was an elitist heresy that came from reading too many European books. If the arguments for municipal commissions most familiar to the twentieth century were not persuasive to writers of the 1878 District government act, what precedents and notions went into the measure?

On a superficial level, Washington's 1878 bill departed so far from prevailing municipal forms that it seems to mock the *Zeitgeist*. The municipal commission is an *administrative* governmental format, while historians depict the Gilded Age polity as relentlessly *popular*. Public participation and interest — as measured by attendance at campaign speeches and rallies, partisan loyalty, and voter turnout — attained levels unmatched since. Most voters and politicians assumed that government should build a tight, ongoing relationship between officials and constituents, even at the expense of efficiency and expertise.[31] The Washington plan broke this cherished bond between citizens and rulers.

On a less apparent level, the District commission epitomized the Gilded Age state. The feeling was widespread that legislatures needed to keep tabs on administrative matters, to guarantee that popular assemblies made policy, not imperious chief executives or arrogant bureaucrats. In fact, a popular argument against civil service reform was that the spoils system made bureaucracy accountable to the majority party. Despite the failure of Andrew Johnson's impeachment (at the heart of which was the issue of executive defiance of legislative will), Congress continued to seek ways to build itself up vis-à-vis the President and to exert a level of supremacy over executive operations that twentieth-century Americans would tend to view as undermining the doctrine of separation of powers.[32]

The debate over a municipal system to replace the Territory makes sense in this context. Congress felt compelled to arrange matters so that the District's next regime would be largely answerable to the Capitol. Far from feeling threatened by this demand, strategic commercial-civic groups in Washington came to agree that the benefits to be gained in exchange for ceding control of local affairs to Congress outweighed the advantages of a return to home rule.

In devising Washington's new government, Congress expanded upon techniques that contemporary legislatures often used when they sought to watch a governmental function carefully. While the general-purpose municipal commission that Congress created for the District was unique in its time, single-purpose boards and commissions abounded in the Gilded Age state. The authority of a ministry, department, or bureau over the category of affairs under its charge is general, imprecise, and perpetual; a commission's duties are in theory defined and delegated in the statute creating it. The desire to keep administrative power defined and delegated helps explain why state governments pursued developmental or regulatory objectives through devices such as canal and railroad commissions. This imperative also contributed to the tendency of cities to evolve mish-mashes of special boards for water, health, parks, schools, police, and so forth.[33] Special commissions were common in the federal government also — for example the Emancipation, Potomac River, and Pennsylvania Avenue boards alluded to earlier. The Civil Service and Interstate Commerce Commissions were late-nineteenth-century federal experiments in active government built upon this model.

Washington's Morrill Bill, named for the Maine Republican who in 1866 introduced the first post–Civil War measure for an appointed federal commission, did not require the typical Gilded Age politician suddenly to think like a progressive. Lot Morrill and his supporters were recommending that Congress govern Washington through an administrative technique already familiar, though from different situations. The difference was that legislatures usually assigned only well-conscribed functions to commissions, rather than the diverse, ceaseless problems associated with governing a large city.

It had been a three-member commission that in the 1790s had managed transfer of the capital to the Potomac site. This offered an obvious historical precedent, but each side in the 1870s debate cited this earlier episode to support its own position. After taking up residence in the new city in 1800, Congress discussed whether to keep the three commissioners and also raised the possibility of a territory with an appointed governor, along the lines of the Northwest Ordinance. An 1802 act, however, attempted to distinguish federal from local affairs by simultaneously chartering the Washington City corporation and founding the office that later became the commissioner of Public Buildings and Grounds. This accorded with a feeling at the time that, while Congress needed a special presence in Washington, except in an emergency residents should govern themselves. "The indispensible necessity of complete authority at the seat of government carries its own evidence with it," Madison wrote in *The Federalist*. Still, "a municipal government for local purposes, derived from their own suffrages, will of course be allowed."[34]

For a long time after the 1802 incorporation, few contemplated reviving the commission format for Washington, even as the price of large national appropriations for local works and services. When officials such as Jacob Thompson, Buchanan's interior secretary, called for the country to adopt a "definite rule or settled policy" concerning Washington, they meant the promise of regular contributions to city services from which the government or its employees directly benefited, such as the police, fire, and school departments, as well as public works. In exchange, the national government would acquire a more active role in Washington's administration, but the manner remained ad hoc. Whenever the federal government reserved the appointment of local officials, this resulted from circumstance rather than principle. For example, Congress had long paid police salaries, while Washington City had built and maintained the station houses; yet the Metropolitan Police Board, appointed by the President, had been established as a security measure during the Civil War. Fire engines and fire houses were paid for by the United States, but Congress left appointment of fire commissioners to the City Council.[35] The Army Corps of Engineers managed the Washington Aqueduct, but the city had its own water department for local service.

Prominent Washingtonians had always been willing to trade the degree of self-government promised by Madison for systematic national expenditures on local services. Still, when Morrill revised the commission scheme in 1866, most residents opposed it as too extreme. For most prominent Washingtonians, the more moderate territorial form appeared to satisfy Congress's stated price of "more direct control and supervision," in exchange for regular contributions. This explains the broad initial support for the 1871 reorganization, a consensus that broke down only because of the mutual suspicions of improvers and old citizens.

The improvers, who had the highest hopes for the Territory, thus had reason to feel that the House had reneged on a deal when it struck from the territorial bill a provision for annual appropriations based upon the value of federal property holdings in the District (which would have provided 40–50 percent of the city's budget). "I have been kicking my heels at the doors of Congress for the last five years to obtain appropriations," Shepherd angrily told the House District Committee, "and have invariably been met with the response: Why not do something for yourselves? Why, are you paupers?" Shepherd insisted ominously: "After we make the start and try to improve the city, Congress should do its part. It cannot rid itself of responsibility in that respect."[36] Shepherd pressed this grievance in the Board of Public Works' 1872 annual report, which charged that from 1802 to 1871 the national coffers had expended only one-tenth of what District taxpayers had spent on improvements. To bolster its case, the board reprinted letters from assorted Founding Fathers favoring national expenditures on the capital city, along with Senator Southard's well-known 1835 argument that since the L'Enfant Plan created unique difficulties for Washington, the federal government should contribute an annual sum based on the value of its local property.[37]

Congress's sluggish response to such appeals increased the improvers' frustration. Not until December 1872 was the Board of Public Works able to persuade the House Appropriations Committee to recommend a substantial contribution to the Comprehensive Plan. The brash Shepherd basically forced Congress's hand by undertaking improvements to federal property and then sending the compliant Major Babcock the bill. Shepherd's gambit violated statutes directing the board not to begin such work without prior authorization, and Appropriations chairman Garfield confided to his diary, "This will no doubt be furiously assailed in the House." Garfield overcame colleagues' misgivings by insisting that, whatever its flaws, the Shepherd program advanced "the convenience and glory of the nation." In 1873, Congress expended $3.45 million on Washington public works, "more money toward the improvement of the Capital than have been appropriated during the seventy years preceding," the House Judiciary Committee discovered a year later. Still, the figure fell well short of what the Shepherd group insisted to be long overdue and, more important, carried no guarantee about the future.[38]

The 1874 joint investigation put all this haggling in a new light. By retreating from an implied promise to stipulate a commitment to the Comprehensive Plan, Congress had helped provoke the questionable expedients detailed by Cluss that the improvers had employed to wring money from the U.S. Treasury. Hitherto skeptical legislators acknowledged a point long made by pro-District politicians — that uncertain commitments and erratic expenditures did a disservice to the country as well as to the city.

The House now asked its judiciary committee to examine "whether some accurately defined basis of expenditure cannot be prescribed and maintained by law." The respected Luke Poland of Vermont responded with a stern report that reiterated Southard's opinions and cited the views of John Adams and Thomas Jefferson, the first Presidents to inhabit Washington, that this "child of the Union" was "solely" dependent on the nation for its well-being. Poland suggested that George Washington and L'Enfant had never imagined the city as a commercial center, which was untrue, and that the founders had "fully contemplated" federal expenditures on the capital's streets, which was unclear. More defensible was the Judiciary Committee's lament that "the utter lack of policy toward the District, which runs through the whole legislation of Congress," had produced the current morass. Congress must "fix upon a definite sum, or proportion, to be contributed by both [the national and local governments]. . . . these appropriations should be based upon some well-defined principle." It was more important that contributions be regular than large. The country's past fitfulness, the committee said, had been "revolting to a proper sense of justice."[39]

Dana's *New York Sun* denounced Poland's "scheme for taxing the public reservations, buildings, grounds, and avenues at Washington like private property." Others found the views of the former Vermont chief justice both sensible and unoriginal. The *New York Tribune,* also no friend of Shepherd, asserted that Washington's next government must "command the confidence of the people of the whole country," but "whatever the form of government . . . the United States ought to, and probably will hereafter, pay its proportionate share of the expenses."[40] For the first time in Washington's history, the country's fiscal responsibility to its capital took center stage during a debate over municipal structure.

While no logical connection existed between proposals for an appointed commission and for a system of annual federal expenditures, participants in this debate assumed that the continuous fiscal commitment Washingtonians sought would necessitate greater federal involvement in District affairs than the territorial system afforded. The best-known alternative format stronger than the territory was the Morrill plan for an appointed commission, so Congress and strategic resident interests understandably reverted to it. When Congress put Senator Morrill in charge of a special committee to prepare a new government, in the summer of 1874, the commission idea and the principle of annual federal contributions had become bound together as one plan. Schemes floated around Washington for modifications that allowed various degrees of local suffrage, but during the 1874–78 reorganization debate no influential person in the city or Congress discussed regular national support except in connection to a commission at least partly appointed by the nation.

While the commission plan promised to resolve the eternal matter of national responsibility for local services and development, it reawakened other tensions and emotions. We saw in the first chapter that the 1866 Morrill bill had been in part a ploy by moderate Republicans to sidetrack the movement, then gaining momentum, for District black suffrage. The scheme's revival in 1874 thus inevitably reopened a bitter, volatile question that the city's blacks and their allies imagined had already been resolved in their favor.

IV

That race-minded proponents of an appointed District commission used the Shepherd scandal as evidence that black suffrage in Washington had failed was bitterly ironic, since the city's black voters had no role in concocting the uproar that supposedly demonstrated their inadequacy. No one in the Territory's inner circle was black, nor were any of the improvers' close business associates. The only notable black territorial official was Howard University law professor John M. Langston, legal counsel to the Board of Health. Observing this, Douglass's *New National Era* expressed "fear" that the improver faction meant "to relieve the Republican Party in the District of Columbia of the influence of its radical element." The appointed and elected chambers of the territorial legislature had at most seven blacks out of thirty-three members, whereas eight blacks had sat in Mayor Bowen's second city council. The elected House of Delegates, widely dismissed as ineffectual, was never even 25 percent black and in any case had little control over the appointed Board of Public Works, which ignored local ordinances it did not care for. "The late Ring," a *Tribune* writer observed in autumn 1874, "was set up by Congress and the Administration without consulting the voters of this District." The reporter, who expressed mixed feelings about black suffrage overall, conceded that the territorial episode held no lesson for the South, since "universal suffrage has had no fair trial in Washington."[41]

Despite Shepherd's moves to disengage his Republicans from Bowen's radical faction, the improvers' enemies still managed to convince themselves that radical excesses somehow lay behind quarrels within the white business community over public works and development. The sentiments and rhetoric reflected the widespread tendency to attribute *all* the wrenching upheavals of Reconstruction to the changed status of blacks. The Democratic *Patriot* labeled Shepherd's improver Republicans, "a combination of African legislators and venal adventurers," similar to the popular stereotype of South Carolina's Reconstruction regime. Improvers, the paper accused, plotted "to establish negro supremacy and through it the rule of ignorance and vice at the capital of the nation." Testimony before Congress suggests that the *Patriot* was simply expressing in partisan terms a common feeling among whites in Washington—that a return to civility was impossible so long as blacks retained a political role. To the *Georgetown Courier,* a Democratic weekly supportive of Shepherd, the main benefit of the 1874 inquiry was that it "so fully convinced" Congress of the "curse" of black suffrage "that it abolishes voting altogether" for *both* whites and blacks.[42]

The racist lens through which white residents interpreted their city's recent history goes far to explain why old-line Washingtonians had by the mid-1870s dropped their earlier hesitation about appointed government. Even before Morrill's special committee began work in July 1874, the well-informed Baltimore *Sun* reported that the old citizens, victorious at last in their feud with Shepherd, would press for a commission: "Citizens who have permanent interests, including the heaviest taxpayers, do not desire that suffrage shall be restored." Such sentiments emanating from old citizens would have been formidable enough, even had they not dovetailed nicely with national political trends. The end of Washington home rule would serve the purposes of Reconstruction's growing horde of enemies. This gave even those congressional Democrats still wary of the accompanying financial commitments a reason to back the proposed commission. Republicans who felt pressed to distance themselves from Reconstruction also had political reasons to favor the scheme, which promised a fiscal policy for Washington compatible with the overall Republican outlook.

When Congress reconvened, in December 1874, the fastidious Morrill presented the Senate with a tedious, 198-page bill that caused desultory debate over minor matters. Supporters still hoped to have a permanent commission in place before the brief, lame-duck congressional session expired in March. Angry Republican radicals would not let less steadfast compatriots off the hook so easily. "It was in this District that colored suffrage was first established," recalled Indiana's Oliver Morton, "and shall it be that this District shall furnish the first example of its destruction?" Conservative Democrats agreed with the fading radical faction as to the measure's significance. Asserted Delaware's Thomas Bayard, "This bill seeks to accomplish the complete abandonment of that most absurd attempt to govern this District through the instrumentality of its most ignorant and degraded citizens." Moderate Republicans tried to divert attention from race. It was not right to "give the District of Columbia another kick and plunge them in deeper" for the sake of manhood suffrage, argued Nevada Senator Stewart. "I hope we shall confine ourselves to the question of good government." Morton, trying to avoid furnishing an ominous "precedent," insisted on an amendment to make the position of commissioner elective. While Morton's proposal lost on a 28-28 tie, the Indiana senator succeeded in ensuring that Washington's new government would be indefinitely postponed.[43] Congress established another select committee in August 1876. In marked contrast with the reorganization debate of a decade earlier, however, local support for the commission scheme grew rather than shrank with time, providing the plan included a 50 percent annual federal contribution.

The still-influential improver faction soon realized that it would lose nothing it cared about by implementation of the commission plan and would gain much. The commission-for-appropriations arrangement would ensure ample funds for extending the infrastructure begun by the Territory. Home rule was a small price to pay for the national financial commitment that from the start had been a political priority of the Shepherd group. Mutual interest in the scheme prompted the reconciliation of improvers and old citizens. In early 1875, pro- and anti-Shepherd residents combined on petitions for the Morrill bill. Cooke, Magruder, Mullett, Willard, and Shepherd sent a memorial for the commission plan with an amendment to retain the nonvoting congressional delegate, "by which the principle of suffrage and representation will be recognized." Shepherd appended a note to say that he personally preferred the "fuller suffrage" of a more liberal substitute offered by his friend, California senator Sargent. Still, the ex-governor thought the Morrill plan more or less expressed "the wishes of all the people of the District." Another petition from Columbus Alexander, and others on both sides, voiced support for Sargent's version, a "more practical, less expensive, and more equitable form of government than any yet proposed." At the same time, the *Critic,* which focused upon federal assumption of the 3.65 bonds, dismissed Sargent's proposal, agreed with Morrill "that suffrage in this District was a sham," and asked Oliver Morton rhetorically, "What if [black suffrage] is a failure?"[44]

Through a four-year delay, occasioned in large measure by the confused state of national politics during the breakdown of Reconstruction, the *Star,* the developers' voice, championed the commission proposal. The paper, which was not anti-suffrage on principle, explained, "The District's people are not at all tenacious as to the form in which suffrage is allotted to them, so long as the 50 percent provision is secured."[45] In dissent, a resident petitioner insisted that only a "comparatively small number of property owners" were "so base as to willingly barter the dignity of American citizenship in order that somebody else may pay their municipal expenses," but such voices were lonely. A new local paper, the *Washington Post,* asserted, "No sensible citizen cares a straw" for elections, since the city would get more from Congress without them, and an Ohio congressman remarked, "Those who live in this city are so anxious to get rid of the indebtedness now existing and to fix the annual proportion of the expense of the Government that they are willing to accept any sort of government."[46]

In his 1877 annual message, President Hayes called for a District government bill that featured "permanent readjustment by Congress of the financial relations between the United States and the District involving the regular annual contribution by the United States of its just proportion."[47] All that now prevented the total abolition of suffrage in Washington was some uneasiness in both parties about completely denying residents the vote. Kentucky Democrat Joseph Blackburn, once a Confederate cavalry officer, managed the House version of the District government bill, debated in spring 1878. This bill provided for both the half-and-half funding arrangement and an appointed municipal commission composed of two civilian residents and a middle-ranking officer of the Army Corps of Engineers, who would be known as the engineer commissioner. As a nod to popular sovereignty, the Kentuckian advocated an advisory council. This body would have had no power to initiate legislation, only to review contracts, expenditures, and taxes determined by the commissioners. As an added safeguard against excesses of democracy, Blackburn proposed that council members meet stiff property and residency requirements and that voters prove a three-year residency and pay a heavy poll tax.[48]

Blackburn's attempt to preserve a facade of home rule nearly defeated the entire plan. Analysis of roll call votes on the 1878 District government act suggests that the Democratic House majority was divided and confused about the bill's budgetary provisions. Southern Democrats gave only lukewarm support to the half-and-half proposal. Northern and Midwestern Democrats leaned towards outright opposition.[49] Anti-centrist Democrats were receptive to arguments like those of John Reagan of Texas, who asserted it to be "inequitable and unjust to impose half the expense of the city on the people of other parts of the country." Democratic leaders needed Republicans to carry their measure. The minority had no qualms about the fifty-fifty idea, but in floor debate and by means of the press, Republicans made it clear they could not accept a District bill that included property qualifications and poll taxes. These were already recognized as tools for disenfranchising Southern blacks, so to sanction them in Washington would cause Republicans more grief over the long run than to abolish elections altogether. The minority took advantage of Democratic bickering over financing to pull parliamentary maneuvers signaling that they would bottle up the bill until unpalatable suffrage restrictions were abandoned.[50] Blackburn had to back down. Washington's government act went to the Senate featuring both the fifty-fifty provision and the Kentuckian's advisory council.

Sentiment in the Senate for the fifty-fifty plan was nearly unanimous. Although Lot Morrill had retired, most remaining Republican leaders had been involved with District matters at some point, and influential Democrats gave vocal support. As the "least injurious" way "to recognize the principle of self-government," J. J. Ingalls of Kansas, the bill's Senate manager, proposed to revive the nonvoting congressional delegate, eliminated with the Territory in 1874, as a substitute for the proposal of an advisory council that the House sent over. Strong feeling in the Senate about District suffrage had disappeared by 1878. Even Morton, before his death in 1877, had grown less determined. After a perfunctory debate, the Senate eliminated elected offices altogether. Despite the relative apathy in the upper house towards District suffrage, Ingalls insisted on a roll call, so that the chamber would make "some authoritative expression" on this significant matter. The final vote to eliminate the franchise in Washington went 40-9-27; all in the minority were Republican. The Senate devoted most of its brief discussion to contract procedures, property taxes, and so forth.[51]

The House conference committee acceded to the Senate's major changes, since they achieved the House's ends through simpler means. With no real argument, Blackburn and the other House conferees acquiesced to the Senate's omission of the advisory council, "doing away," the Kentuckian conceded, "with all exercise of the right of suffrage in the District of Columbia." When the conference report came up for a final House vote on June 8, a 49-50 negative tally from Blackburn's own party was offset by a strongly favorable 80-20 vote among Republicans. Because, unlike the Senate, the bill's House managers sought to avoid a roll call on the suffrage issue, members' true feelings about permanent abolition of home rule in the capital are difficult to measure. Indirect evidence suggests that Democrats opposing the conference report probably objected most to the federal contributions. Republicans, as contemporaries noted, worried more about proposed suffrage restrictions than about the franchise itself. Perhaps fewer than two dozen members voted against the final version of the 1878 bill because it contained no suffrage. Only one member, Republican Mark Dunnell of Minnesota, cited the permanent bill's failure to offer "some relief" from disenfranchisement as his reason voting against it.[52]

V

Thus the federal capital acquired a municipal system that on the surface has more in common with twentieth-century forms of governance than it does with the popular polity of the Gilded Age. It would be a mistake, however, to interpret the District commission as a precursor of progressive municipal rule. Although Washington's commission system reflected the contemporary circumstances, practices, and attitudes, it was an anomaly. If the District commission set no precedent and marked no trend, then has it relevance for anyone apart from Washingtonians? Washington's 1878 government act becomes more than local history when one asks what the episode and its *aftermath* illustrate about the long-run sweep of American state structure and policy-making practice. Examining both how the District commission originated and how it evolved over the next several decades calls into question assumptions widely shared among historians about how American governance transformed around the turn of the century. The District commission, a product of the Gilded Age's mindset and politics, was destined to become a vehicle through which that period's legacy would be perpetuated into recent times.

Nearly all current writers explicitly or implictly posit a distinct break between nineteenth-century and twentieth-century American political practice, structure, and culture. Scholars assert that institutional forms and policy-making practices began to change thoroughly during the Progressive era because powerful social forces rendered the nineteenth-century's framework and approach obsolete. The notion is that with its apparently boundless possibilities and resources, the United States during its first century could afford the nonchalance of popular, distributive governance. The state's main problem seemed to be promoting growth by allocating resources to competing individuals and groups. Politicians and the public felt little need for an administrative state capable of regulating, managing, or redistributing wealth and power, concerns that arise only when resources seem limited. Rapid industrialization and urbanization, the common argument suggests, brought the need for coordinated, professional, activist government, instead of the relatively hands-off forms characteristic of the previous period. Only sophisticated, assertive municipal systems could ensure the health and well-being of huge urban populations. Modern industrial corporations controlled such vast resources and wielded such disproportionate power that the nation had no choice but to embrace regulation as a supplement to the old market discipline.[53]

Viewed from this perspective, turn-of-the-century movements to expand all levels of government, to extend the state's authority into areas hitherto considered private, and to make public administration systematic and professional appear to be nothing other than "responses to industrialism." The great social and economic transformations of the century after 1850 certainly had enormous effects on state organization and policy-making in the United States and other industrial, capitalist countries. Even so, one must not be so awestruck by these momentous developments as to interpret political trends exclusively in terms of them. By following this line of thought too closely, we arrive at the unacceptable conclusion that the internal dynamics of the American polity in the Gilded Age and earlier had little real effect on the subsequent evolution of governmental structure and practice. The familiar scenario for explaining governmental "modernization" seems too abrupt, too dependent on social and economic factors, and hardly affected at all by historical circumstance, pre-existing institutional patterns, and political culture and traditions.

The founding and early history of the District commission point to a route around this dilemma. The 1878 District government act was indeed a product of Reconstruction politics and Gilded Age attitudes and policy goals. Congress acted in accordance with recognizably nineteenth-century ideas about how government should look and work. Even so, Washington's appointed regime did not long remain the creature it was at the start. As unanticipated conflicts and difficulties presented themselves, the regime's backers in Congress and among the local civic elite encouraged it to adopt innovative policy approaches and administrative techniques. Important groups at the heart of the Washington's Gilded Age polity thus played an essential role in sponsoring the advent of modern forms of administrative governance to the capital. Gilded Age politicians and civic leaders did this because they had learned through experience that progressive concepts and methods helped them manage their city. The break we posit between the popular, distributive state of the last century and the administrative, interest group–driven state of our era was in Washington really a merging and (often uneasy) accommodation of the old era and the new.

That supporters of the appointed District commission would have to modify their perspective and improvise on their approach became apparent during the system's first important controversy. Appropriately enough for the unrepresented city, this dispute concerned taxation. At the time of the 1878 act, the chaotic state of Washington's real estate assessments threatened its economic health. In order to find money for public works, the Territory had raised the property tax rate from $1.70 to $2.00 per hundred and pressured assessors to list property at much closer to full market value than the 60 percent or less that was customary in American cities. Between 1870 and 1875, assessments in Washington rose by 40 percent, but probably half of this rise reflected the Shepherd group's drive to squeeze out more revenue.

To make matters worse, territorial assessors revalued lots as they came on the market, rather than systematically. This caused egregious inequities. The interim commissioners found "parcels of property owned by different parties in the same localities, and the real value of which was manifestly the same" listed at wildly different rates. Provisional authorities attempted a revaluation, but they lacked the time and resources to do a proper job. Depreciations resulting from the 1870s depression intensified the ill effects of inflated assessments made during the pre-1873 boom. As the permanent commission took office in summer 1878, the press estimated that up to 40 percent of District real estate was threatened with tax sale.[54]

The shortcomings of the territorial assessment books convinced Congress, despite anger over Shepherd's debts, to relent from the punitive $3.00 tax rate it had set in June 1874 and to adopt a moderate $1.50 rate. In 1878 an unsuccessful proposal to raise the tax rate again caused more debate in the Senate than had either suffrage or federal contributions. Proponents of the $1.50 figure argued that the real estate situation hindered local recovery and thus burdened the nation more. Although Congress stayed with the $1.50 rate and also legislated a reassessment that lowered District values by over 10 percent in one year, demands for relief continued.

Resentment of property taxes was endemic in urban America in the aftermath of the Panic of 1873. Washington's tax situation was extra volatile because of the wild card of Shepherd's special assessments. In 1874, Congress had made the District Engineer and the Treasury's special board of audit responsible for collecting the one-third of the cost of the Comprehensive Plan to be levied against abutting property. Estimates of the eventual yield from these special taxes hovered around $5 million, $3.2 million of which remained unpaid in late 1874. At first, the interim officials did not consider the improvement levies excessive. Engineer Hoxie even recommended raising the proportion borne by property as an equitable way to increase funds available for public works.[55]

Hoxie and the treasury officials auditing Washington admitted that the Board of Public Works had left behind incomplete, contradictory information, but they figured they could sort it out. Property holders, however, reacted furiously when they realized that the interim government meant to collect Shepherd's special levies. Columbus Alexander, the leading tax resister, vowed that "as long as an honest court" was open he would never pay any special tax certificate based upon "false measurements," "issued . . . before the work was completed," or "for work done not according to contract and specifications." As the 1874 hearings demonstrated, this covered nearly every territorial project. Public anger so plagued Hoxie that he undertook a review of the improvement tax assessments. Clerks discovered "gross errors" of between 20 percent and 25 percent on *every* street examined. The city attorney listed fourteen distinct species of errors in the special levies. Bowing to the inevitable, the District halted the assessments in May 1876 and requested authority from Congress to refigure improvement taxes from scratch.[56]

The special levies remained in abeyance while Congress reorganized the city. As the 1878 bill approached passage, members of Congress urged President Hayes to appoint civilian commissioners popular with District taxpayers, in order to secure legitimacy for the new system. Accordingly, Hayes retained the outspoken Seth Phelps, a retired navy captain named to the interim board in 1875, and for the other spot turned to Josiah Dent, a Georgetown lawyer involved in the special tax fight.[57] Congress then passed legislation to enable the capital's new government to revise special assessments and provide "drawbacks" to those who had paid too much or whose property had been damaged by the Board of Public Works. Some residents pressed their lawsuits, but most seized the proffered relief. The commissioners received thirty thousand complaints, relating to "nearly all" Washington's streets. The new regime, desirous of attaining "increased satisfaction and confidence among the tax paying people," undertook the revision in a slow, deliberate manner. Over the next eighteen months, accountants reviewed 416 street projects. The amount of "drawbacks" to taxpayers rapidly approached half a million dollars.[58]

The Treasury Department observed this with a jaundiced eye. Evidently, Congress had learned little from the tribulations of the 1874–76 Board of Audit, because in 1878 it once more turned to the Treasury for help in overseeing Washington. Under the 1878 act, the District treasury was abolished, so local tax collectors had to deposit funds in national coffers. The commissioners could disburse money only after an audit by the U.S. comptrollers of the currency. The commissioners were to submit budget requests to the Treasury, which would then prepare detailed estimates for the House and Senate Appropriations committees. The U.S. treasurer acquired control of the District's "sinking fund," which administered repayment of the municipal debt. The upshot of such provisions was that even though District taxpayers provided half the municipality's revenues, the commissioners received only the degree of control over their finances that was allowed departments with entirely national revenue sources and functions.

James Gilfillan, the U.S. treasurer, wanted to adhere to the dictates of "good management and rigid enforcement" in administering the sinking fund. Gilfillan believed that rich property owners had received a gift from the country in the form of the comprehensive improvements. Washingtonians did not deserve tax relief over and above their public works, especially when the taxes in question were pledged towards redemption of specific certificates in the hands of New York and foreign investors. Gilfillan charged the commissioners with stalling completion of the special tax revision so long and issuing drawbacks in such excessive amounts as to threaten Washington's credit. The treasurer demanded that the District turn over $1.2 million in tax liens that had been frozen when the interim government suspended the special levies in 1876. Gilfillan planned to force the issue by selling this property to cover unpaid taxes. Gilfillan also requested authority to divert money from other budget items to compensate for deficits in the sinking fund resulting from the revisions. He argued further that the commissioners should have no control over the city's debt, as "the attempted exercise of authority at any point by the Commissioners of this District could only lead to confusion, conflict of authority, and damage to the District credit." Finally, the treasurer urged that responsibility for local tax collection be shifted to the U.S. commissioner of internal revenue, whose procedures would certainly be more in line with the treasurer's point of view.[59]

The commissioners labeled Gilfillan's charges and proposals "remarkable." They could not "unjustly encumber the property of citizens with liens on taxes which they did not owe." Commissioner Phelps, who after all had been reappointed by Hayes because taxpayer groups favored him, asserted that he would forward frozen lien certificates "as soon as they are ready for delivery" and that the Treasury must be patient. Even if improvement tax revisions led to substantial losses for the sinking fund, the commissioners, he said, were "not responsible for that result." In any case, the board asserted, they were not obliged to heed Gilfillan's requests, because in his capacity as sinking fund commissioner, the treasurer was technically subordinate to them. Gilfillan found this "so absurd as scarcely to admit of serious discussion." The 1878 act intended the Treasury to watch over the District. Now the prisoner would be the guard.[60]

Gilfillan convinced Rhode Island congressman Nelson Aldrich, a freshman assigned to the District Committee, that the commissioners' actions might be criminal, since the government act outlawed increases in Washington's debt. Aldrich persuaded colleagues to hold hearings, which he ran with youthful energy. Aldrich berated commissioner Dent, "an absolute ignoramus," in Gilfillan's view. The nervous Dent fumbled his testimony, especially when confronted with a minor conflict of interest. "I don't wonder he went back to his office and threw up," Gilfillan gloated. The municipality's discomfiture was short-lived. The House District Committee received petitions from hundreds of prominent and humble residents detailing how the Shepherd assessments approached or surpassed the entire value of their house lots. To Washingtonians, the treasurer was a Simon Legree, who sought "confiscation" through "indiscriminate enforcement of these tax lien certificates." Phelps, by now ex-commissioner, presented the city's case more cogently than Dent: Did the treasurer want Washington knowingly to issue "illegal paper?" Gilfillan was "in entire ignorance of his duties." It was the taxpayers' turn to gloat. Crowed the *Star,* "The Commissioners are quite right in resenting the offensive, impertinent, and insulting tone adopted by [the Treasurer's] office in dealing with them."[61]

Working in tandem with the treasurer's office, Aldrich prepared a denunciatory report. The House District Committee, however, delayed accepting

Aldrich's report until authority for it died when the congressional session expired in March 1881. This was despite Gilfillan's plea not to let the commissioners' "rascality" go unexposed.[62] The District was left to complete its special tax revision unmolested. Ultimately, adjacent property, supposed to cover one-third of the Comprehensive Plan, paid $3.7 million on Shepherd's $18 million program and the interim commissioners' $5 million in project completions.[63] The attempt to use special assessments for a major infrastructure program proved as much a fiasco in Shepherd's Washington as it had in Haussmann's Paris.

Aldrich moved to the Senate, where he and close ally William Allison were destined to emerge as dominant figures, between them controlling the Republican caucus and the Rules, Finance, and Appropriations committees. Along with Allison, Blackburn, and other durable politicians who early in their careers were exposed to Washington's historical problems, the legendary powerbroker came to advocate steady federal involvement in and support for the capital. Four investigations and three reorganizations between 1871 and 1880 had convinced the next generation's leading politicians that Congress had to accept a substantial, constructive, and liberal role in Washington, if the capital were to continue to be functional, prosperous, and "worthy."

The U.S. Treasury, meanwhile, abandoned its effort to regulate the District as though it were a federal department. The Treasury retained management of Washington's accounts. This provided the department a veto over certain types of expenditures, but officials never exercised this power with the vigor or discretion that Gilfillan had advocated. More important, by the mid-1890s, the commissioners routinely submitted budget estimates $2 million over anticipated revenues, in order to have room to bargain. Under the 1878 act, the Treasury should have cut these requests according to its judgment, but it no longer tried. "Not desiring that [the District's] interests should be prejudiced," the Treasury left it to Congress to make cuts that appeared necessary.[64] This enabled the commissioners to make themselves Congress's primary source of information about local affairs, which allowed the municipality to acquire considerably more initiative and autonomy than the 1878 plan envisioned.

The upheavals that began with Shepherd's Comprehensive Plan and ended with the 1878 government act settled the issue of federal contributions in a manner highly congenial to Washington's most formidable business and civic interests. The 1878 scheme likewise laid out an administrative framework that appeared to allow Congress to exert the level of control over the city's day-to-day governance that such an extensive fiscal guarantee appeared to warrant. Aspects of this framework—for example Treasury control of Washington's finances—paralleled the oversight techniques typically employed by Gilded Age Congresses in their ultimately failed attempt to gain a more active presence in the federal departments overall. Disputes such as that over the sinking fund sent a message that if Congress displayed too much inflexibility and insisted too hard that the commissioners answer first to national authorities, so much defiance, evasion, and resentment might ensue that Washington's appointed regime would lose legitimacy with key resident groups and break apart. Although the commissioners owed their jobs to the President and their money to Congress, they could still not be expected to act as agents of national will *against* Washington's people.

During the appointed regime's first decade, legislative committees learned to treat the District commission as a municipal government that could negotiate, rather than a bureau of the United States that was required to obey. Still, Gilded Age Congresses persisted in their effort to remain involved in Washington's daily affairs and to apply to the manifold problems of servicing and governing a large city the rigid, intrusive oversight procedures typical of the period. The tight relationship between Congress and the nation's capital begun in 1878 provided advantages for both, but this association also created dilemmas for the national city and prompted much quarreling in the Capitol.

5

The District Commissioners and Congress

By an inadvertence the name of one of the school-houses of the city of Washington, "The Amidon," is omitted from the clause making provision "for janitors and care of buildings and grounds." . . . [This] omission was a mere clerical error in the engrossment of the bill at the last hour of the last session. . . . The former janitor has continued in service but has not received any pay during the current fiscal year, and his family are suffering great embarrassment and distress.

—Commissioner William B. Webb
to Speaker of the House John G. Carlisle

T HE CIRCUMSTANCES that gave rise to the situation described above epitomized the dilemmas that commanded the attention of the District Commissioners and Congress during the early years of direct federal rule. Washington's 1878 government act was merely an outline; time filled in the details. The executive and legislative portions of the capital's new regime—the appointed commissioners and relevant committees of Congress—wrestled among themselves over the next dozen years to carve out areas of responsibility and to establish policy-making, budgeting, and administrative procedures. Congress's stinginess about delegating authority made it difficult for the commissioners to resolve even the most minor matters without appeal to the Capitol, but congressmen worried that if they permitted Washington's appointed executives too much discretion, they would lose the extensiveness of oversight that the 1878 system was meant to afford them. On the other hand, the commissioners needed to govern day to day, even though their operations were directed not by a board of aldermen able to devote full attention to local affairs but by the national assembly of a continental republic, which of necessity could give the national city only the kind of spotty attention destined to create misunderstandings and errors. Finally, the poor janitor's plight reflected a critical determinant of federal policy towards the District during the first two decades under the commission system—an ongoing quarrel between the House and the Senate over how financially liberal to be towards Washington. Commissioner Webb was being polite here, perhaps out of self-interest: the janitor's pay did not fall victim to a "mere clerical error" but to a guerrilla war over expenditures large and small fought between the wings of the Capitol.

I

As we just saw, the commissioners moved quickly to undermine powers that in theory belonged to the Treasury Department. By shutting out Treasury, the commissioners gained some autonomy to organize bureaus under them as they saw fit. Washington's new rulers needed this discretion, because they right away had to make decisions concerning key city agencies whose duties Congress had defined only vaguely.

One volatile matter left unresolved in the government act was how to enforce health regulations. The Territory's Board of Health, the most recent attempt at sanitary reform, had achieved progress, but at a high cost in terms of public ill-will. As in other cities that established aggressive boards of health after the Civil War, property owners treated the physicians and attorneys on the Washington panel as high-minded busybodies to be ignored whenever possible. The right of cities to compel residents to keep property clean was not yet well established; it still rested chiefly on common law regarding nuisances, which was incoherent and unsuited to modern housing and enterprise.

In 1878, Congress abolished the Board of Health and substituted a "health officer" directly subordinate to the commissioners. When formulating the commission scheme, Congress had more or less promised local elites that the two civilian commissioners would be attentive to the needs of real estate. This is why a few senators growled irritably at the clause demolishing the autonomous health panel. The grumblers feared that the new regime would not merely be more cognizant of property than the Board of Health but might in fact return the capital to pre-Shepherd slovenliness. Vermont senator Edmunds, usually found among the proponents of reform when such matters arose, mystified habitual allies by pressing for the board's destruction. Edmunds asserted that to retain the panel would be "invidious," since the main idea driving the 1878 reorganization was that responsibility should be concentrated in the commissioners as much as possible. Edmunds had nothing against health reform, he said, but Congress had "already agreed to abolish" the myriad autonomous boards that had made the typical Gilded Age city an administrative morass "and to consolidate under the single executive direction."[1]

Edmunds had his way, despite the grumblers. The commissioners received broad powers to formulate and supervise sanitation laws. The first permanent Board of Commissioners named a Dr. Smith Townshend as health officer and authorized him to hire six sanitary inspectors, the maximum allowed by law. Perhaps with his predecessors' travails in mind, the doctor's first request was for imprinted stationery and a pistol. The wary commissioners responded by directing Townshend not to issue citations against insanitary property without telling them.[2] Washington's new rulers had room to work out details. Because of sentiments such as Edmunds's, the commissioners received powers that were extensive, by the standards of American municipal executives. Lot Morrill had used the word *regents* in describing his system. Congress rejected that label as too monarchical, but it accurately described the commissioners' position.

One constraint upon the commissioners' ability to organize Washington as they wished arose from provisions of the government act that dictated collective responsibility. This legal device was supposed to help Congress keep tabs on its capital and in turn to force the commissioners to do the same with city agencies. The Board of Commissioners was bonded as a unit, rendering all legally accountable for the actions of each. The act mandated a unanimous vote on public works contracts and set the quorum at three members. Such provisions forced the commissioners to retain duties that might better have been delegated.[3]

As proponents of the commission schemes popular during the Progressive era would also discover, collective responsibility was both dubious as a legal principle and unworkable in practice. The city would grind to a halt over trivia unless one person could make routine decisions. In its second week in office, the first Board of Commissioners began to divide everyday duties, with Josiah Dent controlling schools, charities, and corrections, and Seth Phelps, chosen the board's president (largely a spokesman position), supervising fire, police, and health. Major William Twining, the first Army Corps of Engineers officer to hold the post of engineer commissioner mandated under the 1878 act, had charge of streets, sewers, and so forth. The board directed employees to refer matters only to the appropriate commissioner. Soon, no department in the city government could communicate with another except through the commissioner in charge.[4]

Later boards expanded on this functional division. As far as lawfully possible, board members avoided each others' affairs. Only the commissioner in charge of a department could order its supplies. The member in charge expected colleagues to ratify his employment decisions. Although the division of duties became routine, the commissioners would reaffirm it whenever a new member joined. In May 1897, when John Wight took office, distribution of municipal functions looked like this:[5]

President Ross	*Mr. Wight*	*Capt. Black*
Gtown. Almshouse	Boiler inspection	Building Division
Was. Asylum	C & O Canal	Chief Clerk, Engi-
Assessments (except water)	Chimney sweeping	neer Dept.
Offices of:	Coal inspection	Contracts
Assessor	Columbia Hosp. for Women	Highway
Attorney	Coroner	extensions
Auditor	Excise Board	Permit Clerk (inc.
Tax Collector	Fire	gas/elec. lines)
Liquor Inspector	Flour Inspector	Sewers/Plumbing
Property Clerk	Harbor Master	Street Lighting

Schools	Hay scales	Streets & Roads
Charities	Health Dept.	Subdivisions
Reform School	Insurance cos.	Super. of Property
St. & alley cleaning	Paupers' transport	Surveyor
	Police	Trees & Parking
	Police rewards	Water
	Salted provisions inspection	
	Sealer of Weights & Measures	
	Steam engineers	
	Telephone and Telegraph Service	
	Wood inspection	

The 1878 law empowered District executives to abolish and consolidate offices, an authority used both to continue the trend towards retrenchment begun under the interim government and to facilitate control. The commissioners reinforced their authority by distributing strict printed rules to employees: Municipal workers had to remain at their jobs during business hours but were not to enter the District Building after 4 P.M. without permission. People could not loaf, read the newspaper, or conduct private business at work. "Beggars, book canvassers, peddlars, solicitors for subscriptions, collectors of private debts" had to be kept out of the building, but congressmen and cabinet officers were "at all times" to be sent directly to the commissioners. Agencies were to keep registers of letters received. Departments heads could pass records to each other only with executive approval.[6]

In such a centralized regime, each commissioner could decide much. Apart from a three-year residency requirement, eligibility for this prestigious post was wide open. Vacancies thus created a scramble. In June 1878, as President Hayes contemplated the initial appointments, the *Washington Post* promised to list all residents who were not candidates, "provided we can find any." Determined candidates competed for support from prominent citizens. Lumber dealer Samuel Wheatley, appointed in 1886, reportedly collected signatures representing $13 million in property. If such efforts grew too enthusiastic, they would negate themselves. The *Evening Star* counted fourteen legitimate candidates, including the incumbents, for two three-year terms beginning May 1897. Within three weeks of his inauguration, President McKinley was "overwhelmed by delegations, all composed of men of standing and undoubted probity." McKinley delayed his choices out of confusion.[7]

Party politicians at first imagined that old-fashioned spoils might determine appointments. In fact, President Hayes hoped to set a precedent that commission appointments address local concerns, not national party politics. At this zenith of partisan politics in the United States, few could grasp a pattern of nominations that defied party exigencies; contemporaries dismissed Hayes's handling of the District as idiosyncratic incompetence. Later presi-

Table 5.1 Background of Civilian Commissioners, District of Columbia, 1878–1910

Seth L. Phelps (served July 1878–Nov. 1879 [interim commissioner Jan. 1875–July 1878]) Democrat, born Ohio, 1824. U.S. Navy captain during Civil War. Afterwards, vice president, Pacific Mail Steamship Company.

Josiah Dent (July 1878–July 1882) Maryland-born lawyer and Democrat. Leader of movement to revise Shepherd-era improvement taxes.

Thomas P. Morgan (Nov. 1879–Mar. 1883) Merchant and manufacturer, born Alexandria, D.C., 1821. Party affiliation unknown. Long active in District politics. Serving as superintendent of the Metropolitan Police when named commissioner.

Joseph R. West (July 1882–July 1885) Lawyer, born New Orleans, 1822, raised in Philadelphia. Republican Civil War veteran. Returned to his native state after the war as a federal officeholder and served a term (1871–77) as U.S. senator representing Louisiana's Reconstruction government.

James B. Edmonds (Mar. 1883–Apr. 1886) Democrat, born upstate New York, 1883. Practiced law two decades in Iowa before coming to Washington, 1878. Property: $28,908 (1889).

William B. Webb (July 1885–May 1889) Republican, born Washington, 1825. Corporate lawyer, law professor, author of *Webb's Digest,* a summary of District laws. In 1861 appointed by Lincoln as the first superintendent of the Metropolitan Police. Property: $26,122 (1889).

Samuel E. Wheatley (Apr. 1886–May 1889) Democrat, born Georgetown, 1844. Partner in Wheatley Brothers, the family lumber firm. Property: $38,470 (1893).

Lemon G. Hine (May 1889–Oct. 1890) Democrat, born Ohio, 1832. Once a newspaper editor in Cleveland, became a key Washington lawyer, as well as a prominent backer of linotype. Twice president of the District bar. Had served on the old Washington Common Council (1868) and the Board of Aldermen (1870). Property: $11,426 (1893).

John W. Douglass (May 1889–Mar. 1893) Republican lawyer, born Philadelphia, 1827. U.S. commissioner of internal revenue during the 1870s.

John W. Ross (Oct. 1890–July 1902) Democrat, born Illinois, 1841. Son of an Illinois congressman. Served in state legislature before coming to Washington in 1883. Lawyer and Georgetown law lecturer until appointed city postmaster by President Cleveland in 1888. Former president, Board of School Trustees. Property: $17,927 (1893).

Table 5.1 (*continued*)

Myron M. Parker (Mar. 1893–Mar. 1894) Born Vermont, 1843. Major figure in District real estate, insurance, and finance. Republican National Committee member, three times president of the Washington Board of Trade. Property: $42,096 (1893).

George Truesdell (Mar. 1894–May 1897) Republican, born New York, 1842. Civil engineering degree from University of Michigan. Trolley entrepreneur, suburban developer. Director of the Board of Trade. Property: $254,454 (1893).

John B. Wight (May 1897–May 1900). Republican, born Washington, 1853. A realtor at time of appointment; previously acted as supervisor of the Columbia Institution for the Deaf and Dumb, now Gallaudet College. Secretary of the Board of Trade.

Henry B. F. Macfarland (May 1900–Jan. 1910) Republican, born Philadelphia, 1861. Son of a well-known journalist. Correspondent for the Boston *Herald* and Philadelphia *Record*. Studied law with William Webb; was son-in-law of John Douglass.

Henry L. West (Oct. 1902–Jan. 1910) Democrat, born Staten Island, N.Y., 1859. Former managing editor of *Washington Post;* father was editor of Washington *Chronicle*.

Sources: City directories, local histories, newspapers, and census records. Since indices for property taxes under the commissioners did not survive, assessed values are given only for those owning more than $20,000 worth, listed in *Evening Star,* Nov. 9, 11, 1889, and more than $10,000, listed in *Evening Star,* Oct. 27–Nov. 4, 1893.

dents attained Hayes's goal of neutralizing partisanship in Washington through a straightfoward practice comprehensible to the run-of-the-mill politico—they divided the two civilian seats between the parties. The board would then turn around and name as its president the member from the President's party. Bipartisanship became so routine that in 1902 Senate District Committee secretary Charles Moore had to remind Senator McMillan, who had been that panel's chairman for more than a decade, that it was an "*unwritten* law [to take] the two civil commissioners from opposite parties. There is no statute governing the matter."[8]

Chester Arthur named Joseph West, a former Reconstruction senator from Louisiana, to what was now considered the Republican spot. Unfamiliar with local Democrats, Arthur gave their place to James Edmonds, who until 1878 had practiced law in Iowa and was suggested by his state's delegation. As Edmonds was not well known among the local elite, his appointment raised cries for home rule. The *Star* published a series of interviews in which civic leaders charged, "The Commissioners hold themselves more responsible to the government from whom they derive their appointment than to any committee of citizens." Businessmen insisted that the regime should not consist of "strangers." Subsequent presidents took this to heart. Of the next ten appointees, only Republican John W. Douglass, who as commissioner of internal revenue in the 1870s had helped break up the Whiskey Ring, lacked a "circle of local acquaintance."[9]

Of the commissioners in the late 1880s, William Webb had been appointed by Lincoln as first superintendent of the Metropolitan Police. An accomplished attorney and legal scholar, Webb's clients included the Washington Gas-Light Company and the First National Bank. Lumber dealer Wheatley "thoroughly identified with the business interests of the District." Lemon G. Hine was a native midwesterner who had only come to the capital after the war, but he had served on the City Council under the defunct corporation and was well known as one of the Washington entrepreneurs behind linotype.[10] The most accomplished early commissioner, John W. Ross, Democrat and son of a congressman, spent four years in the Illinois state legislature before moving to Washington in 1883. Though a relative newcomer when named to the board in 1890, Ross had an entry into local society through his father-in-law, who owned the National Hotel. In addition, while serving President Cleveland's administration as Washington City postmaster during the late 1880s, Ross had gained adequate local stature through his presidency of the Board of School Trustees and his law lectures at Georgetown University.[11]

Throughout the 1890s, Presidents deferred to prominent local businessmen and leading congressional policy-makers when faced with the choice of a civilian commissioner. In effect, the chief executive ceded control of the District commission to James McMillan's Senate District Committee and McMillan's local ally, the Washington Board of Trade, the formidable commercial-civic group founded in 1889. Three straight appointees were officers of the Board of Trade. The case of the one nominee rejected by the Senate during this period illustrates the strength of this alliance. In February 1897, lame-duck President Cleveland named F. P. B. Sands to the Democratic slot on the commission. Downtown businessmen, who sought Ross's reappointment, expressed "a good deal of surprise." "Universal regret" allegedly pervaded the District Building. The press asserted that although Sands was a lifelong Washingtonian, he had never been active in civic affairs; he had won his place "exclusively" by virtue of being son-in-law of a friend of Cleveland.[12]

Businessmen recalled that in 1894–96, Sands had acted as counsel to the incorporators of a proposed rival to the monopolistic Washington Gas-Light Company. When the Senate District Committee rejected the rival charter, Sands fed documents to a South Dakota Populist, who used them to claim on the Senate floor that the District chairman, Republican McMillan, and the committee's two ranking Democrats had conspired with entrenched utility interests to force exorbitant rates on Washington consumers.[13] Reprints of the accusations circulated through the Senate, along with rumors that Sands's real backers included the Pennsylvania Railroad and Pennsylvania bosses Quay and Cameron, which made Sands appear a hypocrite on top of his other failings. The press habitually collected praise from a nominee's acquaintances among prominent residents. Compliments of Sands were pointedly back-handed. "I am sure he is free from any entanglements with trusts or corpo-rations though liberal in his consideration of them," observed the head of a popular neighborhood group. Sands's nomination was referred to a subcom-mittee that included one of the Democrats whose integrity Sands had im-pugned two years before. A week later, the Senate committee voted down the nomination 9-3. In May, McKinley reappointed Ross.[14]

During the Progressive years, two newspapermen were among the civilian rulers of the capital. Journalist and lawyer Henry B. F. Macfarland, though not an officer of the Board of Trade, was an eloquent spokesman for its point of view. Henry L. West, former managing editor of the *Washington Post,* was also a Board of Trade member, but his appointment after Ross's death in July 1902 represented some erosion of the group's control over the appointment process. The Board of Trade's candidate was William V. Cox, bank president and son-in-law of former mayor Matthew Emery. Cox had acted as secretary of the Citizens' Centennial Committee, which began the agitation that re-sulted in the McMillan Plan for redesigning the capital's parks. Cox had "family, property, acquaintance, ability, industry, and good judgment," wrote Senate District Committee secretary Charles Moore.[15]

West, on the other hand, was close to Henry Cabot Lodge, who had unsuc-cessfully urged him on McKinley several times. Lodge would obviously get further with the new President, Theodore Roosevelt, the Massachusetts Re-publican's oldest political friend. Four days after Ross's death, West was al-ready trying to reassure McMillan: "You can rely upon my intelligent and earnest cooperation in your plan." Lodge wired McMillan to express "great interest in West." Cox's backers braced for a "lively" fight. Moore, then doubling as the planning commission's secretary, worried about the plan's political survival and feared that West would prove incapable of rallying sup-port. He pressed McMillan to fight for Cox. West, Moore declared, had never been a friend of McMillan's, was insufficiently "acquainted with business af-fairs," and would make a "very poor" commissioner. Of Cox, on the other hand, Moore wrote to a friend:

> . . . intelligent and progressive . . . a great admirer of Senator McMillan. The *Post* pays no attention whatever to District matters unless there is something particularly big on, and then it sulks, if it does not get the first chance at it. West has always had the idea that he was a bigger man than Senator McMil-lan, and he once remarked in a fit of pique that he would be in Washington long after Senator McMillan left.[16]

The judicious McMillan rejected his trusted aide's advice to pick a quarrel with Lodge, and shortly thereafter he died suddenly, on August 10. West was appointed to the board, and in eight years as commissioner, he kept his word. He energetically defended the McMillan Plan.

National politicians and local civic leaders worked to ensure that local issues, not party patronage, determined the selection of the commissioners. The spoils system did at times affect the function of some subordinate District offices. During the 1870s and 1880s, Republicans protected the Metropolitan Police as a sinecure for the Grand Army of the Republic. The commissioners begged for repeal of a statute requiring that District police officers be veterans of the armed forces. The small postwar army provided a tiny applicant pool, and by 1890, a man would have to have been thirteen at the Civil War's end to meet police entrance requirements. Under Benjamin Harrison, no legislation displeasing to the G.A.R. was possible, so the Supreme Court took pity and overturned the statute, in 1892.[17]

No Gilded Age President used District office appointments for spoils, despite partisan accusations to the contrary. Although by statute the President made appointments to a miscellany of local offices, such as the gas inspector and the superintendent of charities, tradition permitted only a few to go to the chief executive's own friends. Of these, District residents challenged executive control only over the recorder of deeds, a particularly lucrative and visible post. When Presidents began to set aside the recordership for a black supporter, such as Frederick Douglass under Garfield, local opposition turned ugly. The position became a lightening rod for elite racism.[18]

Most documented instances of national politicians using Washington appointments for spoils relate to members of the Senate District Committee. In 1893, for example, Moore recalled to McMillan in a matter of fact way an encounter with the committee's ranking Democrat at the District Building: "Senator Harris was in the office with a constituent for whom he was getting a place."[19] Except for the police, party patronage never caused the city major problems. Still, spoils were a nuisance, so the commissioners tried to short-circuit them by arranging informally for the Civil Service Commission to examine applicants for most city jobs. Despite repeated appeals, no law or executive order followed to legitimize this arrangement. Successive attorneys general ruled that because the District was not a typical federal agency, the President lacked his normal authority to extend civil service to it. District employees had only extralegal protection until well into this century.[20]

II

The ground rules under which the District commission functioned illustrate a pervasive theme of Gilded Age public affairs — the drive by legislatures to participate in administrative matters. If the commissioners were Washington's regents, then the legislature itself was its king, a fact of political life of which District officials were often reminded, not only through the device of collective responsibility, but also through frequent demands from the Capitol for information and accounts. Congress's attempt to push the commissioners to adopt what we would call "hands-on" management brought to light a contradiction built into the 1878 system. Although wanting the Board of Commissioners to have enough control that it could truly be held accountable, Congress was so loath to let any officer loosen the reins on subordinates that the commissioners' ability to govern was undermined.

The commissioners were constrained practically to counting paper clips and pencils. The District's annual report for fiscal 1879, the permanent commission's first year, revealed, for instance, that the health officer had spent $144.40 for file boxes, $37.50 to repair stoves, and $5.00 to repair clocks; the city had used $147.44 for "washing towels, etc." When the commissioners began to lump miscellaneous expenditures as "contingencies," suspicious politicians ordered a contingency audit, which endured from 1885 to 1887 and provided such critical information as that in 1886 the capital government had spent $1.50 for horseshoeing, $1.75 for typewriter ribbons, and $191.26 for dog tags.[21]

Harassing bureaucrats over petty expenditures was largely a game played by congressmen who wished to appear thrifty with the people's money. More serious was the habit of detailing office titles and salaries in appropriations bills. "We give them clerks by name," the chairman of the Senate's District Appropriations Subcommittee exclaimed in 1883, exaggerating slightly. Committees deliberated over requests for added or redefined positions or increased salaries. Outmoded procedures became frozen into budget lines, which of course evolved at a glacial pace. The budget failed to keep pace with changes in technology, professional standards, or the volume of business.

During its first decades, the commission's operations often appeared retrograde and shabby. In 1884, the House District Committee learned that the tax collector's office had not audited its accounts for a decade, in part because of staff shortages. A decade later, the tax collector testified to the House Appropriations Committee that his clerks, at salaries of $1,400 to $1,600, half what they would be getting in a private office, worked overtime half the year and usually lost portions of their annual leave. The lines of residents paying assessments in person often grew so long that no time remained to record taxes paid by mail. Typically, a member of the House panel responded with questions about a seventy-five-year-old employee of the agency, thereby implying that more energetic employees, rather than augmented salaries and staff, would solve the problem. The collector explained that to let go of this twenty-year veteran would be cruel, as the city had no civil pensions.[22]

During the 1880s, the building inspector had but one fieldwork assistant, although by 1886 the annual number of new buildings had risen to more than two thousand. In the next decade, Congress added a handful of assistants; but despite constant overtime and the innovation of doing fieldwork by bicycle, the city could give only cursory supervision to building permits that extended well into the suburbs and by then numbered four thousand per year. In one instance, the day after an inspector certified a row of houses, the assistant engineer commissioner found the contractor putting up the entire block of chimneys without mortar. The builder was relying on the fact that inspectors rarely had time to revisit a site. On most days, people seeking building permits waited three hours, with no assurance that their business would be handled. The inspector's office was supposed to review drawings for both private and commercial buildings, a task complicated immensely by the arrival of steel-frame construction and industrial-scale building. On top of that, the bureau remained responsible for public construction. The District sought architects for the building inspector's staff, but professionals shied away from positions in which they would be classified and paid only as clerks. These shortcomings of the department proved ominous when the collapse of Ford's Theater in 1893 killed twenty-three people, employees of the War Department's records division, which at the time was housed there. Twice in the mid-1890s, coroner's juries blamed inadequate building inspection for accidental deaths.[23]

All District government departments lamented unprofessional salaries and outdated job descriptions. Engineer Department "clerks" were really topographers, surveyors, and mathematicians. Until 1890, the Health Department sent food samples to the city's asphalt inspector, because it lacked a chemist of its own. In 1900, the city attorney reported that he was forced to prepare ten times the number of briefs the office had fifteen years earlier with the same size staff.[24]

The commissioners themselves may have been primary victims of the snail-like pace of reorganization amid expanding duties. In 1890, a prolonged illness of the engineer commissioner did convince Congress to reduce the quorum for most business to two. The same year, the city auditor and the Treasury Department agreed that it was absurd to require the commissioners personally to sign all disbursements. Because of strict statutes governing recordkeeping, the District was required to pay all wages by check, which placed an onerous burden on unskilled laborers, who, in an age before mass consumer banking, faced "difficulty and embarrassment" in finding brokers who would cash their checks without exacting usurious discounts.[25] The city auditor argued that salaries and small bills should be handled by a disbursing clerk, "leaving to the Commissioners, as now, the settlement of the larger and more important obligations to the contractors upon the public works." Anxious that such an arrangement "relieved the Commissioners of responsibilities imposed by the organic act," Congress did nothing about it until 1894, when the auditor reported that the commissioners were signing 33,055 checks per month, so many that no one had time to study them. This created precisely the lack of accountability that the system was supposed to avoid.[26]

Even after Congress authorized a disbursing clerk, clerical matters overwhelmed the commissioners. Until the mid-1890s, the two civilian board members had no personal assistants. District Secretary William Tindall had only five clerks. These clerks had trouble enough keeping up with the mail; it was unthinkable to ask them to make memos of meetings between the executives and the fifteen or twenty people waiting for each at any time. The commissioners had to write many of their own memos and letters, in addition to signing fifty to one hundred endorsements each day. "We have scarcely an opportunity to go out and inspect the work that is going on and the institutions under our charge," complained Commissioner George Truesdell. The commissioners appealed to Congress to authorize Tindall, who had held his post since Bowen's time and had evolved into "a sort of encyclopedia" on District affairs, to act as his bosses' surrogate for routine business, so that the commissioners could leave the office once in a while and see their city.[27]

By common consent, the office space to which the commissioners were often confined was "discreditable." The municipal courthouse on Judiciary Square was built as a city hall in 1820 by architect George Hadfield. Though the building is now much admired, postwar District residents developed a distaste for it. In 1871, the Territory surrendered it to the District Supreme Court. Shepherd moved his office into rented quarters and outfitted them with Gilded Age exuberance. As related in chapter 2, the Territory secured a Pennsylvania Avenue site for a new city hall through a dubious bargain with the Washington Market Company. Congress gave $75,000 to start construction, but Shepherd misappropriated all but $5,000, "which was used to make a slight excavation," Tindall recalled. The interim government had little choice but to move into the old headquarters of the Board of Public Works, the Morrison Building (named for its owner, a city bookseller) on 4½ Street. The permanent District commission inherited the lease, thereby becoming, as a pamphleteer scoffed, the "Triumvirs of Four-and-a-Half Street."[28]

The commissioners petitioned for a new building, but Congress, annoyed by Shepherd's lavishness with his rented quarters, was not in the mood. By 1882, the Morrison Building was "crowded, inconvenient, and combustible." The commissioners reported that ninety-four people worked in fourteen rooms, all but two of which were 16' × 20'. Offices that the public visited were on the third and fourth floors, but there was no elevator, and the wooden stairway was too narrow for two people to use simultaneously. Apart from two portable furnaces in the basement, heat came from stoves and grates. The four fireproof vaults were filled to the brim, so the remaining "books, maps, drawings, measurements, receipts and requisitions, special and general assessment books, in fact nearly all the records since the board of public works was established," were held in offices, where a fire would surely destroy them. The neighboring building, occupied by the police and health departments, the commissioners found to be "inferior."[29]

Congress did not even begin to contemplate a new city hall until the Ford's

Theater tragedy dramatized the perils of decrepit office space. Meanwhile, the District government moved in 1887 to a refurbished lumber warehouse on First Street between B and C streets, northwest. This was "a great improvement," but quarters were still so crowded that on busy days people paying taxes had to line up on the street. Fire remained a threat, especially to miscellaneous records piled in the superintendent of charities' office. In 1895, District officials moved to their last rented home, an insurance company building on Louisiana Avenue, taking along Shepherd's furniture from 1871, which had become rather squalid. Not until authorization in 1902 of the current District Building at 14th Street near Pennsylvania Avenue did the commission finally acquire appropriate surroundings.[30]

III

In fact, during the 1880s and 1890s, Washington's municipal administration was not all that retrograde, compared to those of other American cities. All U.S. cities had trouble keeping up with evolving duties, professional standards, and technology. Other municipalities faced the additional stresses of industrial poverty, large-scale foreign immigration, and mass democratic politics, which were not factors in the capital.

A review of the District budget suggests that despite the appearance of regression, the permanent commission maintained and even improved upon the level of services available at its installation. From fiscal 1879 to 1898, expenditures grew more or less steadily with the city (see tables 5.2–5.4). Expenditures increased per capita as well as in absolute numbers. This is significant, since the 1870s depression initiated an extended period during which per capita expenditures in most large American cities stagnated. The spending spree of Shepherd's Washington had hardly been unique. During the boom that preceded the 1873 panic, as Jon Teaford explains, "urban governments throughout the country embarked on massive projects costing millions of borrowed dollars." When the crash sent property values plummeting, municipalities and their taxpayers found themselves caught "in a vise of financial contraction." Numerous cities teetered on default. Even in the more stable 1880s, "bitter memories of grandiose public spending remained, discouraging officials from digging deeper into the pockets of taxpayers." Not until the end of the century did proponents of municipal capital expenditures regain voter confidence.[31]

On the surface, Gilded Age Washington seems to have been under more pressure for fiscal retrenchment than cities that actually cut back. The 1870s left the District with $21.6 million in bonded debt. This worked out to $127.66 per capita, the largest figure of any American city with over one hundred thousand people (see table 5.5). In 1880, the nationwide per capita municipal debt was $51.09; except for Jersey City, no large municipality came close to the national capital. New York had the third largest debt per capita

Table 5.2 Total Annual Expenditures under the
1878 District of Columbia Government Act,
Fiscal 1879–1902

Fiscal Year	Total Spending	Change from Previous Year (%)
1879	$3,210,047.05	
1880	3,523,867.90	9.8
1881	3,737,049.67	6.0
1882	3,493,280.38	−6.5
1883	3,722,795.94	6.6
1884	3,614,639.76	−2.9
1885	4,020,089.54	11.2
1886	3,854,778.75	−4.1
1887	4,002,396.54	3.8
1888	4,201,569.95	5.0
1889	5,147,686.81	22.5
1890	5,632,496.41	9.4
1891	5,814,237.86	3.2
1892	6,234,938.78	7.2
1893	5,594,012.34	−10.3
1894	6,133,192.17	9.6
1895	6,127,729.17	−0.1
1896	6,345,721.52	3.6
1897	6,307,100.30	−0.6
1898	6,644,804.10	5.4
1899	7,250,971.10	9.1
1900	7,928,749.32	9.3
1901	9,437,829.13	19.0
1902	9,875,521.79	4.6

Source: Auditor's statement in District commissioners' annual
reports, 1879–1902.

among major cities, but it soon rebounded from the Tweed Ring's profligacy.
By 1884, New York had reduced its per capita debt to $75 and was spending
less than 30 percent of its revenue on debt service. Meanwhile, interest and
the sinking fund occupied more than 35 percent of the budget of Washington, "a community with little or no creative wealth."[32]

One might quarrel with this picture of Washington groaning under extraordinary debt. Gilded Age cities conformed to no standard method for cal-
culating debt, so perhaps the District used especially broad criteria.[33] More
important, since the District of Columbia combines functions of a city and a
state, the proper comparison would be between the District's debt and that
of other cities plus their share of the debt of their respective states. To adjust

Table 5.3 Average Annual Expenditures of the District of Columbia, Fiscal Years 1879–1902, by Function

	1879–1884		1885–1890		1891–1896		1897–1902	
	Average Spending	Average %	Average Spending	Average %	Average Spending	Average %	Average Spending	Average %
Offices/Miscellaneous^a	$232,133	6.6	$184,195	4.1	$276,105	4.6	$370,695	4.7
Schools	523,363	14.8	736,870	16.4	968,027	16.0	1,368,590	17.3
Police^b	308,532	8.7	376,069	8.4	553,766	9.2	703,320	8.9
Fire/Telegraph	113,661	3.2	154,123	3.4	197,137	3.3	309,512	3.9
Health/Garbage	33,755	1.0	43,951	1.0	66,389	1.1	97,361	1.2
Charities/Prisons	182,039	5.1	285,266	6.4	465,415	7.7	669,220	8.5
Courts^c	17,973	0.5	17,840	0.4	74,611	1.2	107,181	1.4
Debts^d	1,249,769	35.3	1,292,610	28.8	1,336,433	22.1	1,402,693	17.7
Streets/Sewers^e	746,231	21.1	1,131,590	25.2	1,563,457	25.9	2,143,915	27.1
Water^f	137,798	3.9	235,232	5.3	373,660	6.2	655,348	8.3
Parks^g	—	—	157,661	0.6	164,046	2.7	79,537	1.0

Source: Auditor's statements in District Commissioners' annual reports, 1879–1902.

Note: This chart roughly follows the District's own functional divisions, although budget politics made these erratic. For example, the largest single item, the Sinking Fund, was often classed under miscellaneous. The local jail was in the Washington Asylum, the city almshouse, which is why corrections came under charities.

^a Mainly salaries and office expenses. Some miscellaneous items were classed under the closest functional division, such as the harbor boat under police, the bathing beach under parks, and public pumps under water.

^b After 1890 includes militia.

^c Until 1893 includes only the police court; afterwards includes the District supreme court and others.

^d In addition to the Sinking Fund, includes trust funds, certificate redemptions, and judgments.

^e Also includes bridges, street lighting and sweeping.

^f Includes the aqueduct and the Water Department, although the latter had a separate fund.

^g Until 1890, when the National Zoo was begun, the federal government paid for Washington's parks.

Table 5.4 Average Expenditures of the District of Columbia, Fiscal Years 1879–1902, per Capita

Period	Average Spending	Population[a]	Per Capita
1879–1883[b]	$3,537,408.19	177,624	$19.92
1888–1892	$5,406,185.96	230,392	$23.47
1898–1902	$8,227,575.09	278,718	$29.52

Source: Auditor's statements in District commissioners' annual reports, 1879–1902.
[a]From national census for period in question. See table 1.1.
[b]Starting year not parallel because fiscal '79 was the permanent commission's first year.

for such factors might make the capital's burden appear less severe, but probably it would still be relatively high.

The most plausible explanation for why per capita spending in Washington continued to rise, in the face of a heavy debt burden and a national trend towards retrenchment, was that the half-and-half funding scheme relieved much of the pressure the Shepherd-era debt might otherwise have placed on local taxpayers. In addition, Congress, not an elected local council, controlled the city budget. Invulnerable to whatever no-growth sentiment existed among Washington's taxpayers, Congress could spend what it thought right. The national political leaders who disfranchised Washington promised that in return Congress would underwrite the city's fiscal health and continued development. Gilded Age congressmen have been widely denigrated as an especially short-sighted crew. In fact, the Congress of that period probably attended more carefully to Washington's long-term needs than the residents themselves would have, had they retained the same powers as every other urban public.

Congress kept impressively well the bargain struck in 1878. Under the half-and-half plan, the federal government only agreed to match general revenues from taxes and license fees. If one also considers special fees such as water rates, then Washington always contributed slightly more than the nation (see figure 5.1). Congress argued that it was not obliged to match water rates because in the 1850s the government had agreed to pay for the entire Washington Aqueduct on the condition that the District maintain local service. Congress negated this argument by forcing the city to contribute to the Aqueduct's current expenses and to the controversial Aqueduct Tunnel. Yet Congress refrained from making a more damaging rebuttal to disgruntled residents — that other appropriations bills provided them enormous hidden benefits that the United States did not figure as part of its 50 percent. Until 1890, Washington paid nothing for parks, an increasing burden on other cities. These were managed by the Public Buildings Office with funds from its accounts. Until 1893, Congress charged most municipal court expenses to the federal judiciary. In the 1880s, the Army Corps executed the $3 million Potomac Flats reclamation under the Rivers and Harbors Act.[34]

Serious stress on the fifty-fifty system appeared only in the late 1890s, when expenditure increases began to accelerate, mainly because the District had embarked on the first phase of large-scale capital improvements since Shepherd's reign. In 1884, the commissioners had declared, "Conservatism, measured by the actual necessities of an existing population, must be pursued until growing resources and a reduced debt shall warrant further liberal expenditures." Congress, they proposed, should work "hand in hand" to reduce debt service to an acceptable level while slowly improving services.[35] Unfortunately for the survival of the half-and-half plan, strategic factions in Congress and the city never reached a consensus regarding which services should have first claim on any added funds. As the debt burden lightened,

Table 5.5 Net per Capita Municipal Debt, Twenty Largest Cities, 1880

City	Population	Per Capita Debt
Washington, D.C.	177,624	$127.66
Jersey City	120,722	127.45
New York	1,206,299	90.71
Pittsburgh	156,389	90.38
Providence	104,857	89.39
Cincinnati	255,139	86.20
New Orleans	216,090	82.08
Boston	362,839	77.84
Brooklyn	566,663	67.13
Newark	136,508	66.44
St. Louis	350,518	65.18
Philadelphia	847,170	64.01
Buffalo	155,134	52.93
Cleveland	160,146	40.38
Louisville	123,758	39.19
Chicago	503,185	25.43
Detroit	116,340	19.62
Milwaukee	115,587	18.69
San Francisco	233,959	13.08
Baltimore	332,313	2.57

Source: Tenth Census of the United States, *Report on Valuation, Taxation, and Public Indebtedness* (Washington, D.C.: 1884), vol. 7, pp. 882–90.

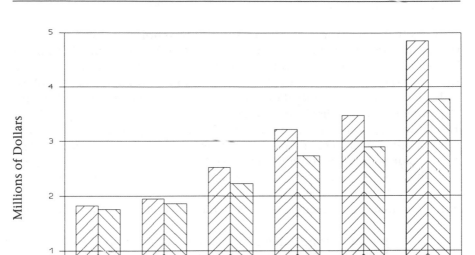

Figure 5.1 Average Contributions to District of Columbia Budget, Fiscal 1879–1902
Source: Auditor's statement in District commissioners' annual reports, 1879–1902.

those hoping to devote extra money to social services found themselves competing again with those who favored public works.

Gilded Age cities usually spent one-third to one-half of their budgets on education, health, and welfare. Washington was towards the low end of that scale. As debt service decreased, funding for schools and charities increased slightly faster than total spending. All other items retained a stable proportion of the budget, except public works, which recovered faster than social services. Its funds exhausted by the comprehensive improvements, Washington used less than 25 percent of expenditures for streets, sewers, and water during the period 1879–1884. By the turn of the century, however, the District was spending about the same on public works as on schools, police, health, and charities combined. Meanwhile, careful management of the sinking fund had diminished Washington's bonded debt to $15.1 million, a reasonable $54 per capita. With municipal debt under control and public works again dominating the budget, congressmen began to express skepticism about continued federal responsibility. Why, they asked, should federal taxes go to enrich further a city already in a stronger fiscal position than their own home towns? Had the new expenditures been on social services they might not have created the acrimony inspired by new public works.

The activities that received the largest expenditures were not necessarily the ones that commanded the lion's share of the commissioners' attention; the distribution of expenditures recounted in table 5.3 only roughly suggests how city executives spent their time. Thorny matters like liquor licenses and street car routes ate up far more time than money. Shortcomings in rubbish collection, which was handled by contractors supervised by the small Health Department, illustrate how the regime pursued solutions to vexing problems. The District spent much of summer 1895 contracting for an incinerator, a rubbish disposal panacea tried in many cities with disappointing results. The commissioners traveled to Philadelphia and Wilmington to view experimental plants. They listened patiently while entrepreneurs from Baltimore, Pittsburgh, and Chicago promoted the Dixon Furnace, which "will apparently burn anything," and the Engle Furnace, which created no "smoke or noxious vapors." [36]

After months of hearings, the commissioners decided on the method of one Samuel H. Brown and turned to the matter of a site accessible to garbage wagons. Foggy Bottom seemed appropriate, but influential residents from nearby northwestern neighborhoods insisted that prevailing winds rendered the "most remote eastern section" preferable. Southwest Washington neighborhood groups also protested, but the commissioners already conceived of that quarter as industrial. The plant was built at the foot of South Capitol Street. By April 1896, the collection contractor was protesting that the furnace never destroyed even two-thirds of what Samuel Brown claimed to be its daily capacity. Brown blamed Washington refuse, calling it "the soggiest and heaviest garbage that I ever saw." Brown also charged that residents hostile to the incinerator's presence plied his employees with drink and plotted to blow up the plant. The city reverted to shipping trash to dumps downriver and fighting with neighboring states. [37]

Congress assigned extensive legislative as well as executive powers to the Board of Commissioners. The commissioners made police, health, building, fire, traffic, and commercial regulations that had the effect of ordinances. [38] With no elected assembly to guide them, the commissioners felt pressed to find ways to reassure residents that these regulations, as well as their recommendations to Congress concerning pending legislation, satisfied some plausible definition of the public will. The board eventually adopted the practice of well-advertised public hearings on important matters. Yet whose opinion had more weight at hearings became a problem. Also, the board refused to vote in public; the triumverate made final decisions later, so that citizens could not know what arguments they used with each other. The commissioners did not even order all proceedings to be recorded until June 1895. [39] As opponents of Brown's incinerator discovered, sabotage was the most efficacious means by which to overturn an unacceptable official act. Pressure existed for a public organization that could serve as a quasi city council and exert discernible influence on the appointed rulers. This pressure resulted in the Board of Trade (discussed further in chapter 7).

IV

Under the 1878 act, Congress reserved to itself many powers held elsewhere by city councils and state legislatures. Allegedly, the diversity and talent of the Congress made it superior to a typical city council filled with ward hacks. Yet a congressmember's primary responsibilities are to constituents, party, state, and nation. For Congress, the capital was of necessity a secondary function, of occasional rather than continual importance, on the level of public lands and immigration.[40] Even the most dedicated members had to set aside District matters in favor of national finance, commerce, or defense. Congress may have offered more collective ability than a municipal council, but it could not possibly provide the same attention as a legislature with horizons confined to the city.

The leadership recognized that if Congress were to exercise its broad powers responsibly, it had to ensure that District business received adequate floor time, despite the desire of many members to focus on other matters. The two houses employed different rules to guarantee floor time to Washington. The Senate placed District bills on its regular committee call. This made it difficult to pass over Washington bills through suspension of the rules and, more important, gave the District Committee chairman opportunities to call up measures when the chamber was full. Senators resisted the idea of assigning special sessions to Washington, on the grounds that colleagues would not attend.[41] The House employed more rigid rules, reserving for District matters one legislative day, which after formalities meant a long afternoon. "District Day" was usually the second or third Monday of the month. Despite apprehension that Washington could not draw a quorum, having a special day afforded the District Committee certainty as to when they could bring their business before the House. The House District Committee encountered too much resistance from other panels to hold its own on the regular legislative call.[42]

In January 1880, the House District Committee resolved to abolish District Day. Committee members reasoned that if they were "on the same footing as to the introduction of bills as the other committees," Washington would "get more time for and a better consideration of its business." The following December, the panel abandoned the experiment and asked for its day back. During the 1880s, the House allowed Washington two days per month during long sessions, but the extra time could not offset apathy among congressmen. Both city officials and residents expressed frustration regarding the "general disposition of the House to trifle away" Washington's time.[43] The local suspicion that the Senate was a more reliable friend was well-founded. The Senate could use informal procedures regarding Washington, since partisan and structural differences from the House inclined the upper chamber to take a more consistent interest.

Democrats controlled the House for eighteen years between 1875 and

1895, while Republicans controlled the Senate for all but four years during the same period. Insofar as there were substantive differences in the major parties' approach to policy during the Gilded Age, Democrats continued to lean towards local-mindedness and anti-centrism, while Republicans retained much of the ambition for building a vigorous national state that had animated the party during Reconstruction. The chamber where Republicans were stronger would clearly be more likely to take an ongoing interest in the nation's city than did its rival, but structural differences between the House and Senate explain at least as much as party ideology.

In part, the Gilded Age Senate developed closer links to and a greater affection for Washington simply because its membership was more stable and its institutional memory longer. Until the electoral realignment of 1896, which began a period of relatively stable membership and hierarchical leadership, the House was volatile and more closely tied to the country than to the capital (which is, after all, what the founders intended). Over half the members of the 43rd and 44th Houses, 1873–75 and 1875–77, were freshmen. Turnover rates dropped to between 30 and 40 percent in the 1880s, but from 1888 to 1896, the party dominance between Republican and Democrat shifted from 166-159 to 88-235 and then back to 244-105.[44]

The Constitution makes swings of such magnitude impossible in the Senate. Senators were far more likely than representatives to enjoy long careers. Over time, the Senate amassed a strong core of legislators who knew a lot about Washington and had many friends there. Senators who had participated in the formation of the District commission, such as Joseph Blackburn and John Ingalls, were around to defend it. As long as William Allison remained Senate Appropriations chairman, the fifty-fifty plan was unchallenged. The House's discontinuity rendered such institutional memory difficult. Apathy towards Washington flourished easily in the chamber that was by nature less acquainted with it. Within fifteen years after the 1878 act, explications of the fifty-fifty plan had to accompany submission of the every District budget. At each session, the scheme ran a gauntlet of measures designed to overturn or undermine it, some sponsored by the relevant appropriations subcommittee itself.

The congressional District committees also reflected the different natures of the houses. They were among Congress's most venerable, dating from the origins of the standing committee system early in the century.[45] During the commission's first decades, the District committees controlled most Washington legislative business, the main exception being the budget, which went through the appropriations committees.

The Senate District Committee was more vigorous and effective than its House counterpart, because of the upper house's smaller size and its prestige and stability. While representatives were limited to membership on one or two committees, senators could be on three or four, so service on the District Committee did not prevent senators from also serving on more prestigious panels. "The only difficulty about giving all your attention to the District of Columbia," remarked chairman McMillan's secretary, Charles Moore, "is that it counts for nothing in Michigan, whereas Finance and Appropriations do count." [46] Although the District Committee was not first-rank in political terms, senators regarded it as a good committee to be on, because the work was interesting. For this reason, Senate leaders had little trouble recruiting influential colleagues to serve. At different points during the 1880s, such Senate powerhouses as Nelson Aldrich, John C. Spooner, and Arthur Gorman filled the ranks. In 1902, McMillan wrote his son, "My present committee brings me in contact with all the people here, which makes it very pleasant, and I have been able to accomplish some splendid work." The Michigan senator even rejected an offer to chair the Commerce Committee, despite the fact that Commerce had better office facilities, handled the immense Rivers and Harbors bill, and had been the stronghold of Senate legends Roscoe Conkling and Zachariah Chandler.[47]

In the House, competition for front-rank committee posts was tight. Places on secondary committees impeded careers. Ambitious members avoided the unglamorous posts. Some representatives now remembered for activities outside the Capitol served on the District Committee early or late in their careers, for instance, Fernando Wood, the dynamic New York mayor, Tom Johnson, the Cleveland progressive, and the first Adlai Stevenson. A number of House District members, such as Aldrich and Blackburn, became successful in the Senate. Yet none of the great Gilded Age congressmen — Randall, Reed, Cannon, et al. — ever served on the District Committee early in their careers.

The House's greater turnover rate and the political price a representative paid for serving on a secondary committee combined to produce the pattern depicted in table 5.6. Between 1863 and 1903, the Senate District Committee was more stable than the House committee, with regard to both the average number of congressional terms a member had served and the proportion of members who had served two or more terms. The higher one rose within the committees, the more this was true. In the Senate, the District chairmanship rotated, until 1879; but from then until 1902, three men, Isham Harris, John Ingalls, and McMillan, held the post. In the House, from 1863 to 1895, only three men remained for two terms as District chairman. After 1895, the House District Committee, like the chamber overall, exhibited more stability. Rudiments of a seniority system began to appear, with Wisconsin's Joseph Babcock serving as chairman through the end of the period studied.

Washingtonians often accused the Speaker of the House (who controlled committee assignments) of using the House District Committee as a dumping ground, an understandable charge, though perhaps unjust, given the political realities the composition of committees reflected. In contrast, residents praised Senate selections. Resident groups developed durable relations with senators, who became versed in local affairs and developed strong views on personalities and issues. The most consequential example was McMillan's al-

Table 5.6 Duration of Service on House and Senate District of
Columbia Committees

	Members Serving	Terms per Member[a]	Two-plus Terms	
			N	%
		1863–1873		
House	36	1.25	7	19.4
Senate	23	1.52	8	34.8
		1873–1883		
House	47	1.17	7	14.9
Senate	21	1.81	12	57.1
		1883–1893		
House	48	1.31	10	20.8
Senate	23	2.04	13	56.5
		1893–1903		
House	45	1.76	23	51.1
Senate	26	2.42	19	73.1

Source: Congressional directories, 1863–1903.
[a]Calculated by dividing the total number of positions on the committee over a ten-year
period by the number of different members who filled those positions. Committees were
appointed for a two-year term at the start of each Congress.

liance with the Board of Trade that in the 1890s pushed for regulated utilities,
renewed public works, suburban street openings, and park improvements.

The House District Committee compensated for turnover in its membership by having standing subcommittees more formal and active than the Senate's. In the 1870s, the eleven-man House committee was divided into an
unwieldy nine sub-panels, but in the following decade, the congressmen arrived at a manageable four: Ways and Means, Judiciary, Corporations and
Improvements, and Education, Labor and Charities.[48] Both District committees established the practice of referring bills to the commissioners for written
recommendations. The committees felt free to ignore proposals from the
commissioners, but they would rarely report in favor of measures the commissioners rejected. Congress made it obvious that proposals had little
chance unless they first went through the commissioners, thus relieving itself
of the vexing duty of arbitrating between disputatious residents. The commissioners did not object to Congress's using them as King Solomon, since it
made them indispensable players in the legislative process.

Indeed, whenever a District committee jumped the gun on a piece of District legislation, it risked freezing all city business before Congress, because if
the commissioners had not reconciled resident differences, each local faction
would find a congressman willing to take its case to the floor. In spring 1886,

a number of prominent Washington businessmen persuaded the House District Committee to report a charter for a cable streetcar line to the full House, even though the commissioners had not had a chance to conciliate substantial opposition from horsecar lines and homeowners along the proposed route. "Uncompromising antagonism" to the cable bill ate up so much of the city's precious floor time that only four bills of consequence passed that session. The commissioners were "disgusted," the *Star* wrote, that "measures which interest comparatively but few persons as corporators or single individuals should command the entire attention of the House to the exclusion of bills that interest the whole community." When supporters pressed the House District chairman to reintroduce the charter bill the next session, the chastened politician demurred: "The idea of chartering a company to run cars over your streets at the rate of 9 or 10 miles an hour strikes me as fraught with very great danger."[49]

V

To a degree, Appropriations Committee management of the municipal budget offset the District committees' flaws. Starting with fiscal 1881, Washington was the subject of an official appropriations bill. This guaranteed hearings by an influential subcommittee and floor time at the height of each session.[50] The drawback to having different committees handle policy and budgeting was, of course, turf battles. Throughout the last quarter of the nineteenth century, an intense dispute took place in both houses over the relation between the Appropriations Committee and other standing committees. This complex dispute involved regional and partisan interests, as well as personalities, but the basic issue was this: other committees accused long-serving Appropriations chairmen—Allison in the Senate and Samuel Randall and Joseph Cannon in the House—of using the budget to usurp policy prerogatives. The tug-of-war between the District committees and Appropriations reflects this broader battle. Until the reign of McMillan, who was Allison's neighbor and friend, the Senate District Committee "always had trouble with the committee on appropriations, because the latter badly needed to be convinced that the District committee knew what it was doing." Cooperation was hindered by the fact that at most two senators per decade were on the two panels simultaneously. McMillan's appointment to Appropriations in January 1902 promised improved coordination, but he died after only one session of service in both posts.[51]

Representatives also almost never held concurrent places on the Appropriations and District committees. Still, the other shortcomings of the House District Committee convinced Washingtonians to oppose distribution* of

---

Distribution of a budget means shifting management of a departmental budget from Appropriations to the relevant functional committee. The great power accumulated by Appro-

their budget in the lower chamber. In January 1892, House Democrats fought among themselves over which committee should control District spending. The *Star* was glad Appropriations won: "While the District committee, because only concerned with District affairs, has theoretically a greater acquaintance with local needs, on the other hand the appropriations committee, on which places are more highly prized, has greater permanence in its composition."[52]

Despite such tensions, Appropriations committees cooperated enough with District committees that "riders" became a common feature of the annual Washington budget bill, popularly known as the "District bill." In theory, Congress was not supposed to do anything in an appropriations bill other than spend money, for a simple reason. Should a measure that had bogged down as regular legislation reappear late in the session as an amendment to a spending bill, a form of legislative blackmail resulted, since Congress needed to pass departmental budgets before adjourning. Riders were most controversial in the aftermath of the Holman Rule of 1876, which expanded the legislative powers of the House Appropriations Committee. Accordingly, members would question whether rules permitted the District bill to authorize new services or public works, to change salaries, or to reorganize city departments. Nevertheless, both Appropriations committees on their own initiative and the District committees working through them employed riders to expedite contested measures.[53]

The rider controversy died down, and Congress displayed fewer misgivings about turning budget bills into grab bags. Under the dubious procedural formula of restrictions on expenditures, Congress enacted significant measures that placed electrical and trolley wires underground, limited support to sectarian charities, and reinvigorated Washington's personal tax. McMillan and Allison grew especially adept at using riders to the District bill to wear down House opposition to expensive projects that would have had no chance had they used the proper route. The senators' resort to the appropriations process to outfox the House reflects another characteristic of the Gilded Age Congress that affected District policy — the divergent attitude the two chambers exhibited regarding fiscal matters of all sorts.

The House staged intermittent revolts against the Democrat Randall or the Republican Cannon, when these notorious "economists" stifled appropriations strongly desired by this or that regional bloc within their respective parties. Resentment against Randall grew so great that in 1885 House Democrats stripped his committee of seven major spending bills and left it a shadow of its former self. Even so, while the lower chamber might chafe against Randall's and Cannon's stinginess, members did agree with them

---

priations chairmen such as Allison, Randall, and Cannon prompted many distribution proposals during the 1880s and 1890s, some of which were successful.

that, as a general rule, the House had a solemn obligation to review departmental requests with skepticism.[54]

The upper house did not duplicate this principled frugality. Senators would not tolerate more than a rare display of Cannon-like stinginess from Allison. In keeping with the Senate's overall inclination towards expansive national government, senators looked at Appropriations more as a concerned big brother than as a mean watchdog. The panel was supposed to remind the Senate that spending had limits, rather than scare it away from spending altogether. As Democrat James Beck argued in opposition to an 1884 effort to distribute the District bill, since functional committees had a "duty" to "promote the interests of their respective Departments," Appropriations was needed as a useful check when other panels pursued duty to excess. In part to accommodate such sentiments, Allison's committee concentrated less on conducting an independent review of departmental estimates than on making upward adjustments in spending bills sent over from the House. "It was a very rare occurrence that the Senate ever proposed a cut in departmental appropriations," wrote one historian. "The House of Representatives, which originated all appropriations bills, undertook the job of reducing departmental estimates."[55]

The Senate Appropriations Committee sent to the floor the first two District bills—fiscal 1881 and 1882—with $8,800 and $9,877, respectively, reduced from the House versions. For fiscal 1884, the Senate panel cut $76,645 from the House version of the bill and $115,116 from the fiscal 1883 municipal budget, with street work especially reduced. For 1885, however, the Senate Appropriations Committee requested an increase of $87,742 over the House bill, with more than half of the increase designated for street improvements. The Senate proposal for 1887 was $209,865 over the House version, an increase in expenditures of $198,844 over the previous year and only $18,341 under the commissioners' own estimates. For fiscal 1889, the Senate added $855,628, or 19 percent over the House version and 20 percent over the previous year. Most of this increase went for streets and schools. By now, the Senate clearly had espoused a "more liberal policy than the House."[56] During the 1890s, the two houses' bills diverged by over $1 million annually. Disparities between House and Senate versions of the District budget led to two or three grueling conferences each year that drove the Senate further towards a generous interpretation of the fifty-fifty system and forced the House into a vigorous defense of its "economist" line.

Senate budget panels accused House counterparts of "puerile and evasive" parsimony.[57] The House Appropriations Committee countered that the Senate was too willing to waste federal money to support real estate promotions and other projects in which the nation and the majority of Washingtonians had little real interest. The House insisted, with some justice, that its policy was generous compared to what officials in other American cities were then spending to improve infrastructure and services and that Senate criticism was misplaced.

Exasperation between the chambers burst into the open in 1887. The House Appropriations Subcommittee "devoted more time and labor to the framing of [the fiscal 1888 budget] than were ever before bestowed on a half dozen District appropriations bills." After "a good deal of trouble," the panel sent to the Senate a new scheduling system, designed to divert street pavement funds from sparsely inhabited land in far northwest portions of the District, where expenditures were thought to serve mostly land speculators, to east Washington, a region of small homeowners that had historically been neglected fiscally. The Senate sent the bill back with sixty-six amendments, including large paving appropriations, useful for "speculative purposes," mostly in the far northwestern section. Iowa Republican David Henderson, a future Speaker of the House and a friend of Allison since 1861, was irate. Henderson and his colleagues went into the conference resolved to oppose gifts to the northwest "nabobs," only to experience the "lecturing propensity" of the senators, who bluntly told the House negotiators that they did not know what they were doing. "I do not want a lecture unless I voluntarily go to one," Henderson told the House. Because "this House is entirely too indolent touching this District and its affairs," the Iowan contended, the lower chamber's point of view, "is hardly looked at" by Senate Appropriations conferees, who "have in a sense become fathers and guardians of all improvements with respect to the District of Columbia, especially those outside the boundary." The senators, the *Post* reported, "made a lot of noise" but eventually yielded to House demands to be "treated like gentlemen." After three conferences, enduring until 2 A.M. of the session's final night, the House gave ground on expenditures but won its main demand—the improvement distribution schedule to divert funds to slighted lower-middle-class neighborhoods.[58]

Henderson and his colleagues had regained initiative, but the House then squandered these gains in partisan wrangling. House treatment of the District bill during the early 1890s represented one of the few instances after 1878 in which partisan politics clearly affected Congress's overall District policy. During the fierce electoral contests of those years, each party felt the urge to turn every appropriations debate into a discourse on its overall superiority. Because of this, some time that the House set aside for the District budget was sidetracked to national issues—ship subsidies, silver, and trusts. Republicans and Democrats on the District Appropriations Subcommittee filled the remainder with mutual recriminations.

In March 1892, Henderson forgot arguments that erupted under his party's majority in 1890–91 and insisted that until then the parties had "worked together in respect to these appropriations without a thought about politics." Committee Democrats, Henderson claimed, had reduced by $1.5 million the commissioners' estimates, without studying their wisdom, simply because the majority "desired to point to a bill that passed this Democratic House as evidence of greater economy." Democrats proposed such severe reductions in the street budget that the city could not possibly have adhered to the paving schedule the House had just recently wrung from its real enemy in the other wing of the Capitol. "There are heavy and wholly unnecessary cuts made in the wrong places in this bill," Henderson concluded, "because of a great impending Presidential campaign."[59] The Republican Senate right away poured salt on the House's wound by voting $700,000 in increases, including a $100,000 subsidy to the 1892 National Encampment of the Grand Army of the Republic, scheduled for Washington in September, conveniently coincident with the campaign. House Democrats took four conferences to whittle the G.A.R. subsidy to $90,000 and to provide that it come entirely from Washington's revenues, without being shared by the nation.[60]

The Senate's liberal — or, as the House would have it, "loose" — view of the nation's obligations to Washington did not always prevail. Skirmishes between the chambers exposed limits beyond which the House would not go in using federal funds to embellish the capital. In 1886, the Senate voted with little dissent to purchase two thousand acres for Rock Creek Park, a proposal on the table since 1867. The House delayed action for four more years, despite criticism that delay multiplied the eventual purchase price. Representatives considered the park a boon to suburban real estate and so held out for complicated provisions to charge benefits to nearby property. Senate District Chairman Ingalls found the House demand "obnoxious," while Democratic leader Gorman thought it a "hardship." In 1890, with "no better adjustment" forthcoming, the upper house caved in. The most ardent Senate opponent of the park was Texas's Reagan, an exception that proves the rule, since in 1878 he had organized House moves to defeat the half-and-half plan.[61]

Also in 1890, the House forced the Senate to accept a provision to charge Washington half the costs of the new National Zoo, which to Ingalls was "a flagrant and glaring injustice," since the zoo was a project of the Smithsonian Institution and not the District. City officials considered the zoo bill a worrisome retreat from the 1878 act, as it forced the District to contribute to a federal agency whose expenses had until then been covered by the United States alone.[62] Through the 1890s, the Senate and House wrestled constantly over how to distinguish between Washington projects that were in the country's interest, and were thus covered by the fifty-fifty scheme, and those that concerned local enterprise alone, and thus were not a proper object for federal money.

VI

In the decades after 1878, the institutional and historical factors emphasized above were largely accountable for the way Congress managed its self-imposed role as Washington's board of aldermen. Members' personal or constituent interests accounted for far less, except with regard to a few individuals and constituencies. In keeping with Congress's historic stress on constituent work, legislators assumed that colleagues had a right — indeed a duty — to champion enterprises from their states that sought or already did business in the national city.

Members also assumed that the Maryland and Virginia delegations should have a privileged voice. Of thirteen House District committees between the end of Reconstruction in 1877 and the end of the period, in 1902, eleven of the committees included representatives from both adjacent states and the remaining two had members from one of the two states. In the same years, the smaller Senate panels included senators from both states on seven committees and from one or the other on five. Virginia and Maryland committee members were allowed to use these places to pursue state interests. Arthur Gorman, famed as the boss of the Maryland Democrats, employed his spot on the Senate District Committee to promote the Chesapeake and Ohio Canal (of which he had once been president) and other Free State enterprises. Senate District secretary Moore "found it desirable in the case of District bills affecting Maryland interests to discuss them with [Gorman] privately, well knowing that he could and would defeat in the Senate measures distasteful to him." Moore proved so successful at evoking the crusty Gorman's "affable" side that Gorman offered to have the Michigan journalist named a commissioner, should Moore want the job.[63]

Before the late 1890s, only the most successful House members could justify buying a home in the District, let alone investing in Washington enterprise. With senators, the case was different. Allison, a childless two-time widower whose private life was sad, resided at 1124 Vermont Avenue. McMillan hosted the nightly "School of Philosophy Club," the Senate leadership's informal poker game/governing group, at his nearby home, 1114 Vermont Avenue. The two friends made investments together; in addition, McMillan had real estate and utilities holdings in Detroit. Yet neither man employed his immense power in Washington for personal material gain. They drew satisfaction from the stature they had acquired in the community. Residents turned to them to iron out problems with national or local authorities. In June 1901, the District ruled that a fence proposed by a Mrs. Townsend at 2121 Massachusetts Avenue violated the building code. A friend of the woman asked Allison to intervene: "The Commissioners will do whatever you *tell them to do.*" Less than a week later, Commissioner Macfarland wrote Allison that, on account of the latter's "great services to the District, I am very desirous to gratify your wishes at all times. It is so in the matter of Mrs. Townsend's fence, and I shall endeavor to come to an agreement with your conclusion, although I have thought differently about it." Two days later, Macfarland informed the senator that the commission had granted the exception: "I may say to you frankly that my vote was determined by your request."[64]

One can imagine the board's response when, in April 1896, McMillan wrote that a carpenter at work near his house was annoying him. McMillan's disinterested endeavors on behalf of Washington aroused curiosity among casual observers of politics, since his conduct in the capital seemed to contradict his role as champion of "interests" and leader of "regulars" in Michigan. In his home city, this industrialist, merchant, and investor was a bitter rival to the popular Detroit mayor and Michigan governor Hazen Pingree, an innovative advocate of the regulation and public ownership of utilities. How could the bane of reform in one city be its bulwark in another? Moore, a former mugwump, who served as McMillan's political assistant throughout his Senate career, felt he needed to rationalize any apparent inconsistency: "While not a reformer in theory, in practice Senator McMillan often became one." The inconsistency was more apparent than real. McMillan despised Pingree's so-called reforms because he thought they established an antagonistic relationship between government and enterprise that would cause Detroit to stagnate. McMillan's activities in Washington aimed at a cooperative relationship with enterprise, in order to promote responsible, measured growth.[65]

Other national figures did take advantage of local opportunities for their own gain, despite potential conflicts of interest. John Sherman invested heavily — and often jointly with his brother, General William T. Sherman — in middle-class residential development, for instance in the areas on either side of North Capitol Street near the present Florida Avenue. The veteran politician never served on the District Committee, but he often intervened in local matters, including those where he had a stake. In 1890, Sherman threw himself into the railroad route controversy. He emphasized to the B & O's vice-president how routes in northeast Washington endangered students of the school for the deaf and did "great and permanent injury to all that part of the City, which would rapidly grow but for your present track." He added, "It is true I am interested in protecting my own property East of your present line, but I think this does not bias me." The distinguished Sherman's image as self-righteous "Prester John" animated gossip about his property dealings that would not have touched a lesser character.[66]

Moore felt that Washington real estate brought the Shermans wealth "by reason merely of the increase in population." Moore meant to contrast this passive approach to development with the dynamic strategy of the so-called California Syndicate. Far and away the most significant circle of political investors in this period, these flamboyant westerners did not wait for the city to reach their land. They used political and financial clout to redirect the flow of investment and the direction of growth.[67]

Nevada's first "Silver Senator," William M. Stewart, began to divert western mining money into Washington real estate in the early 1870s. Stewart's picaresque career started on a farm in New York's Burnt-Over district, then ran through Yale, a stint as a miner in the California Gold Rush, a term as

California's attorney general, and finally to a career as a lawyer for the West's mightiest enterprises, including the Central Pacific Railroad and the Bank of California. Fascinated by the potential of postwar Washington, Stewart was, by early 1871, persuading West Coast clients to put substantial sums into the emerging upper-class quarter around the present Dupont Circle. In 1873, the senator displayed his confidence by hiring Adolph Cluss to build a gaudy 19,000-square-foot mansion, on the north side of the circle, that became known as "Stewart's Castle," or alternately, "Stewart's Folly." Politics and business combined to turn the Nevadan into one of the Shepherd group's chief congressional allies. Stewart became so identified with the improvers that when Republicans considered naming him chair of the 1874 investigation, the cry of "whitewash" forced the party to turn to the unknown freshman Allison. Stewart remained on the panel, where he employed his frontier lawyer skills to discredit Cluss's dramatic testimony against his estranged friends.[68]

Among the clients Stewart had persuaded to invest in Washington was William Sharon, a coarse, cunning prospector who had accumulated a hefty share in the Comstock Lode. In 1875, Sharon suddenly acquired an interest in public service and employed the clout that his wealth gave him in desert politics to take Stewart's seat for himself. By the time Stewart returned to the Senate in 1887, the boorish Sharon had died and the Comstock fortune was in the hands of the tycoon's more urbane, principled son-in-law, Francis G. Newlands.

Under Newlands, the use of western mining money to reshape the nation's city reached its most energetic phase. A native of Natchez, Mississippi, Newlands grew up in genteel poverty in Washington, where his stepfather was a government clerk. Forced by lack of funds to leave Yale after two years, Newlands worked his way through Columbian (now George Washington) Law School and in 1870 migrated to San Francisco. He established himself as a corporate lawyer and married Sharon's daughter, who later died in childbirth. Revolted by how his father-in-law's partners used the Spring Valley Water Company to blackmail San Francisco in the 1870s, Newlands became an advocate of water conservation and land reclamation, causes with which his name is still synonymous. Meanwhile, Sharon's dissipated life led to the Sarah Hill breach of promise suit, one of the most protracted, twisted cases in California judicial history. To move the suit to more favorable federal courts, Newlands, who was named the estate's trustee in Sharon's will, relocated to Nevada, where the family was the second largest landowner. In the 1880s, the lawyer spent his own money building irrigation dams in the desert and providing water and parks for Reno. These activities helped him win Nevada's only congressional seat in 1892.[69]

By this point, Sharon's initial $160,000 investment at Dupont Circle had inflated by four times. Newlands, who did not want the bother of urban rental property, developed an unusual plan to sell the Dupont Circle holding and use the proceeds to establish a model suburb. Stewart quietly helped Newlands assemble a huge tract of farmland on the northwestern outskirts of the capital. By the time Newlands' $1 million Chevy Chase Land Company surfaced in June 1890, it held 1,700 acres in a wedge running from Connecticut Avenue and Rock Creek to three miles into Maryland beyond what is now Chevy Chase Circle. With Stewart's assistance, Newlands secured a charter for the Rock Creek Railway, to run from Boundary Street past the National Zoo and along a proposed extension of Connecticut Avenue. In January 1891, Washingtonians were astounded to read of Newlands's daring scheme, which, as he described it to a reporter, was "to establish a suburban town, connect it with Washington by a railroad line which will furnish quick transit, and then let the improvement at both ends build up the intermediate property." [70]

Newlands organized his enterprise according to the most modern business techniques. He turned to the best experts he could find, including landscape designer Frederick Law Olmsted. The company arranged a shopping district, a school, a library, a post office, a fire station, a community meeting room, a country inn, and a fashionable club. It provided sewerage and water and built an electrical plant for the subdivisions and the trolley. To keep the neighborhood exclusive, the company set minimum house prices and sizes and mandated design restrictions. One of Newlands's partners founded a bank and bought a realty firm, so that by 1900 the land company shared a downtown building (on F Street) with its main realtor and its supplier of mortgages. [71] This degree of vertical integration did not become common among residential developers until the great suburban tracts after World War II.

To keep his trolley afloat through the project's early stages, Newlands lent it money and negotiated transfer agreements with downtown lines. These measures were not sufficient, so Newlands secured a charter amendment that allowed the small suburban line to "contract with any street railway company owning or operating a connecting or intersecting line or lines for the joint management, lease, or purchase" of the *larger* company. Thus, it was Nevada silver money that underwrote transformation of the old Washington and Georgetown Railroad into the Capital Traction Company, which set off a wave of transit consolidations in the District. [72]

Chevy Chase Land Company lots went on sale in 1893; by 1895, twenty-four houses were under construction. The depression of that decade hampered sales, so Newlands had to devote more capital to his dream. Although in all Newlands spent at least $4 million from his own funds and the Sharon estate, the land company was still $1.5 million in debt when he died in 1917. Between 1918 and 1931, sales of more than $7.5 million finally made Chevy Chase one of the most successful of the early planned suburbs. [73]

Newlands encountered little criticism for his use of political position to assist his enterprise, in part because his plan was common knowledge before he was elected to Congress in 1892. The project was well under way before his promotion to the Senate in 1902. While Newlands's activities would violate conflict of interest rules that Congress now applies to itself, he was not the one for whom such rules had to be written. He retained his colleagues' good will by being honest and forthcoming about the "delicacy" of proposing, for example, that government agencies such as the National Bureau of Standards move to the northwest suburbs. He testified candidly to committees in defense of projects essential to his plan, such as the Connecticut Avenue extension. His plan was so innovative, organized, and long-term that good business minds in Congress and the District had to admire it. "Mr. Newlands," a rival realtor conceded to the House Appropriations Committee, "is entitled to more credit than all the rest of us put together." Finally, Newlands's efforts in Congress to improve services and amenities in other parts of the city defused opposition that might have arisen from concern that exclusive Chevy Chase would belong mainly to the rich.[74]

Newlands consistently supported the most comprehensive available forms of city planning. His proposals for Washington and elsewhere encompassed both the City Beautiful movement's emphasis on public space and matters that the City Beautiful approach tended to overlook—land use, traffic, water and drainage, and utilities.[75] The Nevada conservationist, therefore, slipped easily into the role of champion of the City Beautiful–influenced McMillan Plan after the Michigan senator's death in 1902. The developer/senator, in fact, embodied the alliance between politics and business that came to dominate the national city after the Board of Trade's emergence in 1889. Newlands was a one-man example of what progressive governance and political economy would mean for Washington, for good and ill.

Even though Newlands had a stake in Washington and McMillan did not, little difference appears in these senators' thinking about how the country should manage its capital. The Senate's institutional culture and leadership structure favored the background and mindset the pair shared, whatever their particular interests. While in theory there was a conflict between Newlands's role as senator, shaping national policy for Washington, and his role as a developer of residential neighborhoods, in practice the roles coincided. The businessman did what the politician would have wanted, even if they had not been the same person. Legislators who acquired the greatest influence over congressional policy for Washington after 1878 all assumed that, if the nation wanted its city to become more "worthy," the government had to encourage and assist real estate. Chevy Chase was real estate at its grandest.

McMillan and Newlands became sponsors of progressive-style governmental reform in Washington, but not because they rejected or seriously questioned the customary promotional approach to business-government relations. These Senate leaders instead argued that the hands-off "prime mover" posture that traditionally accompanied promotional governance was no longer enough. Government needed to be an active rather than a silent partner in the task of creating a world-class capital. Trained experts and public officials had to work continually and closely with landowners and entrepreneurs to channel their activities in what the two senators understood to be a humane, public-minded direction. The promotional tendency, therefore, remained ingrained in Washington's polity after the abolition of home rule. Congress's activities in the capital after 1878 continued to adhere to this longstanding feature of American political economy, albeit with modifications.

6

The Army Corps and Gilded Age Washington

This Stand-Pipe,
Built by
Inexperienced Army Engineers
with the People's Money
and without Authority of Law,
Is Preserved as a Monument
of Engineering Incapacity
and Official Duplicity

Proposed inscription, September 1887

THE FEDERAL GOVERNMENT'S most significant voice on the District Board of Commissioners was the member of the Army Corps of Engineers to whom one of the three seats had been consigned in the 1878 government act. Congress believed that by giving this commissioner control of Washington's municipal engineering, it was ratifying a custom that had developed over time. The Corps's role in planning and administering the capital's public works had expanded steadily since the 1850s. Even so, the military's role in Washington's Gilded Age polity was in some ways more troubling than the fact that civilian officials were unelected.

During debate over the 1878 act, a few lawmakers argued that the proposed engineer commissioner differed ominously from other civilian duties long delegated to the Corps. Military engineers came into frequent contact with the public through their supervision of flood control and navigation programs, but this circumscribed military involvement in civil affairs did not raise as many dilemmas as placing an active soldier in an executive position in a municipal government. The proposed office was unacceptable, asserted Illinois congressman Lorenzo Brentano, "in a country where the principle prevails that the military power shall always be subordinate to the civil power." Ohio's Jacob Cox admonished, "We seem to have turned back to those old provisions of the Napoleonic imperialism."[1]

Over the next two decades, the Corps's Washington activities came under sometimes bitter criticism. Rarely, though, did critics follow Cox and Brentano in asserting that the officers' position was illegitimate on philosophical grounds. Opponents usually charged that army engineers exercised power in an imperious way or that their training was too narrow to cope with modern urban services and amenities. Most residents and politicians who expressed themselves on the matter favored retaining a Corps of Engineers presence in the capital, though with more limitations than then existed. Even if most contemporaries did not give great weight to anxieties about incipient Napoleonism, these qualms provide a useful place to begin our discussion. While the army officers could strike residents as haughty Baron Haussmanns, the engineers were not trying to apply Napoleonic notions of public service to Washington. Members of the Corps shared the typical political beliefs of nineteenth-century America, including faith in republican self-government and the assumption that the state should aim to facilitate, not dominate enterprise. Army engineers, however, also participated in a military culture that encouraged notions of duty, nation, and public good that diverged from and could conflict with those of politicians or businessmen.

The Corps acquired enormous prestige in Washington during the 1860s and 1870s, but the agency's stature eroded thereafter. The "Aqueduct Tunnel fiasco" of 1888, a scandal resulting from the apparent failure of a six-year effort to expand the water supply, seemed to confirm the emerging case against the engineers. By the 1890s, the officers' archrivals — civilian professionals in municipal engineering, architecture, public health, and other aspects of urban affairs — were showing themselves to be more attuned to the way commercial civic leaders and their congressional allies had come to think about the national city. This, as much as any innate deficiency in the engineers' aesthetic tastes or technical ability, explains why McMillan's Senate District Committee and the Board of Trade increasingly encouraged progressive-style urban professionals to attack the military's position. The resulting agitation helped lead to the 1902 McMillan Plan, which, as chapter 8 describes, dramatically signaled that civilian professionals had arrived as a permanent factor in Washington's governance and that the Corps of Engineers' once-unmatched authority had declined.

I

Army engineers acquired their place in Washington more by circumstance than by design. Civil engineering schools began to appear in the 1840s, but, apart from the Rensselaer Institute, they remained insubstantial until after the Civil War. The American Society of Civil Engineers, founded in 1852, was the only important professional group before the 1870s.[2] As Congress fitfully expanded work on rivers and harbors after 1820, the U. S. Military Academy at West Point formed the one reliable pool of skilled technicians capable of preparing surveys, estimates, and designs. The prestigious engineer divisions (until 1863 the Topographical Engineers formed a distinct entity) attracted many of West Point's most impressive graduates. National politicians respected the engineers' considerable talents and relied on them more and more.

"Internal improvements" work pushed the engineers into a political minefield. Whether the federal government should sponsor public works at all was, of course, a bellwether issue in Jacksonian politics. Over and beyond the economic benefits alleged for federal navigation and flood control projects, such work constituted a form of political currency in the distributive state of the nineteenth century, where parties scrambled to hold together quarrelsome coalitions by doling out pork barrel benefits. As a recent historian notes, even though the Corps nourished a reputation for detachment, the agency of necessity grew highly political, perhaps more adept at navigating Congress than at containing the Mississippi. In a bureaucratic equivalent of a fishbowl, the Corps developed an institutional culture that stressed intense internal loyalty and high standards of performance and behavior. These qualities ensured that appropriations would be spent efficiently, without scandal, which endeared the group still more to edgy congressmen.[3]

The engineers received their first substantial assignment in the District of Columbia in September 1850, when Congress voted $500 "to make such examinations and surveys as may be necessary to determine the best and most available mode of supplying the city of Washington with pure water." Apart from public wells and special pipes that carried spring water to the Capitol and White House, the city of 40,000 had no municipal supply. The Topographical Corps submitted a modest $500,000 proposal to tap Rock Creek, but a fire in the Library of Congress in 1851 suggested that more water was needed.[4]

The task of preparing new plans fell to Lieutenant Montgomery C. Meigs, grandson of Madison's surveyor-general. Meigs was born in Georgia in 1816 but grew up in Philadelphia, where his father was a physician. Fifth in his West Point class, Meigs imbibed the ideals and traditions of the antebellum army so completely that he became a memorable eccentric. According to biographer Russell Weigley, the "rigidity and uncompromising devotion to orthodoxy" that Meigs encountered at the academy, combined with a Puritan family background and a classical education to give Meigs a "self-assured, uncompromising" sense of honor and duty.[5] The young engineer was as upright, proud, and ambitious as a Roman. The example offered by ancient Rome's magnificent engineering feats encouraged Meigs to conceive of public works in monumental terms. The capital of a continental empire should have an imperial water supply, he felt. The young officer pointed out to a hesitant Senate finance chairman that the aqueducts then supplying Rome were 1900 years old, "and in erecting a work to last a thousand years, should we not do it on a scale to supply the city for forty?"[6]

Meigs envisaged one of the most elaborate engineering feats yet attempted in the hemisphere. From a dam at Great Falls, twelve miles up the Potomac,

Capt. Montgomery C. Meigs, c. 1859, as he supervised construction of the Washing-ton Aqueduct. Courtesy the Manuscript Division, Library of Congress.

water would travel through a nine-foot conduit to a receiving reservoir that straddled the border between Maryland and the District. Along the way, it would pass over Cabin John Creek via the world's longest stone masonry arch, an amazing bridge 220 feet long and 105 feet high. From the receiving reservoir, the water would continue to a 37-acre distributing reservoir above Georgetown and then into the city by large mains, including a pipe over Rock Creek via another spectacular bridge, at Pennsylvania Avenue. For an initial $3 million, the capital acquired about 25 million gallons per day when the Washington Aqueduct finally opened in December 1863.[7]

What Weigley calls Meigs's "uncommon talent for lengthy polemics and self-justification by correspondence" proved instrumental in convincing the Senate, in March 1853, to adopt his expansive scheme. In recognition of the lieutenant's energetic fight for his plan, the War Department made him the first superintendent of the aqueduct and soon supervisor of Capitol and Post Office Building extensions as well. Within months, the thirty-seven-year-old Philadelphian had gone from obscurity to being one of the most responsible, acclaimed engineers on the continent. Meigs grudgingly shared credit for the Capitol's new dome and wings with architect Thomas Walter, but there is no doubt, as an official history records, that he "saw the Aqueduct largely as a memorial to himself." Envisioning himself as a modern-day Roman engineer, the designer erected along the route of the aqueduct twelve plaques to himself and his assistants, sprinkled with Latin mottos, "Dei Gratia," "Esto Perpetua," and "Fecit." When the Interior Department (which controlled the project during the war) wanted to implement a minor modification over unyielding opposition from the designer, Interior's engineer, buttressing the department's claim that Meigs was incapable of viewing his creation objectively, informed Congress that Meigs's name or initials were "stamped on nearly every piece of iron or brass connected with the derricks or machinery used for the construction of the work, and the hoisting gear of all stop-cocks and water gates." The most absurd display was at the Georgetown reservoir, where "the rise of each of the iron thirty-nine steps leading down into the pipe vault is composed of the initials, 'M. C. Meigs.' "[8]

Such egotism is easy to ridicule, but the nation profited from it. Meigs, declaring that the "honor and reputation" for the aqueduct "belongs properly to me," defended his project with the tenacity of a centurion against attempts to compromise quality or politicize contracts. The strong backing of Pierce's secretary of war, Jefferson Davis, helped guide the aqueduct through its vulnerable early stages. During the Buchanan administration, Davis, now Senate Military Affairs Committee chairman, sided with Meigs in a running feud with Secretary of War John Floyd, of Virginia, who hoped to wring political patronage out of Washington's water system. Meigs, by now a captain, disobeyed explicit orders to hire certain contractors or workers and to spend money in other ways he considered improper. When Floyd attempted to transfer the restive officer, Senate friends pushed through riders that required aqueduct funds "to be expended according to the plans and estimates of Captain Meigs and under his superintendence," a direct challenge to Buchanan's authority as commander-in-chief. Meigs's "very singular" behavior, the White House asserted, had become "dangerous to the subordination and discipline of the Army." A court-martial would have proved embarrassing, so Buchanan, in the autumn of 1860, permitted Floyd to send the unruly soldier to fortification work in Florida.[9]

Mounting charges of corruption and the confusion of the Secession crisis eventually led Floyd to resign. Meigs was immediately recalled. Accusations surfaced that before leaving the Cabinet for the Confederate Army, the war secretary had facilitated arms transfers to the South and had impeded the organization of Union forces. Although Meigs's fight with Floyd had no sectional aspect and his political friends included Jefferson Davis, the engineer was transformed overnight from insubordinate to patriot. A firm Unionist, Meigs by summer 1861 held the post of quartermaster general, where he performed logistical marvels that surpassed his earlier technical ones.

After the war, Meigs, now a general, retained a lively interest in the capital. His 1867 survey of European street construction, for example, emerged as a major element in Shepherd's Comprehensive Plan. After retirement in 1882, Meigs supervised one more Washington project, the eclectic red brick Pension Building north of Judiciary Square. Younger engineers sought his advice regarding proposed changes to the aqueduct, although his unquestioning faith in his original plan could be exasperating. In 1875, aqueduct superintendent Orville Babcock reported that Meigs's prize-winning Pennsylvania Avenue Bridge was too weak to accommodate streetcars. Forty-two one-hundred-pound decorative wreaths from the cast-iron arches, jarred loose by vibrations, had fallen into Rock Creek. Meigs publicly disparaged Babcock's suggestion for strengthening the bridge as "a useless act of barbarism" and dismissed hazards posed by falling iron blocks. The general's ferocious attack upon his successor helped delay reconstruction of the bridge until 1913.[10]

Meigs's impressive talents and memorable character helped accustom Washingtonians and congressmen to the idea of having military engineers manage the national city's public places and works. When Reconstruction politics led to the ouster of the last civilian public buildings commissioner, B. B. French, in 1867, Congress had few misgivings about transferring his duties to the Corps of Engineers. No agency was better suited to handle "questions of practical science and engineering, of architecture, of science, of taste," remarked Vermont Senator Edmunds, in explaining why a military rather than a civil engineer should succeed French.[11] Such praise obscured the fact that this transfer of authority was an afterthought; French's politics had made his remaining in the position untenable, and a replacement was needed in a hurry. Congress handed the Public Buildings Office over to the Corps at the end of a session, without defining the reorganized bureau's mission, procedures, or relations with the municipal public works officials. Congress thus perpetuated the administrative muddle that, as we saw earlier, became an underlying element in the District improvement scandal.

Meanwhile, the fight for the Union piqued the Engineers' interest in Washington and led them to sharpen their views on what would constitute a worthy national capital. By the time Grant's personal secretary, Major Babcock, took over as combined aqueduct superintendent and public buildings officer, in 1871, military engineers had developed the wide-ranging set of proposals that formed the basis for the Comprehensive Plan. To assist the territorial leaders in their pursuit of a shared goal, Babcock cast aside even the pretense of detachment and threw himself into the fray. If Meigs took the

Corps's ideals of honor and duty to an extreme, Babcock did the same with the Engineers' penchant for political combativeness.

Babcock was an 1861 West Point graduate with wartime experience building bridges and fortifications. The Vermont native, who at age thirty-six was eleven months younger than his friend Shepherd, lacked even surface commitment to political neutrality. In some eyes, Babcock's deep involvement in several notorious Republican intrigues — the Santo Domingo affair and the Whiskey Ring, as well as the District improvement scandal — "brought nothing but disgrace" upon the Corps.[12] Even Grant, whose ostrich-like loyalty perplexed contemporaries, became fed up with Babcock's skullduggery. After risking his own reputation to extricate Babcock from the Whiskey Ring mess, the great hero angrily dismissed him as secretary. Grant, however, allowed Babcock to remain as public buildings officer until the administration went out of office in 1877.

It was fortunate for the Shepherd group that Babcock rejected the stance of neutral engineer. The Board of Public Works badly needed the assistance of a well-placed military engineer to overcome political and bureaucratic resistance to its program. Babcock called upon the Corps's prestige, his influence with the administration and the Republican party, and the respect congressmen had for his engineering skill to push through Shepherd's appropriation requests and to facilitate acceptance of dubious accounts. Babcock's alliance with Shepherd expedited negotiations between local and federal authorities for extending street grades, pavements, sewers, water, and gas mains across federal property. As Cluss's testimony revealed, Babcock's office facilitated the Territory's efforts to charge the United States the maximum amount possible for such work.[13]

Partisan harmony between Shepherd's improver faction and the administration permitted this efficacious cooperation. Improver contractor Albert Gleason recognized the importance of Republican partisanship to Babcock when he proposed to grade federal property: "My record in regard to politics is clear and well known in this community and in that respect I have no hesitancy in presenting my claim to patronage from the government." Gleason may have had adequate political credentials, but he also felt it necessary to stress that Shepherd could guarantee his ability.[14] The contractor respected what Babcock's enemies were reluctant to admit — that the public buildings officer was not interested in Washington's public works for patronage reasons alone. Babcock truly hoped that Washington's amenities and appearance would improve under his care.

While Babcock's political and bureaucratic assistance was essential to Shepherd, he had only an indirect role in the actual construction of the Territory's streets and sewers. Of matters directly under Babcock's purview, parks engaged him most. In Washington City, the federal government owned ninety reservations, totaling 340 acres. These included the Mall and the White House grounds, substantial squares such as Lafayette, Mt. Vernon, and

Judiciary, and dozens of circles, triangles, and odd plots. Prior to the war, authorities had marked and drained some land, but overall unkempt federal parks contributed to the city's shabbiness. The Smithsonian grounds were embellished according to Andrew Jackson Downing's romantic design, but they lacked proper lighting, walkways, or police and remained a resort for "disreputable persons of both sexes" from the nearby Murder Bay slums. B. B. French and Major Nathaniel Michler, the first military public buildings officer, made ambitious plans for walkways, gardens, statues, benches, fountains, and ponds in the central city and as far away as Scott Circle, in the new northwestern neighborhoods, and Lincoln Square, in the eastern portion of Capitol Hill. Political connections and the enthusiasm generated by the Shepherd program gave Babcock a welcome opportunity to implement these schemes.[15]

To bring the reservations "into civilization," the public buildings officer drove away beggars and tore down shanties. He piped in gas for lighting and water for drinking and built tens of thousands of yards of sidewalks, curbs, drives, and fences. Babcock imported bulbs from the Low Countries and had trees and shrubs brought from as far away as Illinois. Interesting trees received "terra-cotta markers of different patterns." A thousand benches appeared, with iron frames and ash-wood seats, copied from patterns used in Baltimore and elsewhere. The benches were bolted down so that the public could not, by moving them, damage the miles of sod that had been planted to replace weeds and wild garlic.[16]

Eels up to three feet long that had been hiding in the fish ponds on the Capitol grounds were killed and replaced with carp purchased from local fishermen. As the carp multiplied, they were transferred to new ponds around the city, including two on the Washington Monument grounds created from remnants of reclaimed marshes. The bureau brought deer to the parks and maintained eagles and owls in cages on Franklin Square, until lack of funds compelled Babcock's successor to ship these "fine specimens" to the Philadelphia Zoo. To combat insects and provide cheerful music, carpenters built birdhouses for English sparrows, purchased at $2 per pair from a New York supplier of "rare animals [and] fancy fowls." Instead of battling rebels or Democrats, Babcock made war on boys who broke the birds' houses and stoned the hapless creatures. To the chagrin of later naturalists, the sparrows caught the fancy of politicians, who obtained permission to catch a few and ship them home, where the now-despised immigrants — "destructive vermin" with "hardly a redeeming trait" — propagated and drove out native species.[17]

In sum, Babcock completed twenty-five reservations, totaling 95 acres, and partially improved 145 more acres of government parks, many of which, he recounted, "were commons and public dumping grounds when I assumed the duties of the position."[18] Grant's intriguing friend instituted improvements to the aqueduct, built bridges over the Potomac and the Anacostia, and supervised work on the State, War, and Navy Building. Yet his feverish groundskeeping and his efforts to facilitate the Shepherd program affected the capital most profoundly. In 1871, when Babcock took over the Public Buildings Office, questions that had been left open when Congress abruptly ousted Commissioner French four years earlier remained unresolved. When a certain project involved both national and local interests, who was primarily responsible? On what basis would federal and District authorities work together regarding programs that concerned both? Acting unilaterally amid enormous controversy, Shepherd and Babcock created a division of labor that proved effective and endured for two decades. District engineers would dominate in municipal matters such as roads, sewerage, and utilities. On the other hand, even after army engineers took over municipal engineering in 1874, the District government had virtually no say over parks, federal buildings, monuments, and other matters within the Public Building Office's domain. Shepherd and Babcock were mainly interested in how to implement their plans quickly, but one side effect of their plotting was a viable division of duties and responsibilities. The army engineers needed only to persist along the lines laid down in the 1870s, and they could, with minimal bureaucratic friction, achieve most features of the worthy national city they had envisaged after the war.

II

By 1880, army engineers ran four separate bureaus concerned with public works in the federal district. Most visible and controversial was the District's Engineer Department, under control of the engineer commissioner. The public buildings officer often served also as superintendent of the aqueduct, as in Babcock's case. The Washington Engineer District handled Potomac River projects. In addition, temporary bureaus managed special projects, such as the Washington Monument, the State, War, and Navy Building, and the Library of Congress.[19]

The job of officer in charge of public buildings and grounds was very prestigious and desirable and was dominated by highly accomplished members of the Engineer Corps. Three of the five men who held the post between 1877 and 1901 had taught at West Point or at the Army Engineer School at Willets Point, New York. Of the exceptions, one was a member of the Quartermaster Corps while the other, Colonel John Wilson, served as West Point superintendent between two terms as public buildings officer, during 1885–89 and 1893–97. Two of the men rose to chief of engineers — Wilson and Colonel Thomas L. Casey, who is famous for finishing the Washington Monument.[20] The term of the office was coincident with presidential terms. There was probably a political element in the officers' designation, but the War Department kept this discreet.

Between Babcock's time and the mid-1890s, federal reservations did not generate much public discussion; the Public Buildings Office went about its business largely out of the public eye. Because later landscape architects, influenced by Beaux-Arts ideals, disdained mid-century romantic eclecticism, they dismissed this steadily productive period as an era of shameful negligence. The great leaps of the McMillan Plan would have been impossible without the gritty preliminary work of surveying, draining, and fencing, so army engineers were understandably offended by the architects' portrayal of their management.

The Army Corps participated only indirectly in the era's most durable landscape design in central Washington, Frederick Law Olmsted's Capitol grounds, which came under the Architect of the Capitol.[21] The old civilian commissioner of public buildings and grounds had handled day-to-day upkeep of several major public buildings. Only in the White House did the military public buildings officer inherit these custodial chores. In addition to directing receptions and minor improvements, the officer had to ensure that the President's environment remained pleasant. Throughout the Gilded Age, this meant waging a guerrilla war with rats. In 1877, Colonel Casey promised $50 to one A. R. Thornett, whose remedy had earned a testimonial from Willard's Hotel. When the rodents continued their forays into the executive kitchen, Casey refused to pay. The first Cleveland administration offered a reward for the best solution. When the contest reached European newspapers, the annihilation of the American President's rodents became an international enterprise. The solutions amused State Department translators but killed few vermin. Mme. Honoré of Savoy advised Cleveland to lure the beasts under a jar and grab them by the tail. A lady from St. Petersburg explained that "un moyen sûr à faire disparaître les rats envahisseurs du répos du Chef de l'État" was to fry bits of sponge in butter, so that scurrying visitors would explode when they ate them. A French cheese merchant advised torturing one unfortunate captive, whose cries would frighten comrades away. One Parisian offered to reveal his infallible secret if M. Cleveland paid his passage to America.[22]

In the twenty years after 1877, the Public Buildings Office was quietly productive. Likewise, while the engineer commissioner's office provoked debate and the aqueduct experienced scandal, the riverfront projects of the Washington Engineer District progressed steadily, without controversy.

Surveys and navigational projects on the Potomac remained the responsibility of the Baltimore Engineer District until the aftermath of the 1872 River Commission, in which the Territory's leaders, the chief of engineers, and the superintendent of the Coast Survey together contrived a plan to reclaim the festering Potomac Flats. The Engineer Corps set up a separate district office for Washington in anticipation of the enterprise, which meanwhile bogged down in Congress during debate over the District commission plan. Soon after their installation, the permanent commissioners stepped up pressure on Congress to begin work. Major William Twining, the first engineer commissioner, modfied the proposal so that the channel closest to the District shore

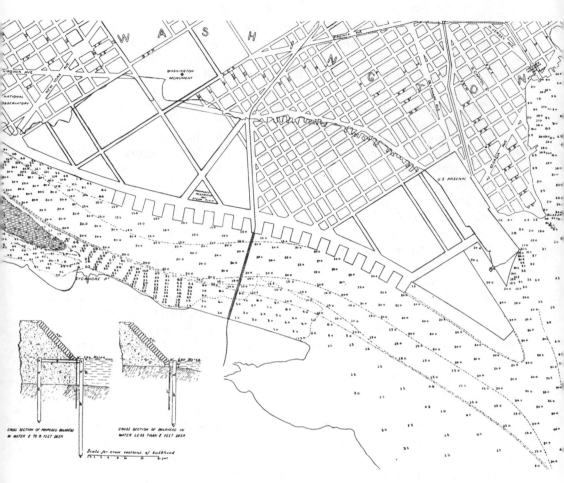

A preliminary drawing, from 1878, of the Flats Reclamation plan. Under this version, the Washington Channel and old riverbank would have disappeared and half the landfill would have been designated for development. Courtesy the U.S. Army Military History Institute, Carlisle, Pennsylvania.

would end in "flushing lakes" or "sluicing ponds," which would prevent stagnation and the silting caused by tides. This is the origin of the Tidal Basin. Despite downtown floods in 1877 and 1881 and accumulating filth from the B Street sewer, Congress kept postponing an undertaking that had come to be regarded as inevitable. "The miserable plea of its expense" was the reason—estimates began at $2 million. Various ideas for generating revenue emerged. These included farming out the project to land developers, a scheme similar to ones that had proved lucrative on Boston's Back Bay. The Washington District of the Engineer Corps fought such plans, insisting in-

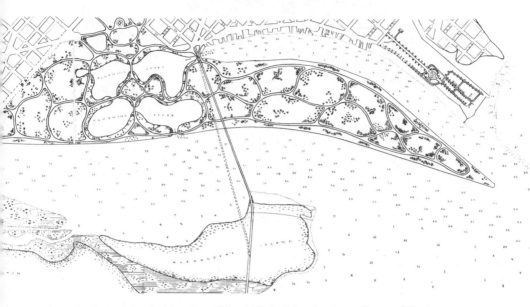

A projection of the finished landfill, published by the Army Corps of Engineers in 1883, when work had just begun. In this version of the plan, the Washington Channel was reinserted, "flushing lakes" — what was to become the Tidal Basin — were added, and the entire reclamation area was set aside for parkland. Courtesy the U.S. Army Military History Institute, Carlisle, Pennsylvania.

stead that at least one-third of the estimated six hundred or seven hundred reclaimed acres be reserved for parks.[23]

The need to clean up the Potomac Flats was underscored when President Garfield, after lying ill for weeks in a humid White House, failed to recover from the gunshot wounds inflicted by an assassin in the summer of 1881. Twining and his colleagues lined up public health experts from throughout the Northeast to assert that the Flats constituted Washington's principal source of malaria. Twining rehearsed why reclamation was a "necessary step so far as the sewerage of the city is concerned." In the process, he persuaded the Senate that a less expensive alternative proposed by the pugnacious George Waring, the nation's best-known sanitary engineer, was based on "ignorance of the facts." After a few months more grousing, Congress provided a $400,000 installment.[24]

To execute the project, Congress naturally turned to its experts on river projects, the Corps of Engineers. Since reclamation of the Flats was exactly the type of job the Corps was geared to perform, it is not surprising that it progressed smoothly. In 1897, after fifteen years, with 621 acres recovered, and with the difficult phase of the project finished, the Engineer Corps boasted that the projected cost was only $236,655 over the original figure of

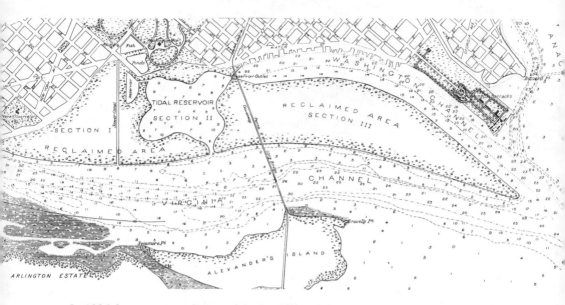

In 1896, between completion of the landfill and Congress's designation of Potomac Park, two obstacles to the park's embellishment—Shepherd's B Street sewer canal (left of tidal reservoir) and the old Long Bridge causeway (right of reservoir)—still traversed the area. Courtesy the U.S. Army Military History Institute, Carlisle, Pennsylvania.

$2.7 million. This was unbelievable, remarked the project's superintendent, "when one considers that the original estimate was made about 1882 and that the work since then has been subject to fluctuations in prices of labor and materials" and other "contingencies." The contingencies included flood damage and erosion in years when Congress neglected to provide any funds.[25]

The army officers supervising the project deployed the Corps's political talents to confound attempts to put land wrought from the river at private disposal. As reclamation progressed, the Engineers and District officials could see less sense in parting with any of the new peninsula that stretched gracefully in front of the old riverbank. "These flats are capable of being transformed into one of the finest parks in the country," they insisted. One obstacle was a convoluted lawsuit by an old associate of Hallet Kilbourn, John L. Kidwell, who believed he held a patent to the swamps, which he gave the bucolic name of "Kidwell's Meadows." The greater threat came from railroads, tempted by empty land in a cramped city. The Pennsylvania Railroad was extremely unlikely to consent to rerouting its line, which ran over the Flats into Virginia via the dilapidated Long Bridge. Yet each annual report of the Washington Engineer District reiterated that the bridge impeded the Potomac's flow and thus threatened the expensive landfill. Engineers reminded the nation that the railroad had gained use of the bridge for free, first as a war measure and later on the promise that it would rebuild the bridge. This campaign ensured that the bridge would eventually be reconstructed, largely at the railroad's expense.[26]

The War Department and the District fought encroachments by additional companies. In April 1894, District commissioner John Ross wrote a fourteen-page letter chastising Senate District chairman Isham Harris over what he said was the sixth proposition that year to open waterfront parks to new tracks. Ross enlisted the Board of Trade in a campaign to create Riverside Park. Politicians found that name "common-place," so when Congress gave final victory to the Corps and its allies in 1897, it chose the name Potomac Park. The Lincoln and Jefferson memorials now share this one-time pestiferous swamp with sports fields, a golf course, and pleasant river walks. Rail lines still disfigure the area, but subsequent automobile roads do more damage.

III

In the decades after 1878, Washingtonians and national lawmakers made few serious criticisms of either the public buildings officers or the engineer officers who oversaw improvements to the Potomac riverfront. The District's engineer commissioners were not so fortunate. The wrangling that surrounded this position arose less from individuals who filled it than from the position itself, which created an inherently tricky relationship between local people and the officers responsible for their public works. While other Corps officers dealing with Washington remained under the authority and protection of the chief of engineers, the 1878 act detached the engineer commissioner from the normal military chain of command and made him a full partner in the District commission. The bill delegated executive authority over the everyday affairs of a populous city to an active member of the military, a situation with virtually no precedent in U.S. history or support in its political thought.

The Engineers were strangers to neither the nation's nor the capital's politics, yet having them build or maintain specific projects does not present the same dilemma as consigning to a military office one-third of a municipal executiveship. While work on rivers and harbors had promotional and developmental uses for cities and states fortunate enough to secure the needed appropriations, the benefits from such improvements were general, spread throughout the local economy. The engineer commissioner and his assistants were charged with ongoing supervision of essential services that connected directly to private property. The military men would need to exercise discretion regarding proposed projects that would enhance some people's property as opposed to others'. An elected official may properly declare himself amenable to a program that favors some interests over others. A military officer pledges himself to the nation, not a constituency, and is not supposed to take stands that are political in this way. What criteria could an officer use to determine whether a project sought by some residents but fought by others was for the country's good or harm? An engineer who sought to transcend parochial concerns and base his actions on national interest rightly risked being regarded as imperious by residents. An officer who threw himself too completely into local quarrels risked undermining his legitimacy, since public acceptance of the Engineers rested on their being above the fray.

Until 1874, the Army Corps had no fixed role in Washington's municipal public works. While the Corps exerted great influence on Shepherd, the Board of Public Works by law included a *civil* engineer. The June 1874 interim government act abolished the board and stipulated that its duties be transferred to a military engineer. Congress imagined that the technical skills and administrative practices the Engineers had developed for rivers and harbors work could be applied to urban public works. The Allison report argued, "Whatever work is done will be well done, and by an officer responsible to the Executive and to Congress."[27] As we saw, Lieutenant Richard L. Hoxie, municipal engineer under the interim commission, did not deal with the mess left by the Board of Public Works in anything like an apolitical manner. Opinion split as to the success of this experiment in "military government." Hoxie's articulate analyses of the shortcomings of Shepherd's program won as many friends as his lavish use of 3.65 bonds to complete that program made enemies.

Skeptics cited Babcock and Hoxie as proof that military engineers were not necessarily more trustworthy than civilians, yet the bipartisan architects of the permanent commission persisted in believing a military presence "the best guarantee," as Representative Blackburn said, of "honest, fair, and impartial" management. Indeed, while Hoxie had in theory been subordinate to the interim commissioners, Blackburn's bill gave the engineer commissioner virtual veto over public works matters. The Kentucky Democrat rationalized Hoxie and Babcock as exceptional for one reason or other. If the point was "to secure a non-partisan civil administration," then "there is no set of men to be found in all this land who have maintained through war and peace an escutcheon more perfectly free from stain or blot." With a member of the Corps of Engineers as the commission's "third man," Washington's public works "ought not to be burdened with politics," he reasoned.[28]

Some lawmakers found Blackburn's reasoning hard to swallow. Ohio's Jacob Cox, a former interior secretary and one of the era's more intellectual politicians, offered a substantive critique. Cox asserted that the Army Engineers' "excellent qualities" manifested themselves best when an officer was "employed under the sanction, the restraints, the kind of subordination, to which he is commonly subjected." Cox speculated that the engineer commissioner would have trouble:

He is unaccustomed to civil administration. He is and should remain a military officer as contrasted to a civilian. The considerations which have most weight in his mind are not those which a civilian would give equal importance to. His methods will be different, his ideas of rule and subordination will be different, his relations to his equals and inferiors will not and cannot be those demanded by our political life. He would cease to be a soldier if in these respects he should become a political governor. The history of our Army, like that of the whole world, establishes this.[29]

Legislators of this mind proposed either to substitute a civil for a military engineer or to maintain the officer in a subordinate position, as under the interim board. Yet the only important restriction on the engineer in the final version of the bill was that he be at least a captain. Blackburn contended that the purpose of this was to guarantee Washington an experienced person, but the provision was also aimed at excluding Hoxie, whose powerful supporters, including Senator Allison and the Sherman brothers, then came to the young man's rescue and arranged that he remain as one of two military assistants afforded the engineer commissioner. Perhaps a friendlier gesture would have been to arrange a transfer far away, because Hoxie had gone from the frying pan to the fire.[30]

The fact that tours of duty in the capital were glamorous and sought-after complicated problems inherent in the engineer commissioner's post. The War Department felt pressure from the ranks to make appointments for reasons other than how well someone might work with other city officials and the local people. In choosing engineers for Washington, the Corps appears to have taken the standing of an individual within the agency as seriously as his likely rapport with the public. Although not as high-ranking and distinguished as the men chosen to serve as public buildings officer, all ten engineer commissioners between 1877 and 1907 had solid records in fortifications, navigation, or topography. Four later became chief of engineers, including Lt. Colonel Henry Robert, author of *Robert's Rules of Order*. Several later had successful careers in civil engineering, including Captain William Black, destined to be both chief of engineers and president of the American Society of Civil Engineers. However, only one commissioner had substantial municipal public works experience before coming to the capital. Colonel William Ludlow had been on extended leave as chief engineer of the Philadelphia Water Department when in 1886 he was brought in to offset rising resident hostility on account of the aqueduct tunnel. Ludlow proved a well-intentioned but, for Washington, unfortunate choice, as we shall see shortly; but his mixed record at Washington did not affect his ascent in the army, and he later served as governor of Havana and president of the Army War College.[31]

Three officers advanced to commissioner after experience as one of the two assistants. These included Captain Lansing Beach, who made strides toward allaying tensions between the Corps and the capital's commercial and civic elites. Yet the tenure of Beach (1898–1901) illustrates as well how the exigencies of military and municipal politics could clash. Beach first became commissioner on an interim basis when the incumbent, William Black, left for the Spanish War in 1898. When the war ended later that year, civic leaders successfully petitioned McKinley to retain Beach rather than recall Black, whose relations with the public had been strained. In 1901, Beach was ordered to Detroit. The Corps considered the tour of duty over and wished to "compliment" his replacement, Colonel John Biddle, then chief engineer in the Philippines. Washingtonians complained that just when an officer had been in the District long enough to learn his job properly, the army sent him elsewhere. Allison sought to have the order retracted, but for Beach to permit defiance of army protocol in his behalf a second time would have endangered his career. The captain politely thanked the formidable senator for his support, but said, "If effort should be made to change the order, I would probably appear to my brother officers of the engineer corps to be trying to hold on to my detail at this very pleasant place." Beach was prudent to respect such sentiments, because in 1920 he became chief of engineers and later built a thriving practice consulting for cities and industries in the United States and Mexico.[32]

The remaining officers assigned as assistants to the engineer commissioner between 1878 and 1902 were less notable, yet they also stood above their peers in the Corps. Although none ranked higher than captain upon appointment, all who made a career in the army eventually became at least lieutenant colonel. Overall, the engineers detached to Washington were an elite group within a unit that was already the army's pride. They epitomized West Point's best contemporary standards and ideals. One consequence of this was that their reports on the national city's public works were written with a clarity and flair that we no longer demand from engineers and that we seem actively to discourage in soldiers and bureaucrats. Officers relieved dry public documents with graceful wit. This is how Captain Hoxie explained his preference for "combined" sewerage over the popular George Waring's scheme for "separate" drainage and waste sewers:

> Similar hallucinations have misled the wisest of men. It is related of Sir Isaac Newton that, having a pet cat which was permitted to share the solitude of his study, he had a hole cut in the bottom of the door to give her free entrance and exit. Missing her from the study for a few days, he was informed the trouble was — a kitten, and starting suddenly from one of those reveries to which science owes so much, he exclaimed, "Well, cut a little hole for the kitten."[33]

As Cox had imagined, members of such a close-knit, high-minded institution did sometimes lack patience for the dismaying give-and-take of city politics. Many officers had healthy relations with residents. However, especially after the accession of Major Garret Lydecker as combined commissioner and aqueduct superintendent in 1882, residents became as quick to disparage the Corps as they once had been to praise it. In a series of press interviews in

1883, leading District businessmen claimed that the officers were "often positively insolent" towards them. Businessmen accused engineers of "contemptuous disregard of our expressed wishes." "The engineer department seems to run the District government," complained a realtor to the *Star*. A respected old citizen concluded, "Of course, Major Lydecker, being an army officer, does not feel towards us as he should."[34]

Suspicion on the part of business and civic leaders was not the only dilemma facing the officers. The fact that the Engineer Department was reorganized at least four times in two decades indicates that the military engineers did not solve the District's public works muddle easily. Even to decide what tasks constituted municipal engineering created problems. Streets, sewerage, and water obviously formed the core. Other duties shifted in and out of the department or landed there for want of somewhere better to go. Since draft animals, tools, and construction materials formed the most valuable parts of the public inventory in the 1880s, the city's property clerk reported to the engineer commissioner, who thus also had to keep track of the city's beef, ham, ice, boots, stationery, and schoolbooks. Important gray areas tended to involve enforcement of technical regulations against private property, for example building inspection and utilities regulation. These duties required not only engineering skill but thorough acquaintance with the local business community, a quality that residents lamented the War Department did not give incumbents time to develop.[35]

The officers devised a crude but workable distinction between "surface" and "subsurface" functions and created two separate divisions. Each assistant engineer was charged with day-to-day management one of these divisions. This arrangement freed the engineer commissioner from operational work, enabling him to fulfill his executive duties at least as thoroughly as his civilian partners. By 1902, the Surface Division included the computing engineer (who handled contracts for paving and grading), the superintendents of streets and alleys, country roads, bridges, the city surveyor, and the parking commission. The Subsurface and Building Division encompassed water service and rates; sewer construction and maintenance; regulation of buildings, elevators, and plumbing; and repairs to city buildings.

Washington's Sewer Department became so widely respected that its civilian superintendent was hired to plan Havana's drainage after the Spanish-American War. Individual segments of the capital's sewerage had been well designed and executed, but until the mid-1890s, the overall system was in stalemate. Impressed by Hoxie's and others' criticisms of the territorial sewers, the Senate gathered an assortment of new plans in 1878. In a display of wishful thinking, Congress and the commissioners then accepted the argument that the Flats reclamation would mitigate the drainage problem for "the life of the present generation." This despite repeated warnings from various sources that the unsightly open channel built by Shepherd to carry the B Street sewer's discharge across the Flats from the old riverbank not only disfigured the future park, but would cause mischief in a flood. Indeed, during an 1889 freshet, the most severe on record, the sewer canal overflowed by thirteen feet and spilled raw waste over the reclaimed ground. By the mid-1880s, Congress had come to understand the need for "well-matured" sewerage but, having recently funded both the reclamation of the Potomac Flats and the aqueduct tunnel, was reluctant to embark on a third expensive enterprise. District engineers had little choice but to concentrate on stop-gap measures that in the long run exacerbated pollution, for example diverting waste to the Anacostia River, which developed its own malarial flats.[36]

Rancorous controversies arose over expedients adopted by the Surface Division to stretch chronically inadequate appropriations for streets, alleys, and sidewalks. These fights illustrate the hazards facing military men who try to navigate private interests the same way politicians do. The Engineer Department attempted to circumvent a three- to four-year backlog on the regular paving schedule by negotiating with residents and developers in the permit system. With the abolition of special improvement taxes in 1878, the municipality had to cover the full cost of projects carried out on its regular schedules. A block that petitioned for a permit, however, could jump the schedule by agreeing to pay half the costs, in effect a back-door reintroduction of the special tax. Since residents of the prosperous northwest and developers in the suburbs obviously had an easier time finding the requisite deposit, east and south Washington groups bitterly complained that permits enabled already privileged quarters to increase their advantages at a time when only one-fifth of streets east of the Capitol had pavements. Congressmen sympathetic to east Washington insisted that the Engineers' course amounted to collusion with real estate syndicates, whose projects might "in time be used by the public" but were at that point "entirely speculative." In contrast, the Engineers viewed the permits as "exceedingly valuable." They offered, in Hoxie's words, a "very unfair but unavoidable means of eking out a small appropriation."[37]

Awkward use of the permit fund to sidestep a tight street budget exacerbated neighborhood rivalries and undermined the officers' image of impartial public service. Yet fiscal discipline had the more desirable effect of spurring technical ingenuity, which led to the development of an asphalt that combined durability, cleanliness, cheapness, and comfort better than had any previous material. Observers who deplore how the automobile has destroyed urban street life retrospectively question the emphasis on smooth roadways that emerged late in the last century.[38] As long as the car stayed a toy, few doubted that Washington's engineer officers had advanced the cause of livability in the city.

Washington's army engineers inherited their interest in asphalt from the Board of Public Works. As we saw earlier, the rebuilding of Pennsylvania Avenue in 1876–77 suggested that natural pitch resulted in a more durable street than the coal-tar mixtures favored by Shepherd. Obstacles still stood in the way of a general asphalt pavement program. The most galling resulted from dozens of miles of wooden block pavements still decomposing on northwest streets at the time of the permanent commission's formation. Plans for improving Capitol Hill streets and those in south Washington, already overdue, sat on the shelf for seven more years while the District devoted most of its street budget to replacing Northwest's "black muck." Also, some still doubted whether asphalt would really prove the material of choice. It cracked in cold weather and "rotted" at the edges, necessitating repair and resurfacing costing up to $150,000 annually.[39]

Old-fashioned alternatives — cobblestone, macadam, and rubble — simply seemed retrograde. Stone blocks were virtually repair free, which offset their high initial cost, and they offered more secure footing for horses than slippery smooth materials. Granite was popular in Europe, but it caused unbearable noise. As in most American cities, "vigorous protest" from Washington homeowners confined stone to commercial streets, where merchants, too, came to hate it. Seventh Street retailers eventually blamed their relative decline on the unwillingness of Congress's notorious skinflint, Joseph Cannon, to let through an appropriation to have their stone blocks removed.[40]

By the late 1880s, the Army Corps had committed Washington to asphalt, either in the familiar sheets or in blocks, which, while easily installed and repaired, were too fragile for well-traveled thoroughfares. Preference for natural asphalt made inevitable a showdown with a network of contractors, known as the Asphalt Trust, who controlled imports from high-quality sources in Trinidad and Switzerland. The key figure in this network was a former Oberlin theology student, Amzi Lorenzo Barber, whose ascent to the title "Asphalt King" began at Washington in 1872, when he left a teaching post at Howard University to try his luck in the Shepherd-era real estate and contracting boom.[41] The Army Corps first clashed with the Asphalt Trust during the interim commission, when Barber and other contractors who had survived the wreckage of the Territory tried to use patents to inflate asphalt as high as $4.30 per square yard. At this point, Hoxie routed the contractors by ignoring the patents, opening asphalt contracts to competitive bids, and daring Barber's combine to sue. The cost of asphalt in Washington plummeted to as low as $1.75 per square yard.[42]

Barber turned the tables on the District by compelling rivals he failed to absorb to come to him for raw materials. Through painstaking negotiations with British colonial authorities, the Asphalt King secured a lease of Trinidad's main pitch lake, a coup that accounts for the giant Barber Asphalt Paving Company having laid half the asphalt in the country in 1896.[43] Slowly, the King nudged his product back to $2.25 per square yard. Congress then stepped in and set a $2.00 ceiling. This stringent limit forced the Engineers temporarily to abandon asphalt for the coal-tar mixtures which had proved disastrous for Shepherd, but with which the Engineers had slightly more success.[44]

In 1893, with prices still hovering around $2.25 for pavement with a standard base, the Corps sent the Barber forces reeling by arranging with a New York company to lay material drawn from a Venezuelan pitch lake just across the Gulf of Paria from Barber's Trinidad stronghold. For three years, Washington enjoyed a paving war. That two members of the combating forces had once worked in the local street department added to the spectacle. Barber's vice president, Lieutenant Francis V. Greene, had been assistant commissioner in charge of the Surface Division in the early 1880s, even opposing Barber at the time. The New York firm's superintendent, an accomplished Belgian engineer named E. J. De Smedt, had been Washington's asphalt inspector through the 1880s. Helped by the Depression, prices dove to unprecedented lows before stabilizing around $1.75 or $1.80. Barber made peace with the New York firm but quarreled with them again over their crude meddling in Venezuelan politics. With the Asphalt Trust in disarray, asphalt became the chosen paving material and one of the capital's distinguishing marks. By 1896, Washington had 120 miles of smooth pavements and only 60 miles of all other sorts. The city ranked second only to Buffalo in yardage of asphalt and was admired by civil engineers around the world for ingenious product testing.[45]

IV

The military feature of Washington's government allowed a degree of consistency in infrastructure policy not easily attained by other American municipalities before the Progressive era, or even since. While the background, ability, and professional standards of civil engineers still varied widely, military engineers shared common training and a high level of ability. As important, because these military engineers remained on active duty while serving in an unelected city government, they were two steps removed from pitfalls normally faced by city engineers during this period. Elsewhere, engineers' long-range plans for systematic services were often thwarted by mayors and aldermen whose horizon was the next election and who shared the popular bias against experts and bureaucrats. Although municipal engineers usually did not need civil service protection to keep them in office,[46] Washington's military engineers were protected from "political" interference to an extent that civilian counterparts elsewhere could only dream about. The truly Haussmannic feature of the capital's Gilded Age government was the relatively unchecked authority that engineer officers exercised over public works.

While army engineers in Washington were isolated from the public accountability, they were not immune to it. Despite the absence of customary channels of popular expression, residents remained able to retaliate against officers who seemed arrogant or who concentrated so much on the impression their Washington work made in the War Department that they forgot local people. The uproar surrounding the Engineers' faltering efforts to expand the water supply illustrates how officers not attentive enough to public opinion could damage their own reputation and encourage influential resident groups to combine against the Corps and attack its accumulated authority.

When authorizing the Washington Aqueduct in the 1850s, Congress attempted to restrict federal responsibility to the community by separating supply from distribution. The government would bring water to Washington and pipe it to federal buildings, but local authorities had to convey it to homes. The Washington City corporation could tap Meigs's mains "provided that no expense shall devolve upon the United States in consequence of said distribution."[47] The municipal water department operated with fees collected from users. As a consequence, while Meigs instituted a coherent plan to bring water *to* the city, he and succeeding aqueduct superintendents had little influence over what happened once it left the distributing reservoir. With little long-range thought, municipal mains were laid according to which sections paid for connections first. Haphazard construction contributed to the inconsistent pressure that plagued the system. The higher, more eastern sections, especially Capitol Hill, suffered chronic shortages before the aqueduct was five years old.

Some engineers insisted that inconsistent pressure arose from poor planning, but others found a plausible villain in public extravagance. In 1880, Washington's daily per capita consumption of water, 155.5 gallons, was by far largest in the nation, exceeding Chicago, the city in second place, by 36.5 gallons per person. Washingtonians used three times as much water per capita as Londoners or Parisians.[48] However, since devices to combat waste, such as universal metering, were enormously expensive to install and of doubtful utility and justice, engineers sought to increase water pressure through mechanical means. Hoxie constructed a system of stop-cocks and a standpipe at 16th Street, northwest, but residents of east Washington claimed that these devices merely diverted more water from Capitol Hill. "With a perversity," mocked one pamphlet, water would not go uphill at Hoxie's behest. "Stupid water, not appreciating the science of hydraulic engineering as applied by this brilliant young engineer," taunted another, "refused and still refuses to rise on Capitol Hill." Such schemes "could only have originated in the fertile brain of Engineer Hoxie." Hoxie's standpipe was grist for the anti-engineer mill until the District abandoned it in 1893.[49]

Colonel Thomas Casey, aqueduct superintendent in the late 1870s, recommended attacking Capitol Hill's problems by building a 36-inch main straight to it. General Meigs countered that such a main already existed, to little avail. For almost the same price, Meigs felt, the government could extend the aqueduct itself beyond the old distribution point to a new "high service" reservoir at 10th or 14th street, above the city. This idea aimed to enhance the system's capacity to store water under pressure at a place accessible to the farthest eastern sections.[50]

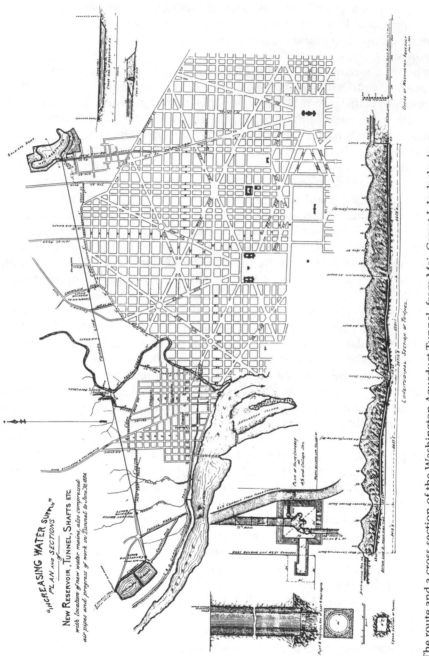

The route and a cross-section of the Washington Aqueduct Tunnel, from Maj. Garret J. Lydecker's 1884 report. Courtesy the U.S. Army Military History Institute, Carlisle, Pennsylvania.

Meigs's idea intrigued Hoxie and Engineer Commissioner Twining, but the pair questioned the wisdom of running a tunnel at the "moderate depth" the general foresaw. A shallow tunnel might limit construction costs and offer access for repairs, but it would meet Rock Creek Valley well above the ground, where it would require either expensive pumps or a 1,500-foot bridge with a siphon. After studying Ellis Chesbrough's deep tunnel beneath Lake Michigan, the source of Chicago's water, Hoxie conceived the idea of extending the aqueduct *under,* not over Rock Creek. Hoxie and Twining suggested a "force conduit," nine feet in diameter, running four miles from the Georgetown distributing reservoir to just east of Howard University, north of the city's geographic center. A large reservoir there would double the District's immediate supply, triple its eventual capacity, and with minimal pumping reach not only deprived sections to the east and south but also developing suburbs to the north. "If borings in this rock are satisfactory," speculated Hoxie, it might be possible to drive the tunnel eighty-five to one-hundred feet below the surface, straight through hard rock.[51]

This assumption that solid rock lay along the proposed route appeared crucial to Hoxie's plan, since the need to build expensive lining in soft, porous rock was the one factor that Hoxie and Twining imagined might drive costs way over their palatable estimate of $1.2 million. Uncertainty on this question meant that Congress could hold only inconclusive hearings. In May 1882, the well-liked Twining died. His replacement, Major Garret Lydecker, was a New Jersey native whose recent assignments had included navigation work on the Great Lakes and the Pacific coast. To improve coordination on the proposed work, Lydecker also took over as aqueduct superintendent, a job until then kept distinct from the District government, although it was often performed by the public buildings officer. In July, legislators demonstrated faith in the Army Corps by setting aside $1.5 million for sundry water projects, with the Corps permitted to make its own decision after further study. Congress, as investigators later noted, never specifically authorized a tunnel.[52]

Lydecker later claimed that the deep tunnel was the only plan he found in his office upon arrival. Yet not long after his appointment, he wrote to the chief of engineers, Horatio Wright, "If compact, solid rock is not reached within a reasonable limit, the project can be modified." Lydecker was convinced that the alternative surface or shallow conduits would prove complicated and expensive. He had "no reasonable doubt" that surveys would turn up firm rock, in which case excavation "would become a simple piece of engineering work."[53]

In March 1883, the aqueduct office reported that surveys were finding "firm rock admirably adapted to tunnelling." In reality, Hoxie's trial shaft at Howard University turned up material "absolutely as rotten as punk." Workmen had to pump out ground water at the rate of ten gallons per minute. In June, four months behind schedule, Hoxie reached what he called bedrock at

116 feet below the surface of the proposed reservoir. This implied a tunnel substantially below the hoped-for level. Lydecker explained the project's "very slow progress" by recalling that he and Hoxie had decided to sink the first trial shaft near Howard University because "every known condition indicated that bed rock would be at a lower elevation there than at any other part of the line and that there also the maximum difficulties of sinking a shaft would be encountered."[54]

Standard procedure now called for referring the project to a review board. Instead, General Wright granted provisional approval pending "further examinations." Despite the spring's frustrations, Hoxie remained optimistic. In July 1883, he backed up Lydecker by remarking that tests "simply confirm the opinion deduced from the known geology." Lydecker then abandoned the idea of a second trial shaft and instead spent the rest of 1883 drawing plans and excavating working shafts. This seems to have irked the feisty Hoxie, who meanwhile had developed the conviction that the only way to limit trouble related to soft rock was to run the tunnel even deeper. Relations between the two became so strained that in early 1884, Lydecker removed Hoxie from the project. Reassigned to the regular Subsurface Division, Hoxie continued to badger Lydecker about the "mistake" he was making.[55]

Captain Hoxie's discontent with his superior became public. The need to save face now rendered objective discussion impossible. Lydecker pulled strings to have his rival reassigned to an insalubrious outpost in the swamps of Alabama. Hoxie and his wife, Vinnie Ream Hoxie, a popular sculptor with many political friends, campaigned in vain to have the order rescinded so that they could remain in Washington and keep her artistic career alive. Captain Hoxie's mentor, retired commanding general William T. Sherman, explained to Mrs. Hoxie that the realities of military politics dictated that the couple resign themselves to the move in order to salvage the young engineer's own career, "for [his] brother officers whose good will is all in all to him would be jealous" if he won the quarrel with Lydecker through influence. After five years in Alabama, Hoxie received choice assignments at Willets Point, Pittsburgh, and Baltimore, but only for a few months in 1905 did he again work in the city where he once caused such a stir.[56]

Burdened with executive duties from his dual posts, Lydecker delegated supervision of the tunnel's construction to Hoxie's replacement, Lieutenant Thomas W. Symons, the only engineer who emerged from the aqueduct tunnel business unsullied, because he voiced misgivings "every day." As the project bogged down and "the confidence of the community" was shaken, Lydecker excused delays and cost overruns by declaring that "no material difficulties" had arisen "that were not contemplated by me as likely to arise in its progress." Meanwhile, Symons reported that the tunnel would be "far from being completed" at the original June 1885 deadline and that costs would escalate "very much on account of the large amount of lining required."[57]

Meigs had suggested that the task of drilling his shallow tunnel would prove neither dangerous nor complex. Lydecker and Hoxie appear not to have considered adequately how additional depth might multiply the danger and difficulty. Five men died during the first two years, although most cave-ins and dynamite accidents ended more fortunately. The expense of drilling under harsh conditions and then of stabilizing "seamy and disorganized rock" was the main reason why, by 1888, the government had already spent the $1.2 million originally estimated for the entire extension — including the Howard University reservoir — on the tunnel portion alone, with no end in sight.[58]

Difficult working conditions led to "constant troubles" with contractors. Although local bids were lower, Lydecker hired a New York firm, Beckwith and Quackenbush. These contractors offered tunneling experience in Boston and California and were at the time also at work on New York's Croton Aqueduct. The overextended New York company, however, gave priority to Croton and subcontracted much of the Washington job. The businessmen quarreled with the engineers over problems similar to those plaguing the Croton tunnel, for example, who would bear the expense when the tunnel deviated from its prescribed course. Lydecker conceded that delays and overruns were partly the government's fault but tried to pin as much as possible on the "extreme slowness" of the builders. After the first year, Symons scolded, "You have never in one month attained a rate of progress as great as the minimum called for by your contract." Symons began to find sections where workmen blasted an area one-third to one-half larger than the conduit's ultimate diameter. To dynamite an excessive cavity was quicker and safer, but it magnified the need for lining. While Symons exhorted the contractors to exercise "proper care" in blasting, he conceded that their claims for compensation for "rock removed beyond the prescribed lines and grades" might be justified under the circumstances. In 1886, Symons secured for himself a transfer to the post of assistant engineer commissioner, where his work on water filtration and street extensions more than offset, in Washingtonians' minds, his connection to the detested tunnel.[59]

Symons's replacement, Lieutenant Curtis Townsend, knew little about tunneling and relied heavily on assistants and inspectors, many of whom Lydecker had hired because they had been pushed on him by congressmen. Meanwhile, Crosby Noyes, the formidable *Evening Star* editor, and other friends of Richard Hoxie stepped up attacks on Lydecker, whom Noyes called the "miserable humbug." Hoxie's charges that Lydecker stole his plan only to ruin it reached the top levels of the War Department and the floor of Congress. Lydecker reminded officials that at the time Hoxie had reported the terrain to be solid. He denied that Hoxie had "protested against commencing the tunnel at the depth at which it has been driven" until after his transfer.[60]

Lydecker labeled his opponent's behavior "unmilitary, unprofessional, and offensive." Yet Hoxie's charges combined with delays and overruns to

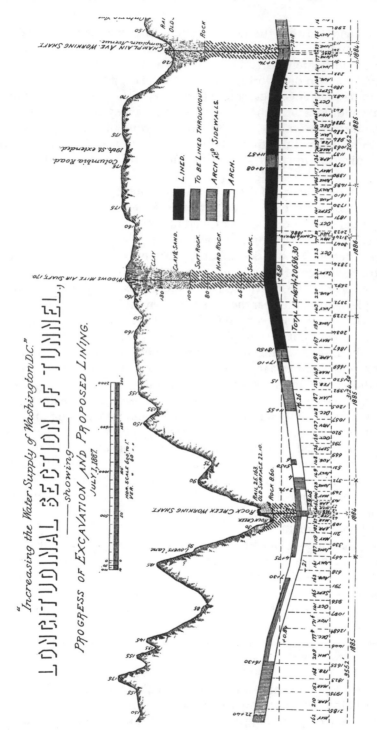

The central section of the Washington Aqueduct Tunnel, from an 1887 progress report on the troubled project. Rock Creek Valley, whose depth convinced engineers to attempt the arduous excavation, appears left of center. Note the extensive lining that Lydecker realized would be needed. Courtesy the U.S. Army Military History Institute, Carlisle, Pennsylvania.

provoke belated internal and legislative reviews. Lydecker insisted that each request for funds would be the last and that the tunnel would still cost less per foot than comparable projects elsewhere. In early 1887, with only 1,275 feet to be excavated and the rest awaiting lining, Lydecker vowed that he was "quite certain" that the work could be completed during that year. In early 1888, the aqueduct superintendent requested another $335,000. Out of patience, Congress attached to this appropriation a November 1 completion date. Lydecker called the deadline "entirely impossible" — it would take six weeks alone to pump out the ground water that had filled the excavation during the previous funding interval.[61]

Lydecker and Townsend pressured Beckwith and Quackenbush to finish the lining right away. Rumors soon spread through the city that harassed workers and dishonest subcontractors were constructing lining without proper backing and using false payrolls to buy silence from politically connected inspectors. In fall 1888, Townsend and Lydecker accompanied the press on an inspection of the tunnel, where reporters found huge gaps behind the lining that they dubbed "McNamara's Cavern," "Lucas's Hole," and "Cave O'Brien," in honor of suspect inspectors. Desperate to avert the impending deadline, Lydecker submitted a new memo: "The rigid examination now in progress has developed some large holes, but such as are already shown up can be made perfectly good at the cost of not more than $5,000." "For monumental gall," sneered the *Post*, Lydecker's memo "takes the cake." The request for a reprieve was incredible, the paper added, since all Washington considered Lydecker responsible for "the greatest scandal that has ever been brought upon the Engineer Corps."[62]

Congress let the project lapse and requested opinions from civil and military engineers as to how bad the mess really was. The consultants guessed that the tunnel would require $900,000 on top of the overruns already incurred. The project's old nemesis, General Casey, who after his Washington Monument triumph had been made chief of engineers, restated his preference for a main directly to Capitol Hill. This was built, but as Meigs had predicted, it failed to fill East Washington bathtubs. A congressional investigation confirmed that "hardly any continuous length of ten feet" of lining had sturdy backing. Legislators were astonished that aqueduct officials could have permitted such "great negligence" in a project already under fire. Lydecker was suspended, but a court-martial merely issued a reprimand and a small fine — a slap on the wrist, the local press contended, that amounted to arrogant dismissal of the city's grievances. In 1891, Lydecker won promotion to lieutenant colonel and in 1907 retired as a brigadier general.[63]

Until the Corps completed the aqueduct extension a decade later, Washingtonians joked that their "cylindrical misfortune" might be worth $3,000 per day as a mushroom farm.[64] Despite mockery and Casey's doubts, a consensus slowly emerged that the tunnel had been a good plan. Civil engineers in other cities encountered similar criticism for grossly underestimating the

expense and difficulty of such excavations. Resolution of comparable problems on the Croton Aqueduct overcame public and official distrust of the
abandoned Washington project. In 1898, Congress authorized the Corps to
resume work on the tunnel. When the reservoir east of Howard University
went into operation in January 1902, seventeen years behind schedule and
several million dollars over budget, those associated with the earlier debacle
renewed their endless feud. The *Star* lent assistance: "Lydecker Tunnel, the
useless hole in the ground, has now become Hoxie Tunnel and is ready to
perform its intended purpose."[65]

The issue was not the intrinsic merits of the tunnel so much as the Engineers' lack of accountability. Such a "disgraceful" display of pride, ambition,
and military politics left Washingtonians feeling "helpless." Citizens lamented that they had little recourse from "cavalier or unjust treatment" by
army officers. Resentment increased after congressmen made it clear that if
the fifty-fifty arrangement were to continue, District taxpayers would have to
pay half of the $2.2 million "literally thrown into a hole." As a House Appro-
priations District subcommittee member explained, "The District of Columbia cannot go into partnership with the United States and be exempted from
its share of the misfortunes."[66]

V

While the army failed to punish Lydecker to residents' satisfaction, it took
other steps to repair damaged relations with Washingtonians. In March 1886,
the War Department removed Lydecker as engineer commissioner, the most
public of his two posts. Colonel William Ludlow, recalled to active duty after
three years with Philadelphia's water works, had ideal credentials and was
appointed to the position; but he had a haughty manner that proved a lightening rod for public hostility. The stylish "dude commissioner" evoked a
traditional prejudice, dating from Jacksonian times, that the Engineer Corps
constituted a "leisure class" of dandies, "with white vests and pantaloons and
an eyeglass dangling at the button hole of their coats." One local pamphleteer charged "His High Mightiness" with using public money for riding
horses, monogrammed gear, and fancy gloves. Ludlow was "boss" of the
commission, wrote an editor, "He makes reports without the consent or
knowledge of his colleagues. He runs the machine like a barrack and sneers
at the taxpayers like common cattle."[67]

Allegations of corruption against various officers now appeared regularly
in the local press. The frequency and content of these charges suggest that
dissatisfaction with the Engineers was real, not that accused officers were actually crooked. During the Gilded Age, for complex reasons of political culture, disputes over policy or structure often degenerated into *ad hominem*
attacks on integrity and motives. Hints appeared that Lydecker's behavior
could be explained by nebulous links relatives had with the out-of-town con-

tractors. Ludlow's opponents focused on the "German Cemetery Outrage," an action in which, supposedly to help a Philadelphia land syndicate, the colonel had tried to speed up extension of North Capitol Street through an immigrant burial ground, a project that had been pending for years.[68]

Ludlow's decision to shift the course of Massachusetts Avenue as it entered the northwest suburbs personally embarrassed President Cleveland, who held property in the region. The President fired the embattled commissioner in January 1888. Still seeking a return to "harmony," the War Department gave the post to Major Charles Raymond, then assistant District engineer, because he was thought to be "easily approached." Some residents remained unimpressed. Within a month, one vociferous editor proclaimed, "The successor of the Lordly Ludlow has already shown his teeth." The editor accused the "Persian satrap" of denying reporters access to public documents. "I am running this office on army principles," Raymond allegedly remarked, "and if I choose will keep no records at all."[69]

Public attacks on "militarism" encouraged civilian portions of the District government to push to win back powers the Engineers had accumulated over the years. The two civilian commissioners keenly resented "the practice of certain officials of the Engineer Department reporting personally to Commissioner Ludlow." The pair demanded clarification of the status of the junior officers serving as assistant engineer commissioners. Were these men attached to the engineer commissioner according to military discipline or to the Board of Commissioners as municipal employees? Armed with fierce arguments from the city attorney, the civilians insisted that Congress amend the 1878 act to emphasize that the assistants were responsible to all the commissioners rather than only their military superior. In 1890, Commissioner John Douglass stressed to Senate District chairman John Ingalls the "great" inconvenience that arose because "the majority of the Comissioners have now no right to call upon said assistants even for information, and can give them no directions concerning District work." The executives wanted to rein in the assistants so that public works no longer ran "almost as an independent office from the rest of the government."[70]

Dissatisfaction with the Corps began to affect legislation. Congress routinely stipulated that certain types of plans and permit applications be submitted directly to the engineer commissioner, who would bring them to the full board after his own review. At the time of the aqueduct extension controversy, Congress was considering bills relating to strategic matters such as subdivision procedures and the mechanization of transit. The civilian commissioners pressured Congress to substitute the phrase "Commissioners of the District of Columbia" for "Engineer Commissioner" wherever it occurred in these measures.[71] Congress did not always comply, but legislative leaders made it clear that they now considered the officers' position at Washington a problem. Maryland's Arthur Gorman, a powerful Senate Democrat, questioned a provision in the 1890 Rock Creek Park bill that gave a special role in land purchases to the chief of engineers and the engineer commissioner. "We all have perfect confidence" in these officials, Gorman argued,

> but to put the money, one-half of which is to come from the tax-payers of the District of Columbia, practically under two Army officers . . . with no control of it by the people of the District and no way to reach it, is going beyond anything heretofore contemplated. I had hoped we would . . . in a very short time, eliminate that military feature from the management of the affairs of the District of Columbia and put it all in the hands of civilians, but under the provisions of this report we are adding to and extending their power and authority.[72]

Unlike Gorman, most prominent Washingtonians and pro-District congressmen remained favorable to an Army Corps presence, yet commercial-civic leaders and their allies in the Capitol sought ways to check the Engineers and above all to loosen their grip on the planning, as opposed to administration, of improvements. The people most willing and able to act as counter-weights to the officers on planning questions were professional consultants in municipal engineering, public health, and architecture. A major factor in the period's overall public works history reared its head in the capital — the rivalry between military engineers and civilian experts.

During the last decades of the nineteenth century, specialists in municipal engineering, public health, public administration, and urban planning began to insist that they constituted distinct professions that offered unique services essential under modern urban conditions. Professional consultants saw the Army Corps's entrenched position in Washington (and on all federal public works) as epitomizing the unenlightened approach to infrastructure that they sought to overcome. In the consultants' eyes, the officers had several fatal flaws. The Corps's rivers and harbors work involved the agency in the piece-meal, "distributive" style of policy-making that characterized the Gilded Age state, while the consultants epitomized the coherence-minded, "administrative" approach we associate with progressivism. The Engineers' training was general, while new-style professionals stressed specialization and expertise. Also, the Corps as an organization seemed slow to absorb recent thinking regarding both civil engineering and civic design. As a historian notes, the notion that the Corps had become an "agency at rest" even with regard to hydraulic engineering, historically its forte, helped to animate proposals appearing in the late 1880s for a federal department of public works, staffed by civilians.[73]

While military engineers and civilian consultants diverged in outlook and approach, they had enough in common to suggest that their differences were not intractible. While adversaries in rhetoric, officers and consultants often cooperated quite well in practice. An 1891 panel of both officers and civilians drew upon innovative Army Corps studies that indicated that underground electrical conduits were already feasible, despite the contrary claims of utilities reluctant to undertake the extra expense. The consultants' report, in turn, proved useful to the District Engineer Department in the ensuing tug-of-war with the corporations and their congressional friends, who tried to sneak through provisions weakening the commitment to conduits.[74] In the aftermath of the distressing 1889 freshet, a consulting board led by renowned sanitary engineer Rudolph Hering submitted a $3.6 million plan to divert sewage from the waterfront and pump it three miles downriver, thereby relieving the most severe shortcomings of Shepherd's drainage system. Both the engineer commissioner's office and the Corps's Potomac River office enthusiastically greeted the Hering plan, which derived much from the officers' own thinking. Military engineers fought tenaciously for appropriations for the sewage diversion project in grueling budget battles during the 1890s.[75]

Since the civilian professionals had their attention focused on the wider struggle over the place of specialists and experts in government and society, out-of-town consultants often lost sight of special factors affecting their conflict with military engineers in Washington. With regard to the national city's public works and services, consultants rarely initiated the attack upon a certain policy or practice of the Army Corps. Instead, congressional policymakers or local civic leaders already at odds with the engineers would enlist the outsiders in disputes that had been under way for a while. The purpose of soliciting a consultant's report in such cases was not to use the professional's expertise to seek from scratch an alternative to the path favored by the Engineers but to validate a course upon which civilian interests were already resolved. The 1890s fight over water filtration, for example, appears on the surface to be an archetypal military-civilian quarrel. In reality, the consultants were adjuncts of local groups with their own agenda and quarrel with the Engineer Corps.

Washington's typhoid rate at the turn of the century was four times that of London and Hamburg and seven times the rate in Rotterdam and Berlin. The third of the population who were blacks accounted for nearly half the annual deaths from bacterial disease. White areas of the District had death rates from typhoid as low as European cities with elaborate water treatment plants. This divergence led the Washington Medical Society and the Board of Trade's Public Health Committee to argue that Washington could go far towards reversing its "unenviable notoriety" for disease simply by making indoor plumbing universally available. Blacks in alley houses and other rundown dwellings counted disproportionately among the one-fourth of local families who lacked running water and depended on wells and privies. Even so, residents distrusted the turbid Potomac water: "its brownish hue brings up visions of wriggling bacteria and lingering diseases." In 1895, a well-publicized study attributed the majority of scarlet fever cases and a large portion of typhoid to the aqueduct. This helped persuade the Board of Trade and the Medical Society that filtration was indeed "an urgent need."[76]

As early as 1886, Captain Symons labeled the aqueduct's healthfulness "doubtful." Military engineers shared the view that filtration would one day be required. Through much of the 1890s, however, the Corps dismayed local physicians and civic leaders by advising delay. While some engineers doubted the dire short-run predictions, the main factor behind this counsel, as the aqueduct superintendent remarked in 1898, was that "filtered water is not a cheap product." Washington no longer led the country in per capita water use, but it remained near the top. With the operating costs of a filtration plant estimated at up to $8.00 per million gallons, officers believed the city could not afford a purification system until per capita use fell by 45 percent, to a "reasonable" hundred gallons a day.[77]

In the meantime, the Corps recommended measures to make treated water less imperative. One idea involved stretching the interval between the Great Falls dam and residents' taps. The Potomac watershed, engineers thought, was still "remarkably free from general pollution." Enough impurities might settle out during a prolonged journey through conduits and reservoirs to render the water adequately safe by the time it reached homes. Water quality had thus provided one of the most forceful arguments for reviving the aborted tunnel project.[78]

Public health experts ridiculed this notion of "self-purification." Gradually, the officers conceded filtration to be necessary in the near future, but they differed with Washington's physicians and businessmen over which system to adopt. Civic groups hoped to cajole Congress into supplying the $2.5 million necessary for an "English" or "Slow Sand" filtration plant, where water was strained through large beds of gravel and sand. The result was not "aesthetic" in terms of appearance and taste, but such systems had all but wiped out organisms from municipal supplies in Europe. In Albany, one of the few American cities to construct such a plant in the 1890s, fatal attacks of typhoid immediately dropped from 10.1 to 1.4 per month. A greater number of our cities, however, had opted for the "mechanical," "rapid," or "American" filter, in which water was strained through steel tanks with a small layer of sand at the bottom. Various alum solutions were added to coagulate impurities and kill bacteria. While early trials of this system had disappointed, recent tests indicated that mechanical filters were nearly as effective as beds of sand at eliminating bacteria and more effective at removing discoloration and sediment. The steel tanks were also easier to clean, meaning that they could remain continually in service. These and similar considerations prompted the aqueduct office to reject proposals to imitate Europe and to come out strongly for mechanical filtration.[79]

Politics as well as science lay behind this disagreement. Accustomed to the obscure thought processes of the Gilded Age politician and the Gilded Age taxpayer's irritable distrust of experts, military engineers assumed that the mechanical filter would be easier to sell. Apart from chauvinism for native technology, construction costs for the American method were less than half that of the European system, although operating costs were 55 percent more.

This might hoodwink Congress's old-fashioned "economists," who gave ground on annual budgets but bristled at capital outlays. Moreover, the purification question depended on the germ theory of disease, which many educated laymen were only beginning to comprehend. When Lt. Col. A. M. Miller, a Washington native appointed aqueduct superintendent in 1898, explained the use of colon bacilli in bacteria counts, the chairman of the House Appropriations District subcommittee asked, "What sort of an animal is he, anyway?" When the engineer remarked that the Potomac at its most turbid, could contain 51,000 colon bacilli per thimblefull, the politician exclaimed, "What room would there be for the water?" Miller's predecessor, arguing in favor of the "aesthetic" mechanical method, had observed that "the average householder would rise up in just wrath if, after being taxed for the establishment of an expensive filter plant, he was furnished with water badly discolored." Since both methods abolished disease, why not choose the more politic?[80]

Miller insisted, "The mechanical filter will, with proper attention, furnish an entirely satisfactory effluent." Washington physicians and civic leaders, as a congressional history later recorded, "vehemently attacked Colonel Miller's recommendation." The engineer would force an "unwise experiment" on the city, the Medical Society claimed. "Alum in large quantities is an effective germicide," they acknowledged, but evidence was inconclusive concerning the ultimate effects of such chemical purifiers upon health. The English method "has stood the test with increasingly good results for a half century."[81]

Resentful that Joseph Cannon–style "cheesepairing" might preclude an international standard of services, the Board of Trade portrayed the sand filter as a test of Congress's capacity for higher patriotism. Senate District chairman McMillan, a close ally of the Board of Trade, took the residents' side against the officers. For the big-thinking McMillan, anything but the best filtration was a concession to reaction and darkness. The Army Corps was playing into the hands of those cheapskates across the Capitol, who should be confronted not assuaged. McMillan and his aide, Charles Moore, organized hearings with authorities in public health and sanitary engineering at the Waldorf Astoria in New York, a convenient location in which to attest to the effectiveness of natural filtration. "Much to the chagrin of the War Department," Moore recalled, McMillan supplemented these hearings with a consulting panel that included Rudolph Hering, the sanitary engineer who had replanned Washington's sewerage, as well as engineers who had worked on the Albany plant and a similar facility at Lawrence, Massachusetts. Although "the average yearly bacterial efficiency of the two systems would be about equal," the consultants reported, European filters were "supported by long precedent."[82]

In this controversy, out-of-town experts did not act independently; they served as weapons in the arsenal of the Corps's antagonists in the city and the Capitol. Miller lamented that his plan fell victim to "strong opposition" from "the Washington Board of Trade, the Washington Business Men's Association, and the Medical Society." The officer could not conceal his frustration at "being overruled completely," but he participated in good faith in planning the European plant, constructed in McMillan Park, that opened in 1905.[83]

During the Shepherd period, the improver faction and its friends in national politics had cheerfully deferred to military engineers as arbiters of the worthy national city. By 1878, the Corps's prestige had grown so great that residents expressed few misgivings about adding municipal engineering to the already lengthy list of duties performed by the Corps in the national city. The first dozen years of the commission system shook the officers from their Civil War–era pedestal. In a revealing inaccuracy, prominent Washingtonians by the 1890s were remembering the engineer commissioner as having been *imposed* by Congress as part of the price of the fifty-fifty deal. At the time, Congress had scrutinized the proposal more carefully than the public had.[84]

In the 1890s, individuals such as Captain Beach still attained popularity. The Engineers' uniform continued to inspire patriotic pride in the generation of businessmen and politicians whose adult lives began during the Civil War. Yet deference to the Corps's technical and aesthetic judgment had turned to skepticism. The Engineers' generalist approach to the urban environment now seemed clumsy and crude next to the confident precision of specialized municipal engineers and the expansive grandeur of Beaux-Arts architects and park planners. In addition, national politicians and local commercial and civic elites were arriving at the view that private consultants were more reliable allies than army officers, whose proud history and strong institutional culture at times resulted in a truculent high-mindedness that new professions in need of well-placed patrons could ill afford. Perhaps the capital would have been better off if these famous antagonists had chosen to ally. After all, the Engineer Corps was the actor on Washington's local scene who most deeply shared the professionals' belief in a broad public interest transcending the aims and concerns of private groups. Working at cross purposes, neither could offer a counterbalance to the promotional approach to public works and development.

7

An Unsectional Public

Every well-informed legislator knows that the Washington Board of Trade represents the residents of the national capital; that it gives careful consideration to all public measures which touch local interests; that it will do the right thing and nothing which is not right, and that it grinds no private ax. Thus firmly entrenched, the board fears no assault upon its motives or methods. Asking for legislation, it may reasonably expect to receive.

— George H. Harries, Secretary of the Board of Trade

O N SEPTEMBER 17, 1890, New Hampshire Republican Henry Blair pleaded with the Senate to provide congressional representation to the District of Columbia. By consenting to "set up a despotism in its own heart," Blair portentously proclaimed, the Republic had foolishly engaged in a "stupendous and dangerous inconsistency." The senator warned that republican Rome had sunk "in one dead plain of slavery," because over centuries its leaders had tolerated practices "untrue to the republican form of government." Drift towards tyranny could become America's "unhappy fate" unless Congress repaired "the foul work consummated by legislative rape of the rights of man in this alleged temple of liberty in 1878."[1] The Senate heeded Blair's prophesy as much as its ancient counterpart had heeded Cicero's. Blair's resolution, quickly buried, was the only time in the first three decades of the District's appointed rule that a measure to restore any form of suffrage to the national city reached the Senate floor.

Suffrage proposals for Washington gained little support in Congress. The city's congressional friends wished to preserve the embattled half-and-half plan, which would certainly fall by the wayside in a return to home rule. Since the capital's friends had a stake in denying suffrage, the move would have to come from its enemies, not a likely source. Every so often, a hostile lawmaker suggested restoring home rule as a way to overturn the despised fifty-fifty system, a motive that did not inspire citizen support.

Also at work was the tendency of institutions to avoid yielding power, even when the reason for assuming it has faded. The House Appropriations Committee, which often expressed unease with the open-ended nature of the half-and-half commitment, sponsored measures throughout the 1890s to define federal fiscal responsibility to the national city more narrowly. While the House panel was willing to whittle down the 1878 deal, it avoided outright attack, because this would inevitably entail devolving some authority over municipal finances to the citizens themselves. "You might as well talk about giving local self-government to any dockyard or navy-yard in the United States, as to the District of Columbia," asserted the Democratic chairman of the House Appropriations District subcommittee, in response to an attempt in 1894 to repeal the 1878 system. "Whenever this proposition has been brought up here it has been whistled down the wind by the best talent of both political parties." The Constitution, the Founding Fathers, and legal precedent all dictated that "the Government should have absolute and unlimited control."[2]

The basic fact was that Congress would not return the vote to Washington unless the people agitated for it. Washingtonians recognized that their government was an anomaly, but a broad range of resident groups actively supported the status quo. In response to an 1895 inquiry as to whether Congress should call a referendum on home rule, Commissioner Ross accurately reported, "The existing form of government is generally regarded as superior in economical and good administration to any form of municipal government in this country." Blair found "absolute political despotism" to be "all the more alarming because so many are in love with it."[3]

However deplorable the idea might seem to principled democrats, the District commission was a legitimate regime as far those it governed were concerned. The majority of citizens acquiesced to the system with few complaints. This created an unusual situation, of interest to students of both urban and national political history. Americans generally take the primacy of the representative parts of our polity so much for granted that we do not even try to imagine how politics would work in a populous jurisdiction in our country if elections did not exist. Yet even in Gilded Age America, when the making and implementing of policy was emphatically participatory by comparison to our time, politics could flourish without parties and campaigns.

Local politics, in the sense of people agitating to influence public policy, survived in Washington despite the end of suffrage. Still, until the early 1890s, mechanisms for gauging public opinion and transforming it into policy remained haphazard and unsatisfying. Within a decade after the 1878 act, the commissioners and pro-District elements in Congress realized that Congress was ill-suited to perform the aldermen role it had reserved to itself. Pressure built among residents and within the institutions of government for a quasi city council that could present itself as a credible embodiment of public opinion, in lieu of the elected local legislature few really wanted.

Residents first attempted to exert systematic influence through coalitions of neighborhood-based groups that called themselves citizens associations. This effort failed, because the neighborhood coalitions suffered from the same centrifugal tendencies that made the period's ward-based city councils a synonym for incoherence, while they lacked the statutory responsibilities that compelled those elected councils to overcome "particularism" sufficiently to keep cities running. However, at the time of Blair's speech, in September 1890, the Washington Board of Trade, the organization that for the next quarter century would symbolize Washington to itself and the country, was nearing the end of its first year. A commercial-civic group composed of downtown businessmen and professionals, the board quickly impressed the commissioners and Congress with its ability to put together workable proposals for new public works and services, to compose differences within the community over a given project so that the city presented a single face at the Capitol, and in general to come across as "unsectional" and worthy of respect.

A formidable alliance emerged between the board and James McMillan's Senate District Committee. The two groups encouraged regular cooperation between the public sector and the capital's real estate, commercial, and utilities interests. They fostered in Washington a municipal administration that became widely respected for honesty, imagination, and effectiveness. Over the long run, though, the national city paid a price for having the "businessmen's" government that many contemporaries felt would cure the inefficiency, ignorance, and corruption that allegedly plagued other municipalities. Washington's polity became even more infused with the assumption that government ought to act as a partner and promoter of enterprise, rather than guardian of an overall public good that sometimes transcended what a community's businessmen felt that good to be.

I

The man who succeeded to Senator Blair's New Hampshire seat in 1891 was Republican Jacob Gallinger, an associate of McMillan on the Senate District Committee from 1891 until McMillan's death in 1902. Gallinger expressed distaste nearly as strong as his predecessor's for the municipality he oversaw, calling the commission system "government of the few, by the few, and for the few." Yet he brushed aside calls for Congress to undo its 1878 handiwork, observing, "Most of the large property owners of Washington are content to be deprived of suffrage — that inalienable right about which we talk so much — and are satisfied to let Congress do the thinking and legislating for them."[4] The acquiescence of the propertied class to appointed rule allowed its continuation, because only the propertied were organized and self-aware enough to have led a home rule campaign. Other voices were too weak or not sufficiently committed.

Blacks lost the most from Washington's disfranchisement, an understandable result, since the commission existed in part to shut the minority out of municipal affairs. Blacks had "just as much chance to obtain recognition as a donkey would of going through the eye of the needle," a black weekly, the *Washington Bee,* asserted in 1883. The city's rulers, the paper charged, cared "as much for a negro as a rat terrier does for a mouse."[5] The proportion of blacks in the District's population, one-third, remained what it had been in the 1870s. In 1890, the capital had the largest proportion of blacks among the nation's twenty-five largest cities. Only New Orleans, at 26.6 percent, came close. Baltimore was 15.4 percent black, Philadelphia 3.8 percent.[6] Blacks had active influence over the segregated schools but were all but ignored with regard to development and public works.

While black businessmen, ministers, and such were often present in the commissioners' chambers, there were exceedingly few instances during the regime's first decades when the commissioners met a delegation representing minority concerns on economic or development issues. Such a meeting occurred January 19, 1897, when officials greeted a group of ministers seeking alley house reform. That year, blacks accounted for 93 percent of residents of the capital's notorious alley houses. Even in this matter, black needs did not easily dominate debate. After four years of agitation, Congress in 1892 had prohibited new construction in alleys less than thirty feet wide and lacking water, sewerage, and lighting. The well-being of inhabitants was discussed, but equally influential were arguments that because alleys were "harboring places for undesirable, if not dangerous tenants," they depreciated property values in the neighborhood. Once the alley bill was passed, bankers and realtors who had supported it (some of whom had previously built housing now prohibited) petitioned Congress for legislation to facilitate widening alleys to the requisite size, allowing further alley construction, to benefit "many localities in a moral and sanitary way, beside greatly enhancing property values."[7]

With return to home rule unlikely, prominent local blacks sometimes proposed that they be given a minority seat on the commission. As this was even more improbable, the best that African-American papers such as the *Bee* could do was rally support for white commissioners who seemed sympathetic. Republican John Douglass, commissioner from 1889–1893, showed "disregard to race prejudices . . . by his appointments of colored men to responsible positions in the District government." Even so, in 1898, the *Bee* opposed a municipal civil service because it might freeze the number of black clerks at two.[8]

In May 1895, Commissioner George Truesdell, a transit entrepreneur and suburban developer, remarked at the annual Board of Trade shad bake, a major event attended by businessmen and politicians, that "restless and dissatisfied" home rule advocates carried "no weight in the community."[9] Every once in a while, a prominent resident would publicly express misgivings about appointed rule, but such intermittent pangs of doubt produced little action. In 1883, antipathy to Engineer Commissioner Lydecker and complaints that President Arthur's civilian appointments were "strangers" induced Commissioner Joseph West to propose that a majority of the commissioners be elected. Of two hundred businessmen questioned by the *Star* regarding West's proposal, most felt that elected officials should have only a minority role in any revamped municipality. Even for this, one realtor remarked, there was "no crying need." The *Star* concluded, "While a considerable number of our citizens favor qualified suffrage, there are not many disposed to return to the undiluted 'Murder Bay' suffrage" (a euphemism for black voting).[10]

Racism remained a factor in elite backing for appointed rule, but, as in the original debate during the 1870s, the fifty-fifty budget arrangement clinched the support of prominent citizens. Pro–home rule residents charged "cowardly, timid, and selfish" businessmen with caring more about "the almighty dollar" than liberty: "When one mentions suffrage, they say, 'We don't want suffrage here, because if we have it Congress won't appropriate money as they now do.'" A resident signing himself "America" wrote to the *National Republican,* less enamored of the commission than the pro-developer *Star,* that the rich lacked incentive to seek a compromise that might allow a revival of self-government while retaining some measure of federal contributions: "By their money and social influence, [prominent Washingtonians] are pretty sure to be able to control an appointed government."[11]

By the 1890s, all daily papers favored an appointed commission, on both economic and political grounds. The press explained that fixed appropriations meant steady growth and partial immunity to fluctuations in the national economy. Journalists emphasized how the commission's record of propriety contrasted with the "rottenness" that pervaded municipalities "in which the 'popular will' is supposed to be ever potent." Newspaperman Henry Macfarland, successful as a commissioner in part because of his articulate defenses of the appointed system, remarked in an address prepared for the centennial celebration of 1900 that "although many good citizens have regretted that in the National Capital taxation without representation is the principle of government," under the commission, Washington

> has become the most beautiful capital in the world. Free from the slightest suspicion of scandal, successive boards of commissioners of the highest character have administered the affairs of the District more efficiently and economically than the affairs of any other city. . . . The compact between the National Government and the people of the District of Columbia for the equal division of its expenses has worked so well that no adverse comment is now made upon it.[12]

Theodore Noyes, son and successor of the venerable *Star* editor, Crosby Noyes, would, after 1910, become a figure in a more assertive (though still ineffectual) home rule movement; yet as Board of Trade president in 1898–99, the younger Noyes echoed the view that the community's priority was preservation of the half-and-half plan, not home rule. Other board presidents, including department store owner S. W. Woodward, asserted that most residents understood why federal appointees "must control the affairs of the city which is the seat of the National Government" and credited the regime for the fact that "no corrupt rings exist, as in most other cities."[13]

Smaller businessmen and property owners gave few signs that they desired change more than their wealthier compatriots. In 1888, the neighborhood-based citizens associations established a central committee to enhance the influence of homeowners. This committee proposed a ward-based council, appointed by the President, as a way to "improve the present form of government," while avoiding "unlimited suffrage." Even this degree of representation caused so much dissent that the umbrella group split up. "With all its admitted shortcomings," one dissenter argued, the commission was the most effective government the city had ever had. In 1894, the neighborhood groups tried another experiment in united action, establishing the Joint Executive Committees of the Citizens Associations, composed of the leaders of nine citizens associations. While this short-lived panel berated Congress for not fulfilling its fiscal obligations under the 1878 act, the Joint Executive treated the commission system itself as untouchable, a manifestation of "thoroughly informed congressional wisdom."[14] The District commission might disturb republican consciences, but Washington's people could live with it. This anomalous regime appeared to offer the thoughtful, effective municipal administration that American cities with self-government sought in vain.

Behind numerous municipal reorganization schemes that arose across the country in these years lay a deep conviction that complex, modern cities required strong, integrative authorities capable of overriding the parochial interests entrenched in ward-based councils. As historian Samuel P. Hays writes, the Progressive-era vogue for elected city commissions, as well as the more durable city manager and "strong mayor" schemes, all manifested "a drive for integration and centralization in [municipal] decision making," which paralleled those larger "forces making for integration in economic, professional, and social life." Contemporaries wondered — and urban Americans still wonder — whether taking power away from neighborhood spokesmen and concentrating it in a citywide executive enriches urban democracy or ruins it. When was the legendary ward boss the champion of his constituents' human needs against impersonal bureaucracy and an indifferent upper class and when was he merely a bulwark of short-sighted localism? The period's best-known urban affairs writers, however, nearly all argued that by affording public officials some degree of protection from direct popular pressure, a city could ensure itself more efficient services and more far-sighted, innovative public works.[15]

Urban affairs writers came to cite Washington, where shielding officials from public accountability had gone to its logical extreme, as an example of the good that unimpeded professionalism could accomplish. Few outsiders recommended that other cities follow the capital to the point of abolishing self-government altogether, but a broad spectrum of Washingtonians appeared content with a system that delivered water, picked up garbage, and suffered no "razor-cutting, shoulder-hitting mob-rowdyism."[16]

II

The treatment of Washington residents by their governing institutions — the District commission, Congress, and the Army Corps — led to many complaints and conflicts, yet the community in effect consented to pursue its grievances through "the courts and humble petition."[17] Washington's people perceived how, in an administrative polity such as their city had become, effective action required interest-group organizations capable of being constantly present in the offices and minds of authorities. The advantage that trade associations and public interest groups have over the general electorate in today's Washington is the ability to be on the spot while officials deliberate and implement policy. Yet, in keeping with what historian Hays calls the "particularistic" impulse of Gilded Age city dwellers, Washingtonians made no serious effort during the dozen years after 1878 to influence their regime through citywide civic associations or political parties. Until the founding of the Board of Trade in 1889, the only groups that exhibited substantial energy were the neighborhood-based homeowners groups that were known as citizens associations.

The most venerable such group, the North East Washington Citizens Association, formed in the 1860s as a response to the Baltimore and Ohio's aggravating street grade tracks. The Board of Public Works' "discrimination" in favor of northwest Washington during the territorial period prompted similar groups in Capitol Hill and South Washington. Citizens groups proliferated and broadened in scope after the commission took over. The South Washington Improvement and Protective Association, for example, lobbied for new railroad routes, the rebuilding of Long Bridge, and reclamation of the Potomac Flats, in addition to better streets and sewers.[18] During the 1880s and 1890s, the number of these groups fluctuated between fourteen and twenty-two.

Emphasis on sectional grievances hampered the neighborhood movement from the start. Above all, this narrowness of focus discouraged participation from the capital's wealthiest, most populous neighborhoods, in particular the area known as Northwest, the northwestern section of L'Enfant's Washington City. Why should taxpayers in Northwest bother with a movement premised on the notion that they were unduly privileged? Georgetown was the only western section with a thriving club. In the 1880s, Northwest had approximately 42 percent of the area and 57 percent of the population of Washington City and Georgetown. Citizens associations also arose to represent the suburbs, such as Brightwood, Mount Pleasant, and Brookland, that were emerging within the District boundary but outside the original two cities, Washington City and Georgetown. This outlying area of the District, once known as Washington County, has about five times the area of the old cities, but as late as 1888, it contained only 24,364 of the District's 218,157 people, and 3,645 of its 38,585 taxable buildings. The 1894 Joint Executive movement involved three large east and south Washington groups, the Georgetown organization, and five suburban clubs, but no organization from Northwest. The citizens associations could not credibly claim to represent either property or people.[19]

The first priority of each association was its backyard, which set neighborhood groups at odds with one another. Competition between neighborhoods for attention and money proved a "perpetual cause of jealousy and heartburning" for the commissioners and Congress. The District and Appropriations committees received so many petitions for neighborhood improvements that they could review none with care. Out of self-preservation, Appropriations limited its contacts with resident delegations. The job of sifting requests was pushed onto the commissioners, whose budget hearings turned into parades of delegations wanting this street sewered or that trolley line approved. "Jealousies and rivalries between the several sections of the city, each urging its own claims for preference and disparaging those of the others," imposed upon commissioners a "harassing and thankless task."[20]

Whenever neighborhood groups tried to work together on overall city problems, acrimonious debate resulted. Either too few associations participated to give weight to a position, or neighborhood interests conflicted. One insurmountable difficulty concerned railroad tracks, since all plans to relieve the northeast increased burdens on the southwest, and vice versa. In 1881, Engineer Commissioner Twining submitted the first project for a Union Station — at Maryland and Virginia avenues, southwest. Twining aimed to solve two galling problems in a stroke by clearing the Mall of tracks and giving people a reason regularly to cross the underused park. The South Washington Improvement Association objected: Twining's plan, they claimed, would consign "exclusive occupancy" of their quarter to depots and sidings. If Union Station were to be below the Mall, it had to be farther east, towards the Capitol, in order to free "the most desirable portion of South Washington." Northeast groups, meanwhile, made it an article of faith that "the citizens" favored a station south of the Mall.[21] The ensuing stalemate lasted two decades. When, in 1901, the Senate Parks Commission, the consulting board that developed the McMillan Plan, finally convinced the Pennsylvania Railroad to leave the Mall for Union Station's present Massachusetts Avenue, northeast, site, one newspaper chided that Northeast residents would be "a set of mummies" if they did not "vigorously protest." The North East Association called architect Daniel Burnham's Union Station plan "hideous and monstrous."[22]

Since the citizens associations were most vigorous in neighborhoods that felt slighted by the authorities, all the groups agreed on one point — that the public works budget slanted egregiously towards Northwest. Although far more impartial than the Board of Public Works, the civilian commissioners were almost entirely from Northwest and from portions of the business community engaged in real estate development. The Army Engineers expressed intentions to spread work evenly, but the officers also accepted that public works had an economic development function. Washington's rulers thus had minimal sympathy for sectional complaints, especially since this criticism frequently bordered on personal slander. Through the mid-1880s, the commissioners asserted that charges of continued "discrimination" were "not warranted by facts." They blamed slowness at redressing Shepherd's imbalances on the need to devote most funds to replacing rotten wood pavements. In 1885, with only about half a mile of wood left, the Engineer Department suggested that, although Northwest paid 80 percent of taxes, it should receive only 50 percent of the improvement allocations until other areas caught up. When this did not appease the associations, District engineers published "rather remarkable" data purporting to show that since 1878, the proportion of improvement funds spent in each section approximated the average of the proportion of each section's population, area, and tax assessments.[23]

The neighborhood associations' claims could be refuted with statistics. Still, the Engineers tried to mollify the neighborhoods by distinguishing between general and special improvements. The former consisted of streets of "public importance," improved at the city's discretion, while the latter were attended to according to a "formula" designed to spread funds among sections equitably. The neighborhoods responded that since this formula was based on *existing* property values, the District would deny them the stimulation that Shepherd had earlier given his preferred quarters. The associations decided they could not trust the commissioners and demanded that Congress dictate an improvement schedule to the commission. When the House reacted favorably, the result was the quarrel over alleged Senate bias towards Northwest that was discussed in chapter 5.[24]

The citizens associations presumed that one could build a political coalition based upon property ownership. The interests of developers and merchants clashed with those of householders, themselves hard to unite. Groups from Capitol Hill, northeast Washington, and south Washington, where homeowners were mainly skilled workers, small businessmen, and government clerks, were under the aegis of proprietors of real estate, lumber, hardware, and grocery concerns. Subdividers sponsored suburban associations, whose leaders included both ordinary homeowners and merchants and professionals eager to build a neighborhood clientele. Municipal and federal officials were left to mediate intra- as well as interneighborhood disputes.

Congress and the commissioners often received memorials for and against the same local project. In 1891 the House Appropriations District subcommittee could not decide between the North East Association and realtors Myron Parker and Brainard Warner. The realtors had gathered dozens of signatures to show that "residents and property owners of East Washington" wanted a section of Third Street, northeast, to be paved. The association had resolved against this project, on the grounds that it compromised the neighborhood's case against the B & O's street-level tracks in the vicinity. The Senate already had consented to the pavement as a "personal favor" to Parker, the Board of Trade's founding president and a member of the Republican National Committee. Parker "was interested in the erection of a block of houses" on each side of the street.[25] More intractible were intraneighborhood disputes over proposed transit routes. Homeowners along the planned line would accuse subdividers and transit entrepreneurs (often the same individuals) of plotting to invade their "quiet and repose" and undermine their street's "charm." Residents of slightly more distant streets would take the side of the trolleys and charge the anti-trolley faction with causing them "serious hardship."[26]

Even in the most "particularistic" jurisdictions, elected representative bodies sometimes manage to transcend constituent interests. Their volunteer status, on top of their sectionalism, was fatal to the neighborhood groups' efforts to set up a quasi legislature. During 1888, the joint Citizens Representative Committee of One Hundred "largely destroyed its usefulness" with meandering discussions of municipal reorganization. When some neighborhoods stopped sending delegates, the president became so exasperated that he unilaterally suspended meetings. Some members accused him of precipitating failure, but a supporter said in agreement, "Each association ought to be fully represented if we [are] to continue as representatives of the people." The 1894 Joint Executive failed quickly. In 1902, an organizational meeting for yet another central association drew delegates from only six neighborhoods. Those attending noted wistfully that if all neighborhoods participated, Congress might "be bound to pay some attention."[27]

III

Though inevitable, inter- and intraneighborhood disputes, created headaches for congressmen responsible for District policy. In late 1888, as the Citizens Representative Committee fell apart, a senator friendly to Washington asserted, "The squabbles of the citizens [over railroad routes] have disgusted many of us who are really as anxious as they are to see this troublous matter settled." How could the city's friends possibly push complex legislation through a distracted Congress when "no two representative [residents] can agree?"[28]

In April 1890, the *Post* voiced a similar concern: "Hitherto, the wants of the District have been made known to the law-making and appropriation-granting powers in a desultory and not always harmonious way through various associations of citizens, as often pulling apart as together." The paper expressed hope that henceforth the city would hold lawmakers' attention better. The reason for this optimism was that, since its formation in late 1889, the Board of Trade had encountered remarkable success as the capital's spokesman to the nation. In his first annual report in 1890, board president Myron Parker hinted at a major reason for this success — encouragement from the capital's official rulers. "The necessity for [such] an organization," Parker wrote, "was manifest to all." The board answered "the common remark in both Houses of Congress that there was no general organization in Washington representing in a public, impartial, unsectional way, the necessity and wishes of the community."[29]

Nearly all American cities in the quarter-century after 1890 experienced movements among downtown businessmen and professionals to create nonsectional community organizations with continuing influence on local government. "Downtown" here connotes not a location, but an outlook that encouraged civic activism while defining the city's well-being in an aggregate way, as viewed from the center. The Washington Board of Trade thus manifested the impulse towards organizing, centralizing, and professionalizing the urban and national polity that formed a major strand of progressive thought.

The group gave itself a misleading name. The board functioned not as a commercial but as a commercial-civic association. Anyone familiar with the urban South will grasp the distinction. In a Northern or Midwestern city, a board of trade might well act, as the name implies, as a coalition of wholesale and retail merchants. In the South, where urban businessmen and professionals hoped through collective action to transcend the region's historic backwardness, such groups often as not developed into a sort of political party or governing alliance. Southern chambers of commerce and boards of trade strove to incorporate not just commercial interests but as many strategic elites as could be digested. Their umbrella nature enabled such groups to accumulate "the requisite power and resources," according to historian Blaine Brownell, who identified this phenomenon, "to determine urban policy and translate their thinking into action." While the commercial-civic impulse spread throughout urban America, the coherence and articulateness it acquired in the capital may signal that Washington's elites shared a "New South" as much as a mid-Atlantic regional outlook. During the late nineteenth and early twentieth centuries, the District slowly rebuilt traditional business and social links with the South that had been disrupted during the war and the Shepherd period.[30]

Other civic associations besides the Board of Trade sprang up in the national city between 1890 and 1910. The capital produced two citywide but more strictly business groups — the Business Men's Association and the Chamber of Commerce. The Civic Center was an alliance of gentleman reformers with professionals in health, education, and social work, such as led the progressive movement in nearby Baltimore.[31]

Despite the diversity of groups and approaches, most Washingtonians came to accept the Board of Trade's claim to be the primary place where "influences which can promote the welfare of Washington seek and find representation and the opportunity for active public labor." The press was instrumental in launching the group. Credit for its founding often went to Beriah Wilkins, a former Democratic congressman from Ohio who earlier in

1889 had bought a share in the *Post* and assumed the position of editor. Wilkins wrote the circular letter that prompted the inaugural meeting. The "representative businessmen" who responded to Wilkin's call needed little persuading that the recent inglorious collapse of the Citizens Representative Committee left a void. Civic leaders such as Parker, Henry Willard, Brainard Warner, Charles Glover of the Riggs Bank, and ex-commissioner Samuel Wheatley responded so enthusiastically that Wilkins did not even have to serve as an officer of the group he inspired.[32]

Aware of shared interests with similar movements elsewhere, the Washingtonians joined the National Board of Trade and engaged in the standard activities of commercial associations. The by-laws defined the group's object as "the consideration of, and action upon, matters concerning the commerce, prosperity, and advancement of the material interests of the National Capital," with "special attention to the promotion of public improvements." The board sent delegates to monetary and mining conventions and corresponded with sister groups promoting better merchant marine and food and drug laws, the Isthmian canal, and a federal department of commerce and industry. The group acted as a board of promotion, to attract tourists and conventions. In 1898, when the National Board of Trade, National Food and Drug Congress, Episcopal General Convention, and National Education Association all met in the capital, the board's secretary proudly proclaimed Washington, "Convention City."[33]

Despite parallels to other boards of trade, President Warner explained in 1894, "The mission of this Board is very different from the aims of corresponding bodies elsewhere," because of the capital's "exceptional" political and economic structure. Leaders reminded their fellows that the commission system left them with "unique and different" responsibilities. "Chief" among these, according to Warner, was "proper presentation of the interests of the city before the several committees of Congress." Board of Trade members were requested to employ their individual and collective prominence to "endeavor, as far as possible, to explain the relations of [the District to] the General Government to each and every member of Congress with whom he is acquainted."[34]

From the start, the group set out to fill the void left by the omission of a local legislature in the 1878 government act. In early 1890, board president Parker told neighborhood representatives that the organization intended to adopt "the plan of a common council and board of alderman." The association created standing committees on parks, health, charities, public order, libraries, and schools, in addition to public works, utilities, commerce, and finance. This initiative had the desired effect. The board won support in Congress simply because it consisted of knowledgeable persons capable of producing polished bills on complicated matters. The act setting up the local superintendent of insurance was known as a "Board of Trade bill," as was

1894 legislation to reform the assessor's office. The organization made itself a leading consultant on the strategic matter of taxation. The commissioners, already overburdened with executive and regulatory duties, were happy to have a capable group that could relieve the pressure upon them to review and promote legislation. District executives began to meet with board delegations as a mayor would a city council committee, so that by 1898, board president Theodore Noyes could claim that one of the group's strengths was that it kept "in close touch with the Commissioners."[35]

The eternal railroad question became one of the first areas where the board built a cooperative relationship with congressional policy-makers. During the 1880s, the unsettled state of railroad routes meant that the District had no legal means to regulate freight facilities. The commissioners had been granting temporary permits to the Pennsylvania and the B & O, but measures to legitimize those permits were pinned down in crossfire among the corporations, pro- and anti-railroad factions in Congress, and neighborhoods. In 1890, the Senate District Committee consigned this morass to McMillan, then a low-ranking freshman. The senator softened a shamelessly pro-railroad bill then on the table. McMillan hoped to legalize the freight yards that had spread through south Washington while ensuring that they did not eat up the neighborhood, as people there feared. McMillan, moreover, refused to accede to Pennsylvania Railroad demands to reaffirm occupancy of the Mall and based his work on the assumption that a comprehensive settlement of the vexing problem of grade crossings could follow shortly.[36]

The Board of Trade's Railroad Committee made itself useful to McMillan by consolidating disparate neighborhood concerns into a relatively consistent resident position. Board members retained the confidence of resentful inhabitants by proclaiming that "outlaws, grabbers, and robbers" ran the Pennsylvania Railroad. Meanwhile, the board reassured the companies and Congress by acceding to McMillan's basic assertion that railroads were "public servants entitled to facilities." Negotiations with the B & O reached an impasse, but Pennsylvania executives recognized that despite the angry rhetoric, McMillan's plans indeed afforded the company ample facilities. South Washington would suffer the bulk of freight, but at least cars would no longer unload in the streets. The board refused to back McMillan's final conference report on Pennsylvania freight sidings in January 1891, because it did not deal with the long-term issues of grade crossings and the Mall tracks.[37] Yet, given the ill-will between the public and the companies and among residents themselves, McMillan's peers were impressed that he could get through any rail legislation that left the concerned parties speaking to one another. The Pennsylvania freight bill helped McMillan's progress to both the District chairmanship and to a trusted place in the Republican party's hierarchy.

This and similiar experiences cemented an important friendship. The

Board of Trade's alliance with McMillan's Senate District Committee, arising from mutual usefulness as well as shared perspective, was a key factor in building the board into "the greatest of District of Columbia institutions." The commercial-civic group did all it could to enhance McMillan's stature with Washingtonians. The Senate District Committee returned the favor by treating board proposals with extra respect and by siding with the board in disputes with House "economists" and with the Corps of Engineers. McMillan also ensured that another of his committees, Commerce, remained favorable to the District, which facilitated campaigns for having riverfront reclamations paid out of the Rivers and Harbors bill.[38]

Secretary George Harries, a journalist turned utilities executive, wrote in 1900 that the "conservative energy and irreproachable character" of the board had "impressed themselves deeply on those who make our laws." McMillan, the Detroit railroad car manufacturer and utilities entrepreneur, was naturally sympathetic, but the group had to employ the arts of persuasion on others. Pamphlets on the 1878 act circulated through Congress. The group distributed tens of thousands of copies of a free handbook, aimed at tourists, offering "useful information" about Washington. In addition to rail schedules and bank hours, this handbook contained a plea, supported by statistics and pertinent quotations from historical documents, that the country "deal fairly with the District." When the board's new headquarters opened on G Street between 14th and 15th, northwest, the secretary sent engraved invitations to congressmen, judges, and District officials, "inviting them to make free use of the rooms at any time it might suit their pleasure, for correspondence, meeting friends, or business engagements," a valuable service given the woeful shortage of federal office space. Especially "promotive of good feeling between the national and local partners" were the annual spring shad bake and winter reception, the highlight of which were speeches on Washington's needs.[39]

It was essential for the commercial-civic group to portray the capital's deficiencies as an injury to national honor. Washington had come a long way from the "dirty little third-rate Southern town" the *Nation* had found it to be in 1871. Could anyone blame a congressman who, especially during the grueling depression of the 1890s, wondered if the United States did not have higher priorities? If the Board of Trade could not make a convincing case that something deeper than local pride or ambition was at stake in its proposals, the half-and-half system's skeptics and enemies might persuade a majority in Congress that Washington's people could pay for their needs by themselves. In 1900, board president John Joy Edson insisted, "There are no improvements or needs, however desirable or important, that should be secured by consenting to an appropriation wholly out of the revenues of the District." In Edson's view, "the direct and proper course for District officials and citizens" was "never to assent" to departures from the half-and-half principle.[40]

IV

The Board of Trade could maintain its hold on Congress and the commissioners only if it could reasonably claim to represent, if not everyone in Washington, at least the city's "vital" interests. In conformity with this ambition, board organizers adopted a membership policy more liberal than would have prevailed in, say, their social clubs. Anyone was welcome who could meet the hefty $25 initiation fee and $10 annual dues ($25 for firms). The group affirmed a nonracial policy as late as 1916, though by the early 1920s it had adopted segregation. It did not move to exclude women until 1924. This openness was tempered by self-selecting admission procedures: an applicant had to be nominated by a member and approved by the membership committee and board of directors. A Jew, Isadore Saks of the department store family, became a director, but the early board contained fewer than five women or blacks at any time.[41]

In the belief that numbers conferred legitimacy, founding president Parker set a target of one thousand members. In the first two years, four hundred joined. The depression that began in 1893 stymied growth, so that still under five hundred belonged by 1895. The group first lowered, then suspended its dues and relied upon levies, though this threatened to cause an embarrassing operating deficit. "Don't resign; stick to us," the membership committee pleaded with hard-pressed businessmen in 1896. Concerned about slow growth, the committee recommended suspending cumbersome membership rules to allow active recruitment. With the return of prosperity came renewed confidence, and by 1901 membership was 650 and rising. At this juncture, it was felt that active solicitation ill became "the dignity of the Board of Trade."[42]

Despite occasional doubts about how many specific business interests the board managed to incorporate, observers agreed that the organization was popular with its essential targets. The board attracted all the important local-based enterprises that backed commercial-civic movements in other cities that have been studied. Historian Carl Harris found that the leadership of a comparable organization in Birmingham, Alabama in the early 1900s included 25–33 percent merchants, 20 percent realtors, and 15–20 percent professionals. Bankers and manufacturers composed the remainder. Truly small businessmen, such as grocers, saloonkeepers, and artisans, were not encouraged to join and almost never did.[43] Washington's Board of Trade contained virtually the same mix, except that the Washington group drew few manufacturers, a reflection of the unimportance of manufacturing to the local economy. Both at the depths of the mid-decade depression and in the midst of turn-of-the-century prosperity, merchants, lawyers, and realtors made up 55–60 percent of the Washington board. The addition of bankers, contractors, physicians, and government officials, brings the percentage to 75.6 in 1895 and 75.7 in 1900.

Table 7.1 Occupations of Washington Board of Trade Members

	1895		1900	
	N	%	N	%
	484	100.0	655	100.0
Architecture	5	1.0	7	1.1
Asphalt paving	2	0.4	6	0.9
Auctioneering	3	0.6	4	0.6
Banking/Brokerage	25	5.2	39	6.0
Civil engineering	5	1.0	2	0.3
Contracting/Building	22	4.5	14	2.1
Editing/Journalism	9	1.9	12	1.8
Hauling/Storage	4	0.8	4	0.6
Hotels	13	2.7	14	2.1
Investment/Retirement	11	2.3	14	2.1
Law/Patents	67	13.8	105	16.0
Livery stables	5	1.0	4	0.6
Manufacturing	17	3.5	5	0.8
Medicine	18	3.7	29	4.4
Plumbing/Building supply[b]	6	1.2	17	2.6
Printing/Publishing	5	1.0	13	2.0
Railroads	6	1.2	8	1.2
Real estate/Loans/Insurance	75	15.5	99	15.1
Sales[a]	147	30.4	163	24.9
Undertaking	3	0.6	2	0.3
U.S. or D.C. administration	12	2.5	47	7.2
Other[c]	24	5.0	47	7.2

Source: Washington Board of Trade, annual reports, 1895, p. 131; 1900, p. 189.
[a] In 1900, included 6 commission merchants, 4 confectioners, 7 druggists, and 4 florists.
[b] Plumbing supply for 1895, building supply for 1900.
[c] For 1900, includes 18 "Managers and Agents."

Although many cities produced similar movements, the capital's unique governance enabled its Board of Trade to rise to greater heights of power than its counterparts achieved. Commercial-civic organizations everywhere had advantages over other citizen groups seeking to affect the formation and implementation of policy, on account of the disproportionate prominence, resources, and unity of their members. The tendency of the institutional framework of governance in most American cities to foster multiple power centers limited the ability of commercial-civic movements to consolidate as continuous a grip on the municipal polity as happened at Washington. Even progressive-style efforts to implement "businesslike" municipal structures did not necessarily result in government as "downtown" saw fit, since professional public administrators could build power bases for themselves and since business groups frequently supported municipal reorganization for complex reasons not directly related to a governmental format's responsiveness to business.[44] Like other American cities, Washington harbored a diversity of interests and perspectives, but the capital's centralized, nonelected institutions firmly rewarded those who concentrated influence and punished those who dispersed it. Moreover, those who made and implemented the capital's laws were predisposed, by the promotional tendency in our political culture, to accept the board's insistence that its downtown perspective coincided with the general welfare.

So long as the board received the lion's share of influence and respect, it was willing to abide alternate forms of civic action. Board leaders believed they stood for "unsectional" concerns, "the common good of all," while the neighborhood-based citizens associations focused on "matters peculiarly sectional and local." Theodore Noyes argued, "The spheres of activity of the associations and the board instead of colliding are distinct and supplemental."[45] Railroad routes, industrial sites, and public works funds brought the downtown movement into collision with the neighborhoods. Mitigating such conflicts, however, were the board's and the citizens' overlapping membership; many businessmen and professionals had citywide interests that they expressed through the board and sectional concerns that led them to join a neighborhood group.

Since the Board of Trade argued that factories, warehouses, and railroad sidings should be concentrated in South Washington, that neighborhood would on the surface want nothing to do with the citywide group; yet Charles Church, one of south Washington's delegates to the short-lived 1894 Joint Executive Committees of the Citizens Associations was at the same time chairman of the Board of Trade's Rivers and Harbors Committee. Serving with Church on that board committee was the long-time leader of south Washington's citizens association, realtor J. Harrison Johnson. Johnson's brother, lumber dealer E. Kurtz Johnson, and Kurtz's partner, William Wimsatt, were both Board of Trade directors in 1894. Overall, five of south Washington's eight Joint Executive delegates belonged to the Board of Trade.

None of the Joint Executive delegates from the historically aggrieved Capitol Hill area was a Board of Trade officer in the mid-1890s, and only one of the twelve from that part of town was a member of the board. Yet, by 1900, three of the twelve were on the board, one as a director and committee chairman. In 1902, building supplier Thomas W. Smith simultaneously served as president of the East Washington Citizens Association and Board of Trade president. In addition to owning a mill that employed one hundred men, Smith was vice president of the National Capital Bank and owned hundreds of thousands of dollars worth of District real estate. Smith was not atypical; downtown businessmen saw that they had a stake in making their presence felt in their neighborhoods, and people active on the neighborhood level could also feel the need to exert influence on a citywide basis.[46]

Of the seventy delegates to the Joint Executive whom I managed to trace, only four were committee chairmen on the Board of Trade, but seventeen were members of the board in either 1894 or 1895. Over three-fourths of the board's forty officers, directors, and committee chairmen at the start of 1894 were from Northwest and Georgetown; this was true of only 24 percent of the Joint Executive. This illustrates Northwest's economic dominance and the neighborhood movment's opposition to what it perceived as official favoritism towards that section. Both movements consisted of established residents, mostly middle aged. The board members tended to be of longer residence. Thirty-eight of the forty Board of Trade officers had been in the City Directory ten years before, which was true for only 77 percent of the Joint Executive, but turnover rates for both groups compare favorably with those of the elites in other American cities in the nineteenth century. Virtually the same proportion of each group was still in the capital ten years later. Whatever their disputes, the board and the Joint Executive both contained dedicated Washingtonians.

The Board of Trade was just in contending that it offered wider-ranging experience and a more cosmopolitan perspective than did neighborhood activists like those on the Joint Executive (see table 7.2).[47] While nearly 60 percent of the Joint Executive were natives of the Washington region, more Board of Trade leaders were born in the Northeast and Ohio than in the District and surrounding states. The background of the board's leadership in its first decade suggests that the 1870s improver movement had to some extent succeeded in infusing Washington enterprise with the Northern orientation and spirit that Shepherd and his allies thought essential. Another study finds that half the group's founding directors in 1889 were born in the North and that the median date of their arrival in the District was 1872, the height of the territorial period. The board would not always remain so Northern in character. By the 1920s, native Washingtonians accounted for about half of its officers. It may not be a coincidence that during that decade, other Washingtonians often accused the board of having become inbred and less enlightened than in its vibrant early years.[48]

Some members of the Joint Executive of the neighborhood groups also had broad experience. The leaders of the 1894 Joint Executive were Ellis Spear, former U.S. commissioner of patents, and William Birney, former municipal attorney for the District. A Civil War veteran, Spear was a Maine native and Bowdoin graduate. Birney, son of the abolitionist James Birney, had led an adventurous life that included participation in the French Revolution of 1848.[49] Yet none of the Joint Executive had as thorough an acquaintance with the country's or the city's business as did the Board of Trade leaders.

The board's 1894 list of officers epitomizes the group's cosmopolitan character and downtown orientation. President Brainard Warner, a Pennsylvania native with political connections, began his career in the 1860s as a revenue collector. After a stint as editor of a Pennsylvania temperance journal and as law clerk to Thaddeus Stevens, Warner entered the capital's real estate business during the territorial boom. By the 1890s, Warner ran perhaps the largest realty firm in the District. In addition to his property interests, Warner was President of the Washington Loan and Trust Company and financed street car lines. First vice president Samuel W. Woodward had run a dry goods store in Chelsea, Massachusetts, with Alvin M. Lothrop until 1880, when the pair opened what became Washington's greatest department store. The second vice president was former commissioner Wheatley. General Counsel Alexander T. Britton, a New York native and Brown graduate, was a former Interior Department expert in public land law. The treasurer, O. G. Staples, built resort hotels in the Thousand Islands before purchasing Willard's Hotel from Board of Trade director Henry Willard (the former Board of Public Works vice president). In 1909, the *National Cyclopedia of American Biography* called Staples the "largest owner of hotel property in the United States today." Secretary John B. Wight was the former supervisor of the Columbia Institution for the Deaf and Dumb and was named a commissioner by McKinley in 1897. Wight's replacement as board secretary, George H. Harries, was highly visible in the District militia and other civic groups and played an important role in the effort to consolidate Washington's fragmented electrical and transit businesses.[50]

Board directors in 1894 included the "big three" of Washington banking—Charles J. Bell of American Security and Trust, John Joy Edson of Washington Loan and Trust, and Charles Glover of the Riggs Bank. None was a native of the area. Bell, born in Dublin in 1858, was the cousin of Alexander Graham Bell, for whom he worked setting up telephone systems in England before entering banking in the American capital in 1882. Bell and Glover came to hold interlocking utilities directorships, and each served as president of the Washington Stock Exchange.[51] Directors Crosby Noyes and Theodore Noyes of the *Star* and former congressman Wilkins, editor and part-owner of the *Post*, represented the major evening and morning papers. Another former congressman active on the board was Jeremiah Wilson, the Indiana Republican who in 1874 had convinced Adolph Cluss to testify against Shepherd. The 1874 investigation must have impressed Wilson greatly, because he remained in Washington after leaving Congress to enter the real estate and paving businesses, in addition to establishing a successful law practice. During the 1890s, Wilson testified before the commissioners and Congress as president of the Cranford Paving Company, which, ironically, had its origins in the paving ring that Wilson had attacked during the territorial years.[52]

Board members in banking and insurance—enterprises typical of commercial-civic leaders—occupied an equivalent place to the Joint Executive's government officials, physicians, and printers—representative of the city's solid homeowners. Both bodies included realtors, merchants, and lawyers, but different types were prominent in each. Evan Tucker and Michael Weller of the Joint Executive were becoming citywide realtors, but the scope of the other

Table 7.2 Characteristics of the Board of Trade and the Joint Executive, 1894

	Board of Trade		Joint Executive	
	N	%	N	%
Mean age	49.95	37	49.39	51
Median age	48	37	50	51
	Birthplace			
	37	100.0	52	100.0
District of Columbia	7	18.9	21	40.4
Maryland, Virginia,				
West Virginia	7	18.9	10	19.2
Northeast[a]	14	37.8	10	19.2
Ohio[b]	3	8.1	1	1.9
South[c]	2	5.4	2	3.8
Abroad[d]	4	10.8	8	15.4
	Persistence in City Directory			
1884	38	95.0	54	77.1
1894	40	100.0	70	100.0
1904	29	72.5	50	71.4
	Area of Residence			
	40	100.0	70	100.0
Northwest	27	67.5	4	5.7
Northeast	2	5.0	10	14.3
Southwest	2	5.0	8	11.4
Southeast	0	0.0	3	4.3
Georgetown	4	10.0	13	18.6
Washington County	3	7.5	31	44.3
Maryland, Virginia	2	5.0	1	1.4
	Occupation, 1894			
	40	100.0	70	100.0
Banking, insurance	9	22.5	3	4.3
Contracting, building				
supply	7	17.5	4	5.7
Crafts, skilled labor	0	0.0	5[e]	7.1

Table 7.2 (Continued)

	Board of Trade		Joint Executive	
	N	%	N	%
Government	0	0.0	12	17.1
Journalism	3	7.5	0	0.0
Law, claims agency	6	15.0	9	12.9
Manufacturing	0	0.0	3[f]	4.3
Medicine	0	0.0	4	5.7
Real estate	4	10.0	6	8.6
Transit	1	2.5	1	1.4
Wholesale and retail sales	9	22.5	19	27.1
All others	1[g]	2.5	4[h]	5.7
	Prominence			
In *National Cyclopedia*	14	35.0	3	4.3
In local biographical dictionaries	22	55.0	12	17.1
	Assessed Real Property, 1893[i]			
Number above $10,000	28	70.0	22	31.4
Aggregate[j]	$1,880,178		$589,534	
Mean[j]	$67,149		26,797	
Median[j]	46,825		24,489	

Sources: Board of Trade *Annual Report,* Jan. 10, 1894; 53rd Cong., 2nd sess. (Feb. 1, 1894), S. Misc. Doc. 67; and city directories, contemporary accounts, local histories, and biographical dictionaries. See also note 47.

[a] Includes New England, Pennsylvania, New York, and New Jersey.
[b] Only Midwestern state represented.
[c] Includes Alabama, North Carolina, and Tennessee.
[d] Includes England, Scotland, Ireland, and Germany.
[e] A pressman, a printer, a tailor, a carpenter, and a woodworker.
[f] Includes proprietors of a carriage building company, a paper mill, and a brick factory.
[g] A hotel proprietor.
[h] A bookkeeper, a teacher, a policeman, and a civil engineer.
[i] Since no official index of assessments for this period appears to have survived, property information comes from lists of large (value over $10,000) property holders as published in the *Evening Star,* Oct. 27–Nov. 4, 1893. The Joint Executive figures include one estate of $7,686, which represents Evan Tucker's half of property shared with his brother.
[j] Of the 28 large property holders.

Four commercial-civic leaders from turn-of-the-century Washington, as noted cartoonist Clifford K. Berryman portrayed them. *Top left:* George H. Harries, utilities executive, Board of Trade secretary, president of the Board of School Trustees, general in the District National Guard. *Top right:* Crosby S. Noyes, owner and editor of the *Evening Star. Bottom left:* Myron M. Parker, realtor and financier, Republican National Committee, founding president of the Board of Trade, District Commissioner, 1893–94. The cartoon lampoons Parker's investments in Mexican mining ventures. *Bottom right:* George Truesdell, engineer, suburban developer, utilities executive, District Commissioner, 1894–97. Published in Clifford K. Berryman, *Cartoons and Caricatures* (Washington, D.C.: H. B. Thompson, n.d.); courtesy the Washingtoniana Division, District of Columbia Public Library.

realtors in the neighborhood movement was confined to one region or a few subdivisions. On the other side, the board's George Truesdell, appointed commissioner in March 1894, was a university-trained civil engineer who co-ordinated transit lines and subdivisions in new suburbs such as Eckington. Truesdell's operations were grand for the period, though less extensive and coordinated than Francis Newlands's Chevy Chase. Warner, Glover, Myron Parker, and Thomas Smith combined downtown, inner city, and suburban holdings. While it is impossible to trace exactly, the forty Board of Trade leaders in 1894 probably held in aggregate three times as much property as the seventy neighborhood delegates. Four from the board held between $197,000 and $272,000 in the 1893 assessment, but the wealthiest citizens' representative held only $51,046.

The merchants on the board were the likes of Woodward and Saks. The Joint Executive group's merchants included Arnold Holsten and Frederick Kramer, who ran vegetable and flower stalls in the Center Market, and George Pyles, a dealer in dry goods and groceries in Anacostia. Except for Birney and Spear, none of the lawyers on the Joint Executive had a citywide practice, while the board's attorneys and claims agents all represented substantial clients. Over half the board's officers, directors, and committee chairmen merited profiles in one of two contemporary local biographical compendia: the *Post*'s *Washington: Its Men and Institutions,* published in 1903, and the Washington edition of *American Biographical Dictionaries,* published in 1908. Only 17 percent of the Joint Executive made it into one of these books. The *National Cyclopedia of American Biography,* which profiled a wide variety of persons from business and public life, saw fit to include fourteen Board of Trade leaders but from the Joint Executive only Birney, Spear, and realtor and anti-quarian Michael Weller.

During the first quarter-century of the appointed commission, the key trends in Washington's popular politics were the citizens associations, which usually espoused the perspective of neighborhoods, and the Board of Trade, which embraced the commercial-civic point of view. The skill the Board of Trade exhibited, combined with the ideological sympathy of strategic members of Congress, gave the downtown movement greater leverage than it would have attained in a more typical municipal system. There is no reason to suppose, however, that the national city's people would have directed their energies along markedly different channels had complete or partial home rule been restored. With home rule or without it, tension between the commercial-civic and neighborhood tendencies would have remained a major focus of Washington politics.[53] If Washington had regained an elected council, the same sort of neighborhood notables who ran the citizens associations would probably have won a majority most of the time. Civic-minded professionals and citywide businessmen such as led the Board of Trade would probably have occupied most remaining seats. A council with this composition would have reflected the balance of interest, sentiment, and opinion in the local white population. Immigrant politics, a large matter elsewhere in the country, would not have been a major concern. The direction that would have been taken by the black community had it suddenly regained the franchise is more difficult to imagine. While the capital in 1890 had the highest proportion of blacks among the nation's twenty-five largest cities, it had the lowest proportion of foreign-born residents.[54]

V

"Within the last few years," board president Theodore Noyes remarked in 1899, "there has been comparatively little of the old wrangling before Congress of contending delegations of citizens." In the newspaperman's view, that "harmonious cooperation" had replaced "jealous discord" demonstrated that the business group had achieved the "primary purpose" for which it was founded. Most residents, Noyes felt, recognized the value of the board's special place in the national city's governance: "What has been accomplished through the cooperation of the District Commissioners, the Board of Trade, and the Congressional committees dealing with District affairs has been an object lesson in the value of harmony."[55]

The board was, of course, not always as harmonious as Noyes claimed. Some members grumbled at the effusive preaching of officers such as Noyes. In 1897, the membership committee, concerned about criticism that "conclusions reached by the board itself as a body have narrowed down to the opinion of a few," recommended more frequent, open-ended meetings. Contentious proposals could prompt "general and lengthy debate," with speakers angrily trying to rule each other out of order.[56]

Still, few who knew Washington well would dispute Noyes's basic assertion that his group was more adept than other resident organizations at "united, organized, and systematic effort." The board helped build a viable system of cooperation between the capital's public and private sectors. As a result, the local polity demonstrated "strength and effectiveness" in dealing with complicated questions involving the direction and character of development. Under the commercial-civic movement's guidance, District business would continue to focus on enterprises that fit well with Washington's special role as the nation's administrative and symbolic home. In return, municipal and federal authorities would perform regulatory and planning functions so as to encourage, not constrain, enterprise. The public-private governing alliance that the board and McMillan's Senate District Committee created stressed benevolence and civic-mindedness to a remarkable degree, yet, in part because this alliance quickly achieved so much, Washington's experience in the 1890s seemed to validate the basic tenets of promotional governance — that the public and private sectors naturally complement each other and that the proper relationship between state and enterprise is "harmonious cooperation."[57]

The board succeeded better than neighborhood-based groups or more narrowly commercial groups would have in achieving a rough consensus concerning how much and what kinds of industry the city should accommodate. Despite muttering from a few who still harbored George Washington's "greatest commercial emporium" idea, the Board of Trade adhered to the understanding that emerged during the Shepherd years, and it worked to direct local attention towards enterprises consistent with the "needs and uses of the national government." Spokesmen such as realtor Brainard Warner stressed the group's resolution to promote only "such manufactures as would not be detrimental to the city in any respect."[58]

The board had standing committees on commerce and manufactures and on mercantile interests, but only the latter did much. Retailers such as Isadore Saks used the Mercantile Interests Committee to promote tourism, downtown improvement, and favorable licensing and trade laws. They argued that Washington's prosperity would follow, not from imitating Baltimore, Pittsburgh, or Cleveland, but from emphasizing the city's special attractions as the "fountain-head of the National government" and as a center of "art, science, and literature."[59]

A strong indication that the board put little stock in the notion of an industrial Washington is the fact that prominent, influential members rarely joined the Commerce and Manufactures Committee. They preferred panels devoted to public works, social services, finance, and development. Those who did serve on Commerce and Manufactures won approval for pushing light industry or commerce intended for regional consumption, particularly the coal, grain, lumber, and building supply trades that had long dominated the Potomac waterfront. More aggressive efforts to attract the "hurly-burly of commerce" encountered apathy or resistance from the rest of the group. If some board members regretted that congressmen, not wanting to nurture a rival for their constituents, refused to consider tax breaks for industrial investment in the District and did little to develop water power on the Potomac, others retorted that "Washington is not, and, perhaps, never can be a great commercial city." In 1896, the manufactures committee itself declared advantageous "the assured absence of large commercial and manufacturing interests," since it increased Washington's attractiveness as an administrative, residential, and cultural center.[60]

By 1900, Washington represented a fascinating counterexample to Max Weber's belief that commerce created the environment most conducive to the development of a thorough sense of identity in a city's elite. Washington's elite, as embodied by the Board of Trade, had no interest in enterprises that compromised the "grandeur or beauty" of a political capital. Of the country's twenty-five most populous cities, only Washington did not rank in the top fifty in value added in manufacturing. Washington's employment structure and investment of capital and labor in industry had by 1880 already diverged from those of cities dependent on manufacturing and trade. In 1900,

Table 7.3 Employment in the District of Columbia and Cities of Comparable Size, 1900

Occupation	Detroit		Milwaukee		New Orleans		Washington	
	N	%	N	%	N	%	N	%
Total Labor Force[a]	115,223	100.0	111,556	100.0	111,690	100.2[b]	126,161	100.6[b]
Agriculture	721	0.6	588	0.5	2,519	2.3	1,488	1.2
Professional Service	6,693	5.8	5,533	5.0	5,036	4.5	9,420	7.5
Domestic/Personal Service	27,653	24.0	24,958	22.4	45,655	40.9	48,876	38.7
Trade/Transport	33,591	29.2	30,092	27.0	31,791	28.5	40,553	32.1
Mechanical/ Manufacturing	46,565	40.4	50,355	45.1	26,689	24.0	26,604	21.1

Source: U.S. Bureau of the Census, Twelfth Census of the United States, "Special Report on Occupations," Tables 42–43.
[a] All totals include male and female.
[b] Discrepancies caused by rounding percentages.

Table 7.4 Manufacturing in the District of Columbia and Cities
of Comparable Size, 1900

	Detroit	Milwaukee	New Orleans	Washington
Number of Establishments	2,847	3,342	1,524	2,754[a]
Capital	$71,751,193	$110,363,854	$46,003,604	$41,981,245
Average Total Wage Earners	45,707	48,328	19,435	24,693
Wages Paid	$18,718,081	$20,240,656	$7,645,167	$14,643,714
Product	$100,892,838	$123,786,449	$63,514,505	$47,667,622

Source: U.S. Bureau of the Census, *Twelfth Census of the United States,* "Report on Manufactures," vol. 8, pt. 2, pp. 992–1004.
[a] Includes government establishments, e.g., Government Printing Office, U.S. Navy Yard.

the federal district's employment structure and investment in manufacturing was most akin to that of New Orleans, a telling comparison, since the Louisiana port was generally considered stagnant, while Washington was flourishing, but in its own direction.[61]

In exchange for eschewing industrial and commercial activity, businessmen on the board assumed, the nation would create a healthy environment for investment in enterprises appropriate to the capital. Above all, the board felt, the country had a duty to ensure the liveliness of the local real estate market, even though the main focus of developers' activities was shifting from L'Enfant's original federal city to suburbs beyond Florida Avenue in the old Washington County. Since this argument in effect implied that Congress's fiscal obligations had no discernible limit, proposals put forth by the board in the mid-1890s for a new wave of federally funded service extensions proved quite controversial. The consensus that had prevailed since the 1870s, that the nation had a stake in Washington's ongoing improvement, began to erode, and the board and its congressional allies had to seek ways to reinvigorate it.

VI

The health of the District real estate market depended not only on continued expansion of public works and services. Much infrastructure essential to developers lay in private hands, in the form of franchises for gas, electricity, and transit. The alliance between major commercial interests and local and federal authorities enabled Washington to resolve questions regarding public regulation of utilities with relatively little of the bitterness and scandal that surrounded these matters in other American cities.

Utilities prompted complex debates involving five sets of participants: the companies themselves, other business interests, consumers, District officials, and Congress. Special political pressures on the franchise-granting authority, Congress, complicated the regulatory problem further. The national trend around the turn of the century was for state legislatures to establish semi-autonomous utilities commissions, potentially transforming issues of price, quality, and service from political into administrative or technical decisions. Congress gradually moved in this direction over the two decades after 1900. Yet during the 1880s and 1890s, the angry national debate over what constituted a trust more or less forced the congressional District committees to keep on establishing prices and standards through the clumsy medium of direct legislation. The middle-of-the-road conservatives who controlled District policy understandably dreaded having outspoken anti-trust colleagues publicly label them the dupes of robber barons, if those to whom regulation of local utilities had been delegated became mired in a scandal.[62]

The Washington Gas-Light Company sparked the angriest, most prolonged debates, in large measure because its management was neither integrated into nor accepted by the capital's mainstream commercial elite. Washingtonians helped to finance and manage the firm, but since 1852 "foreigners"—from Philadelphia—had held the upper hand in both financial and technical matters. "Foreign" ownership provoked suspicion. In 1892, John R. McLean, former publisher of the Cincinnati *Enquirer* and one-time Democratic candidate for governor of Ohio, organized a local take-over of the company. Repatriation under such auspices reassured no one. Although McLean had extensive banking and real estate interests in Washington, he kept aloof from civic organizations such as the Board of Trade. Not that commercial-civic leaders had much interest in McLean's friendship. Peers suspected him of lacking scruples, a reputation confirmed by his scandal-mongering tenure, beginning in 1905, as publisher of the *Post*.[63]

Washingtonians' suspicions of the gas company were substantiated in episodes of that public-be-damned arrogance of which Gilded Age corporations were capable. The company had averaged nearly 17 percent dividends from the early 1850s through the early 1880s, its first three decades. Rumors proliferated that these "miraculous dividends" were on heavily watered stock. In 1886, a Senate committee, attempting to determine how much the stock was watered, found that the relevant books had been sold to a Philadelphia scrap paper company for $100, reportedly because they were "moldy" and "no longer of use." Customers accused employees of treating complainants "brutally." In 1894 one homeowner wondered how he had incurred an $18 bill in a month when his house was vacant. Unsatisfied with the explanation, the customer threateningly responded that soon the District would have an electric lighting company. Company clerks laughed, "When you do, we shall own it." Although the consumer price of gas in 1895, $1.25 per thousand cubic feet, was the seventh lowest of sixteen large cities, evidence abounded that the utility could make a healthy profit at $1.00 or even $0.75.[64]

Public ownership of utilities won sympathy from home rule advocates and even from a special committee of the Board of Trade. While Senator McMillan, an investor in utilities, unequivocally favored regulated monopoly, some District Committee colleagues thought public ownership worth studying. Everyone could agree to study municipal gas, because there was no chance it would happen. At the 1886 Senate hearing, the gas company president had revealed why when he remarked that he would happily consent to a buyout, "if the company got a good price." Commissioner John Ross later noted that the financial "embarrassments which would probably attend the attempt to obtain control of the plant" rendered the idea infeasible. Legal complications and daunting condemnation costs crippled the movement for public ownership of utilities all over the United States. By 1900 there were only eleven public gas companies and no public trolley systems. Only three cities over 100,000 owned electrical plants.[65]

In lieu of public ownership, non-elite resident groups demanded the old panacea of a competing company. A second gas company, however, was unacceptable to the Board of Trade and to most congressmen on the District committees, though bills to charter rival companies did win favorable committee reports from time to time. The most determined opponents of gas competition were the commissioners themselves. Successive boards of commissioners rejected every such proposal with the admonition that it was "unwise to authorize the tearing up of street pavements for the purpose of laying a second set of gas mains."[66] The District defended its pavements so obstinately that congressmen came to believe "that disease and death always follow in the wake of such excavations." Opponents of competition supported their stand with the mix of arguments known as "natural monopoly theory." In cities such as Detroit and Baltimore, they pointed out, attempts at competition had led to intercorporate shakedowns and buyouts that reinstated monopoly. The inflated cost of these transactions fell on the public. The same Board of Trade report that discussed public ownership in friendly terms succinctly stated the case: "The multiplication of gas or electric light companies . . . but increases fixed charges to be paid by consumers and creates double service and expense where public economy demands the existence of a single institution."[67]

Congress's District policy-makers had an additional reason to oppose gas competition. While utilities regulation caused nasty arguments within the District committees, nearly all committeemen could unite in demanding that other colleagues leave them alone with this perplexing issue and not yield to the temptation to meddle in another committee's affairs in order to score points. The reason that the Senate District Committee was so embittered against F. P. B. Sands, the nominee for commissioner rejected in February 1897, was that, as a lobbyist for a new gas company, he had incited Senate anti-trusters to impugn committee members on the Senate floor. The gas company was not as nefarious as was rumored, New Hampshire's Gallinger insisted. Under congressional tutelage it provided decent quality gas at reasonable prices. Unless it had solid evidence to the contrary, Gallinger added, the Senate should presume that the District Committee consisted of "intelligent, honorable, and high-minded men whose findings are entitled to the fair and unprejudiced consideration of their colleagues."[68]

The Senate District Committee attempted to mollify its critics by verbally chastising the gas company and pushing for a $1.00 per thousand cubic feet price ceiling. McLean's political friends, however, repeatedly strangled "dollar gas," adding to complaints that Congress was incapable of managing Washington utilities. In 1896, McMillan finally pushed through a compromise proposal that implemented the $1 limit, but over five years rather than right away. Since hard lobbying had delayed the price change for years already, even loyal allies, such as the *Evening Star,* scolded McMillan for caving in to "the few at the expense of the many." The exasperated senator reportedly warned McLean to "keep away from Congress," if he hoped to go on "making as much money . . . out of the District gas companies."[69]

On the other hand, McMillan and his allies had reason to be satisfied. Battles between utilities and cities were notoriously convoluted and vicious. In the gas controversy, Washington achieved a straightforward solution in a relatively aboveboard manner. Since Washington's officials were appointed, which removed the obstacle that urban democracy places on open cooperation between public and private sectors, they could work out public solutions to the quandaries that officials and utilities elsewhere sometimes handled with bribery and collusion, as in Samuel Insull's Chicago or reformer Frederic Howe's Cleveland. As Howe berated his friends in Cleveland's gas industry, their exercise of covert influence undermined the accountability of officials to the public, "destroy[ing] responsible government."[70] Since the purpose of the representative system is to give the public control over the actions of government, where policy is made according to concealed criteria, there might as well not be elections. The commission system brought negotiations between officials and utilities out in the open and thereby permitted a sort of responsible government, albeit at the cost of representation itself.

Because the gas company's management held itself aloof from Washington's mainstream business community, public-private cooperation did not come about smoothly. By contrast, the manner in which the corporate leadership of the city's electrical and transit companies intertwined with the local commercial-civic movement facilitated reorganization of these enterprises in ways that satisfied national and local interest, with comparatively little wrangling and suspicion.

Innovative Engineer Corps reports on the feasibility of underground electrical conduits encouraged Congress and the commissioners to press for elimination of all overhead electrical wires.[71] Installation of underground lines, however, depended upon adoption by the District of legal and technical requirements for corporations to follow. A dispute between the District and its usual allies in the Senate over which of two competing power companies to endorse delayed adoption of essential regulations for years on end. The commissioners, reflecting the concerns of real estate interests, saw quick expansion of service to outlying regions as a priority and thus leaned towards the Potomac Electric Power Company, a heavily capitalized out-of-town corporation linked to General Electric, over the weaker, but local United States Electric Company. McMillan and his colleagues insisted that the commissioners prevent the Potomac Company from laying too many lines until an accord was reached that allowed the two sets of investors to live together peacefully.[72]

The success of alternatives to the widely deplored overhead trolley—the cable system and the "Budapest" conduit system—confirmed Washington's rulers in their belief that transit, like electricity, should bury its power source. The momentous capital investment this change would entail, however, created a stalemate that paralleled that in electricity. Even after the important Capital Traction merger of 1895, thirteen separate trolley companies remained at work. The difficulty of cajoling each to adopt expensive new technologies—let alone getting them to agree upon territory and transfers—created a "deadlock in legislation," as Francis Newlands, one of Capital Traction's sponsors, lamented. Real estate investors such as Newlands found the electrical and transit impasses very frustrating, because they counted on these services as an "important aid to suburban development."[73]

On shoestring budgets, often with second-rate equipment, subdividers had "girdled, encircled, and crisscrossed" Washington's outskirts with lines such as the Brightwood, the Eckington and Soldiers' Home, and the Georgetown and Tenallytown. These lines and the small electrical plants that fed them and lighted the developments never had a prayer of making money; they existed to promote the subdivisions. "The road was built as you know to develop suburban property," the president of one such line maintained to the House District chairman. It "can't stand the expense of an under-ground system."[74] When the 1893 depression exposed how far subdivision could outrun settlement, the promotional tramways loomed as white elephants. Hard-pressed subdividers needed to muddle along either until land sales picked up or until the utilities deadlock resolved itself, so that the large transit and electric companies could proceed with buying out the realtors.

One developer whom the electrical and transit impasses caught in this bind was George Truesdell, the Board of Trade director, who became commissioner soon after the depression hit. While commissioner, Truesdell testified to the House about the troubles of his Eckington project: "I did not contemplate the maintenance of a street lighting system perpetually." Torn between personal predicament and official duty, Truesdell reexamined the policy on overhead wires. In June 1894, he suggested to Congress that "notwithstanding the public prejudice existing against" the trolley, it "is to-day the cheapest, the most satisfactory, and generally the most popular system in the country." Most of Truesdell's Board of Trade friends, however, sided

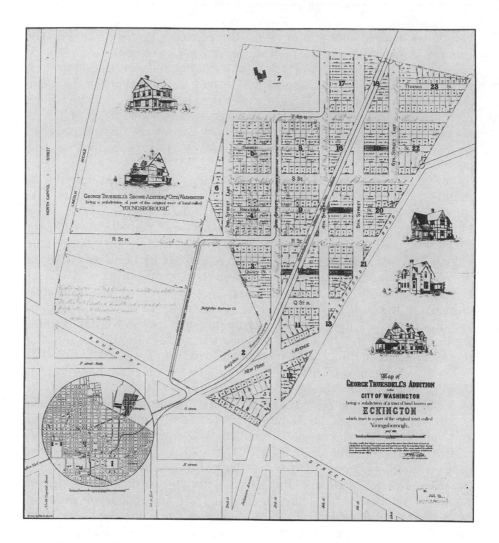

Detail from developer and District Commissioner George Truesdell's plan for Eckington, in northeast Washington. A branch of the Baltimore and Ohio Railroad bisects the project. A feeder trolley line, the Eckington and Soldiers Home Railroad, enters from the left. Courtesy the Geography and Map Division, Library of Congress.

against him and with Commissioner Ross, who defended the "beauty of the streets" against companies "looking for traffic alone." The *Star* labeled objections to underground wires "unadulterated nonsense" and insisted, "No sensible community wants the trolley."[75]

Given the expense of building underground conduits, the only solution appeared to be consolidating the electrical and transit companies into a couple of giants who would carve the District into secure territories. In effecting this move, the close group identity of the city's commercial-civic elite proved indispensable. An example of the intertwined character of Washington's downtown business and a key figure in the utilities consolidation was the Board of Trade's Welsh-born secretary, George Harries. In January 1901, Harries appeared before the House Appropriations Committee wearing the hats of president of the Board of School Trustees, general of the District Militia, and, significantly, vice president of the United States Electric Company. Harries also served as an officer of various large and small transit companies, including the Metropolitan Railway.[76]

After Truesdell's term as commissioner ended in 1897, he and the ubiquitous Harries and other prominent developers and utilities investors cooperated with a Philadelphia syndicate to form interlocking directorates of small street railroads and to arrange for the suburban lines to buy power from their downtown counterparts. Senator McMillan encouraged this trend; suburban transit, he believed, deserved support "as a means of developing real estate values."[77] Also, consolidation by merger and lease would create McMillan's preferred solution of regulated oligopoly or monopoly, while avoiding another ruckus in Congress over District trusts.

Out-of-town and local investors succeeded in combining the electrical companies in 1900. Settlement of the underground conduit question, pending for twelve years, came within months of the merger, on terms applauded by the commissioners, since it guaranteed them considerable oversight and ample space for municipal wires, all at little cost to taxpayers. The prospect of quick extensions won over the neighborhood associations, especially in suburbs impatient for service. Meanwhile, with the consent of Newlands and his associates, McMillan backed legislation to merge Capital Traction's competitors and the two electric companies into a giant firm, which, after a false start, became Washington Railway and Electric, or "Werco." Instead of fragmented transit, the capital now possessed two District-wide companies. Sprawling, uneconomic routes caused Werco to suffer chronic financial problems, but it proved strong enough to resist the national holding companies and preserve substantive local control until the Great Depression.[78]

Although the capital's utilities policies during the 1890s arose from direct negotiation among elite businessmen, sympathetic municipal officials, and mainstream national politicians, they were more comprehensive and probably more accepted by the community at large than those devised by elected municipal governments that were crippled by factional conflict or troubled by charges of inside influence. Washington's success in securing locally owned utilities and in compelling removal of overhead wires suggests how much a nonelected government could win for the public through its freedom to deal openly with enterprise.

Perhaps, as Frederic Howe and others eloquently argued, public ownership would have best promoted both public well-being and civic consciousness.[79]

Yet, given the prevailing legal and administrative environment and political culture, few municipal officials in turn-of-the-century America would have pressed forward with large-scale takeovers of private utilities, even if they had had the resources. While the public's wariness of trusts rendered utilities suspect among the urban electorate, most public officials undoubtedly shared the view of entrepreneur and politician McMillan that such businesses formed an essential part of urban enterprise and that cities should work *with*, not around or against them. The promotional alliances that McMillan and the Board of Trade favored seemed natural and were probably all but inevitable. The reader can decide whether public life in our cities was demoralized more by having this relationship camouflaged in an elected system or manifest in an unelected one.

The Board of Trade in its early decades provided Washington with broad-minded, imaginative commercial-civic leadership; but whatever the group's propagandists contended, *downtown* was not synonymous with *unsectional*. By their nature, commercial-civic elites represented circumscribed interests and a particular vision of how a city should grow and operate. Washington's downtown movement had critics in both the community and Congress. These skeptics questioned whether ambitious public works schemes formulated by the board in the 1890s were in either the nation's or the city's interest. They raised doubts about whether extensive federal support for the developmental activities of local enterprise was still needed to maintain a worthy capital. Washington's ruling group responded by forging an alliance with renowned civil engineers, architects, and park planners, who put together a dramatic, effective case for reinvigorating the national commitment to Washington. This partnership between established politicians, developers, and financiers on one side and reform-minded urban professionals on the other also fixed the conditions and constraints that governed urban planning in the national city in the new century.

8

Promotional Government and Urban Planning

The report of the Burnham Commission was not intended to be
comprehensive. . . . There is no end to what might be said about the control
of the growth of the city into the suburbs.

— Frederick Law Olmsted, Jr., 1906

MANY MEMBERS OF CONGRESS merely tolerated the half-and-half
budget plan without feeling any devotion to it. Public works proposals, therefore, could easily ruffle legislative feathers, especially if
the project in question created an unprecedented service or covered a larger
geographic area than addressed in the 1878 government act. In disputes over
new projects, the capital's commercial-civic leaders and their allies in the
Capitol would seize the moral high ground by portraying resisters as pig-
headed "economists." Congressmen who resisted, however, were sometimes
manifesting shrewdness, not just provincialism.

Enlightened opinion agreed with the view of Frederick Law Olmsted, Sr.,
that parks helped city dwellers "maintain a temperate, good-natured, and
healthy state of mind" that countered the "hardening" influence of modern
urban life. So why was the House "implacable" in its opposition to Rock
Creek Park?[1] Like most big city parks, Rock Creek would be located not near
poor, crowded neighborhoods but on the outskirts of prosperous northwest
Washington. Those residing near it already had more access to soothing nature than other Washingtonians. Following the land boom that accompanied
construction of Manhattan's Central Park, investors, sometimes to their cost,
trumpeted parks as a boon to nearby property values. Critics of Rock Creek
Park imagined that its promoters were putting a civic face on a commercial
venture, that the undertaking was intended mainly "for the benefit of speculators who own the land adjoining." Put so starkly, the charge was unfair;
propertied Washingtonians also supported the park for civic reasons. Yet even
politicians who favored the undertaking could not avoid noticing that it
would take "2000 acres out of the market," as Senator William Stewart reminded his fellow Chevy Chase investor, Francis Newlands.[2]

After refusing several times to concur in Senate bills to purchase the designated land, the House consented to Rock Creek in September 1890, twenty-
three years after it was first proposed. Approval came only after the Senate

yielded to a "pernicious" House demand that owners of adjacent property be forced to pay a "benefit" tax to offset the nation's customary 50 percent contribution to District improvement projects. The task of assessing these "benefits" fell to a special commission under the auspices of the chief of engineers.[3]

In keeping with the capital's chaotic experience with improvement taxes, property holders overwhelmed Rock Creek's condemnation proceedings with lawsuits and obstructed the assessment of "benefits." Realtors such as the Chevy Chase Company's E. J. Stellwagen and former Board of Trade president Brainard Warner demonstrated to the Rock Creek Commission that even if benefits to nearby property could be proved, "it would be impossible to apply that value in dollar and cents to the particular abutting tracts." By 1898, resignations from exhausted members had depleted the special panel. The realtors had a point about the assessments being arbitrary, Chief of Engineers Wilson wrote to the House District chairman. The time had come, he said, to forget the money and push ahead with landscaping the park.[4]

Any congressman who actually expected benefit taxes to pay for Rock Creek Park knew little about Washington. Many lawmakers were perhaps less concerned with the money the special tax might yield than with the message it sent to District real estate investors and their friends in the Capitol: speculating "nabobs" and profligate senators could not go on browbeating the House by insisting that all their costly schemes were "national" enterprises. This dispute foreshadowed a fight that flared up repeatedly during the 1890s, the resolution of which would determine the character of Washington's governance through the early part of the coming century. What were the limits — geographic, economic, and political — of the nation's obligations to its city?

By the 1890s, the political environment that had given rise to the 1878 government plan was disappearing. The national city had achieved the self-sustained growth that had once eluded it. Even so, Washington's commercial-civic leaders and their supporters in Congress persisted in the assumptions and practices that had drawn them into alliance in the first place. They insisted that the country should continue in its promotional role of nurturing enterprise and facilitating development in the capital city. Throughout the decade, the Board of Trade, the District Commissioners, and the Senate District Committee pressed expensive plans to extend infrastructure and services to the District's outlying regions. While most arguments for Rock Creek Park revolved around social welfare and civic pride, other programs, such as the board's controversial highway extension plan, were expressly intended to promote suburban real estate. "Localist" congressmen questioned whether the nation had as broad and perpetual an obligation as McMillan and his crew seemed to think. Diverse residents wondered whether the commercial-civic movement had confused its own well-being with that of the city overall.

To vindicate their claim that promotional governance still served both capital and nation, those in Congress and the city who favored ambitious, but embattled new projects secured the backing of well-known consultants in municipal engineering, public health, landscape architecture, and urban planning. A paradox resulted. The people, techniques, and ideas we think of as characterizing progressive urban government gained a foothold in Washington because an established leadership needed them to maintain its position and to justify its ambitions. For their part, new-style urban professionals, exhibiting understandable eagerness to play a part in planning and running the national capital, persuaded themselves that their local patrons shared their ambitions for redirecting Washington's polity. The newcomers lost sight of the extent to which their presence in Washington depended on their accommodating themselves to assumptions and tendencies they did not really share.

The circumstances that resulted in the 1902 McMillan Plan to reshape Washington's parks and public places illustrate well this pattern of collaboration and accommodation. Local backers of the Senate Parks Commission perceived and used this historic report by famous architects and landscape designers as a way to inspire and reaffirm the country's apparently waning commitment to expanding and upgrading the capital's amenities and services. As the McMillan Plan was a defining moment in American urban planning, scholars have thoroughly examined the 1902 document and its aftermath; but they have generally done so from the perspective of the planners, focusing too much on what it reveals about early planners' aesthetics, ideology, professional standards, and political sophistication and not enough on how the plan evolved from the political history of the national city itself.

The McMillan Plan's critics usually trace its weaknesses to shortcomings in the concepts and procedures of the first generation of American urban planners themselves. There were indeed shortcomings in early planners' attitudes and methods, but the local conditions that prompted the hiring of outside consultants constrained these experts in ways that they only vaguely understood and could not hope to offset. These constraints stemmed in large measure from the promotional relationship between state and enterprise that lay at the heart of Washington's local polity. Because they came to Washington under the auspices of an entrenched governing group whose underlying aims were only superficially compatible with their own, innovators in municipal administration and urban planning gained the freedom to introduce new methods but not new assumptions regarding how the city should grow and what it should become.

In turn-of-the-century Washington, the most consistent sponsors of expertise and professionalism were McMillan's Senate District Committee and the Board of Trade. To their sponsors, cosmopolitan experts in municipal engineering, public health, or public administration embodied "progress." They made the side with whom they allied appear big-thinking and enlightened, which aided those who sought an up-to-date justification for perpetuating an arrangement that made sectional Washingtonians and provincial politicians uneasy. For over a decade, pro-District congressmen and the Board of Trade had turned to famous experts to shore up their side of disputes over new works and services. In fact, the prominent part taken on the 1901 McMillan Commission by Frederick Law Olmsted, Jr., followed from the role played by Olmsted Associates in the mid-1890s in the effort to implement the Board of Trade's controversial highway extension plan. To invite the nation's most distinguished firm of landscape architects to help extend the L'Enfant Plan had been a major gesture in favor of the national government's continuing in the promotional role it had played in Washington since the Shepherd period.

In addition, the capital's commercial-civic leadership turned to outside consultants because their customary source of public works expertise — the Army Corps of Engineers — now seemed an undependable ally. The Engineers saw eye-to-eye with Washington's civilian rulers most of the time, but they had their own traditions, loyalties, and political base. For their part, civilian professionals perceived the Army Corps not as a potential friend with a shared interest in improved public works but as a technically inferior and aesthetically backward rival. The professionals were therefore willing to offer themselves as an alternative to the engineer officers. By disparging the Corps's management of the capital, the professionals helped spark a noisy quarrel that weakened both sides and caused them to lose sight of ideals and goals they had in common.

I

The proposal for Rock Creek Park stirred controversy because it pointed up the difficulty of determining where the national portion of the federal district ended. Decades of argument favored maintaining, in a worthy condition, the original federal city planned by L'Enfant, but it was not so evident that the United States had as vital an interest in Washington County, the fifty square miles of the District of Columbia outside L'Enfant's Washington and the colonial port of Georgetown. Beginning in the late 1870s, subdividers, builders, suburban residents, and the local press insisted that the United States would gain from surveying and servicing the suburbs. Suburban improvements were no "scheme gotten up in the interest of any particular syndicate or section." By readying outlying districts for settlement, the United States could render the capital more prosperous and governable and set a positive example for the country.[5]

In 1890, one of Washington's black business leaders informed the House District chairman that an appropriation for a certain suburban road "would increase adjacent values more than 500 percent, enable people in the city to get homes at prices they can reach, relieve the plethoric condition of the city, and tend to lessen crime (that which is the result of overcrowding in alleys) and raise the moral condition of the people." While white developers rarely took black housing needs into account when projecting new subdivisions, this businessman presented a familiar mix of social and economic arguments that made sense to Americans of all races who worried that social upheaval might arise from rapid urban growth. In 1892, Senator McMillan, who had promoted transit, parks, and housing in Detroit, supported a suburban transit proposal for Washington by quoting a *Scribner's* writer who contended that since "it makes the poor man a landholder," suburban transit "is doing more to put down socialism, in this country at least, than all other things combined."[6]

Service extensions to outlying districts provoked controversy for a variety of reasons, some peculiar to Washington and others general to all cities. To begin with, there was strong consensus that despite Washington County's irregular topography, the street pattern there ought to "conform" to the L'Enfant Plan, but how could sprawling suburban streets be made to harmonize with a geometric design conceived for a compact city? Also, who would determine the pace and priority of extensions and according to what criteria? Those like McMillan who believed government ought to assist in developing real estate values favored a pace and pattern of improvements that accorded with the preconceptions of investors. Such an explicit emphasis on the land market might further strain relations between the commercial-civic faction and the Engineer Corps, which was willing to aid growth but bristled at hints that it acted on real estate's bidding. This emphasis would also heighten the suspicions of homeowners' groups that the appointed municipal regime was entirely too close to downtown enterprise. Resulting demands from older neighborhoods that preference go to the original city in turn played into the hands of the half-and-half system's congressional enemies, always on the lookout for precedents suggesting that the country had little responsibility for services outside the original capital.

These dilemmas became evident during the first major phase of suburban expansion, which began in earnest only after the 1870s depression. Suburban real estate, a source of conflict later on, had little bearing on the upheavals of the 1860s and 1870s. Farms, interspersed by estates and country retreats, dominated Washington County through the end of Reconstruction. Farsighted investors did begin to register county subdivisions right after the war, but the most visible players in District real estate during the territorial period had focused on Washington City proper, especially on a mile-wide semicircle northwest of Lafayette Square. Shepherd owned a county estate (which the disputatious businessman fittingly called Bleak House), yet he paid little systematic attention to areas outside Georgetown and Washington City, either in his personal affairs or in his capacity as head of the Board of Public Works.

When suburban expansion finally began in earnest, it replicated the inner city pattern, northern and western areas flourishing at the expense of southern and eastern ones. The shrewd Francis Newlands had seen this pattern emerging during his youth in Washington in the 1850s and 1860s. Like some other observers of nineteenth-century cities, he attributed this phenomenon to some inherent propensity of cities to grow westward.[7] In fact, the tendency arose from identifiable economic and historical conditions, not from the general nature of cities.

During the 1850s, organizers of Uniontown, south of the Anacostia River, attempted to capture a specific real estate market by creating payment plans affordable to the skilled workers in the Navy Yard, directly across the Anacostia Bridge. While set on picturesque high ground above the Anacostia, the area later stagnated economically, on account of what economists call "adverse neighborhood effects." Authorities habitually selected the marshy banks of the Anacostia as the site for institutions that sections with more political pull refused to accept, such as St. Elizabeths, the federal hospital for the mentally ill. Patients there endured horrendous outbreaks of malaria on top of their other afflictions. Between Uniontown and St. Elizabeths was Barry Farm, established in 1867 by the Freedmen's Bureau to provide homes for five hundred families. The presence of even a stable community of black homeowners diminished property values.[8]

Also in the 1850s, Amos Kendall, the Jacksonian politician and telegraph entrepreneur, offered two-acre lots in "Kendall Green," beyond 7th and M streets, northeast. Kendall donoted part of the land for the Columbia Institution for the Deaf and sponsored an omnibus line to make the project accessible, but the northeast's growth remained unexceptional, even after the war. There were northeast suburbs, such as George Truesdell's Eckington and the railroad and streetcar suburbs of Brookland and University Heights, but they suffered from proximity to the freight yards and street-level tracks of the Baltimore and Ohio.[9] Chevy Chase and Takoma Park straddled the Maryland line, but the balance of Montgomery and Prince George's counties, Maryland, was nearly as untouched as northern Virginia, which remained as poorly connected to the heart of Washington as it was at the time of the 1846 Alexandria retrocession. Development deeper into the surrounding states was beyond the reach of the streetcars of the Gilded Age.

Suburban growth in Gilded Age Washington took place mainly in the area bounded by Rock Creek on the west, Boundary Street (now Florida Avenue) on the south, Howard University and the Soldiers' Home on the east, and the Maryland line on the north. Nowadays, "Northwest" includes regions beyond Rock Creek, but even the Chevy Chase Company's huge tract, straddling the current upper Connecticut Avenue, remained relatively untouched until the 1906 opening of the Taft Bridge over Rock Creek. Another region current Washingtonians include in "Northwest" — beyond Georgetown and the Naval Observatory, from Tennallytown down to the Potomac — awaited such turn-of-the-century improvements as the Massachusetts Avenue Bridge.[10]

One far-sighted player in the post–Civil War property boom was Samuel P.

Brown, Lincoln's navy agent, who later served on the Board of Public Works. In 1866, Brown subdivided farmland into a development he called Mount Pleasant. Two miles beyond the wealthy community emerging around Dupont Circle, between the 14th and 16th streets extended, this was a good site for less pricey lots aimed at "clerks in the government employ." Brown joined in founding the Metropolitan Railroad largely to bring horsecars to this property. Mount Pleasant constituted one-third of three hundred acres of subdivisions registered on the outskirts of the federal city in the year after the war ended. Tracts such as Meridian Hill, Columbia Heights, Washington Heights, and Denison and Leighton's quickly filled the territory within two miles of Boundary Street.[11]

Mount Pleasant was an identifiable neighborhood by the mid-1870s. Areas as far north as Brightwood and Takoma Park had active community organizations by the early 1890s. Between 1870 and 1880, the county population grew 60 percent, from 11,117 to 17,753. In the same decade, the District overall grew 34.9 percent. The county grew 54.4 percent in the 1880s, reaching 27,414, while the District grew 29.7 percent. In 1889, the District assessor counted 1,161 houses south of the Anacostia, 1,874 houses between the Anacostia and Rock Creek, and 768 west of Rock Creek. In the 1870s and 1880s, blacks accounted for between 30 percent and 35 percent of the District's total growth, but they represented over 40 percent of the increase in the county. This suggests that while the white middle class was indeed moving to the outskirts in impressive numbers, the county still filled a more traditional function of suburbs by offering refuge to marginal groups denied prime housing sites.[12]

Apart from Brown, the 1870s improvers did not involve themselves heavily in suburban development. Younger associates of the Shepherd circle, such as Brown's sons, Austin and Chapin, Brainard Warner, and Amzi Lorenzo Barber, did play a large role. These suburban developers worked through shifting partnerships, employing the same approach used by their predecessors at Farragut Square and Dupont Circle. Barber, whom we met earlier in his incarnation as the "asphalt king," acted as agent for Senator John Sherman in several ventures. Warner and Barber worked together on LeDroit Park, a white-only enclave before it became Washington's leading black middle-class neighborhood.[13]

Little distinguished the operations of Washington's early suburban developers from those in any other American city. An investor would purchase an estate or farm, survey the land, plot streets and lots, and register the subdivision with the city surveyor. After a lag of five or ten years, depending on the building cycle and other contingencies, the owner or his realtor might contract for some houses. The subdivider much preferred to market lots to individual purchasers, who were themselves responsible for building the house, or to turn tracts over to speculative builders, who might divide the risk with realtors or take it upon themselves. While subdividers did not expect to pro-

vide finished houses, they were supposed to assure access to modern utilities — paved and lighted streets, water and sewerage, gas and electricity. The
dependence of subdivisions on steady expansion of muncipal services gave
suburban developers everywhere an incentive to involve themselves vigorously in local politics.[14]

Subdividers were also expected to ensure access to downtown, which explains the propensity of Gilded Age real estate entrepreneurs to bankrupt
themselves with transit. Regulation of impecunious streetcar companies
caused friction among District officials, developers, and the public. Similar
problems arose over other utilities in private hands, especially gas and electricity. The most weighty disputes, however, surrounded publicly owned and
financed improvements — streets, water, and sewerage.

By the mid-1880s, municipal engineers and health officials were drawing
attention to outer Washington's need for pavements, streetlamps, water, and
drainage. District officials argued that Mount Pleasant required water and
sewerage as much as Capitol Hill: "But a brief period can elapse before an
urgent need for these necessities must be answered, or the development of
the District, and by possibility public health, will be seriously affected." In
1889, Captain Thomas Symons, the assistant engineer commissioner who
had earlier won residents' confidence with his candid appraisals of the aqueduct tunnel, called for a million-dollar suburban street program, despite the
fact that four-fifths of east Washington streets remained unimproved. That
year, the suburban street budget had been $70,393.[15]

Population did not outrun pavements, water, and sewerage as quickly as
these nervous pronouncements implied. Maps published annually by the Engineer Department show gradual extension of paving. Between 1888 and
1891, the District laid nearly 200,000 square yards of pavement in the suburbs, although the 5.25 million square yards in Washington and Georgetown
still dwarfed this. In 1891, the municipality spent $165,514 on twenty-eight
suburban projects, one-fifth of its street budget. The county then contained
12 percent of the District's people. The District had not yet solved Capitol
Hill's water conundrum when, in 1893, it began a "high service" system, in
which water was pumped to a reservoir, near Tennallytown, and then east as
far as Brookland. Charles Glover, an influential Riggs Bank executive and a
substantial investor in suburban property, assuaged suspicions of this project
by personally contributing half the cost of the land.[16]

At the time of the 1890 Hering report, the $3.6 million plan to divert se-
wage from the city's waterfront, sewer mains already reached Meridian Hill
and Columbia Heights, adding their wastes to the Potomac. Most sewage
from beyond the original city line flowed into Rock Creek, making Foggy
Bottom one of Washington's unhealthiest quarters and inspiring schemes to
cover the creek all the way to Massachusetts Avenue. With the Hering plan
making slow but inexorable progress, army engineers put aside this drastic
expedient in favor of laying suburban mains that would one day feed into

Hering's unified system. Even though the crucial Potomac interceptors remained several years from completion, the Engineer Department continued through the turn of the century to lay sewers in outlying districts, sometimes for neighborhoods that did not yet exist. In 1902 and 1903, Engineer Commissioner John Biddle advised the Senate Appropriations Committee to give the Arizona Avenue sewer, in the far northwest, priority over projects in the northeast. Although only 1,600 people then lived in this sewer basin, Charles Glover's property was in the area. One restive Appropriations Committee member, "Pitchfork Ben" Tillman of South Carolina, accused the engineer of "building things for development . . . when the city proper is neglected." Glover defended the Arizona Avenue sewer to the House Appropriations District subcommittee as a benefit for nearby American University, of which he was a trustee. The committee chairman, a Vermont Republican concerned about a pending municipal deficit widely blamed on suburban service extensions, asked the banker, "When a deficit arises in your bank, what do you do?" Glover shot back, "We do not have any."[17]

Another proponent of the Arizona Avenue sewer told the Senate, "There are thousands—yes millions—of dollars ready and willing to be expended out there in the way of buildings and subdivisions."[18] Given prevailing attitudes towards using public works to bolster real estate, such arguments inevitably wore down efforts to spread funds equitably or to examine the national interest thoroughly. With the commissioners, the Army Corps, and strategic factions in Congress sympathetic towards extensions, subdividers would eventually get the assistance they wanted without having to fight hard for it. Central city taxpayers and congressmen opposed to the fifty-fifty plan would have tried to slow extensions in any case. Opposing interests had no plausible grounds to deny services forever to subdividers, as long as work on the outskirts stayed gradual and not obviously at the expense of the city proper.

Developers understood that the practice instituted in 1878 of the public sector bearing the full cost of the capital's pavements and sewers had resulted from different circumstances. Suburban investors were asking that country and city pay a portion of the costs, but they expected to contribute as well. Developers, in fact, were so eager to put up their own money rather than wait for publicly financed projects that they made extensive use of the permit system, under which the District split costs with property owners on a discretionary basis. As described earlier, east and south Washington citizens charged that such cooperation between the District and suburban realtors amounted to favoritism, but city engineers saw it as sensible policy. Washington would have to do the work someday; why not encourage parties willing to share the cost?[19]

The "sad lack of uniformity" of outlying streets, however, and the prospect of services being extended piecemeal as developers worked out deals with the District, caused real estate developers and their allies in government to fear that outer Washington would "resemble a patchwork."[20] The national city's commercial-civic movement felt self-confident enough to launch a public fight for a comprehensive, "uniform" expansion. Extension planning, however, proved too complex and contentious for even the Washington Board of Trade to finesse with its customary verve.

II

Common-law precedents allowed municipalities only weak controls over the platting of new roads. Basically, subdividers could do as they pleased. Not one street in the first nine hundred acres of subdivisions north of Boundary Street harmonized with the L'Enfant Plan. In 1879 the assistant engineer commissioner warned that if "misfit" subdivision did not end, "the District government will be required at no distant day to expend large sums for damages incurred in straightening out the streets of these villages." "Individual owners must be stopped at once," wrote an editor, "or Washington will soon present a patched and piebald appearance." Developers pressed the government to establish guidelines for them. Offending developers, such as Austin Brown, asserted that the capital should copy Haussmann's foresight in plotting boulevards in new quarters on Paris's northwestern outskirts. By delaying too long, he warned, Washington, potentially as magnificient as Paris, would end up as "haphazard" as other American cities.[21]

To bring subdivision under control, the District would need legislation empowering it to regulate subdivision at its initial stages. The city attorney informed the commissioners that under prevailing law, recourse was limited: "A proprietor may plat and replat at pleasure, bound by his sales and contracts to purchasers only."[22] The District tried for a while to avoid assuming control of nonconforming streets, but this negative maneuver meant indefinite postponement of sewers, water mains, and street lighting that police and health officials, let alone residents and realtors, considered essential. In January 1886, the District commission tested its muscle against Barber and Warner's LeDroit Park—according to Symons a "thorn in the side"—which blocked the extension of Rhode Island and New Jersey avenues to Howard University and the Soldiers' Home. The District failed to remedy this "hopeless case," but it succeeded in grabbing the attention of Congress. Considering the paucity of legal precedents, both houses acted expeditiously. In August 1888, the House and Senate agreed on a bill to prohibit registration of subdivisions not "in conformity with the general plan of the city."[23] At last Washington had a weapon against those who would "mutilate and butcher" L'Enfant's and George Washington's vision. Captain Symons warned that subdividers could continue to plot roads as they liked, but unacceptable streets would never become public. A few mavericks tried to evade restrictions by submitting plats to the recorder of deeds, a presidential appointee, rather than to the city surveyor, who was under the commissioners, a loophole Congress closed in 1894.[24]

For both officials and investors, prohibition of uncontrolled subdivision was only a first step. Symons explained that the 1888 law prevented "further desecration," but would not "remedy the evils already done." Every north-bound county thoroughfare in the mile and a half between North Capitol and Sixteenth streets was either blocked by a subdivision or continued at only half its city width. The commissioners and the Corps of Engineers began to argue that to condemn and replat existing nonconforming streets was both necessary and inevitable. Serious talk of replatting, in turn, put a "heavy cloud" on property already subdivided, which prevented "many people from buying property and building houses in the region," because they felt "no security they will not be disturbed." This, along with the boom anticipated in the wake of a coordinated extension program, prompted strong support among developers for a quick solution. Symons estimated that the matter could be settled for $1 million, if the District replatted only major thorough-fares. The *Post* agreed with Symons's view that straightening other than "main avenues and principal streets" might not be worth the effort. Legisla-tion, the paper advised, should leave "ample discretionary powers" to the District, "as in many instances the acceptance of streets now in existence will be no detriment to the public even though they are narrow and do not con-form to the plan of the city exactly." If replatting was not unreasonably am-bitious, reporters believed, realtors might go along with army engineers' sug-gestions that a third or half of the expense be offset by special assessments.[25]

Washington had run head-long into the thorny problem of extension planning. Cities obviously invited trouble if they expanded according to whatever arrangement subdividers could strike with authorities at any mo-ment. In both Europe and America, however, municipal governments were stumped by the problem of how to impose orderly street systems on outlying districts that were on the verge of development. Of the large cities in the eastern United States, only Philadelphia had clear authority to compel sub-dividers to adhere to a preconceived pattern, a legacy of William Penn's effort to create an ideal New World metropolis. Elsewhere, courts sided with owners who defied extension plans that did not please them, leaving it to banks to force such nonconformists into line by refusing to lend to them. The period's most ambitious extension plans appeared in Germany. In cities such as Berlin and Cologne, planners learned the hard way that heavy-handed schemes, not coordinated with building regulations and based on an inadequate notion of the local land market, could encourage the rise of suburban tenement dis-tricts every bit as gloomy as those in the old city.[26]

Could the imaginative public-private partnership that ran Washington manage suburban expansion better than Germany's ambitious public ser-vants? By now, the Board of Trade had taken over the task of speaking for Washington real estate. The board's Street Committee, chaired by Truesdell, dismissed taking anything less than a comprehensive approach. Truesdell, Warner, and realtor Myron Parker, the board's founding president, convinced

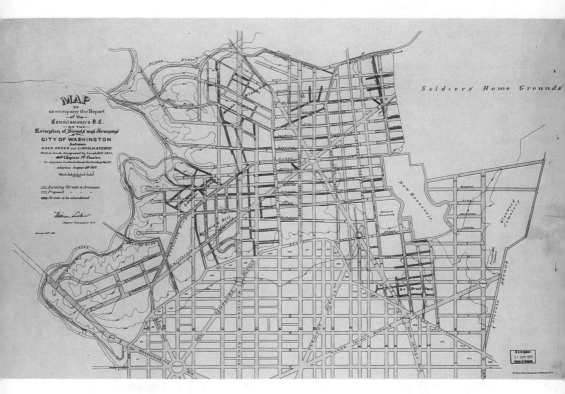

Detail from an 1887 proposal for projecting a regular street pattern onto the "misfit" subdivisions north of Florida Avenue, northwest, making them "conform" to the L'Enfant Plan. Courtesy the Geography and Map Division, Library of Congress.

army engineers, the civilian commissioners, and leaders of both District committees that the largest property owners favored a scheme whereby the entire county would be mapped as soon as possible, beginning with the misfit tracts. Condemnation would start within thirty days of the filing of plans, so the market would be little disturbed. Special assessments would cover one-third of the cost, leaving two-thirds to be divided between the United States and the District under the half-and-half system. To guard the national interest, all maps would be reviewed by a high commission consisting of the secretaries of war and the interior and the chief of engineers. The District would finance this "comprehensive highway plan" in one shot with a bond issue of approximately $3.2 million.[27]

Both congressional District committees reported bills worked out with Truesdell's panel. However, the Board of Trade bill, as it was called, unraveled as it moved through Congress. The Senate District Committee was forced to drop the bond issue when it sparked an irrelevant partisan debate over the federal debt. In the House, the absence of bond provisions limited election-year meandering, even though partisan disputes over that year's District appropriation bill had been the most rancorous since 1878. The provision that two-thirds of the expense be covered by the public under the half-and-half formula encountered two objections in the House. "When it comes to taxing the whole people of this country to pay for beautiful squares and magnificent streets outside this original general plan," asserted a Tennessee congressman, "I hold that those who are benefited ought to pay the expense." Because District taxpayers do not choose their rulers, argued William Jennings Bryan, "we should be more careful than we might be if we were their direct representatives." Unless the bill were changed so that special assessments would cover at least half, Bryan continued, "we shall be making the people of the city pay a very large expense for the benefit of speculators."[28]

With these considerations in mind, the House amended the bill so that as much funding as possible would come from assessments on adjacent property and the remainder *exclusively* from District revenues. The conference committee, which included Senators Harris and McMillan and House District Committee chairman John Hemphill, rolled back the assessed portion to 50 percent and tried to soften the prohibition on federal contributions. Hemphill implored the House not to insist on its ban; Congress could decide whether proposed openings merited federal help on a case-by-case basis. Representatives, however, demanded a statement at the outset that "this magnificent scheme and the expenditures attendant thereon should not be charged upon the Federal Treasury." The House delayed the conference report nine months, until February 1893, when the Senate acquiesced to a clear stipulation that any portion of the highway plan not covered by special taxes "shall be charged to the revenues of the District of Columbia."[29]

This was a turning point in Washington governmental history, the first time since 1878 that Congress refused outright to pay fifty percent for a major improvement. By contrast, previous so-called departures from the half-and-half system—such as the National Zoo and the aqueduct tunnel—had required that Washington share expenses, even though precedent would have dictated that funding come exclusively from United States revenues or, as in the case of Rock Creek Park, that alternate funding sources be sought to lessen the federal role.

Commissioner John Ross considered asking for a presidential veto but decided instead to endorse the measure to President Harrison and seek redress during the next congressional session. Later, as the extensions helped push Washington into a state of chronic deficit, critics accused Ross of allowing the city to take a "dangerous plunge" at the behest of the Board of Trade. This accusation, though unfair, was based upon evidence. On March 1, 1893, the day before President Harrison signed the Highway Act, Myron Parker became Ross's colleague on the commission, the first of three straight appointees to the commission who, as Board of Trade officers, had been instrumental in formulating or defending the extension plan. When Truesdell became commissioner in 1894, Parker took his place as chair of the board's Streets and Avenues Committee. Truesdell's successor, John B. Wight, had represented the board in discussions with Congress and the District on the suburban scheme. These links fueled rumors that Ross had consented to a project Washington could ill afford because a committee of the Board of Trade wanted it.[30]

III

The affiliation of Olmsted Associates, the renowned firm of landscape architects, with Washington went back to the 1870s, when Frederick Law Olmsted, Sr., supervised redesign of the Capitol grounds. Later he had acted as landscape adviser to the National Zoo. Chevy Chase employed its own landscape architect, but the meticulous Newlands, aware of Olmsted's innovative work on suburban projects such as Chestnut Hill near Boston and Riverside near Chicago, still conferred with the planner. The House, however, hesitated to contribute even the $100 per day, the "usual pay of an expert," charged by Olmsted Associates for advising the District's special highway extension bureau.[31] Since the impetus to hire the firm to help plat outer Washington came as much from Senator McMillan as from District real estate speculators, perhaps congressmen balked at picking up Olmsted's tab as a way of taking a swipe at the Michigan Republican.

In keeping with his familiar ideas on what made a congenial, successful suburb, Olmsted counseled Newlands that, given northwest Washington's hilly landscape, a grid system would "delay and obstruct satisfactory improvement," while picturesque, winding streets would ensure "full value of your company's land." Working on the Zoo and Chevy Chase had drawn the great designer's attention to outer Washington's problems at an early stage in the extension controversy. As the Highway Act moved through committee, Olmsted counseled Newlands's political colleague and real estate partner, Senator Stewart, on how to word the bill to provide flexibility for geographic conditions.[32]

Stewart, Newlands, and McMillan solicited Olmsted's help mostly because of his reputation and experience, but also because they doubted the competence of the Army Corps, which would supervise the highway extension program unless other arrangements were made. McMillan, who knew Olmsted from his term as Detroit park commissioner, strongly backed proposals by Newlands and others that the designer be secured. "It seems to me that the Engineer Corps of the Army thinks itself entirely able to handle the work of street extension without outside assistance," Charles Moore wrote his boss soon after the Highway Act went into effect, "but the California Syndicate [i.e. the Chevy Chase group] are strenuous about having Mr. Olmsted employed, as I assured [Commissioner] Parker you also were." In 1894, Mc-

Millan sponsored a measure providing $5,000 (the House trimmed this to $3,000) to retain the firm as consultants to the District. Illness soon forced Olmsted, Sr., into semi-retirement. His sons, Frederick, Jr., and John, took charge of the family firm and pressed ahead with suggestions for the capital's suburbs.[33] In the case of highway extension, despite the apprehensions of landowners and their congressional allies, civilian experts and military engineers saw the problem similarly and so cooperated cordially. During the 1880s, the Army Corps had worked with the Coast and Geodetic Survey on a topographical map highlighting "picturesque features" of the outskirts of Washington. Engineer Commissioner Charles Powell's correspondence with the Boston firm reveals strong preference for Olmsted's type of "curvilinear plan," although engineers and consultants did concede some grid-like sections to developers who insisted upon them.[34]

Resistance to the extension program came not from military engineers protecting their turf, but from "many poor persons" who maintained that the House's draconian financing provisions threatened them with "serious losses and in many cases absolute ruin." In three of the four sections into which the highway plan divided the county, most property was still in large parcels. Subdividers in these sections, eager to bring their lots on the market, promised to donate land needed for streets, meaning that condemnation costs would be miniscule. The Board of Trade estimated that these three sections could be opened for $300,000, total. In the first section, the area of "misfit" subdivision between Rock Creek and North Capitol Street, numerous investors and residents were stuck with unsaleable lots on mortgage during a depression. In the Denison and Leighton's subdivision, 100 parcels were held by 60 persons. Meridian Hill had 400 parcels in the hands of 250 owners. All these lots would float in limbo while the proposed new plats wound through administrative hearings and then the courts. At the end of that ordeal, lot holders might, if the House's system stuck, find themselves liable for the benefit the new street plan presumably offered them. Dozens of frustrated Washingtonians, convinced that Congress sought to take their property "without pretending to make any compensation . . . as prescribed by the Constitution," paid a visit to their attorneys.[35]

By shifting the federal portion of the extensions onto "poor people" with lawyers, the House had guaranteed that the highway plan would create a legal and financial morass. Soon, the fate of lots was being decided by a jury of the holders' peers. No self-respecting citizen would grant a low condemnation award to a fellow resident whose house was to be taken or lawn cut in two, let alone assess the fifty-percent benefit called for by the legislation. Attorneys for owners in nonconforming subdivisions strengthened their hand by disingenuously painting clients, some of whom were landlords and investors, as "persons of small means . . . most, if not all of [whom], opposed the passage of the highway extension act." The city attorney spent the next eight years pleading with juries to set condemnations and benefits at the prescribed ratios. Awards so overran initial estimates that the District could not afford to accept the verdicts unless the House backed down on its funding ban, which it was not prepared to do. The Supreme Court eventually declared the benefits formula constitutional, but it was, as a House District Committee later observed, "impossible of execution." [36]

In 1895, the commissioners and the Board of Trade prepared new legislation to "render operative" the Highway Act. In a ploy intended to broaden support, they proposed using a single bond issue to underwrite both the extensions and completion of the Hering sewer system. In conjunction, the Senate District Committee called for abrogation of the ban on federal assistance. The House remained adamant in refusing to dig into the U.S. Treasury to open outlying streets. Meanwhile, many residents expressed intense resentment at the attempt by downtown civic leaders to equate sewer improvements everyone thought essential with the controversial Highway Act, derided by the 1894 Joint Executive of the citizens movement as a "brilliant" scheme that "stirs the blood of patriotism." The east and south Washington homeowners groups insisted that Congress should authorize bonds only for public works "which will benefit actual occupants." [37]

Divisions within the neighborhood movement once again hampered efforts to find a coherent alternative to the Board of Trade's plan. The Brightwood Avenue Citizens Association asserted, "No bill will be satisfactory to the Northern Section of the District that does not include both sewerage and street extension." Mount Pleasant leader Ellis Spear explained why suburban citizens groups split with their central city compatriots over such a significant matter. The condemnations were inevitable, Spear wrote Board of Trade president Warner, so anything more piecemeal than the highway plan would be "the mistaken compassion which led the man to cut off the dog's tail a little at a time." [38]

Even the commercial-civic movement experienced a rare public argument. In 1895, Warner reiterated, "Unquestionably the general provisions of this bill are endorsed by a very large majority of the people, and especially of the wealthy taxpayers, who are deeply interested in securing favorable action." Yet the board's own general counsel, A. T. Britton, asserted in a business journal he edited that "a vicious and extravagant plan of street extensions" should not be "so dovetailed into the sewer system that the one must carry the other." [39]

Five years into the Highway Act, not one parcel had been acquired or street paved. By late 1896, the commissioners estimated that delays and court challenges had driven the cost of fixing misfit subdivisions to $8 million. The Board of Trade suggested scaling back replatting to a maximum expenditure of $4 million. The board's dogged attempts to salvage the Highway Act, however, undermined public deference to it. At angry public meetings in early 1898, neighborhood spokesmen asserted that the Board of Trade only represented itself. Congress should stop listening only to the board's "ideas of what the people of the District want." One neighborhood leader called the 1893 bill a crime. Local people "did not have confidence in the board of trade," the man claimed. Former House District chairman Hemphill, now a Washington attorney, replied that it was unjust to label "such a body of citizens" criminals; the extensions had simply proved of "greater magnitude than had first been anticipated."[40]

Hard-pressed lot holders in northern suburbs begged Congress either to provide funds for immediate condemnation or rescind the highway plan. The Board of Trade retreated. The prohibition on federal funding was fatal to the scheme. A board committee wrote, "If [misfit] subdivisions can be corrected only at the expense of our people, then in our judgment they should not be corrected at all." The House District Committee proposed replacing the 1893 bill with a strengthened version of the uncontroversial 1888 act, but the Senate, the commissioners, and developers found abandoning five years of surveys "unnecessarily destructive." In June 1898, Congress voted to cancel only those maps "which had given rise to trouble and expense." Outside of the misfit areas, the city could finish its plats. The notion of immediate condemnation and dedication was abandoned, however. The maps now served merely as a guide for what officials were to consider in conformity with L'Enfant's plan. Registration of subdivisions again took place only when developers brought them in, as provided in 1888. The result was the discontinuity between boards of commissioners that had prompted the Board of Trade to call for comprehensive extension in the first place.[41]

Still wanting their streets, suburban developers lobbied for special legislation to open key roads projected under the Highway Act but delayed during the funding muddle. A gaggle of street extension bills arrived in the Senate, where McMillan gave them a favorable report and passed them to Allison, who quietly attached them to the current District budget. The senators were conniving to implement the highway plan by subterfuge. The House smelled the rat: the projects survived conference committees only with the prohibition on federal contributions and the mandate for 50 percent benefits assessments pasted prominently on their backs.[42]

Where a single developer owned parcels of land, the District could extend an avenue without a battle over condemnation and benefits. In other instances, the commissioners regarded the street as local and did not mind enforcing the assessment, which operated "to keep down excessive awards of juries and also the number of bills" for extensions.[43] In well-publicized cases, however, the commissioners resisted enforcing the benefits for the same reason that the 1893 act fell apart: the project was "not one that the people who were actually living there would ever have undertaken or sought." Thirty houses stood in the way of extending 16th Street to Rock Creek Park, at $1 million the "most expensive thoroughfare the District has ever opened." After four years of deliberation, the Senate District Committee advised the commissioners to accept a verdict of $730,000 in condemnations and $109,000 in benefits, an award the committee thought obviously fair. An irate Commissioner Macfarland argued that *all* of this "national boulevard of extraordinary width" should be covered by Congress, rather than none. "Alleged benefits," a group of realtors protested to the House Appropriations Committee, continued to be "imposed upon abutting owners, without regard to actual benefits, but solely in pursuance" of an arbitrary policy.[44]

All sides could rattle at each other harmlessly so long as the District budget remained in the black, but in fiscal 1901, Washington ran its first deficit in a decade, $220,183 on actual expenditures, three times that on authorized appropriations. The next year, the national city fell short by $1.5 on expenditures and $2.4 million on appropriations. The commissioners and residents blamed the deficit on extensions undertaken without federal assistance. Washington was in the red, Macfarland charged, because revenues were "continuously diverted by Congress." "There was never a deficiency," wrote the *Evening Star*, "until Congress violated the half-and-half principle." Senator Gallinger agreed, "Had Congress decided that the General Government should share with the District the expense of taking land for the extension of streets, there would have been little, if any, deficit." In fact, the disputed extensions accounted for only $2 million of the shortfall. The remainder resulted from congressional willingness to move forward with long-delayed water and sewer improvements, as well as from efforts to help city departments overcome antiquated staff definitions and office procedures.[45]

McMillan tried to conciliate his friends in the city, assuring them that "it was important that certain streets should be opened," despite House intransigence. All around the Senate District Committee chairman, tempers flared. The House Appropriations District subcommittee accused the commissioners of derelict indulgence of propertied interests. "Citizens come in here, as they did when the original highway act was passed, and say, 'Put this through and put the whole expense on the District,'" the panel's chairman alleged. "You ought to have organized a force to fight them." The commissioners indeed began to delay the suburban street openings pouring into and out of the Senate. By early 1903, nearly thirty streets were on hold, awaiting resolution of the budget deadlock.[46]

To combat the impression that Washington no longer needed federal support and instead had taken to abusing it, the commissioners developed a list of $13.6 million in pending "extraordinary projects." In addition to sewerage and water filtration, these included a municipal hospital, a business high school, reclamation of the Anacostia Flats, bridges over Rock Creek and the Potomac, and high-pressure fire equipment. Even the House admitted the imminent necessity of a $2.5 million city hall, slated for the site of Capital Traction's old cable powerhouse, at 14th and E streets, northwest, which had burned in 1897. Under agreements reached in 1900, District taxpayers were to pay $1.75 million towards removing B & O and Pennsylvania Railroad grade crossings. That Washington could not bear all these expenses alone was

The *Evening Star* of April 2, 1902, voiced the frustration of Washington's business and civic leaders at congressional insistence that the city raise $2 million annually through new taxes. The cartoon, entitled "The District Must Set the Pace," quoted Representative Cannon: "As to that great project—we shall go just so fast in beautifying the city of Washington as the people of the city of Washington are willing to go and no faster." Courtesy the Newspapers and Current Periodicals Division, Library of Congress.

"self-evident." Rather than "living from hand to mouth," the District requested $10 million in advances from the U.S. Treasury, to be repaid with interest over twenty years. With the old Shepherd-era debt down under $15 million, the federal city could bear a new debt. A long-term loan from the United States, Macfarland insisted was the only way to restore fiscal stability while keeping services and administration up-to-date.[47]

The House District chairman urged colleagues to look upon long-term advances as a "business proposition." Still, the chamber would only consent to rolling advances, repayable in three or four years. This merely perpetuated budgetary turmoil. Anxious that they would never receive overdue raises and added help, District employees pleaded with Congress "not to allow the conflict between the House and the Senate over the larger items" to prevent "small increases" in various departments. Lawmakers were not moved. "We increased 15 salaries out of the entire legislative, executive, and judicial branches of this Government," a House Appropriations member scolded Macfarland during hearings on the 1902 budget, "and you come in with your little bill and ask for an increase of 367 subordinate force." The former journalist replied, "The mere fact that for ten years [an employee] has been getting an inadequate sum is no reason to continue" the injustice. The House responded by recommending an across-the-board 10 percent salary cut for fiscal 1903.[48]

Deficits placed upward pressure on taxation, which frayed nerves even more. In return for authorizing even short-term advances, Congress required Washington to raise $2 million per year in new taxes. McMillan justified this hefty hike by pointing out that the District had collected more revenue during depressed 1894 than during prosperous 1901 — $3,390,000 versus $3,387,636. Part of the new levy came from abolishing an outmoded tax break exploited by investors holding county land listed as agricultural. About one quarter came from increased license fees, including $25 charged to "mediums, clairvoyants, soothsayers, fortune tellers or palmists." The capital's soothsayers must have seen stormy times in their crystal balls, since, ominously, another quarter of the added revenue was to come from a reinvigorated personal property tax. Washington business, like commercial interests everywhere, felt few scruples about evading this "iniquitous" levy. While the Board of Trade and other business groups organized to fight "inquisitorial" imposts, the District jumped from a moderate sixtieth to fifth or sixth among the nation's cities in per capita taxation.[49]

IV

During these squabbles, the McMillan Plan was authorized, prepared, and exhibited. While noting how local circumstances shaped this important episode, historians of urban planning usually focus their attention on design principles employed by the commission's members or on the "City Beautiful" ideology that the McMillan Plan reflected. These scholars thus unwittingly adopt the global perspective of the out-of-town consultants who compiled the report and underemphasize the viewpoint and aims of the policy-makers and local notables who commissioned it. John Reps, the major historian most favorable to the McMillan Plan, argues that it "emerged almost inevitably from the background of its authors and under the strong influence of the environmental setting," by which he means architectural, not political factors — "the strong elements of the L'Enfant Plan and the existing major structures." For Reps, "yet another influence" was the White City at the 1893 Columbian Exposition in Chicago, by which "the taste of the entire country had been re-directed" with regard to architecture and city design. Behind this analysis is the notion that impetus for endeavors such this came not so much from local interests as from professionals and publicists leading the national movement for civic beautification. The McMillan Plan served above all as a "demonstration project" in the urban professionals' campaign to persuade civic leaders to moderate their customary privatism and to think systematically about the urban environment.[50]

There are many criticisms of Reps's view. One critique popular in recent years unfortunately still considers the McMillan report and comparable projects elsewhere at an ambiguous, global level. City Beautiful planning now appears as a messenger for, rather than a moderating influence on corporate capitalism. According to Marxist scholar Richard Foglesong, commercial-civic elites such as the Board of Trade were receptive to the City Beautiful because "urban beautification and its supportive ideology fulfilled capital's need for a legitimating civic ideal." The icons contrived by City Beautiful architects and landscape designers — boulevards, statues, parks, and civic centers — supposedly functioned to spread bourgeois values and sanction the capitalist order. In this view, the "political objective of the McMillan Plan" was "to glorify, educate, and commemorate, to do for national patriotism what later City Beautiful plans would seek to do for local patriotism."[51]

Since the City Beautiful movement started from the premise that proper urban design could tranform the "behavior and moral outlook" of city dwellers, the underlying message conveyed by the Beaux-Arts forms that the movement favored certainly is relevant.[52] Yet how groups and interests besides professional architects and landscape designers read and used these plans depended on their own political situation as much as on the ambiguous symbolism contained in neoclassical statues and buildings, Renaissance squares, and baroque parks. The dominant classes were not alone in finding serviceable ideas in City Beautiful plans. Anti-corporate writers, professionals, and politicians — indeed virtually every American captivated by the notions of "municipal improvement" and "civic beautification" — for years found symbolic support for their own positions in documents like the McMillan Plan.

Whatever its symbolism and artistry, the 1902 parks report had direct utility for the consultants' sponsors, the promotional faction centered around McMillan's Senate District Committee and the Board of Trade. The aggressively publicized report by renowned designers of parks and public buildings provided dramatic support for the embattled new round of expensive public works that Washington's governing alliance sought. It countered the erosion of a twenty-five-year consensus. To the District commissioners, the undertaking was "an important expression of the new feeling in Congress." The pro-developer *Evening Star* was more blunt: "The congressional cheesepairers for once will find themselves embarrassed in the matter of an excuse for opposition." The park plan promised redress for "shabby treatment of the District in times past."[53]

Concerned with the spreading sense that the half-and-half arrangement had become outmoded and abused, Washington's downtown movement sought to revive and adapt the belief that the capital's public works were a national enterprise. The Board of Trade decided to use the centennial of the capital's removal to Washington, scheduled for December 12, 1900, to glorify the "completed" phase of the national city's development and reaffirm the country's devotion to it for the "coming century." A board delegation proposed to President McKinley, "So important an event could well be marked by the erection of a type of architecture which will inspire patriotism and a broader love of country." The businessmen incorrectly supposed that their best chance for a "permanent structure" was the memorial bridge from the Potomac Flats to Arlington Cemetery. Under consideration since 1886, the Memorial Bridge was destined not to be built until the 1920s.[54]

"No other labor of the centennial year is more inspiring or promising of notable results," board president Theodore Noyes contended in 1899, "than that of developing Washington as the city of parks and the forest city by a vigorous campaign." Yet, by apparent contrast to the Memorial Bridge, prospects seemed gloomy for the "great river park system" that Noyes envisioned. "What ought to be done," McMillan told the *Star* in April 1899, "is to consolidate all these parks into a single system, to be in charge of a parking commission," with representatives from the Army Corps, the commissioners, and the public. In April 1900, however, McMillan nearly scuttled all hope for a unified park system when he introduced bills, agreed to by the railroads, to eliminate grade crossings. Intended as a "satisfactory and permanent solution" to the problem of street-level railroad tracks, which had agitated Washington for decades, the bills would have left the Pennsylvania's tracks on the Mall, a permanent obstacle to serious landscaping in central Washington. "The city has adjusted itself" to the Mall tracks, McMillan rationalized. More revealingly, the Senator asserted that he knew no Washingtonian "who would prefer to have no change" than to have this measure passed. He implied that, if the Pennsylvania insisted on keeping its Mall route as the price for abolishing its grade crossings, many prominent residents felt the city had no choice but to accede. Civic groups, including the Board of Trade, indeed had acquiesced to the Pennsylania's demand to retain use of the Mall, because the railroad refused to abandon its murderous street-level routes otherwise. Only a few downtown merchants actively approved the Pennsylvania's Mall site. Other resident groups felt that a mighty corporation had bullied them, and they blamed McMillan for failing to dislodge the usurper.[55]

To offset this frustration, McMillan suggested a grand "Centennial Avenue" through the Mall, from the Capitol, past an elegant new railroad depot, and across the proposed memorial bridge. McMillan's avenue proposal gave an opening to those who refused to accept the Mall as lost to the Pennsylvania Railroad. Major Theodore Bingham, the public buildings officer, a vivid character who would one day serve as New York City's police commissioner, condemned McMillan's compromise with the railroad as "unpatriotic, and even irreverent." Tireless, often self-righteous in his advocacy of L'Enfant's design, Bingham prepared his own drawings of the Mall. His idea was to confine the railroad to the smallest possible space, if it could not be removed altogether. McMillan tried to calm passions by proposing a joint Corps of Engineers and civilian board of consultants. The House blocked this move and turned the $6,000 appropriation over to Bingham, who then hired a New York landscape designer to prepare sketches for moving the Pennsylvania depot south of the Mall, exactly the location the Army Corps had been advocating since 1881.[56]

An admirer of romantic designs, Bingham based his drawings on Andrew Jackson Downing's layouts, which had intrigued him for some time.[57] Bingham's sketches drew vigorous criticism from Glenn Brown, national secretary of the American Institute of Architects (AIA). Brown, an authority on household plumbing, detested Bingham, who once published under his own name Brown's plan for upgrading the White House plumbing. Brown had become interested in the L'Enfant Plan while writing a book on the Capitol. Although as adamant as Bingham that railroads did not belong on the Mall, Brown, a zealous convert to the mannered Beaux-Arts approach to architecture, considered neoclassicism to be in the spirit of the capital's founders and denounced the romantic eclecticism traditionally favored by army engineers such as Bingham. "The training and education of the engineer[s], which best fits them for war, river and harbor work, and the construction of bridges and fortifications," Brown wrote, "unfits them to act as judges and critics on questions of taste and beauty." The height of Engineer Corps influence in Washington was, Brown felt, "the dark era of our art history." The architect published his own "suggestion," which not only hid the railroad but also proposed destruction of the Smithsonian Castle, the new Post Office tower on Pennsylvania Avenue, and other "unfortunate" structures from the mid- or late-nineteenth century.[58]

Brown arranged for the AIA to hold a "propaganda convention" in Washington to coincide with the December 1900 Centennial. Leaders of the profession, including Frederick Law Olmsted, Jr., gave papers that proposed to reorganize the capital's public buildings according to Beaux-Arts formulas, which stressed public grounds that opened onto impressive vistas and monumental buildings arranged in formal groups, "compositions." The architects denigrated the competing tastes of Major Bingham in particular and the Army Corps in general. They claimed to be "mortified" by a "deterioration in the character and design" of public buildings and an "absence of respect for the early forms." One speaker repeated a misconception common among AIA members that "the original idea of the city was for a long time forgotten." Army engineers, who among their activities had helped prepare a critical edition of the L'Enfant Plan, published in 1887, understandably regarded this as libel. The McMillan Commission later refused to perpetuate this misunderstanding and instead noted "steady improvement in the character of the Mall" under thirty years of military management.[59]

The AIA's session on Washington was printed as a Senate document, with an introduction by McMillan's aide, Charles Moore. During the convention, McMillan and his local allies persuaded the architects to support the senator's proposed expert study of parks and public places. This time, it was decided, the certainly combative, allegedly boorish Army Engineers would be excluded; civilian professionals would fill the panel. On December 14, 1900, the day after the architects presented their studies, the Board of Trade resolved "earnestly" to recommend "a Commission of three or five building and landscape architects, each eminent and experienced in his profession" to prepare "suitable and adequate plans for the development of the capital city, in subordination to the plan of its founders, and yet sufficiently expanded in dimensions to typify a century's growth of the Republic."[60]

Since the early 1890s, when Newlands, Stewart, and McMillan began corresponding with the Olmsteds about highway extension, Washington's leading policy-makers and property investors had claimed that the nation's most respected experts on urban design supported their image of Washington's future. The proposed commission of experts would carry this alliance between outside consultants and the capital's commercial-civic movement to unprecedented heights. Given the range of questions relating to the national city's geography and appearance that the consultants would be authorized to investigate, their report had the potential to overwhelm all critics of the McMillan group's view of a worthy Washington. That such a result would be a coup for the improvement faction as well as the planners was obvious to congressional enemies of the open-ended view of the country's role in the District and to the Corps of Engineers, stung by the architects' attacks. Caught in the middle, the District commissioners recommended a broad-based study panel that would encompass both the professionals and Major Bingham. The public buildings officer had to be included, Macfarland admonished, because he would "be at all times available for the giving of information to Congress." A study that ignored him would make a dangerous enemy.[61]

The House became intractable and the Senate confused. McMillan gave up on a joint resolution and instead waited until an executive session in March, when, acting by itself, the Senate authorized him to "secure the services of such experts as may be necessary" to prepare a scheme "for the development of the entire park system of the District." The congressional park commission hence became the Senate Parks Commission.[62]

The Senate District Committee agreed with representatives of the AIA that the study should feature the younger Olmsted and Daniel Burnham, principal designer of the Columbian Exposition's White City and a leading figure in civic beautification. Burnham would have overall charge of the work. Olmsted would concentrate on outlying parks, of which he already had an understanding because of his Highway Act studies. Olmsted also collaborated on writing the final report with Moore, who became the commission's secretary.[63] This was a golden opportunity for Burnham, his first chance to apply to a real place the ideas he had begun to develop when designing the Chicago fair eight years earlier. Burnham secured participation of his partners on the White City, architect Charles McKim, of McKim, Mead, and White, and Augustus Saint-Gaudens, sculptor of the Adams statue in Rock Creek Cemetery, though illness prevented the latter from making a major contribution. In June 1901, Burnham, Olmsted, McKim, and Moore embarked on a summer junket through Europe, where they studied both current town planning and the baroque gardens and public squares that had influenced L'Enfant. At Fountainbleau, Vaux-le-Vicomte, and Versailles, where L'Enfant had grown up, Olmsted photographed the work of André Lenôtre, the seventeenth-century architect of royal gardens. These pictures served as illustrations in the final report.[64]

The American Institute of Architects helped in every way it could, not only because Brown took a proprietary interest in a movement he had helped start, but because the study promoted one of the profession's primary objectives: reduction of the influence of political appointees and military engineers over public buildings and grounds. Conviction that only the "best artistic talent" should design public buildings animated the dogmatic criticisms of army engineers that marred the 1900 convention. The AIA worked with Burnham and his colleagues on an integrated public relations campaign, at that time an innovative political tactic. The consultants arranged the timing of articles and editorials with sympathetic editors. The highlight of the publicity campaign was a lavish exhibition at the Corcoran Gallery in winter 1902, with an opening attended by President Roosevelt. Timed to coincide with McMillan's presentation to the Senate, the exhibit featured costly three-dimensional models prepared by a Boston craftsman and an impressive wall display put together by McKim.[65]

For the consultants themselves, the Washington report proved a personal and professional triumph. Sophisticated publicity spread news to commercial-civic groups in Cleveland, San Francisco, and Chicago, who in the next decade acted as patrons for city plans by Burnham. From being one figure in the diverse campaign for civic beautification, the Chicago architect came to be seen as the key figure in a unified City Beautiful movement. At the time of Burnham's death, in 1912, proponents of other forms of urban planning had only begun to chip away at his reputation as America's leading town planner.[66]

V

The "magnificent plan presented by the Park Commission" received loud acclaim and only muted criticism from residents. The aspect of the study most pleasing to Washingtonians was that it "was instrumental in securing an ideal solution of the railroad problem." About this time, the B & O happened to enter a temporary merger with the Pennsylvania. The latter corporation's main reason for refusing to move its depot from the Mall had always been that it would leave a rival closer to downtown. Not wanting the opportunity to slip, Burnham hastened to London in order to meet with Pennsylvania president Alexander Cassatt (brother of artist Mary Cassatt). Burnham persuaded the urbane businessman that he had a patriotic duty to unite the two roads in a grand depot, designed by Burnham himself, on a new plaza north of Massachusetts Avenue. The final Union Station bill, passed after McMillan's unexpected death in August 1902, provided for abolishing grade crossings, rebuilding the decrepit Long Bridge, and clearing the Mall of tracks, all for not much more in public money than was set aside for grade crossings and the Potomac bridge alone under McMillan's "unjust" legislation of the previous year. Only the affected neighborhoods in northeast Washington offered resistance.[67]

Public acceptance of the plan was also facilitated by the fact that it contained few specific proposals that had not been under discussion for some time. "The plan was not original," Moore recalled two decades later. "Actually and professedly," the consultants sought "to adapt" L'Enfant "to new and enlarged conditions."[68] In concrete terms, the 1902 report called for Washington to unify and embellish the Mall, remove the Pennsylvania Railroad tracks from the Mall, embellish Potomac Park and construct Arlington Bridge, abolish the Murder Bay slums, concentrate new federal office buildings on Capitol Hill and in central Washington, develop a system of outlying parks and parkways, and fill the Anacostia Flats. The Board of Trade, the District commission, pro-District elements in Congress, and the Army Corps had long favored all these projects, though in different measure and for different reasons. In essence, the McMillan Plan integrated the sum of thinking from local quarters within the context of the emerging City Beautiful idea. In the local political context, the McMillan Plan acted as an eloquent declaration that the nation had an ongoing interest in Washington's prosperity and development. Whatever their enemies charged, the report implied, the capital's current governing elite meant to extend, not subvert, George Washington's dream.

While the McMillan Plan contained familiar pieces, its form was novel, which explains the considerable interest it generated. In the view of some, the document "marked the birth of comprehensive city planning" in the United States.[69] Never before had an official consulting panel gathered together such a range of feasible proposals regarding what a real American city should do next to better itself. The McMillan Commission, moreover, operated from the assumption that its recommendations were interdependent and could affect the city's life, as well as its appearance, in a profound way. In retrospect, the panel's claims for its handiwork seem exaggerated. The Parks Commission did not even draw upon every technique available at the time for planning a city in a comprehensive manner. By the First World War, critics within the profession that by then called itself urban planning argued that the 1902 Washington report, like all City Beautiful projects, was not comprehensive, because it focused too much on the arrangement of public places and had little to say about industry, housing, traffic, and other essential matters. To adherents of the "city practical" or "city efficient," Burnham's approach seemed not so much a starting point as a distraction. The real founders of planning, in this view, were the municipal engineers and public health experts who over the previous generation had constructed the country's water, street, and sewer systems and written its health and housing codes.[70]

In the late nineteenth century, every large Western country, with the partial exception of Victorian Britain, wary of Georgian grandeur, went through a phase in which public officials and civic elites put enormous energy and resources into boulevards, squares, parks, and monuments, in order to give cities an elegant, dignified atmosphere and, as the phrase went, to bring "light and air" into overgrown old neighborhoods. France had Haussmann and his followers. German municipal authorities, influenced by the concept of "practical aesthetics," ruthlessly destroyed unspectacular, though vibrant and historic, quarters in order to "disencumber" major churches and public buildings. By 1900, France was the only country where Haussmannism remained strong; the baron's legacy created "massive inertia," in part because the Third Republic's insecure elected town governments had their hands full finishing projects the Second Empire's arrogant authoritarians had begun. Municipal authorities in Germany and Britain were experimenting with publicly owned utilities, strong building and health codes, zoning, public housing, and other techniques for actively influencing the direction and nature of development. In those countries, town planning had begun to suggest an operation more thorough than unifying parks and rearranging monuments and squares.[71]

Even so, the McMillan Plan won admirers on both sides of the Atlantic, largely because it effectively presented its recommendations as an interrelated set that covered the entire city. Consultants often submitted reports on a city's park, water, or street system or on its housing or health problems, but rarely had they been asked to report on a city as a whole.[72] Moreover, government officials, writers on urban matters, and indeed virtually everyone in the Western world, regardless of politics or social position, agreed with Burnham and his friends that their attempt to fill Washington with compositions, vistas, and other impressive effects was anything but an empty aesthetic exer-

cise. City Beautiful planners and architects gave expression to and were beneficiaries of a widespread feeling that an attractive urban environment would
foster civic spirit and other social ideals that the harsh life of the modern city
seemed to wear away.[73]

A few skeptics objected to City Beautiful dogma about urban design. A
scathing 1908 critique labeled the report a "showy sham" that would "revive
the decadent, obsolete Lenôtre formalisms and rigidities." The call to eliminate "discordant notes," such as the Smithsonian Castle and the Library of
Congress dome, prompted the well-founded charge that in seeking to "restore, develop, and supplement" L'Enfant, the Burnham panel took a cavalier
attitude toward a century of intervening history. The report audaciously suggested that the early Republican buildings around Lafayette Square, such as
St. John's Church, built by Benjamin Latrobe in 1816, and the homes of Daniel Webster and Dolly Madison, be destroyed to make room for monumental
federal offices. "To what end is this sacrifice to be made?" the *Star* asked
regarding the proposal to "sweep through" Downing's Smithsonian grounds.
"There is no lack of vistas of the Capitol."[74]

The most determined opposition came not from those who disputed the
plan's beauty, social message, or historical judgment but from politicians and
agencies irritated by the document's existence. After McMillan's parliamentary maneuver enabled the study to proceed despite House resistance, House
Appropriations chairman Joseph Cannon allegedly vowed "to see the Mall
sown in oats," rather than let senators and architects outfox him. Opponents
suspected that "Uncle Joe" was "conscientiously opposed to spending Government monies for art," but noted as well that the legendary reactionary
was determined to preserve the "rights of the House." Cannon fought all
projects related to the McMillan Commission, even Union Station, which he
seems to have favored personally. For a decade, Cannon resisted the commission's proposal to construct the Lincoln Memorial in the old Potomac Flats,
proclaiming "that God damned swamp" an unworthy site. Contemporaries
speculated that this old-time political operator was equally motivated by
prejudice against new-style professionals and by a desire to exercise his customary prerogative over the nation's tribute to his state's hero.[75]

Cannon told the Board of Trade "that the rapidity of the execution of the
plan would depend upon the degree in which the District raised money by
taxation," a reference to the tax debate then underway. A few months later,
however, the appropriations chairman set out to suppress the project "behind
a door of financial impossibility." He projected costs at $200 million, a figure
he had to invent, because the consultants had deliberately offered neither
estimates nor a timetable. Burnham and his co-workers agreed beforehand to
make their report "as general as possible as not to offer many points of attack" to intransigents such as Cannon. "Obviously it is impossible to make
even an approximate estimate of the costs of improvements which are to be

The McMillan Commission's 1902 plan for "that God damned swamp." Under Speaker Joseph Cannon's prodding, the House held up construction of the Lincoln Memorial in the old Potomac Flats at the western end of the Mall for a decade. The Memorial Bridge, also shown here, first proposed in the 1880s, was not built until the 1920s. Courtesy the Law Library, Library of Congress.

completed in an indefinite future," the report contended, "nor is such an estimate necessary."[76]

McKim believed that McMillan meant the park plan to "be made official by act of Congress." Cannon's opposition precluded this. The report would have to exert what the AIA's Brown called "moral force." Panel members for several years kept involvement in District public works to a minimum, so as not to open themselves to the charge that they were a self-aggrandizing ring. Other than Union Station, the only major Washington projects involving a commission member during the plan's aftermath were McKim's 1902 restoration of the White House and McKim, Mead, and White's 1902 design for new buildings at the Washington Barracks. The Burnham group instead took the stance of detached advisors and, in the manner of a modern interest group, depended upon public relations, letter-writing campaigns, and articles in periodicals to maintain pressure on supportive politicians, such as Newlands and Secretary of War Elihu Root. The politicians' duty was "to see every possible peg driven in to fasten future development" to the plan, Root wrote

McMillan. The consultants' job was to hover about the government and goad it.[77]

The panel's role as hovering critic led to irritation among federal officials, who would be responsible for the plan's execution and expenditures, even though credit would go to the planners. Cannon thus gained tactical allies who were otherwise sympathetic to Washington and who favored professionalism, expertise, and administrative reform in other matters. Even after 1910, when the Commission of Fine Arts became the authorized guardian of the McMillan Plan, Newlands worried that politicians and officeholders still regarded architects and planners as "audacious intermeddlers in governmental functions." While Presidents Roosevelt and Taft were supportive, cabinet secretaries conspired to "disarrange" the "Mall scheme." Roosevelt and Newlands barely managed to dissuade the Agriculture Department from citing its new building within the boundaries projected for the Mall's park area. The otherwise progressive secretary despised Burnham as an annoying meddler in "other people's affairs."[78]

The annoyance of cabinet secretaries paled before the exasperation of the Army Corps of Engineers. Since the 1880s, civilian professionals had sought ways to strip the Corps of its role in planning public works and designing public buildings. The McMillan report was perhaps the most damaging blow yet struck in this campaign. Although the four consultants were less strident than Brown and the speakers at the 1900 AIA covention, they shared the aversion: officers had "pet views," McKim felt, and a "clannish horror of outsiders." In 1906, in a blunt attack on the Corps's "meaningless," "shortsighted" management of Potomac Park, Burnham and his associates asserted to Secretary of War Taft that the capital's public spaces should be entrusted only to "persons of recognized standing as landscape architects." Washington suffered, he claimed, from "the unguided efforts" of officers, who lacked "technical training in park work."[79]

The publicity campaign surrounding the McMillan Plan brought with it a string of humiliations for the Office of Public Buildings and Grounds, the Corps's agency responsible for the Mall and other national places and monuments. In an especially unpleasant incident, the public buildings officer, Major Bingham, who hoped to leave his mark on the capital, prepared an ambitious but awkward proposal for remodeling the White House. He presented a model of his proposal, ridiculed as a "mongrel, unrecognizable contraption," at the Centennial Celebration in December 1900. Brown and Moore permitted Bingham's model to remain on exhibit only long enough that architects assembled for the AIA convention had time to condemn it unanimously. Moore then "consigned [Bingham's plans] to a storeroom, whence they never emerged" and worked to have the remodeling task assigned to McKim.[80]

Bingham could not but interpret such moves as slaps in the face. McMillan tried to mollify the engineer, but the damage was done. The truculent public buildings officer and his like-minded successors insisted that they would happily carry out as much of the consultants' report as was "practicable." Meanwhile, work they were already doing would fit admirably into any plan that might one day be fortunate enough to win congressional assent. As the chief of engineers responded to the Burnham group's 1906 attack, "Unless Congress should sanction the costly plans proposed by the park commission," the engineers would go forward with gradual embellishments which would "add to the beauty and public usefulness of the grounds in a greater degree and within less time than would an attempt" to carry out the Burnham panel's "extensive scheme" piecemeal.[81]

The assault by the professionals and their local friends forced the engineers into an alliance of convenience with Cannon and the House's "economists." Likewise, by alienating the Army Corps, the consultants made themselves ever more dependent for defense of their program on Senate leaders such McMillan and Newlands and on Washington's commercial-civic elite. By posing the issue as modernity versus backwardness in technical skills and aesthetic standards, the professionals drove a wedge between themselves and the major player in the Washington polity who came closest to sharing their expansive notions of the public interest and the public sector.

VI

Burnham and his colleagues, Moore wrote, understood that "perhaps even a century would elapse before" important features of the McMillan Plan could be carried out. Some recommendations, such as to surround Lafayette Square with public buildings and to connect the Civil War fortifications outside the city with a parkway, were never implemented. The influence of the plan is most evident around the Mall. The Lincoln and Grant memorials and the National Gallery of Art show the positive side of the City Beautiful's preference for neoclassical monuments. On the other hand, "discordant" notes that consultants wanted removed, including the Post Office tower and the Library of Congress dome, now count among Washington's favorite landmarks. Tourists marvel at the view of the Mall from the Capitol, but critics, such as planning historian Mel Scott, suggest that a less rigid treatment — perhaps reminiscent of Downing and the elder Olmsted — would have been equally impressive and more respectful of the country's history and political system. The McMillan Commission, Scott writes, produced "an elaborate set piece immune to the whims of time and chance." Rather than monarchical "conceits" that "reduced the citizen to insignificance," Scott would prefer a layout recalling "the rough frontier, the diversity of regions and peoples" and befitting "a city honoring men who revolted against a tyrant."[82]

Regardless of whether the 1902 plan's artistry is appropriate or perverse, the commission and its backers in the AIA did fulfill one of the enterprise's chief aims. Architects, planners, and assorted intellectuals acquired an ongoing role in planning public buildings and grounds. Even before the expert panel was assembled, Congress and federal officials, including the Army Corps, had been moving towards design competitions, with architects among the judges, as opposed to the old system of having public buildings drawn by staff technicians, like those working in the Office of the Supervising Architect of the Treasury. For the District Building, finally authorized in 1902, a jury that included the engineer commissioner, the supervising architect of the Treasury, Burnham, and the AIA's national president invited entries from architects in Washington, New York, Philadelphia, and Boston. In 1910 Congress made professional influence official by establishing the Commission of Fine Arts, consisting of "well-qualified judges of the fine arts." Moore, who would serve two decades as the panel's chairman, noted with satisfaction that all seven founding members belonged to New York's highly cultured Century Club, five had gone to Harvard, and the remaining two had worked for McKim, Mead, and White — not just well qualified but well connected, a professional elite.[83]

Political circumstances provided an opportunity for urban professionals to enhance their position at Washington, but later commentators accused City Beautiful groups such as the McMillan and Fine Arts commissions of ignoring the "city practical" until destructive economic and social forces grew so thoroughly entrenched in the physical fabric and political economy of our cities that urban planning could do little to make serious headway against them. This charge exaggerates both the narrowness of the City Beautiful and the broad-mindedness and efficacy of competing approaches. A few adherents may have conceived of the City Beautiful merely in terms of monuments and buildings, but most prominent advocates never claimed that civic centers and park systems, such as the McMillan Plan envisioned, were ends in themselves. Thoughtful, articulate proponents of civic beautification expected that "the unified treatment of the city's architecture" would engender "city sense," in the words of Progressive urban affairs writer Frederic Howe. By this, Howe meant that impressive public buildings and attractive public places might induce people to view their city as an interdependent commonwealth rather than an agglomeration of private interests. Infused with this more comprehensive perspective, the city's inhabitants might then be inspired to handle more arduous, contentious matters in a humane, enlightened fashion.[84]

The consultants who devised the McMillan Plan imagined that their program might inspire this civic spirit. Charles Moore, who in his varied career as journalist, Senate aide, publicist for urban planning, and Fine Arts Commission chair, straddled the worlds of regular and reform politics, foresaw that "a central composition, dignified, beautiful, and of great extent" might assist in a larger object: "a harmonious and consistent building up of the entire city of Washington, instead of the piecemeal, haphazard and unsatisfactory methods that had theretofore prevailed." Of the 1901 panel, Olmsted, Jr., had thought most about Washington as a totality, in part because of his work on highway extension, and exhibited the most sophisticated notion of how to translate the capital's public space into civic spirit. Half of the 1902 report details Olmsted's ideas for "outlying parks and park connections" from Rock Creek to the Anacostia Flats, how parks could anchor existing and future neighborhoods. Olmsted varied park designs not only with symbolic effects in mind but according to how he imagined his parks might be used by different social classes. He later explained that the 1902 plan was never meant to be "perfectly comprehensive," only "sufficiently" so. Such a document could never say all that was needed about parks and public spaces, its main focus, let alone cover more than "one or two aspects" of how to "control the growth" of Washington into its suburbs, a matter "which has as many sides as the varied activities of modern city life." The plan offered a starting point. On that level he stuck by it "emphatically."[85]

Olmsted worried that the excessive publicity received by the commission's dramatic Mall scheme had "withdrawn attention from the individually less important but much more immediately pressing problems of park acquisition on the outskirts of the growing city," which he saw as a necessary step towards bringing Washington's overall environment under control. Olmsted's anxiety that the McMillan Plan was being interpreted too narrowly illustrates the dilemma posed by the political circumstances under which professionals, experts, and planners gained their place in Washington's governance.[86]

The governing alliance formed by the McMillan faction in Congress and the Board of Trade had reasons for wanting to sponsor projects such as those of the Senate Parks Commission that only partially overlapped the professionals' reasons for wanting to work on them. In order to preserve the influence granted them, the outside consultants had to put most of their effort into the parts of their proposals most serviceable and agreeable to their sponsors. Even as the plan was being prepared, McMillan sensed the potential and limits of the Burnham group's project. He observed to Moore that while the report would prove a "grand" success, a credit to all involved, the Mall proposals were especially likely to be carried out.[87] As most of us would in such a situation, Burnham and his friends concentrated on projects likely to produce results in the forseeable future and put off less tractable problems for a better day.

New-style urban professionals acquired no latitude for a systematic pursuit of the civic idealism that lay at the heart of the City Beautiful movement. With regard to the McMillan Plan and similar schemes it inspired elsewhere, Frederic Howe remarked hopefully, "The belief in the city as a home, as an object of public spirited endeavor, has superseded the earlier commercial ideas that characterized our thought."[88] Yet, even as they were winning their well-publicized fight for the Mall, the consultants, especially the perceptive Olmsted, feared they might lose the war. In our century, reality has exceeded Olmsted's fears.

By the time of the Federal Triangle project in the 1930s, a respected plan-

The District of Columbia, 1901. Map was prepared for the Senate Parks Commission and shows the extension of residential development into the old Washington County within the District of Columbia. Shaded areas show new parks and parkways the commission contemplated creating. Courtesy the Geography and Map Division, Library of Congress.

ner, Elbert Peets, had noticed that the heart of the capital, the group of government buildings that surround the Mall, was evolving into a "city-within-a-city." Frustrated at the way the federal government was "turning away from the city," Peets unfairly blamed the McMillan Commission for setting in motion a "programme of isolation" that left the great bulk of Washington to "welter in its chaos." He charged that by concentrating public buildings and monuments around the Mall, Burnham and his colleagues had negated the potential of the original L'Enfant Plan to "put the impress of the national capital on every part" of Washington, to make city and capital "serve . . . each other."[89] Washington's turn-of-the-century planners did focus their primary energies on the Mall, but with the intent of imprinting upon that dramatic focal point a vision that could spread itself gradually over the city and even the nation. Instead, civic spirit and national-mindedness gained their foothold in central Washington only to be assailed there: just blocks from the Mall, the twin forces of privatism and promotionalism reign — positive forces when checked and channeled, but agents of havoc when made king.

Conclusion

> For a generation the city of Washington has known no serious scandal. Its departments are intelligently and economically administered. Its official class is dignified and of a high order of talent. True, Washington is governed in an autocratic way. Three Commissioners appointed by the President perform the functions usually entrusted to the Mayor and the heads of the city departments, while Congress itself is the Board of Aldermen.
>
> — Frederic Howe, 1905

T
WO MONTHS PRIOR to Washington's centennial celebration, on September 8, 1900, Galveston experienced a devastating hurricane. Six thousand people were killed and four thousand homes destroyed. Galveston's mayor and city council, which in previous years had allegedly "out-Tweeded Tweed," appeared "impotent" in the face of the disaster. A central relief committee organized clean-up under martial law. After a while, civic leaders began to propose that the business of the city remain indefinitely in the hands of a small committee that combined executive and legislative powers. In the succeeding months, the Texas legislature debated a new charter for the suffering port. A bill advocated by the Galveston Deep Water Committee, composed of large commercial interests, and by smaller businessmen on the Galveston Chamber of Commerce proposed establishment of a five-man commission appointed by the governor. Opponents in the legislature, however, would not countenance a measure that held "in derision the Declaration of Independence." The charter passed only with an amendment providing that two of the five commissioners be elected. Two years later, a state appeals court ruled that the commission still "violated the principle of self-government." The legislature then directed that the entire board be elected.[1]

Despite these vicissitudes, the "Galveston experiment" caught the attention of reform periodicals such as *McClure's* and progressive organizations like the National Municipal League. It appeared to offer a mechanism for pulling the rug from under political machines entrenched in ward-based councils. It also seemed to provide municipalities with a governmental structure that permitted efficient management of public works and services. These were two basic progressive aims. The commission format drew more notice in its incarnation as the Des Moines Plan, which emerged from a successful 1907 campaign by "leading citizens and better classes" to install "nonpartisan, business government" in the Iowa capital. By the First World

War, nearly five hundred cities had adopted it. Most were small, but six, including Buffalo, New Orleans, and Jersey City, had over 200,000 people.[2]

"Acknowledged to be one of our best-governed cities," Washington offered proof that small commissions could manage large, complex cities. Galveston businessmen had studied the District. Supporters of commission rule soon began to insist that there was little direct connection between the capital's system and what they proposed for other cities, that the Washington regime had "originated in an entirely different way from that of the commission form of government." After defeat of the appointive feature of the Galveston charter, advocates realized that state legislatures would hesitate to impose nonelective government on voters in the absence of an acute crisis. Since even the elected variant of the commission flew in the face of the tradition of diffused, participatory urban rule, proponents were already hard-pressed to refute charges that commission government was antirepublican. Although an instructive administrative example, the "military control" at Washington was a rhetorical embarrassment in a land whose governmental creeds derived from Jefferson and Jackson, not Napoleon or Richelieu. "There is no more self-government at Washington than in St. Petersburg," Drake University professor F. I. Herriot, an anticommission political scientist, admonished the citizens of Des Moines. Many of Herriot's readers would have found this comparison apt.[3]

Moreover, from the perspective of many proponents of elected commissions, the example of Washington was misleading as well as politically embarrassing. To numerous urban reformers, the capital's appointed regime defied the point of municipal reorganization, which was to reinvigorate urban democracy, not undermine it. A major reason the commission system's detractors found the plan antidemocratic was that it directly attacked the strong bond that had developed over the decades between local government and working class, lower-middle-class, and ethnic neighborhoods. At-large elections of a small governing panel of necessity gave preponderant voice to citywide perspectives. Since in practice *citywide* often meant *downtown*, elite commercial-civic groups, such as chambers of commerce and boards of trade, were among the plan's most vocal supporters. The enthusiasm of businessmen merely confirmed the critics' suspicions, yet certain activists and scholars who could hardly be called mouthpieces for corporate capital also found aspects of the commission plan worthwhile. For example, Charles Beard, the eminent historian and consultant on urban government, expressed concern that at-large commissions gave inadequate representation to the ordinary voter. At the same time, however, this legendary scholarly iconoclast participated in several expert studies that endorsed at least the principle of small, at-large commissions. Beard was among those urban progressives who felt that well-conceived municipal reorganization could render city government businesslike without leaving it subservient to business. The Des Moines idea had promise, Beard wrote. "It centralizes power and responsibility in a small group of men constantly before the public and subjected to scrutiny of public criticism."[4]

In order to bring urban democracy into the metropolitan age, thinkers such as Beard felt, new institutional forms needed to supersede structures created during Jackson's time and addressed to the facts and concerns of that bygone era. The familiar city corporation, with its unwieldy ward-based legislature, figurehead mayor, herd of elected recorders, comptrollers, etc., and cacophony of special-purpose boards, engendered neither efficiency nor accountability. Until the most visible elected figures were powerful and accountable, the argument went, urban democracy would remain strong in form but illusory in practice. Cities had grown so huge and unfathomable that to focus voters' attention on a few officeholders, whose policies were known from one end of the metropolis to the other, now seemed the best device for engaging the whole community. Whatever its shortcomings, the commission plan accomplished this goal. Progressive urbanists discussed the form tried in Galveston and Des Moines, among a number of alternative schemes, such as the strong mayor charter and the short ballot, all of which aimed at concentrating power and responsibility in identifiable, constituted authorities rather than shadowy, extralegal bosses. To us it may seem contradictory that the progressives campaigned simultaneously for the commission and city-manager formats and for practices that enhanced direct democracy — such as initiative and petition, recall, and home rule — but from their perspective, these measures supplemented each other.

In 1911, political scientist Ernest R. Bradford, who believed commissions a "clear improvement" over previous forms, cited two reasons why he thought other cities should not imitate the federal capital's "partial" commission. In Washington, Congress retained ordinance powers, which rendered policy-making plodding and incoherent. Also, Bradford understood the commission plan as a way to increase public participation and official accountability. A system where inhabitants "have no direct voice in the management of municipal affairs" was obviously unacceptable. While some proponents indeed wanted to use the commission and city-manager formats as conservative devices for "retooling the machinery of urban government to fit the needs of the business world," Beard and his like hoped that these restructuring schemes would aid in creating a truly democratic metropolis. For such people, Washington's 1878 system would have appeared not an example but an aberration, albeit an instructive one.[5]

Washington newspapers also understood that the elected Des Moines commission was not a descendent of their appointed system but an alternative model, viable for Washington should the national city have the opportunity to return to self-government. In his memoirs, however, journalist Lincoln Steffens, who was famous for arguing that business caused more corruption in government than the scorned immigrant voter or the coarse ward boss, recalled that he had planned to muckrake the District commission "to show the city experimenters how that experiment with commissions had worked out." Steffens was offended by the fact that "in order to get rid of" the black vote, the republican capital "had abandoned all pretense of democracy." Yet he was virtually alone in finding the District commission "scandalously corrupt."[6] Others had misgivings about the denial of self-government and its roots in racial politics, but most observers agreed that Washington was the only American city whose operations consistently approached the competence and honesty of German municipal departments, at that time held up by intellectuals as the standard.

The reputation of Washington officials for skill and integrity impressed Frederic Howe, a thoughtful, compelling champion of municipal democracy and working-class voters. "In recent years," Howe wrote approvingly, the city in general had "changed its character and slowly enlarged its functions." Because the provision of new services "increased demands upon municipal government," the public's "social sense is being organized." As a professional reformer, therefore, Howe was bound to approve of an American city that was "probably as well governed as any European municipality." Despite acknowledging the autocracy of Washington's government, Howe thought that its officials demonstrated "the power of cooperative effort," belief in which, he imagined, could cultivate a "rebirth of democracy" elsewhere.[7]

"Many persons are convinced that mass government will not work in municipal affairs," Howe noted dismissively. He then proceeded to describe his own program of structural and social reforms designed to turn the modern metropolis into a democratic showcase. Sadly, subsequent experience offers more support to those he dismissed than to the optimistic reformer. American cities since Howe's time have experienced not a rebirth of democracy but an excruciating physical and social disintegration. Howe wrote that, in the modern world, cities were no longer an "incidental problem"; they were the "measure of our civilization."[8] In these terms, the squalor of our cities' amenities and their decadent, menacing atmosphere stand as a reproach upon and threat to our way of life. Any sensitive observer of the career of our cities since Howe's day will wonder whether the American form of democracy is not the enemy of the city, rather than its hope.

An especially painful aspect of this story is that despite all their talent and good will, American city builders of the period 1860–1920 were not able to contrive a political, legal, and economic foundation to perpetuate their impressive material achievements. Howe argued, I think correctly, that attractive public spaces, impressive public works, and accessible public services form an essential component of the "city sense" that makes a democratic metropolis possible. Our cities' disheartening squalor must, according to this reasoning, reinforce the cycle of decline by pushing the public towards even more privatism and withdrawal rather than towards civic consciousness. Several writers have recently asserted that late-nineteenth-century American urban government was an "unheralded triumph," because municipal officials and engineers accomplished the institution of social services and public works in a very brief period against enormous political, economic, and technological obstacles. One suspects that the people who oversaw this expansion would find their victory hollow, because it proved so transient and so ineffective at altering the balance between private- and public-mindedness in our urban culture.[9]

In Great Britain, France, and Germany, meanwhile, modern city services and public works originated within municipal political systems that were, by comparison to the United States, oligarchic, bureaucratic, or authoritarian. While the cities of other industrial, capitalist countries certainly face severe problems, they have survived war, dictatorship, and the break-up of empires better than American cities have weathered industrial prosperity, the rise to world power, and stable popular government. We must consider whether the relative success of others in holding their cities together is attributable to the later arrival and relative weakness of urban electoral democracy or to their different legal and political cultures and administrative practices with regard to real estate, utilities, and commerce. It would be a sad comment on the hope of democracy if a humane city could grow only in soil fertilized by feudalism, authoritarian administration, or class rule.

The effect of American-style representative government on our cities' physical layout and economic character is difficult to measure, because even in the relentlessly democratic United States of the nineteenth century, popular institutions were only part of a matrix of authority, law, and bureaucracy. This complicated structure has always rendered the reality of self-government at all levels of our polity different from the theory. Admittedly, the emergence of popular politics in the early nineteenth century had substantial consequences for urban political economy; but administrative, legal, and market-based factors also exerted much weight in shaping municipal politics and government.[10] By focusing on the institutional and cultural environment that both nurtured and constrained this country's pioneers in municipal administration, engineering, public health, and urban planning, we gain a better sense of why these innovators failed in perhaps their most fundamental task: establishing the concentrated responsibility and sense of interdependence necessary for stable urban development.

The early advent and great extent of representative democracy in the United States distinguish it from industrial, capitalist countries that built more durable cities. Americans are aware of a variety of ways in which our style of democracy has perhaps contributed to urban stagnation. A partial indictment of urban self-government might include the visionless influence peddling that we call machine politics, the tendency of taxpayers to resist even the most useful capital expenditures, the intermittent anti-city biases displayed by rural-dominated state legislatures, and the resistance of independent suburbs to metropolitan consolidation.

Still, liberal-minded people may draw some comfort from this analysis of

Washington's post–Civil War development, since it suggests that while representative democracy was a contributing factor in our cities' sad fate, it was not the determinant one. Among historical factors that can be blamed for Washington's sharing ailments of other American cities, democracy had no direct influence between 1871 and the 1960s. Far more evident throughout that the period was the promotional tendency ingrained in the way the American state handled development issues. This mix of attitudes, laws, and administrative practices, which was ubiquitous in this country's public sphere in the last century, made our governments — regional and national, as well as local — proficient at fostering economic growth but less adept at channeling that growth towards shared public purposes.

The post–Civil War movement for a worthy federal capital, which resulted in Alexander R. Shepherd's Comprehensive Plan of Improvements, hinged upon a promotional view of nationalism. The assumption that government ought to identify itself with enterprise and undertake public works that boosted private investment had woven itself into politics, bureaucracy, and law over many decades. Shepherd's improvers regarded the territorial program of public works to stimulate real estate to be of such dire importance that step-by-step they subordinated and then sacrificed the exercise of self-government to it. Every strategic interest and institution in late-Reconstruction Washington — Congress, the Grant and Hayes administrations, both major parties, and Washington's "old citizens" — either actively encouraged or eventually acquiesced in this trend.

No group of residents offered a determined challenge to the commission system that superseded Shepherd's Territory, despite the Gilded Age public's alleged devotion to the remnants of Jacksonism. Many resident groups organized to influence the commissioners and the congressional District committees. Still, the two major forces in public politics in late-nineteenth-century Washington, the local-minded citizens associations and the purportedly unsectional Board of Trade, consented to pursue their disparate goals through lobbying and other techniques of interest-group politics and rejected the idea of submitting disputes to the people at large. The interests of the downtown commercial-civic movement conformed readily to the procedures of appointed government and the attitudes and political requirements of key policy-makers in Congress, so the Board of Trade quickly became the community's quasi city council. For decades after 1878, the capital's local politics reinforced, rather than challenged, the denial of self-government.

In no other American city were governing institutions so removed from public pressure. If Congress, the commissioners, the Army Corps, and commercial-civic leaders had agreed that they should pursue the metropolitan commonwealth envisioned by progressive urbanists, then a short-sighted, "particularistic" public could not significantly inhibit them. Reform-minded urban professionals were heard from, and the improvement faction that coalesced around James McMillan and the Board of Trade did implement half of the reformers' program. By sponsoring expert consultants and by battling congressional conservatives they attained for Washington a level of administrative and public works excellence that was rare. What unified the improvers, however, was their attachment to the promotional function of public improvements. Indeed, the Army Corps often found itself the odd man out in Washington's post-1878 governing group in part because the Corps's sense of nationalism and duty to the broad public interest sometimes competed with the promotional tendency.

Ingrained assumptions and practices regarding the state and development made impossible the second half of the progressive urbanists' program — the use of public works and services to encourage a humane city whose residents appreciated their interdependence and understood the complexity of their environment. The District was an innovator in street design, water, and sewerage, but these services were extended to outlying districts in ways that enhanced the disintegrating effects of an unmanaged land market. The Army Corps won worldwide acclaim for innovative work in street paving, but well-built roads served as a frustrating centrifugal force. The McMillan Commission introduced town planning to the United States, but, critics insist, the 1902 park plan represented surrender of all but a small slice of the republican capital to the chaos of privatism.

Most fateful for the District in the long run was the unwillingness to attack a pattern of race politics that effectively defined one-third of Washington's residents as something less than full members of the polity. The combination of circumstances, attitudes, and interests that led to the District commission's formation in 1878 deprived black civic and business organizations of the opportunity to participate in deliberations over the city's direction on a scale that even remotely reflected the needs and significance of that segment of the population. Race politics finally destroyed the commission system in the 1960s, but not before this pattern of exclusion had contributed to debilitating distortions in private economy and social life.

In the national city, as elsewhere in urban America, reform-minded officials and civic leaders were able to pursue individual, even contradictory and self-defeating, programs with energy and intelligence; but when they sought to institute coordinated, comprehensive measures, they encountered insurmountable obstacles. Democracy could not have been the main reason the federal district manifested the "incoherence" and "fragmentation" many historians and political scientists consider ubiquitous in the formation and implementation of public policy in the United States.[11] The implication is that the promotional approach, which served the country well in other aspects of economic development, has been the Achilles heel of American urban governance. Perhaps we are now paying the price for having approached situations that required coordination and interdependence with a mentality in which coordination was considered stifling. Perhaps other industrial, capitalist countries built more durable, humane cities because their state tradi-

By the turn of century, streetcars powered through underground conduits had replaced horse tramways on Pennsylvania Avenue and now-familiar landmarks stood
in place of the ramshackle shops, offices, and boarding houses that Mark Twain and
others had ridiculed. The Post Office Tower (*right rear*) was completed in 1899; the
Willard Hotel (*left*) would be completed in 1901. Courtesy the Washingtoniana Division, District of Columbia Public Library.

tions encouraged vigorous bureaucratic oversight of the urban economy and
because their urban political cultures distinguished civic pride from entrepreneurial enthusiasm more clearly than ours.[12] At the same time, our counterparts' own historical predispositions created dilemmas we have not had
to face.

Regardless of the District commission's underlying defects, knowledgeable contemporaries agreed upon its comparative operational efficiency. Washington's "streets are clean, well lighted, and well protected by the police," Howe wrote. "Its school system is among the best, and its health, fire, and many other departments are beyond serious criticism." The capital's appointed rulers were at least as proficient as elected authorities elsewhere at regulating unruly transit companies and pugnacious utilities.[13] This observation brings us to a concluding thought regarding the Gilded Age drive to build a capital worthy of the nation. The District commission functioned at least as well as other American municipalities, but critics had a point when they insisted that the system constituted a discreditable anomaly. Washington mocked the country's ideals when it should have epitomized them.

Americans have a hard time imagining that a group of their compatriots would deliberately decide that one of our major jurisdictions ought to be *permanently* governed in an unrepresentative way. Admittedly, the political atmosphere of the late-Reconstruction period was unusually confused and tense; still, Congress debated the commission proposal for four years. When they acted, in 1878, it was calmly and with minimal dissent. Prominent Washingtonians worked actively for the 1878 act and cheerfully greeted its passage. Once the commission was in place, most Washingtonians adapted readily and completely. Residents designed their civic, commercial, and neighborhood associations to operate within the new framework. After a while, few cared greatly whether elections returned. The District's home rule movement never attained the scale or intensity one would have expected from the city of George Washington, John Adams, and Thomas Jefferson. "It would be supposed," exclaimed New Hampshire Senator Henry Blair in 1890, "that the capital of the foremost Republic on the face of the earth . . . would itself be a model republic." Blair believed in his country's total and permanent dedication to popular sovereignty. Washington's story casts doubt on the ubiquity and immutability of that faith.[14]

We began with the 1863 raising of Thomas Crawford's statue of Freedom atop the new Capitol dome. At that time, Horace Greeley's *New York Tribune* remarked solemnly that the immense bronze woman could serve as "a mentor, a censor, a scoffer, or a satirist" for the flesh-and-blood people below.[15] During the lively parades and lavish ceremonies that marked Washington's gala centennial celebration in 1900, the capital's prominent residents and leading policy-makers joined with friends from around the country to express confidence that, despite certain shortcomings, the national city had at last come to justify its founders' vision and now projected a proud face to the world. Freedom's comments on these proceedings, from her lofty position atop the Capitol, might have been worth hearing.

Note on Sources

Unpublished Sources

A LONGSTANDING PLAN to move papers of the District of Columbia from the National Archives to a separate municipal archives has suffered one delay after another. As of this writing, the District records I used remain in the national repository, where they are listed as record group (RG) 351. Many volumes of minute books, letter press copies of letters sent, and registers of letters received survive from the Gilded Age. These initially seem dull as dishwater, but they repay patient effort. A major turning point in the documentation of Washington's local government occurred in the mid-1890s, when the District acquired typewriters. Before then, except when a meeting was of unusual significance, minutes merely listed with whom the commissioners had met and what was decided. Equipped with the new machines, secretaries recorded details of discussions and the rationale behind decisions.

More varied were records of the Office of Public Buildings and Grounds (RG 42). Correspondence of the pre-1867 civilian bureau is on microfilm. The Army Corps of Engineers, who took over this agency in 1867, kept everything, from lists of whose wife was to receive fresh flowers from the Botanical Garden at what interval to samples of rat poison sent from France. I learned of the worldwide campaign against Grover Cleveland's unwelcome houseguests on a slow day in the Archives, when I innocently opened a carefully wrapped hand-painted box labeled *"crainte d'humidité"* and spilled the contents over the reading room floor. The clerk who preserved this powder a century ago deserves a commendation — it was still perfectly dry.

Although nineteenth-century congressional committees did not always keep records as diligently as the Army Engineers, Congress played such a pervasive role in District affairs that the manuscript records of the Senate (RG 46) and of the House (RG 233) provide information about more facets of Washington's politics, economy, and life than any other unpublished source. The Commission of Fine Arts Papers (RG 66) cover the aftermath of the McMillan Plan, as well as the influential career of long-time chairman Charles Moore. The records of the chief of engineers (RG 77) proved most useful for tracing the ups and downs of the Washington Aqueduct. Other official papers consulted include manscript census records at the Archives and the "Bioessays" at the Office of History of the Army Corps of Engineers, Fort Belvoir, Virginia.

Personal papers provide uneven coverage of a Gilded Age politician's career. Most public business in nineteenth-century politics occurred in face-to-face encounters, rather than through memos, drafts, and position papers. The involvement of congressmen from around the country in Washington's affairs shows up in their private papers mainly when they were out of town and aides or friends were updating them on a matter left unfinished or recently arisen. I made a very worthwhile midwestern swing to see James McMillan's papers at the Detroit Public Library and William B. Allison's at the Iowa State Historical Society in Des Moines. The trip was generously funded by the Everett McKinley Dirksen Congressional Leadership Research Center of Pekin, Illinois.

James Garfield was an unusually meticulous recordkeeper, for a Gilded Age politician, but even he seems to have removed key documents pertaining to the DeGolyer-McLelland controversy from his papers, now in the Library of Congress (and also available on microfilm). A minority of the papers in the Library's Alexander Shepherd collection pertain to his activities as leader of the territorial movement, although his family kept enormous scrapbooks of clippings that praised or defended him. Francis G. Newlands's papers in the Manuscripts and Archives Division of the Yale University Library were a singular disappointment for my purposes, as they offer only a sketchy portrait of the formation and early development of the Chevy Chase Company.

The civil engineers, planning consultants, and assorted urban professionals whose presence in Washington increased as the century progressed represented a style of politics in which paper played a more central role, so the coverage provided by Library of Congress collections on such as Frederick Law Olmsted (microfilmed and in the process of publication), the Olmsted Associates, and Charles McKim feel more comprehensive. Charles Moore, an experienced journalist who earned a doctorate in history from George Washington University, carefully arranged his private papers, also in the Library of Congress, according to correspondent and subject. He later drew heavily upon them when writing his interesting biographies of Daniel Burnham and McKim.

The only military engineer active in the District who left a personal record as extensive as his civilian counterparts was Montgomery Meigs, whose papers, microfilmed at the Library of Congress, more than justify his contemporary reputation as a stubborn, curmudgeonly controversialist. Richard Hoxie's wife, Vinnie Ream, was a sculptor popular in political circles. The Library's collection of her and her husband's correspondence with General William T. Sherman, Senator Daniel Vorhees, and other military and political figures provides insight into the public works imbroglios Hoxie managed repeatedly to mix himself in, as well as into the system of military patronage that alternately helped and hindered a young engineer's career.

Finally, Constance M. Green's papers in the Library show how this major figure in the early urban history movement developed her ideas for her two-volume "biography" of the capital, *Washington: A History of the National Capital, 1800–1950,* published by Princeton University Press in 1962 and 1963. Other important personal collections include those of Nelson Aldrich, Sayles J. Bowen, William E. Chandler, and Benjamin B. French in the Library of Congress; Rudolph Hering and William R. Hutton in the National Museum of American History; and Orville Babcock in the Newberry Library.

Of business and association papers, the Historical Society of Washington houses the Capital Traction Papers as well as minutes books from Shepherd's antagonists, the Citizens Association. The Board of Trade Papers at George Washington University, though far from comprehensive for this period, are worth consulting.

Published Sources

An advantage in studying Washington, especially the period after installation of the District commission, 1874–78, is that municipal reports, official communications, and legislative reports and investigations were published as part of the Congressional Serial Sets, which are readily available in microform. These constitute the set of documents most frequently employed in this study. Congress's willingness to put the resources of the Government Printing Office at Washington's disposal affords historians an unusually thorough picture of the internal workings of a Gilded Age city and lessens our dependence on newspapers, memoirs, and other sources that of necessity give incomplete coverage to administrative matters.

When citing documents in the Serial Sets, I have provided the title of the document, or if that is unwieldy, an abbreviated title, the Congress and session numbers, the date submitted (in most cases), and the category and number assigned. For example, Commissioner Dent's explication of the District's side of its dispute with the U.S. Treasury over the enforcement of special improvement taxes (discussed in chapter 4) is "Letter of the District Commissioners on the Sinking Fund of the District of Columbia," 46th Cong., 2nd sess. (Mar. 30, 1880), S. Misc. Doc. [Senate Miscellaneous Document] 68. Senator McMillan's report explaining his grade crossings bill that would have left the railroad tracks on the Mall (discussed in chapter 8) is denoted "To eliminate grade crossings on the Baltimore and Potomac Railroad," 56th Cong., 1st sess. (Apr. 10, 1900), S. Rept. [Senate Report] 928. The 1890 Hering Commission plan for Washington's sewers is *Report on the System of Sewerage in the District of Columbia*, 51st Cong., 2nd sess. (June 1890), H. Exec. Doc. [House Executive Document] 445.

Among official publications not listed in the Serial Sets, I made extensive use of the *Congressional Globe*, *Congressional Record* (which superseded the *Globe* in 1873), appropriations hearings on the District of Columbia Bill, and publications of the Census Bureau.

Of nongovernmental printed sources, most fundamental are the annual reports of the Board of Trade. These are accessible at the Washingtoniana Room of the District's Martin Luther King Memorial Library.

After the collapse of the *National Intelligencer* in 1869, the District newspaper most committed to local news was the *Evening Star*, edited by Shepherd's old friend, Crosby Noyes. Though a fine newspaper, the *Star* was thoroughly "downtown" in orientation, which means that competing views are hard to follow in the District press. The *Washington Post,* which first appeared in the late 1870s, went through several owners of varying talents in its early days. While I consulted many other papers, I most often used the daily and Sunday *Chronicle,* the *Critic* (published in the 1880s by Hallet Kilbourn), and the *National Republican.* The *Washington Bee* was the most durable black newspaper. Widely circulated out-of-town papers, such as the Baltimore *Sun* and New York's *Daily Tribune* and *Sun,* played a major role in the territorial controversy.

That noble Anglo-American tradition, venting one's spleen in a pamphlet, flourished in the federal city a century ago. The Historical Society of Washington has many pamphlets on local affairs dating from these decades, including the Suter-Noyes collection, which focuses on the home rule question. A fair number found their way to the Johns Hopkins University's Milton S. Eisenhower Library, where nineteenth-century pamphlets are grouped into special collections for history (anything listed as D1.A in the catalog), political economy (HB30.A), and political science (JA36.A).

Useful published diaries include Benjamin B. French, *Witness to the Young Republic: A Yankee's Journal, 1828–1870,* edited by Donald B. Cole and John J. McDonough (Hanover, N.H.: UP of New England, 1989); and *The Diary of James A. Garfield,* edited by Harry James Brown and Frederick D. Williams (East Lansing: Michigan State UP, 1967). Also, *Mr. Lincoln's Washington: Selections from the Writings of Noah Brooks, Civil War Correspondent,* edited by P. J. Staudenraus (South Brunswick, N.J.: Thomas Yoseloff, 1967). Contemporary or near-contemporary analyses of the District's governance and public works may be found in Walter F. Dodd, *The Government of the District of Columbia* (Washington, D.C.: John Byrne, 1909); John Addison Porter, *The City of Washington: Its Origin and Administration* (Studies in Historical and Political Science series) (Baltimore: Johns Hopkins Press, 1885); and Carroll D. Wright, "The Economic Development of the District of Columbia," *Proceedings of the Washington Academy of Sciences* 1 (Dec. 1899): 161–87. John W. Reps, *Washington on View: The Nation's Capital since 1790* (Chapel Hill: U of North Carolina P, 1991) provides an overview of guidebook and tourist writing on nineteenth-century Washington.

The most entertaining, persuasive memoirs of turn-of-the-century Washington politics came from the pen of Charles Moore. Moore's *Autobiography* remains unpublished, but there are manuscript copies in his papers at the Library of Congress and in the Fine Arts Commission papers, Record Group 66 at the Archives. Moore's loosely structured memoir/history, *Washington, Past and Present* (New York: Century, 1929), presents the McMillan Plan as the culmination of the movement for a worthy national city. Though it has been superseded by modern biographies, Moore's *Daniel Burnham: Architect, Planner of Cities* (New York: Houghton Mifflin, 1916) is indispensable to scholars of the period, as it makes a masterful case for what later became the standard view of the protagonist's place in the emergence of the American urban planning profession. The same author's *Life and Times of Charles Follen McKim* (Boston: Houghton Mifflin, 1929) likewise reached a national audience. Less persuasive but still perceptive is *Memories, 1860–1930: A Winning Crusade to Revive George Washington's Vision of a Capital City,* by architect Glenn Brown (Washington, D.C.: W. F. Roberts, 1931).

Early volumes of the *Records of the Columbia Historical Society* contain first-hand sketches of major figures in the upheavals of the 1860s and 1870s, including Shepherd and Sayles Bowen (both by the omnipresent William Tindall), James G. Berret (by himself), and Lewis Clephane, Matthew Emery, and Richard Wallach.

For the collective biographies and sketches of factional leaders discussed in chapters 2 and 7, I also relied on *A History of the City of Washington: Its Men and Institutions,* edited by Allen B. Slauson (Washington, D.C.: Washington Post, 1903); and *American Biographical Dictionaries—the District of Columbia* (Washington, D.C.: Potomac Publishers, 1908); in addition to the standard biographical dictionaries. These sources were supplemented by biographical sketches culled from general histories of Washington, such as *Washington, Past and Present: A History,* edited by John C. Proctor (New York: Lewis Historical Publishing, 1930); William Tindall, *Standard History of Washington* (Knoxville, Tenn.: H. W. Crew, 1914); and William B. Webb and H. W. Crew, *Centennial History of Washington, D.C.* (Dayton, Ohio: United Brethren Publishing, 1892).

Of all general Washington histories prior to Constance Green's, Wilhelmus B. Bryan, *A History of the National Capital,* volume 2, *1815–1878* (New York: Macmillan, 1916) proved most useful by far. A near contemporary, Bryan implicitly grasped the improvers' mentality and approach to development. Bryan provides important details, passed over by Green, regarding the organization of the capital's private sector and its evolving relations with local and national governmental institutions.

Abbreviations

Aqueduct Tunnel Invest.:	*Investigation of the Washington Aqueduct Tunnel*, 50th Cong., 2nd sess., S. Rept. 2686
Board of Audit Invest.:	*Investigation of the Board of Audit of the District of Columbia*, 44th Cong., 1st sess., H. Misc. Doc. 103
BPW-AR:	District of Columbia Board of Public Works, *Annual Report*
CEngsAR:	Chief of Engineers, *Annual Report*
CG:n-n:	*Congressional Globe* (Congress-session)
CR:n-n:	*Congressional Record* (Congress-session)
DCComsAR:	District of Columbia Commissioners, *Annual Report*
DCComsLS:	District of Columbia Commissioners, letters sent, record group 351, National Archives
DCComsMins:	District of Columbia Commissioners, minutes, record group 351, National Archives
DCComsRLR:	District of Columbia Commissioners, register of letters received, record group 351, National Archives
DCTComsMins:	District of Columbia Temporary Board of Commissioners, minutes, record group 351, National Archives
House Invest. (1872):	*Affairs in the District of Columbia*, 42nd Cong., 2nd sess., H. Rept. 72
HRApproHrgs:	*Hearings of the House Subcommittee on the District of Columbia Appropriations Bill*
Joint Invest. (1874):	*Affairs in the District of Columbia*, 43rd Cong., 1st sess., S. Rept. 453
LawsLegAssem:	Laws of the Legislative Assembly, Territory of the District of Columbia, record group 351, National Archives

MayorLS:	Office of the Mayor, Washington City, letters sent, record group 351, National Archives
OpinCorpCoun:	Opinions of the Corporation Counsel, District of Columbia, record group 351, National Archives
PBO:	Records of the Public Buildings Office, record group 42, National Archives
PBO-AR:	Commissioner of Public Buildings and Grounds, *Annual Report* (until 1867 appended to Interior Department, *Annual Report*)
RCHS:	*Records of the Columbia Historical Society*
RG:	Record group at the National Archives
RecHRep:	Records of the United States House of Representatives, record group 233, National Archives
RecSen:	Records of the United States Senate, record group 46, National Archives
SenApproHrgs:	*Hearings of the Senate Subcommittee on the District of Columbia Appropriations Bill*
Sinking Fund Invest. (1880):	*Testimony on Charges against the Commissioners of the District of Columbia*, 46th Cong., 2nd sess., H. Misc. Doc. 39
TDCGovLS:	Territory of the District of Columbia, Office of the Governor, letters sent, record group 351, National Archives
WashAque:	Office of the Washington Aqueduct, Records of the Chief of Engineers, letters sent, record group 77, National Archives
WBT-AR:	Washington Board of Trade, *Annual Report*

Notes

Preface

1. Probably, Monte S. Calvert, "The Manifest Functions of the Machine," in Bruce M. Stave and Sondra A. Stave, eds., *Urban Bosses, Machines, and Progressive Reformers* (1972; 2nd rev. ed., Malabar, Fla.: Robert E. Krieger, 1984), pp. 45–55.

Introduction

1. On the concept of metropolis, see Anthony Sutcliffe, ed., *Metropolis, 1890–1940* (Chicago: U of Chicago P, 1984).

2. David Pinkney, *Napoleon III and the Rebuilding of Paris* (Princeton: Princeton UP, 1958). Cecil O. Smith, Jr., "The Longest Run: Public Engineers and Planning in France," *American Historical Review* 95, no. 3 (1990), 657–92.

3. *Harper's New Monthly Magazine,* Dec. 1859.

4. Charles Burr Todd, *The Story of Washington, the National Capital* (New York: Putnam's, 1889), p. 177. P. J. Staudenraus, *Mr. Lincoln's Washington: Selections from the Writings of Noah Brooks, Civil War Correspondent* (South Brunswick, N.J.: Thomas Yoseloff, 1967), pp. 344–45. Margaret Leech, *Reveille in Washington, 1860–1865* (1941; Alexandria, Va.: Time-Life Books, 1980), pp. 6–15. *Harper's New Monthly Magazine,* Dec. 1859.

5. PBO-AR, 1861, p. 850. Staudenraus, *Mr. Lincoln's Washington,* pp. 116–17. James H. Whyte, *The Uncivil War: Washington during the Reconstruction* (New York: Twayne, 1958), pp. 13–14.

6. John W. Reps, *Monumental Washington* (Princeton: Princeton UP, 1967), pp. 18–21. BPW-AR, 1872, p. 4. Constance M. Green, *Washington: Village and Capital, 1800–1878* (Princeton: Princeton UP, 1962), pp. 13–16.

7. Reps, *Monumental Washington,* p. 26. James Sterling Young, *The Washington Community, 1800–1828* (New York: Columbia UP, 1966), p. 19.

8. George Washington, quoted in "The Site of the National Capital," *Harper's New Monthly Magazine* (1870), reprinted in Frank Oppel and Tony Meisel, eds., *Washington: A Turn-of-the-Century Treasury* (Secaucus, N.J.: Castle, 1987), p. 41. Carroll D. Wright, "The Economic Development of the District of Columbia," *Proceedings of the Washington Academy of Sciences,* vol. 1 (Dec. 29, 1899), pp. 181, 184. U.S. Census Bureau, *Twelfth Census of the United States,* "Report on Manufactures," vol. 8, pt. 2, p. 115.

9. CEngsAR, 1868, pp. 913–24. PBO-AR, 1864, pp. 686–87. House Invest. (1872), p. 622. William A. Croffut, "Lincoln's Washington: Recollections of a Journalist Who Knew Everybody," *Atlantic Monthly,* Jan. 1930, 55–65. Green, *Village and Capital,* pp. 12–13. Whyte, *Uncivil War,* p. 4.

10. Wilhelmus B. Bryan, *A History of the National Capital* (New York: Macmillan, 1916), vol. 2, pp. 262–63.

11. *Harper's New Monthly Magazine,* Dec. 1859. Trollope, da Serra, and Dickens quoted in Reps, *Monumental Washington,* p. 41.

12. CG:41-2 (Dec. 22, 1869, Feb. 18, 1870), pp. 303–4, 1392–1400. Memorial regarding International Exhibition bill, 41st Cong., 2nd sess., H. Misc. Doc. 4. Bryan,

History of the National Capital, vol. 2, pp. 591–92. Elizabeth J. Miller, "Dreams of Being the Capital of Commerce: The National Fair of 1879," RCHS, vol. 51 (1984), pp. 71–82.

13. Todd, *Story of Washington,* pp. viii, 96. Charles Moore, *Washington, Past and Present* (New York: Century, 1929), p. 50.

14. WBT-AR, 1891, pp. 6–7.

15. William V. Cox, ed., *The Centennial Celebration of the Establishment of the Seat of Government in the District of Columbia* (Washington, D.C.: GPO, 1901), p. 22.

16. Cox, *Centennial Celebration,* pp. 64–71.

17. Cox, *Centennial Celebration,* p. 115. Walter E. McCann, "The Rise and Growth of Our National Capital," *Frank Leslie's Popular Monthly,* Feb. 1887, 131–40. DCComsAR, 1898, pp. 25–30. George Tillson, "Asphalt and Asphalt Pavements," *Transactions of the American Society of Civil Engineers* 38 (Dec. 1897): 231–33.

18. The term *commercial-civic elite,* which aptly describes "downtown" business and professional movements such as the Washington Board of Trade, comes from Blaine Brownell, *The Urban Ethos in the South, 1920–1930* (Baton Rouge: Louisiana State UP, 1975).

19. The notion that a "promotional" orientation structured the way American governments — state and local as well as national — dealt with development matters during the nineteenth century grew out of an academic debate on historical trends in public sector–private sector relations that took place during the 1950s and 1960s. Major contributions to this debate are reviewed in Robert A. Lively, "The American System: A Review Article," *Business History Review* 29 (1955): 81–96; and Harry N. Schieber, "Government and the Economy: Studies of the 'Commonwealth' Policy in the Nineteenth Century," *Journal of Interdisciplinary History* 3 (Summer 1972): 135–51. A recent review appears in Richard L. McCormick, *The Party Period and Public Policy* (New York: Oxford UP, 1986), pp. 204 ff.

20. Many urban history surveys employ this framework. Among the most thoughtful and readable are Raymond A. Mohl, *The New City: Urban America in the Industrial Age* (Arlington Heights, Ill.: Harlan Davidson, 1985); and Maury Klein and Harvey A. Kantor, *Prisoners of Progress: American Industrial Cities, 1850–1920* (New York: Macmillan, 1976). The phrases quoted come from two influential accounts: Samuel P. Hays, *The Response to Industrialism* (Chicago: U of Chicago P, 1957); and Martin J. Schiesl, *The Politics of Efficiency: Municipal Administration and Reform in America, 1800–1920* (Berkeley: U of California P, 1977).

21. The best-known example is Sam Bass Warner, Jr., *The Private City: Philadelphia in Three Periods of Its Growth* (Philadelphia: U of Pennsylvania P, 1968). Warner's "private city" concept has implications that parallel much of what I am arguing.

22. Some writings employed here draw upon an "exceptionalist" framework to interpret American state development, but I prefer to talk of distinctive or distinctively strong features. Michael McGerr, "The Price of the New Transnational History," *American Historical Review* 96, no. 4 (Oct. 1991): 1056–67, describes conceptual advantages of distinctiveness as opposed to exceptionalism.

23. Robert M. Fogelson, *The Fragmented Metropolis: Los Angeles, 1850–1930* (Cambridge: Harvard UP, 1967). Sam Bass Warner, Jr., *The Urban Wilderness* (New York: Harper and Row, 1972), p. 3. Eric Monkkonen, in *America Becomes Urban* (Berkeley: U of California P, 1988), p. 25, refuses to concede that American cities *are* fragmented, in addition to appearing so: "As much as [the concept of fragmentation] may reflect urban disorder and chaos, it may equally suggest that the observer has failed to see order and cohesiveness, lacking the necessary perceptual conditioning to unify a set of observations."

24. Barry Karl, *The Uneasy State* (Chicago: U of Chicago P, 1983). Stephen Skowronek, *Building a New American State* (Cambridge: Cambridge UP, 1982), p. viii.

Chapter 1 Washington and the Wartime Union

1. Baltimore *Sun*, Dec. 2 and 3, 1863. Margaret Leech, *Reveille in Washington* (1941; Alexandria, Va.: Time-Life Books, 1980), p. 345. Constance M. Green, *Washington: Village and Capital, 1800–1878* (Princeton: Princeton UP, 1962), p. 268.

2. Diary for Dec. 3 and 6, 1863, B. B. French Papers, box 3, reel 2, Library of Congress. Lincoln, quoted in Leech, *Reveille in Washington*, p. 345. *New York Daily Tribune*, Dec. 4, 1863.

3. Wilhelmus B. Bryan, *A History of the National Capital* (New York: Macmillan, 1916), vol. 2, pp. 331, 371, 556. Thomas J. Cantwell, "Anacostia: Strength in Adversity," RCHS, 1973–74, 330–70.

4. Mark Twain and Charles Dudley Warner, *The Gilded Age* (1873; New York: Harper and Row, 1915), vol. 1, pp. 263–69.

5. Horace Greeley, quoted in James H. Whyte, *The Uncivil War: Washington during the Reconstruction* (New York: Twayne, 1958), p. 16. Henry Adams, *Education of Henry Adams* (1918; New York: Time Book Div., 1964), vol. 1, pp. 46–47, 108–9.

6. Green, *Village and Capital*, p. 295. The estimated population of Washington City alone was 140,000 in 1864, nearly twice the entire District in 1860.

7. Carl Abbott, "Dimensions of Regional Change in Washington, D.C.," *American Historical Review* 95, no. 5 (1990): 1370.

8. Twain and Warner, *Gilded Age*, pp. 268–69.

9. CG:37-2 (May 15, 1862), pp. 2141–46. *National Intelligencer*, Oct. 20, 1866.

10. "Testimony . . . as to the Condition of the Potomac River Front at Washington," 47th Cong., 1st sess., S. Misc. Doc. 133. "Reclamation of the Marshes of the Cities of Washington and Georgetown," 47th Cong., 1st sess. (Jan. 26, 1882), H. Rept. 83.

11. Frederick Gutheim, consultant, *Worthy of the Nation* (Washington, D.C.: Smithsonian Institution P, 1977), pp. 53–55. Andrew Jackson Downing, quoted in John W. Reps, *Monumental Washington* (Princeton: Princeton UP, 1967), pp. 50–53.

12. *National Intelligencer*, Sept. 14, 1867. Frederick Law Olmsted to Senator Justin Morrill, draft letter, Jan. 22, 1874, Olmsted Papers, Library of Congress, reel 14. Reps, *Monumental Washington*, p. 51. Petitions for canal improvement, 38th Cong., 1st sess., S. Misc. Doc. 84. Public Buildings and Grounds Committee Papers, RecHRep, 38A-E17.1. Green, *Village and Capital*, p. 309.

13. Olmsted to W. H. Hall, draft letter, Mar. 28, 1874, Olmsted Papers, reel 40. Green, *Village and Capital*, pp. 195–96. Harry James Brown and Frederick D. Williams, eds., *The Diary of James A. Garfield* (East Lansing: Michigan State UP, 1967), vol. 2 (1872–1874), Mar. 22, 1874, p. 33. *Evening Star*, Apr. 18, 1890.

14. William R. Smith to Benjamin B. French, Jan. 1864, Public Buildings and Grounds Committee Papers, RecHRep, 38A-E17.1. Letter from the Commissioner of Public Buildings, 37th Cong., 2nd sess. (Mar. 1, 1862), H. Misc. Doc. 57. "Improvement of the Washington Canal," 41st Cong., 2nd sess. (May 1870), S. Misc. Doc. 142. Green, *Village and Capital*, p. 5.

15. "Improvements to the Washington Canal," 39th Cong., 1st sess. (Apr. 2, 1866), S. Exec. Doc. 35. "Report of the Executive Committee of the Smithsonian on the Washington City Canal," 40th Cong., 2nd sess. (May 15, 1868), S. Misc. Doc. 95. Bryan, *History of the National Capital*, vol. 2, pp. 107–13, 122–32. *National Intelligencer*, Sept. 12, 1866.

16. Donald E. Press, "South of the Avenue: From Murder Bay to the Federal Triangle," RCHS, 51 (1984), pp. 51–70. Green, *Village and Capital*, p. 251. CG:39-1, (Mar. 20, 1866), pp. 1507–8. Whyte, *Uncivil War*, pp. 31–32.

17. Whyte, *Uncivil War*, p. 14. Leech, *Reveille in Washington*, pp. 321–22. "Isadore Saks," *American Biographical Dictionaries — the District of Columbia* (Washington, D.C.:

Potomac Publishers, 1908), p. 476. Allan B. Slauson, ed., *A History of the City of Washington: Its Men and Institutions* (Washington, D.C.: Washington Post, 1903), pp. 255–56.

18. Resolution of the Washington City Council, RecHRep, 37A-G3.5. CG:41-2 (June 17, 1870), pp. 4535–37.

19. *National Intelligencer,* Nov. 5, 1862, Feb. 2, 1863.

20. James Sterling Young, *The Washington Community, 1800–1828* (New York: Columbia UP, 1966), pp. 75–76.

21. *National Intelligencer,* Oct. 16–17, 1866. Mayor Magruder to the Common Council and Board of Aldermen, Apr. 12, 1858, MayorLS.

22. CG:21-1 (Aug. 21, 1852), pp. 2288–92. *National Intelligencer,* Dec. 7, 1863. Diary for Dec. 5, 1863, B. B. French Papers, box 3, reel 2.

23. Theodore Samo to B. B. French, May 1865, PBO, entry 1, reel 27. Samo to Randolph Coyle, June 5, 1867, WashAque, entry 271, vol. 1. CEngsAR, 1867, pp. 530–31; 1880, pp. 2348–52. DCComsAR, 1875, pp. 269–74. "Additional Water Supply on Capitol Hill," 46th Cong., 2nd sess. (Mar. 6, 1880), S. Misc. Doc. 51. "Waste of Water in the District of Columbia," 46th Cong., 2nd sess. (Mar. 5, 1880), S. Misc. Doc. 52. Diary for Apr. 3, 1870, B. B. French Papers, box 4, reel 3.

24. *The Nation,* Mar. 30, 1871. CG:41-3 (Jan. 23, 1871), p. 683.

25. Nelson M. Blake, *Water for the Cities* (Syracuse: Syracuse UP, 1956), pp. 238–42, 266. Stuart Galishoff, "Triumph and Failure: The American Response to the Urban Water Supply Problem, 1860–1923," in Martin V. Melosi, ed., *Pollution and Reform in American Cities* (Austin: U of Texas P, 1980), pp. 33–55. Joel A. Tarr, "Building the Urban Infrastructure in the Nineteenth Century: An Introduction," in *Infrastructure and Urban Growth in the Nineteenth Century* (Chicago: Public Works Historical Society, 1985), p. 77. David Owen, *The Government of Victorian London* (Cambridge: Harvard UP, 1982), p. 134.

26. Joel A. Tarr et al., "The Development and Impact of Urban Waste Water Technology: Changing Concepts of Water Quality Control," in Melosi, *Pollution and Reform,* pp. 59–82. Joel A. Tarr, "The Separate versus Combined Sewer Problem: A Case Study in Urban Technology Design Choice," *Journal of Urban History* 5, no. 3 (1979): 308–39. Eugene P. Moehring, *Public Works and the Patterns of Urban Real Estate Growth in Manhattan, 1835–1894* (New York: Arno, 1981), pp. 19–22, 43–45, 87–94. Alan D. Anderson, *The Origin and Resolution of an Urban Crisis: Baltimore, 1890–1930* (Baltimore: Johns Hopkins UP, 1977), pp. 66–73. James B. Crooks, *Politics and Progress: The Rise of Urban Progressivism in Baltimore, 1895–1911* (Baton Rouge: Louisiana State UP, 1968), pp. 133–36. Jon A. Peterson, "Environment and Technology in the Great City Era of American History," *Journal of Urban History* 8, no. 3 (1982): 343–54.

27. Jon C. Teaford, *The Unheralded Triumph: City Government in America, 1870–1900* (Baltimore: Johns Hopkins UP, 1984), p. 225.

28. Moehring, *Public Works,* pp. 109–14. Gutheim, *Worthy of the Nation,* p. 81. Clay McShane, "Transforming the Use of Urban Space: A Look at the Revolution in Street Pavements, 1880–1924," *Journal of Urban History* 5, no. 3 (1979): 281–86. CEngsAR, 1867, pp. 544–48. *Evening Star,* May 15, 1880. Walter W. Crosby, "Macadam Road Surfacing in the Past and for the Future," *Proceedings of the First International Road Congress* (Paris, 1908).

29. Moehring, *Public Works,* pp. 112–14.

30. Martin V. Melosi, *Garbage in the Cities* (College Station: Texas A&M UP, 1981), pp. 44–46. By the end of the nineteenth century, one-third of American cities paid from the general fund the entire cost of street improvements, one-third assessed it all, and one-third split the cost with property owners. Experts in municipal finance recommended the split system on grounds of practicality and justice. In Europe, only Germany and Belgium had successful special assessment systems, Germany's on the

half-and-half principle. J. L. van Ornum, "The Theory and Practice of Special Assessments," *American Society of Civil Engineers Transactions* 38 (Dec. 1897): 336–422; Victor Rosewater, *Special Assessments: A Study in Municipal Finance* (New York: Columbia College Studies in History, Economics, and Law, 1893). For a contrasting view that appeared too late to incorporate fully here, see Robin Einhorn, *Property Rules: Political Economy in Chicago, 1833–1872* (Chicago: U of Chicago P, 1991).

31. Moehring, *Public Works,* pp. 248–53.

32. Regarding the evolution of public services and the origins of town planning in the great European countries: Anthony Sutcliffe, *Towards the Planned City* (New York: St. Martin's, 1981); David Pinkney, *Napoleon III and the Rebuilding of Paris* (Princeton: Princeton UP, 1958); Anthony Sutcliffe, *The Autumn of Central Paris: The Defeat of Town Planning* (London: Edward Arnold, 1970); Brian Ladd, *Urban Planning and Civic Order in Germany, 1860–1914* (Cambridge: Harvard UP, 1990). On capitals versus other large European cities, see Anthony Sutcliffe, "Environmental Control and Planning in European Capitals, 1850–1914: London, Paris, and Berlin," in Ingrid Hammerstrohm and Thomas Hall, eds., *Growth and Transformation of the Modern City* (Stockholm: Swedish Council for Building Research, 1979), pp. 71–88.

33. Susan B. Hanley, "Urban Sanitation in Preindustrial Japan," *Journal of Interdisciplinary History* 18, no. 1 (1987): 1–26. Shan-Ichi J. Watanabe, "Metropolitanism as a Way of Life: The Case of Tokyo, 1865–1930," in Anthony Sutcliffe, ed., *Metropolis, 1890–1940* (Chicago: U of Chicago P, 1984), p. 415.

34. For this paragraph and the next: CG:37-2 (Mar. 3, May 6–7, 13, 15, 1862), pp. 1043 ff., 1952–53, 1985–90, 2111, 2141; Docket of the House District Committee, Dec. 19, 1861, RecHRep, 37A-E4.4; *Laws Relating to Street Railway Franchises* (Washington, D.C.: GPO, 1896), pp. 47–51; Bryan, *History of the National Capital,* pp. 362–66, 492–93; John W. Boettjer, "Street Railways in the District of Columbia" (Master's thesis, George Washington U, 1963), chap. 2; Leroy O. King, Jr., *One Hundred Years of Capital Traction,* (n.p.: Taylor Publishing, 1972), pp. 3–9; John H. White, Jr., "Public Transport in Washington before the Great Consolidation of 1902," RCHS, 1966–68, pp. 216–30.

35. Glen E. Holt, "The Changing Perception of an Urban Pathology: An Essay on the Development of Mass Transit in the United States," in Kenneth T. Jackson and Stanley K. Schultz, eds., *Cities in American History* (New York: Alfred A. Knopf, 1972), 324–43. John P. McKay, *Tramways and Trolleys: The Rise of Urban Mass Transport in Europe* (Princeton: Princeton UP, 1976).

36. L. U. Reavis, *A Pamphlet for the People* (St. Louis, 1869); and Reavis, *A Change of National Empire* (St. Louis, 1870), both in history pamphlets, Johns Hopkins U library. CG:40-2 (June 15, 1868), p. 3174. Green, *Village and Capital,* pp. 328–30. Whyte, *Uncivil War,* pp. 70–71.

37. Whyte, *Uncivil War,* p. 17. George Townsend, quoted in Abbott, "Dimensions of Change," p. 1376.

38. Petitions on District of Columbia government, RecSen, 39A-J.1 (1867) and 41A-H5.2 (Mar. 20, 1869). Walter F. Dodd, *The Government of the District of Columbia* (Washington, D.C.: John Byrne, 1909), pp. 31–38.

39. Proceedings of the Levy Court, vol. 3, esp. letter of Shepherd to *Chronicle* in front cover and meeting of Sept. 7, 1863, RG 351.

40. Henry A. Addison, *An Address to the People of Georgetown* (Georgetown, 1855). Metropolitan Railroad Company, *First Annual Report,* 1854. House District of Columbia Committee, "Minority Report of G. W. Hughes of Maryland," 36th Cong., 1st sess. (May 24, 1860), H. Rept. 565, in William R. Hutton Papers, Museum of American History.

41. Flyer by "J" on the Baltimore and Ohio, and other documents, District of Columbia Committee Petitions, RecHRep, 42A-H4.4. Charles Moore, ed., *Federal and Lo-*

cal Legislation on Canals and Steam Railroads, 1802–1903, 57th Cong., 2nd sess., S. Doc. 220.

42. "Correspondence with the Baltimore and Ohio Railroad Company on additional routes between Washington and New York," 37th Cong., 2nd sess. (Feb. 1862), H. Exec. Doc. 79. "Railroad Communication between New York and Washington City," (Nov. 13, 1861), H. Misc. Doc. 65. "Railroad Facilities between New York and Washington," 37th Cong., 2nd sess. (Mar. 13, 1863), H. Rept. 61. "Railroad from Washington City to New York," 37th Cong., 3rd sess. (1863), H. Rept. 63. "Resolutions of the Legislature of New York . . . ," 38th Cong., 1st sess. (Feb. 3, 1864), S. Misc. Doc. 24.

43. John Work Garrett to Mayor Wallach, Nov. 28, 1866, copy along with related documents and petitions in RecSen, 45A-H5. *National Intelligencer,* Oct. 12, 1866.

44. Mayor Magruder to the Common Council and Board of Aldermen, Mar. 1, 1858, Mayor Berret to the Common Council, Jan. 28, 1861, MayorLS. Bryan, *History of the National Capital,* vol. 2, pp. 293–94, 308.

45. Mayor Berret to the Common Council, June 10, 1861, MayorLS. Bryan, *History of the National Capital,* vol. 2, pp. 501–2.

46. CG:38-2 (Jan. 27, 1865), p. 450; CG:40-2 (Apr. 7, 1868), p. 2265. Petition of Property Owners on I Street N, Jan. 19, 1867, RecSen, 39A-H4. Secretary of the Interior, *Annual Report,* 1865, p. 862. *Evening Star,* Aug. 1 and 18, 1865. *National Intelligencer,* Sept. 11, 1867. Bryan, *History of the National Capital,* vol. 2, pp. 566–67.

47. CG:39-2 (Mar. 1, 1867), p. 1698. CG:40-2 (Apr. 7, 1868), pp. 2263–67. CG:41-2 (Apr. 1–2, 1870), pp. 2332, 2376. Secretary of the Interior, *Annual Report,* 1865, p. 862. CEngsAR, 1867, pp. 523 ff. William V. Cox, "Matthew Gault Emery: the Last Mayor of Washington, 1870–1871," RCHS, 20 (1917), 19–59. Gutheim, *Worthy of the Nation,* pp. 78–84. Whyte, *Uncivil War,* p. 104.

48. Samuel Southard, "Report on District Affairs," Feb. 2, 1835, reprinted in BPW-AR, 1872, pp. 16–27.

49. *Evening Star,* Dec. 6, 1860. *National Intelligencer,* Dec. 11, 1863. Petition in favor of the improvement of Indiana and Louisiana Avenues, with accompanying documents, June 1867, RecSen, 40A-H5.1.

50. CG:32-1 (Aug. 21, 1852), p. 2289. CG:41-2 (May 20, 1870), Appendix, pp. 361–65.

51. Diary for Jan. 7, 1868, B. B. French Papers, box 4, reel 3; Benjamin to Henry F. French, Dec. 24, 1861, box 6, reel 5. PBO-AR, 1864, p. 682.

52. B. B. French to Montgomery Meigs, Sept. 30, 1861, letters sent, PBO, entry 6, reel 7. Leech, *Reveille in Washington,* p. 536. Bryan, *History of the National Capital,* vol. 2, p. 468. Green, *Village and Capital,* p. 201. An abridged version of French's journals: Donald B. Cole and John J. McDonough, eds., *Witness to the Young Republic: A Yankee's Journal, 1828–1870* (Hanover, N.H.: UP of New England, 1989).

53. Diary for July 17 and Sept. 22, 1863, B. B. French Papers, Apr. 14, 1864, boxes 2–3, reel 2; Benjamin to Pamela French, Oct. 29, 1867, box 6, reel 6. Bryan, *History of the National Capital,* vol. 2, pp. 366–67.

54. *National Intelligencer,* Mar. 7, 1860.

55. William Forsyth to B. B. French, Jan. 27, 1866, letters received, entry 1, reel 27, and John Blake to Secretary of the Interior, July 21, 1860, letters sent, PBO, entry 6, reel 7. PBO-AR, 1861, p. 854; 1864, p. 684; 1865, pp. 801–6; 1866, pp. 550–52. French to General John Martindale, Nov. 24, 1863, with petition of citizens for improvement of Maryland Avenue, 1863, RecSen, 38A-H4. William Forsyth to French, Oct. 5, 1863; French to Rep. John Rice, Mar. 23, 1864, RecHRep, 38A-E17.1. Minutes of the District of Columbia Committee for Jan. 19, 1866, RecHRep, 39A-F6.4.

56. Benjamin B. to Pamela French, Apr. 10, 1864, French Papers, box 6, reel 6. French to Stevens, Jan 20, 1865, with enclosures, Public Buildings and Grounds Com-

mittee Papers, RecHRep, 38A-E17.1. Minutes of the District of Columbia Committee for Dec. 16, 1865, RecHRep, 39A-F6.4. CG:39-1 (July 20, 1866), p. 3970.

57. PBO-AR, 1864, p. 682; 1866, p. 548. Nicolson to French, Feb. 15, 1866, letters received, PBO, entry 1, reel 27.

58. Minutes of the House District Committee, Jan. 10—Feb. 2, 1866, RecHRep, 39A-F6.4. "Appropriations and Expenditures in the District of Columbia from July 16, 1790, to June 30, 1876," 45th Cong., 2nd sess., S. Exec. Doc. 84, p. 72. Diary for Jan. 20 and 29, 1866, French Papers, box 4, reel 3.

59. Benjamin to Henry F. French, Oct. 13, 1861, June 16, 1862, French Papers, box 6, reel 5.

60. Diary for July 5 and 31, Dec. 3—6, 1863, Feb. 28, Apr. 25, 1864, Apr. 1, 1865, B. B. French Papers, box 3, reel 2; Benjamin to Pamela French, Apr. 10, 1864, box 6, reel 6.

61. CG:39-2 (Feb. 23, Mar. 2, 1867), pp. 1523—25, 1983. Diary for Feb. 1—Mar. 31, and May 12, 1867, box 4, reel 3, and Benjamin to Henry F. French, Mar. 19, 1867, box 6, reel 6, French Papers. Maj. Charles C. Jones to Col. John M. Wilson, May 18, 1888, PBO, entry 87, box 18.

62. Diary for Mar. 14 and 30, Dec. 8, 1867, French Papers, box 4, reel 3. "Appropriations and Expenditures in the District of Columbia," 45th Cong., 2nd sess., S. Exec. Doc. 84, p. 72.

63. P. J. Staudenraus, *Mr. Lincoln's Washington: Selections from the Writings of Noah Brooks, Civil War Correspondent* (South Brunswick, N.J.: Thomas Yoseloff, 1967), pp. 172—73, 186. CR:40-3 (Mar. 3, 1869), pp. 1828—29. *Washington Sunday Chronicle,* Feb. 26, 1888. Leech, *Reveille in Washington,* pp. 174 ff.

64. Bryan, *History of the National Capital,* vol. 2, p. 475. Also the following articles in RCHS: "Address of Ex-Mayor Berret," 2 (1899), 206—18; Allen C. Clark, "Richard Wallach and the Times of His Mayoralty," 21 (1918), 195—244; James H. Whyte, "Divided Loyalties in Washington during the Civil War," 1960—62, pp. 103—22

65. "Emancipation of Slaves in the District of Columbia," 37th Cong., 2nd sess. (Feb. 2, 1862), S. Rept. 12. Thomas R. Johnson, "Reconstruction Politics in Washington: 'An Experimental Garden for Radical Plants,'" RCHS, 50 (1980), 180—90. On Washington's black community during this period, Melvin R. Williams, "Blacks in Washington, D.C., 1860—1870" (Ph.D. diss., Johns Hopkins U, 1975); and Constance Green, *The Secret City* (Princeton: Princeton UP, 1967), chaps. 4—6.

66. "Report of Commissioners on Emancipation in the District of Columbia," 38th Cong., 1st sess., H. Exec. Doc. 42. Minority Report on District Emancipation bill, 37th Cong., 2nd sess., H. Rept. 58. CG:37-2 (Mar. 20, Apr. 2, 1862), p. 1299, 1496. Mayor Wallach to the Provost Marshall, Oct. 29, 1862, MayorLS.

67. Petitions regarding Equal Suffrage, RecSen, 39A-H4. CG:38-1 (May 12, 1864), pp. 2246. CG:39-1 (Dec. 20, 1865, Jan. 10—18, June 15, 27, 28, 1866), pp. 89, 175—78, 232—64, 311, 3191—92, 3432—39. CG:39-2 (Jan. 7, 1867), pp. 303—8.

68. Mary Bowen to Harriet Underhill, Aug. 31, 1845, Nov., 14, 1846, to Phebe and Julia Barker, Jan. 28, 1849, Sayles Bowen to Julia Barker, Jan. 14, July 24, 1856, box 1, Bowen Papers, Library of Congress. Diary for Jan. 7, June 1—2, Oct. 13, 1868, French Papers, box 4, reel 3. William Tindall, "A Sketch of Mayor Sayles J. Bowen," RCHS, 18 (1915), 25—43. Tindall had worked for Bowen and later was the District's secretary for over thirty years. Whyte, *Uncivil War,* pp. 34—35. Johnson, "Reconstruction Politics in Washington," RCHS, 183.

69. *Evening Star,* Sept. 14, 1865, May 26, 30, June 2, 1868.

70. *Evening Star,* June 2—9, 1868. CG:40-2 (June 13—15, 1868), pp. 3117 ff., 3173 ff.

71. Tindall, "Sketch of Mayor Bowen," RCHS. Whyte, *Uncivil War,* p. 70. Green, *Village and Capital,* pp. 317—19. Johnson, "Reconstruction Politics in Washington," RCHS, 185—86.

72. John W. Forney, *Speech to the 3rd Ward Republican Club* (Washington, D.C.: 1870), in history pamphlets, Johns Hopkins U library. Cox, "Matthew Gault Emery," RCHS. Tindall, "Sketch of Mayor Bowen," RCHS. Washington *Evening Star*, Jan. 30, 1892.

73. Richard Hildreth, quoted in Eric Foner, *Free Soil, Free Labor, Free Men: The Ideology of the Republican Party before the Civil War* (New York: Oxford UP, 1970), p. 51. Johnson, "Reconstruction Politics in Washington," RCHS, 187–90.

Chapter 2 Improvers and Old Citizens

1. WBT-AR, 1902, p. 5. On Shepherd's background, William Tindall, "A Sketch of Alexander Robey Shepherd," RCHS, 14 (1911), 49–66. Shepherd's own papers in the Library of Congress relate mostly to his later life in Mexico. See Mrs. E. E. Billings, "Alexander Shepherd and His Unpublished Diaries and Correspondence," RCHS, 1960–62, 150–66. Readable accounts of the District Improvement controversy include James H. Whyte, *The Uncivil War: Washington during the Reconstruction* (New York: Twayne, 1958); and William M. Maury, "The Territorial Period in Washington with Special Emphasis on Alexander Shepherd and the Board of Public Works" (Ph.D. diss., George Washington U, 1975). The latter is summarized in William M. Maury, *Alexander 'Boss' Shepherd and the Board of Public Works* (Washington, D.C.: George Washington U Center for Washington Area Studies, 1975).

2. CR:43–2 (Feb. 12, 1875), p. 1207.

3. Washington *Critic*, Sept. 20, 1887.

4. Speeches of Brainard Warner and Henry Macfarland, Mar. 3, 1909, in Shepherd Memorial Booklet, Shepherd Papers, box 13, pp. 37–38, 40. Louis Brownlow to Constance M. Green, Apr. 17, 1962, Green Papers, box 1, Library of Congress.

In the late 1970s, when a street project destroyed the small triangle in Pennsylvania Avenue where the Shepherd statue had stood since the 1930s, the statue reportedly was left on a stack of tires at a District sludge treatment plant. For a decade, some local historians thought the statue lost, but eventually the city recovered and re-erected it—as seemed appropriate—near a Department of Public Works Building on Shepherd Avenue in Anacostia. See Washington *City Paper*, Nov. 28–Dec. 4, 1986.

5. Carroll D. Wright, "The Economic Development of the District of Columbia," *Proceedings of the Washington Academy of Sciences* 1 (Dec. 1899): 178.

6. *New York Sun*, Apr. 2, 23, 1873.

7. Tindall, "Sketch of Alexander Shepherd," RCHS. *Evening Star*, Sept. 12, 1865, July 11, 1901. W. B. Webb and H. W. Crew, *Centennial History of Washington* (Dayton: United Brethren Publishing House, 1892), p. 356. Whyte, *Uncivil War*, p. 21.

8. CG:38-1 (Mar. 13, 1864), pp. 1139–40. Walter Clephane, "Lewis Clephane: A Pioneer Washington Republican," RCHS, 21 (1918), 263–77. Joint Invest. (1874), testimony, p. 875. District of Columbia Committee Papers, RecHRep, 40A-F7.1. *Evening Star*, Feb. 12, 1897. *Washington Post*, Feb. 20, 1898. *National Cyclopedia of American Biography*, vol. 13, p. 80, vol. 15, p. 124. Whyte, *Uncivil War*, pp. 21, 34. John W. Boettjer, "Street Railways in the District of Columbia," (Master's thesis, George Washington U, 1963), pp. 27–30.

9. Tanya Edwards Beauchamp, "Adolph Cluss: An Architect in Washington during the Civil War and Reconstruction," RCHS, 1971–72, pp. 338–51. *National Cyclopedia of American Biography*, vol. 4, p. 507. Frederick Gutheim, consultant, *Worthy of the Nation* (Washington, D.C.: Smithsonian Institution P, 1977), pp. 99–102, 108. David Shribman, "The Marxist Who Left His Mark on the Capital," *New York Times*, Feb. 18, 1984.

10. Whyte, *Uncivil War*, pp. 143–44, 178–79. Gutheim, *Worthy of the Nation*, pp. 102–3.

11. *Evening Star,* Apr. 4, 1903. Washington *Chronicle,* Jan. 11, 1869.

12. Joint Invest. (1874), charges, esp. p. 41; testimony, pp. 295−322. House Invest. (1872), pp. 206, 537.

13. Joint Invest. (1874), testimony, pp. 1524−26, 1571. A thorough description of the business, political, and social connections that bound the Shepherd group together appears in Maury, "Territorial Period in Washington," esp. chap. 4 and pp. 198 ff. Like most Washington historians, Maury interprets this built-in "identity of interest" as evidence that a "ring" indeed dominated the territorial movement and that collusion was widespread in the execution of the Comprehensive Plan.

14. House Invest. (1872), pp. 206, 403. Joint Invest. (1874), testimony, pp. 701−3, 716, 1525−26.

15. Diary for Apr. 14, 1864, B. B. French Papers, Library of Congress, reel 2, box 3. *National Cyclopedia of American Biography,* vol. 10, p. 510. Eleutheros Cooke quoted in Henrietta Larson, *Jay Cooke, Private Banker* (Cambridge: Harvard UP, 1936), pp. 101−4. Ellis P. Oberholtzer, *Jay Cooke: Financier of the Civil War* (Philadelphia: George W. Jacobs, 1907), esp. vol. 2, p. 207. Whyte, *Uncivil War,* pp. 22−23, 192−93.

16. For this paragraph and the next, Washington Market Co. Investigation, RecHRep, 41A-F2.8. District of Columbia Committee Papers, RecHRep, 45A-F8.2. Public Buildings and Grounds Committee Papers, RecHRep, 45A-F28.7. Henry Cooke to Chandler, Aug. 30, 1870, Edward R. Tinker to Chandler, Sept. 12, 1870, Chandler Papers, book 18, Library of Congress. CG:40-3 (Feb. 15−16, 1869), pp. 1217−18, 1247. CG:41-2 (May 16, 1870), pp. 3500−3502. CG:41-3 (Dec. 20, 1870), pp. 189−90. "Specifications for the building to be erected by the Market Company," 41st Cong., 2nd sess., H. Misc. Doc. 81. "Affairs of the Washington Market Company," 43rd Cong., 1st sess. (June 13, 1874), S. Rept. 449. "Incorporation of the Washington Market Company," 43rd Cong., 2nd sess. (Mar. 3, 1875), H. Rept. 277. "Amending or Repealing the Charter of the Washington Market Company," 46th Cong., 2nd sess. (Apr. 8, 1880), H. Rept. 1011. Albert Riddle to the District Commissioners, Dec. 26, 1882, Jan. 2, 1883, OpinCorpCoun, vol. 3. Wilhelmus B. Bryan, *A History of the National Capital* (New York: Macmillan, 1916), vol. 2, p. 421. Constance M. Green, *Washington: Village and Capital, 1800−1878* (Princeton: Princeton UP, 1962), p. 353. Beauchamp, "Adolph Cluss," RCHS, 348. James Goode, *Capital Losses: A Cultural History of Washington's Destroyed Buildings* (Washington, D.C.: Smithsonian Institution P, 1979), pp. 262−64.

17. For Mullett's background, see *National Cyclopedia of American Biography,* vol. 27, p. 452; and *Evening Star,* Oct. 20, 1891. *New York Sun,* May 27−28, 1874. Glenn Brown, *Memories, 1860−1930: A Winning Crusade to Revive George Washington's Vision of a Capital City* (Washington, D.C.: W. F. Roberts, 1931), p. 205. Gutheim, *Worthy of a Nation,* p. 88. John W. Reps, *Monumental Washington* (Princeton: Princeton UP, 1967), p. 61. Jon A. Peterson, "The Origins of the Comprehensive City Planning Ideal in the United States, 1840−1911" (Ph.D. diss., Harvard U, 1967), p. 156.

18. New York *Daily Tribune,* Sept. 15, 1873. Whyte, *Uncivil War,* pp. 92−93.

19. *Evening Star,* June 30, 1871.

20. House Invest. (1872), p. 422. Bryan, *History of the National Capital,* vol. 2, p. 608. Maury, "Territorial Period in Washington," pp. 96−98.

21. CG:39-1 (June 15, 1866), pp. 3191−92. CG:40-1 (Mar. 12, 1867), p. 68. House Invest. (1872), p. 692. *National Cyclopedia of American Biography,* vol. 28, p. 326. Petitions on the Washington City Charter, RecSen, 39A-H4 and 39A-J1. Whyte, *Uncivil War,* p. 61.

22. *National Intelligencer,* Oct. 22, 1867. "Petition of the Citizens of the District of Columbia," 41st Cong., 1st sess. (Mar. 20, 1869), S. Misc. Doc. 24. Bryan, *History of the National Capital,* vol. 2, p. 572.

23. CG:41-2 (Mar. 7, 1870), p. 1738. CG:41-3 (Jan. 24, 1871), pp. 685−88. *Evening Star,* July 16, 1897. Bryan, *History of the National Capital,* vol. 2, p. 574.

24. CG:41-3 (Jan. 24, 1871), pp. 685–88.

25. CG:41-3 (Jan. 20, Feb. 17, 1872), pp. 639–47, 1363–65. *Evening Star,* Jan 21, 1871.

26. Whyte, *Uncivil War,* pp. 101–4.

27. House Invest. (1872), pp. 292–98, 688–702. Diary for Feb. 3, 1870, box 4, reel 3, French Papers. *Daily Patriot,* Apr. 20, June 6, July 1, 1871. *Evening Star,* Apr. 6, June 30, July 7, 1871.

28. Green, *Village and Capital,* p. 341. *Patriot* quoted in Whyte, *Uncivil War,* p. 113.

29. Green, *Village and Capital,* p. 341.

30. *Evening Star,* April 19, 1871. *New National Era,* April 6–20, 1871. *Daily Patriot,* Mar. 30, 1871. *Biographical Dictionary of the American Congress,* p. 734. Mary R. Dearing, *Veterans in Politics: The Story of the G.A.R.* (Baton Rouge: Louisiana State UP, 1952), pp. 116–17, 131–33. Maury, "Territorial Period in Washington," pp. 18–26. Whyte, *Uncivil War,* pp. 106–10.

31. House Invest. (1872), esp. pp. 406–9. BPW-AR, 1872, p. 3. New York *Daily Tribune,* July 18, 1871. *Daily Patriot,* June 21–27, 1871. Maury, "Territorial Period in Washington," pp. 27–29.

32. House Invest. (1872), esp. pp. iii–iv. BPW-AR, 1872, p. 4. BPW-AR, 1873, p. 6. *Daily Patriot,* July 12, 1871.

33. *Daily Patriot,* Nov. 14, 1870, Feb. 18, Mar. 22, 1871. House Invest. (1872), pp. 293, 310–11, 319–21, 335–36, 537. Minutes for Oct. 27, Nov. 16, 1871, Records of the Citizens Association, Historical Society of Washington. Whyte, *Uncivil War,* pp. 98, 126.

34. Records of the Citizens Association, Minutes for Aug. 18, 1871. *Daily Patriot,* June 27, 30, 1871. House Invest. (1872), pp. 282 ff., 610–16. *Evening Star,* Nov. 21–23, 1871.

35. *Daily Patriot,* July 21, 1871. *Evening Star,* June 29, July 17, 1872.

36. The leadership of the Citizens Association, as reflected in the minute books for Aug. 18 and 25, 1871, in the Historical Society of Washington: Columbus Alexander, John B. Blake, James L. Barbour, James W. Barker, Daniel Breed, George W. Cochrane, Joseph J. Coombs, Walter S. Cox, John H. Crane, J. A. Cushing, Henry S. Davis, Thomas J. Durant, Charles E. Edmonston, William Fendall, Emil S. Friedrich, Albert Grant, Noble D. Larner, George Mattingly, Francis Mohun, William H. Phillip, Esau Pickerell, George H. Plant, Albert G. Riddle, George W. Riggs, Michael Talty, William H. Tenney, William B. Todd, Enoch Totten, John van Riswick, E. E. White, Albert A. Wilson, and Jesse B. Wilson. Two members, A. Watson and A. Klopfer, were not fully identified.

Improvers, the list of whom I developed as described in the text, included: 1) District officers: Governor Henry Cooke, delegate Norton Chipman, city attorney William A. Cook, tax collector William H. Slater, tax collector Lewis Clephane, secretary Edwin L. Stanton [the war secretary's son], secretary and city attorney Richard Harrington, Sinking Fund commissioner Moses Kelly. 2) The Board of Public Works: Samuel P. Brown, Adolph Cluss, James A. Magruder, Alfred B. Mullett, Alexander R. Shepherd (later also governor), and Henry A. Willard (John B. Blake was not included in my calculations of the improvers, as he was appointed to the board in 1873 because he was a Citizen). 3) Key board employees: George W. Balloch, George W. Beall, William Forsyth, Charles S. Johnson, Benjamin N. Meeds, Bartholomew Oertley. 4) Officers of the legislature: Peter Campbell, Charles L. Hulse, Arthur Shepherd, William Stickney, plus delegate John W. McKnight. 5) Businessmen: John O. Evans, Albert Gleason, William S. Huntington, John L. Kidwell, Hallet Kilbourn, James M. Latta, William F. Mattingly, James B. Naylor, Henry R. Searle, Samuel Strong, John W. Thompson, and J. V. W. Vandenburg.

Property information for these men came from the General Assessment for 1871,

RG 351. Personal, address, and occupational information came from city directories, testimony at hearings, contemporary accounts, memoirs, and profiles in the *Records of the Columbia Historical Society* and from newspaper obituaries. Information was added from the various histories and biographical dictionaries of Washington cited in the Note on Sources. Wherever possible, age and birthplace came from U.S. Censuses, but this source biased the study in favor of youth, because of the spotty nature of the Soundex Census index before 1900. Likewise, District newspapers only began running detailed obituaries after the mid-1880s, nor are there indices of obituaries printed before then.

37. The total was $79,997,454. Wright, "Economic Development," 187.

38. House Invest. (1872), p. 298. *Daily Patriot,* July 20, 1871. Kenneth T. Jackson, *Crabgrass Frontier: The Suburbanization of the United States* (New York: Oxford UP, 1985), pp. 128–32.

39. Washington *Critic,* Feb. 26, 1881. *Evening Star,* June 28, 1883, Jan. 27, 1897, Feb. 14, 1898. *Washington Sentinel,* Feb. 14, 1898. *National Cyclopedia of American Biography,* vol. 9, p. 322. Bryan, *History of the National Capital,* vol. 2, p. 520. John C. Proctor, ed., *Washington Past and Present: A History,* (New York: Lewis Historical, 1930), vol. 3, p. 657.

40. Lewis Clephane's great-uncle, a portrait painter, was established in Washington by 1797. Clephane's son, Lewis Painter Clephane, was also a professional artist. Andrew J. Cosentino and Henry H. Glassie, *The Capital Image: Painters in Washington, 1800–1915* (Washington, D.C.: Smithsonian Institution P, 1983), pp. 21–22. Clephane, "Lewis Clephane," RCHS, 21 (1918), 263–77. *Evening Star,* July 16, 1897. Bryan, *History of the National Capital,* vol. 2, pp. 370. *National Cyclopedia of American Biography,* vol. 22 p. 450. *Daily Patriot,* Apr. 3, 1871.

41. *New National Era,* July 27, 1871. Report of the Emancipation Commission, 38th Cong., 1st sess., H. Exec. Doc. 42. Tindall, "A Sketch of Alexander Robery Shepherd," RCHS, 14, p. 50.

42. Whitelaw Reid to Durant, Apr. 14, 1875, Durant Papers, New York Historical Society. On Durant's wartime experiences, Joseph G. Tregle, Jr., "Thomas J. Durant, Utopian Socialism, and the Failure of Radical Reconstruction in Louisiana," *Journal of Southern History,* 45, no. 4 (Nov. 1979): 485–512.

43. *Biographical Dictionary of the American Congress,* pp. 1608–9. *National Cyclopedia of American Biography,* vol. 2, p. 371.

44. House Invest. (1872), Grant's testimony, esp. pp. 109 ff. *Grant's Letter to the Governor* (pamphlet dated Aug. 17, 1871 in Territorial File, Washingtoniana Room, D.C. Public Library). *Evening Star,* Jan. 5, 1889, Nov. 12, 1898. Maury, "Territorial Period in Washington," p. 155. Gutheim, *Worthy of the Nation,* p. 106.

45. *Evening Star,* Nov. 9, 1889, Feb. 9, 1894, Nov. 12, 1898; *National Cyclopedia of American Biography,* vol. 2, p. 371, vol. 9, p. 322.

46. *National Cyclopedia of American Biography,* vol. 10, p. 510. *Washington Post,* Dec. 26, 1881.

47. *National Cyclopedia of American Biography,* vol. 28, p. 452. Beauchamp, "Adolph Cluss," RCHS.

48. *National Cyclopedia of American Biography,* vol. 15, p. 124, vol. 22, p. 450. *Evening Critic,* Nov. 5, 1881. *Washington Post,* Feb. 20, 1898.

49. The Kilbourn case begins at p. 1705 of CR:44-1 and continues through the session. Speeches on the civil liberties and political ramifications of the case begin at p. 160 of the appendix. See also H. Rept. 242 and H. Misc. Doc. 174 of that session. *Evening Star,* May 13, 1902, Apr. 14, 1903.

50. Joint Invest. (1874), arguments, pp. 1–3, 117.

51. Kathryn A. Jacob, "High Society in Washington during the Gilded Age: Three Distinct Aristocracies" (Ph.D. diss., Johns Hopkins U, 1987).

52. Records of the Citizens Association, Minutes for Nov. 16, 1871. House Invest. (1872), pp. 248–52, 267–73. LawsLegAssem, July 10, 1871. Receipts from Babcock to Shepherd, box 1, Babcock Papers, Newberry Library, Chicago. Democrats accused supervising architect Mullett of arranging for Shepherd to install gas fixtures and patent roofing on favorable terms in such distant cities as Madison, Des Moines, and Portland, Maine. *Democratic Campaign Textbook: The Republican Party Reviewed* (New York, 1876), pp. 352–59.

53. Joint Invest. (1874), testimony, pp. 1024–27.

54. *Daily Patriot,* July 1, 1871.

55. *Daily Patriot,* May 17, June 30, July 1, 7, 16, 1871. House Invest. (1872), pp. 1–10. Terrence J. McDonald, *The Parameters of Urban Fiscal Policy* (Berkeley: U of California P, 1986), pp. xi, 116–57.

56. Bryan, *History of the National Capital,* vol. 2, p. 596. *Daily Patriot,* Sept. 25, 1871.

57. *Evening Star,* Oct. 14, 1871. House Invest. (1872), pp. 587, 625–26.

58. *Evening Star,* Oct. 29, 1872.

59. *Evening Star,* Oct. 9, 1871.

60. *Daily Patriot,* May 6, 1871,

61. New York *Daily Tribune,* Sept. 15, 1873.

62. Alfred D. Chandler, *The Visible Hand: The Managerial Revolution in American Business* (Cambridge: Harvard UP, 1977). On the growth of large-scale organization in the real estate industry, see Marc A. Weiss, *The Rise of the Community Builders* (New York: Columbia UP, 1987). On the development business in Washington, see Melissa McLoud, "Craftsmen and Entrepreneurs: Washington, D.C.'s Late Nineteenth-Century Builders" (Ph.D. diss., George Washington U, 1988).

63. Respected discussions date the emergence of modern municipal engineering departments to the last quarter of the nineteenth century. Jon C. Teaford, *The Unheralded Triumph* (Baltimore: Johns Hopkins UP, 1984), chap. 8; Stanley K. Schultz and Clay McShane, "To Engineer the Metropolis: Sewers, Sanitation, and City Planning in Late-Nineteenth-Century America," *Journal of American History,* 65, no. 2 (1978): 389–411.

64. David Owen, *The Government of Victorian London* (Cambridge: Harvard UP, 1982), p. 88. Joint Invest. (1874), testimony, pp. 1024, 1936.

65. House Invest. (1872), p. 251. Roosevelt, a Democrat, was Theodore's father's brother. *Dictionary of American Biography,* vol. 7, pp. 482–86. Also, Robert B. Roosevelt, "Tammany the Second" and "Washington City Ring," pamphlets reprinted from the *Congressional Record,* Jan. 24 and Feb. 11, 1873, in Territorial File, Washingtoniana Room, D.C. Public Library. New York *Daily Tribune,* May 11, Dec. 5, 1872.

66. *Evening Star,* July 29, 1873.

67. John G. Sproat, *The Best Men: Liberal Reformers in the Gilded Age* (New York: Oxford UP, 1968), pp. 148–52.

68. Louis Napoleon quoted in Charlene M. Leonard, *Lyon Transformed: Public Works of the Second Empire, 1853–1864* (Berkeley: U of California P, 1961), p. 5. Louis Girard, *La Politique des Travaux Publics du Second Empire* (Paris: Librarie Armand Colin, 1952), pp. 108–41 *passim.* Cecil O. Smith, Jr., "The Longest Run: Public Engineers and Planning in France," *American Historical Review* 95, no. 3 (1990): 657–92.

69. Carlton Hayes, *Historical Evolution of Modern Nationalism* (New York: Richard Smith, 1931), pp. 248, 267–72. Friedrich List, *The National System of Political Economy,* Sampson S. Lloyd, trans. (1885; Fairfield, Conn.: Augustus M. Kelley, 1966), pp. xxix, 97–102. Hans Kohn, *Nationalism: Its Meaning and History,* rev. ed. (Princeton: D. Van Nostrand, 1965), pp. 54, 129–35. W. O. Henderson, *Friedrich List: Economist and Visionary, 1789–1846* (London: Frank Cass, 1983). For the historical context of this sort of state-centered nationalism in Germany, see Mack Walker, *German Home Towns* (Ithaca: Cornell UP, 1971).

70. List, *National System of Political Economy*, pp. 378–81.
71. Eric Monkkonen, *America Becomes Urban* (Berkeley: U of California P, 1988), pp. 138–41. Carl Abbott, *Boosters and Businessmen* (Westport, Conn.: Greenwood, 1981), pp. 206–8.
72. Carter Goodrich, *Government Promotion of American Canals and Railroads, 1800–1890* (New York: Columbia UP, 1960), p. 289. Abbott, *Boosters and Businessmen*, p. 9.
73. Morton Keller, *Affairs of State: Public Life in Late Nineteenth-Century America* (Cambridge: Harvard UP, 1977), pp. 98–101, 106.

Chapter 3 Energy and Engineering

Epigraph: Clipping dated Dec. 28, 1905, in Commissioners' Scrapbook, Washingtoniana Collection, District of Columbia Public Library.
1. House Invest. (1872), pp. iv, xvii. *New York Sun*, Apr. 5, 1873. William E. Chandler, *Suggestions of Mr. William E. Chandler, Counsel for the District of Columbia*, pamphlet dated Apr. 24, 1872, in history pamphlets, Johns Hopkins U library. Robert B. Roosevelt, "Washington City Ring," and "Tammany the Second," pamphlets in the Territorial File, Washingtoniana Room, District of Columbia Public Library. Leon B. Richardson, *William E. Chandler — Republican* (New York: Dodd, Mead, 1940), p. 120. James H. Whyte, *The Uncivil War: Washington during the Reconstruction* (New York: Twayne, 1958), pp. 130, 158–60.
2. *Evening Star*, July 29, 1873. These figures come from the board itself and may be found in its annual report for 1873, in outline on p. 1 and in detail scattered throughout. They appear as well as in Joint Invest. (1874). Despite their source, no one has ever disputed them, although the board's work was thoroughly audited and inspected between 1874 and 1876. William M. Maury reiterates these figures in "The Territorial Period in Washington with Special Emphasis on Alexander Shepherd and the Board of Public Works" (Ph.D. diss., George Washington U, 1975), esp. pp. 206–8, without questioning their veracity.
3. For example, *Evening Star*, Sept. 21, 1872, Feb. 14, Apr. 11, Apr. 30, 1873. See also scrapbooks in the Shepherd Papers, Library of Congress. *New National Era*, Dec. 12, 1872, Feb. 13, 1873. *Sunday Chronicle*, Apr. 13, 1873. *National Republican*, Jan. 5, 1872, June 23, 1874.
4. Harry James Brown and Frederick D. Williams, ed., *The Diary of James A. Garfield* (East Lansing: Michigan State UP, 1967), vol. 2, Dec. 7–10, 1872, May 14, Dec. 12, 1873. Baltimore *Sun*, Nov. 24, 1873, June 2 and 22, 1874.
5. House Invest. (1872), p. 298. *Evening Star*, July 19, 1872. "Certain Reports Relating to Street Improvements in the District of Columbia," 43rd Cong., 2nd sess. (Mar. 3, 1875), H. Misc. Doc. 96. "Revision of Special Assessments," 46th Cong., 3rd sess. (Feb. 14, 1881), H. Misc. Doc. 11. "Authorizing Commissioners to Accept Payment . . . of Certain Special Assessments," 53rd Cong., 2nd sess. (Sept. 5, 1893), S. Rept. 97.
6. For residents' complaints, House Invest. (1872), esp. pp. 231–43. Regarding Edmunds and Bayard, Joint Invest. (1874), testimony, pp. 1985–97. Governor Cooke's annual message, May 2, 1872, TDCGovLS. LawsLegAssem, June 20, 1872. For relevant precedents, see Stanley K. Schultz, *Constructing Urban Culture* (Philadelphia: Temple UP, 1989), pp. 46–47.
7. Lucy R. Freeman to Shepherd, Aug. 15, 1873; Emily Briggs to Shepherd, Apr. 29, 1873, Shepherd Papers, box 4.
8. *Daily Chronicle*, Jan. 26, 1876. *Evening Star*, Sept. 24, 1887. Whyte, *Uncivil War*, pp. 147, 154. Wilhelmus B. Bryan, *A History of the National Capital* (New York: Macmillan, 1916), vol. 2, p. 615.
9. "Payment for Destruction of the Northern Liberty Market," 54th Cong., 1st sess.

(May 12, 1896), S. Rept. 926. *Evening Star*, Jan. 29, 1876. Bryan, *History of the National Capital*, vol. 2, pp. 614–15. Whyte, *Uncivil War*, pp. 147–48. Maury, "Territorial Period in Washington," pp. 162–65.

10. New York *Daily Tribune*, July 18, Aug. 9, 1871.

11. New York *Daily Tribune*, May 2, Sept. 15, Dec. 9, 1873, Jan. 28, 1874. *New York Sun*, Apr. 7 and 26, 1873, June 7, July 11–14, 1874. *Evening Star*, June 27, 1873. Whyte, *Uncivil War*, pp. 262–63.

12. New York *Daily Tribune*, Apr. 2–10, 17, 19, 26, 29, 30, May 2, 3, 10, 17, 1873.

13. New York *Daily Tribune*, Apr. 8, July 12, 1873. *New York Sun*, Apr. 25, 1873. *Sunday Morning Chronicle*, June 22, 1873. Governor Cooke's 1871 annual message, in TDCGovLS, vol. 1. House Invest. (1872), p. 585. LawsLegAssem, June 20, 1872, June 20, 1873. Joint Invest. (1874), report, pp. ix–xiv, xxii, governor's answer, pp. 470–77, charges of the memorialists, p. 62, arguments, pp. 76–77.

14. *Evening Star*, June 9, 1873. New York *Daily Tribune*, Aug. 9, Nov. 22, 1873. Baltimore *Sun*, Aug. 9, Sept. 1, 1873. Shepherd to Baker, esp. Jan. 31, Feb. 2, 1874, TDCGovLS, vol. 3.

15. CR:43-1 (Feb. 2, 1874), pp. 1125–28. *National Republican*, June 24, 1874. George Tichenor to Allison, Feb. 14, 1874, Allison Papers, new list, box 3, Iowa State Historical Department.

16. Joint Invest. (1874), pp. vii–xiv, governor's statement, pp. 461–69, testimony, p. 1861. Papers relating to the District investigation, RecSen, 43A-E22. Board of Audit, *Annual Report*, 1875, 44th Cong., 1st sess., H. Exec. Doc. 1.

17. Joint Invest. (1874), report, p. vii, arguments, pp. 70–72. Governor Cooke's 1871 Message, TDCGovLS, vol 1. New York *Daily Tribune*, Apr. 26, 1873. BPW-AR, 1872, pp. 7–8. House Invest. (1872), pp. 585–87.

18. House Invest. (1872), pp. iv–v. Joint Invest. (1874), report, pp. vi–viii. New York *Daily Tribune*, Apr. 26, 1873.

19. BPW-AR, 1872, pp. 12–13. Joint Invest. (1874), report, pp. viii–ix, testimony, pp. 1013–14, 2143–46, 2356.

20. The DeGolyer-McClelland case begins on p. 933 of Joint Invest. (1874). New York *Daily Tribune*, Apr. 9–30, 1874. Garfield to Shepherd, June 18, 1872, Shepherd Papers. Also, Garfield's correspondence with Shepherd and George Chittenden from June to Nov. 1872, reel 24, and the DeGolyer-McClelland file, reel 134, the Garfield Papers, Library of Congress. Brown and Williams, *Diary of Garfield*, June 28, 1872, p. 70. Whyte, *Uncivil War*, pp. 212 ff. Allan Peskin, *Garfield* (Kent, Ohio: Kent State UP, 1978), pp. 377–81. On congressmen as lobbyists, Margaret Thompson, *The "Spider Web": Congress and Lobbying in the Age of Grant* (Ithaca: Cornell UP, 1985).

21. Peskin, *Garfield*, p. 381. B. A. Hinsdale to Garfield, Apr. 24, 1874, H. Austin to Garfield, Apr. 21, 1874, reel 28, Garfield Papers.

22. Joint Invest. (1874), esp. testimony, pp. 168, 222–25, 251–60, 455, 482–93, 503–7, 1057–58, 1347.

23. Joint Invest. (1874), report, p. xi, testimony, pp. 2122–28. "Certain Reports Relating to Street Improvements," 43rd Cong., 2nd sess., H. Misc. Doc. 96, p. 5. Baltimore *Sun*, June 27, 1874.

24. Joint Invest. (1874), testimony, pp. 2172–73. New York *Daily Tribune*, June 17, 1874. Maury, "Territorial Period in Washington," p. 77. On Tweed's organization of contracting and public works, see Alexander B. Callow, *The Tweed Ring* (New York: Oxford UP, 1966).

25. Joint Invest. (1874), report, p. xi, testimony, pp. 2092–95, 2320–27. Whyte, *Uncivil War*, pp. 219–22, 229–30.

26. Joint Invest. (1874), testimony, pp. 1958 ff., 2049 ff. Board of Audit Invest., pt. 1, pp. 478–80. *National Republican*, May 22, 1874.

27. Whyte, *Uncivil War*, pp. 221–22.

28. Joint Invest. (1874), report, p. xxv–xxix. *National Republican,* May 22–25, 1874. *Evening Star,* May 25, 1874. New York *Daily Tribune,* May 26–June 2, June 10–19, 1874. Baltimore *Sun,* May 21–June 2, 1874. *New York Sun,* May 27–28, 1874.

29. *The Nation,* June 25, 1874.

30. House Invest. (1872), pp. 579–80, 736.

31. Maury, "Territorial Period in Washington," pp. 132–34.

32. David Pinkney, *Napoleon III and the Rebuilding of Paris* (Princeton: Princeton UP, 1958), p. 5. On how Haussmann selected his staff, see Henri Malet, *Le Baron Haussmann et la Rénovation de Paris* (Paris: Éditions Municipales, 1973).

33. "Address of Ex-Mayor Berret," RCHS, 2 (1899), 215.

34. CEngsAR, 1867, pp. 523–30. Regarding Roman paving, Michler is quoting from an unnamed source.

35. CEngsAR, 1867, pp. 523–30, 544–48. Frederick Gutheim, consultant, *Worthy of the Nation* (Washington, D.C.: Smithsonian Institution P, 1977), pp. 78–81.

36. BPW-AR, 1873, pp. 39–40. DCComsAR, 1888, p. 30; 1896, pp. 584–86.

37. Governor Cooke's 1871 message, TDCGovLS, vol. 1. Joint Invest. (1874), charges of the memorialists, pp. 5–6. DCComsAR, 1899, vol. 1, pp. 25 ff.

38. DCComsAR, 1875, pp. 232–39. DCComsAR, 1884, p. 166–67.

39. Clay McShane, "Transforming the Use of Urban Space: A Look at the Revolution in Street Pavements, 1880–1924," *Journal of Urban History,* 5, no. 3 (1979): 288–90. BPW-AR, 1873, pp. 37–38. House Invest. (1872), pp. 110–12.

40. Franklin T. Howe, "The Board of Public Works," RCHS, 3 (1900), 274.

41. CEngsAR, 1868, p. 901. CEngsAR, 1871, pp. 978–79. DCComsAR, 1899, pp. 25 ff.

42. DCComsAR, 1875, pp. 232–37. BPW-AR, 1873, pp. 37–38. House Invest. (1872), pp. 539–64, 605. Howe, "The Board of Public Works," p. 274.

43. House Invest. (1872), pp. 559–62.

44. CEngsAR, 1867, p. 546. Gutheim, *Worthy of a Nation,* p. 81.

45. DCComsAR, 1875, pp. 232–36. DCComsAR, 1878, p. 241. DCComsAR, 1899, pp. 25 ff. George W. Tillson, "Asphalt and Asphalt Pavements," *Transactions of the American Society of Civil Engineers* 38 (Dec. 1897): 214–45.

46. *Report of the Joint Committee on Manufactures of the Legislative Assembly* (Washington, D.C.: Chronicle Publishing, 1872). *Evening Star,* Oct. 29, Nov. 8, Dec. 17, 1872.

47. Mayor Wallach's letter with accompanying documents, in Secretary of the Interior, *Annual Report,* 1865, p. 861. *Evening Star,* Sept. 8, 1865. "Report of the Executive Committee Appointed by the Regents of the Smithsonian Institution on the Washington City Canal," 40th Cong., 2nd sess. (May 15, 1868), S. Misc. Doc. 95.

48. CEngsAR, 1868, p. 902.

49. Smithsonian Canal Report, 1868, S. Misc. Doc. 95. "Improvement of the Washington Canal," 42nd Cong., 2nd sess., S. Misc. Doc. 142. House Invest. (1872), p. 636.

50. "Memorial of Benjamin Severson, Engineer . . . ," 40th Cong., 2nd sess. (June 16, 1868), S. Misc. Doc. 103. "Report of Mr. Severson, Engineer of the Washington Canal," 40th Cong., 3rd sess. (1869), H. Misc. Doc. 36. Washington *Daily Chronicle,* Jan. 4, 9, 22, 1869.

51. Papers regarding Georgetown and Washington Canal and Sewerage Company, RecHRep, 41A-F7.4. "To incorporate the Georgetown and Washington Canal and Sewerage Company," 40th Cong., 2nd sess., S. Rept. 167. "Minutes of the Commission to Improve the Washington Canal," RG 351, entry 108. CEngsAR, 1870, p. 521. House Invest. (1872), pp. 138–50.

52. House Invest. (1872), pp. 138–50, 571–75.

53. Ibid., pp. 199–205, 211–30, 348, 606–59.

54. Ibid., p. 200. DCComsAR, 1875, pp. 239–45. DCComsAR, 1878, pp. 251–60. "Estimates for Relieving Defects in the Main System of Sewerage in Washington City," 45th Cong., 3rd sess., S. Misc. Doc. 17, p. 3. "Plans for the Improvement of the Sewer-

age and the Sanitary Condition of the District of Columbia," 45th Cong., 3rd sess., S. Misc. Doc. 19.

55. *Report on Sewerage in the District of Columbia,* 51st Cong. 2nd sess. (June 1890), H. Exec. Doc. 445, p. 13. DCComsAR, 1875 p. 242; 1884, p. 176. "Plans for the Improvement of the Sewerage," 45th Cong., 3rd sess., S. Misc. Doc. 19, p. 40.

56. "Estimates for Relieving Defects," 45th Cong., 3rd sess., S. Misc. Doc. 17, p. 12. "Plans for the Improvement of Sewerage," 45th Cong., 3rd sess., S. Misc. Doc. 19. DCComsAR, 1884, pp. 175–76; 1897, vol. 2, p. 103. Joel A. Tarr, "The Separate versus Combined Sewer Problem: A Case Study in Urban Technology Design Choice," *Journal of Urban History* 5, no. 3 (1979): 308–39.

57. The litany of charges against the territorial sewer system led public works historians Stanley K. Schultz and Clay McShane to argue that Shepherd had "wasted" the money spent on sewers by ignoring "the use of experts in the construction and administration of his system. My evidence, on the contrary, suggests that Shepherd elected to follow a politically expedient course in a situation where no clear expert consensus existed. Schultz and McShane, "To Engineer the Metropolis: Sewers, Sanitation, and City Planning in Late-Nineteenth-Century America," *Journal of American History* 45, no. 2 (1978): 397. "Estimates for Relieving Defects," 45th Cong., 3rd sess., S. Misc. Doc. 17, p. 1.

58. "Improvement of the Harbors of Washington and Georgetown," 42nd Cong., 3rd sess. (Dec. 17, 1872), S. Misc. Doc. 15.

59. Constance M. Green, personal notes for chapters 11–14 of *Washington: Village and Capital,* box 4, Green Papers, Library of Congress. Some historians believe that the post–Civil War generation of Washington businessmen did intend their city to enter the North's manufacturing and trade network. Elizabeth J. Miller, "Dreams of Being the Capital of Commerce: The National Fair of 1879," RCHS, 51 (1984), 71–82; and Carl Abbott, "Dimensions of Regional Change in Washington, D.C.," *American Historical Review* 95, no. 5 (1990), 1375–80.

60. For this paragraph and the next, Constance M. Green, *Washington: Village and Capital* (Princeton: Princeton UP, 1962), p. 345.

61. *National Republican,* Jan. 5, 1872. *Georgetown Courier,* June 13, 1874. *New National Era,* Feb. 20, 1873. Baltimore *Sun,* Nov. 24, 1873. *Evening Star,* July 29, 1873. Arthur Shepherd, "Why General Chipman Should Be Re-Elected to Congress," speech of July 29, 1872, in history pamphlets, Johns Hopkins U library. *Daily Patriot,* Sept. 8, 1871. Norton Chipman, *The Administration Vindicated* (Washington, D.C.: 1871), and *Chipman's Reply to Roosevelt,* reprinted from *Congressional Record,* June 3, 1872, in history pamphlets, Johns Hopkins U library. *Evening Star,* Jan. 29, 1876.

62. House Invest. (1872), pp. 586–87, 736. This, of course, is the moral of Robert Caro's celebrated *The Power Broker: Robert Moses and the Fall of New York* (New York: Alfred A. Knopf, 1974). While Caro's biography vividly portrays ethical dilemmas facing an overly ambitious public works official (who had, incidently, impeccable academic and social credentials), some historians have qualms about the way the author places Moses in American urban history. Joann P. Krieg, ed., *Robert Moses: Single-Minded Genius* (Hempstead, N.Y.: Long Island Studies Institute, 1989).

63. The 1874 joint committee overlooked testimony from a contractor who asserted that the treasurer of the Board of Public Works, Magruder, had solicited a bribe to expedite his bills. Joint Invest. (1874), testimony, pp. 482–93.

64. "Alleged Safe Burglary in the Office of the U.S. Attorney in the District of Columbia . . . ," 43rd Cong., 1st sess. (June 23, 1874), H. Rept. 785. Baltimore *Sun,* Apr. 25, 1874. Whyte, *Uncivil War,* pp. 213–14, 227–28, 263–67.

65. Whyte, *Uncivil War,* pp. 263–67. Also, *New York Sun,* June 12, 17, 1874. For accounts of the first safe burglary trial, New York *Daily Tribune,* Oct. and Nov., 1874, passim. Boxes 7 and 8 of the Babcock Papers, Newberry Library, concern the Whiskey

Ring and safe burglary scandals and contain correspondence from Nettleship and others in the Secret Service. These documents do not confirm the charges against Babcock regarding the safe burglary.

66. *Report of the Commissioners on the Freedman's Savings and Trust Company,* 43rd Cong., 2nd sess., H. Misc. Doc. 16, p. 96. *The Freedman's Bank,* 44th Cong., 1st sess., H. Rept. 502, esp. pp. 75–86. Carl R. Osthaus, *Freedmen, Philanthropy, and Fraud* (Urbana: U of Illinois P, 1976), pp. 156–64. Walter L. Fleming, *The Freedmen's Savings Bank* (1927; reprint, Westport, Ct.: Negro Universities P, 1970), p. 74. Frederick Douglass, *The Life and Times of Frederick Douglass* (1892 ed. reprint, New York: Collier Books, 1962), pp. 400–406.

67. *Report of the Commissioners on the Freedman's Savings and Trust Company,* 43rd Cong., 2nd sess., H. Misc. Doc. 16, pp. 36–39. House Select Committee, *The Freedman's Bank,* 44th Cong., 1st sess., H. Rept. 502, pp. vii, 76–77, 102–3, 123–24. David M. Cole, *The Development of Banking in the District of Columbia* (New York: William-Frederick, 1959), pp. 325–27. Fleming, *Freedmen's Savings Bank,* p. 73.

68. Joint Invest. (1874), Report, p. vii. CR:43-2 (Feb. 12, 1875), pp. 1207–8.

69. Hawkins Taylor to Allison, June 30, July 18, Aug. 12, Sept. 6, 1874, S. Hooper to Allison, July 7, 1874, Albert Swalm to Allison, July 21, 1874, Chipman to Allison, June 23, 1874, Allison Papers, new list, boxes 3–4. *New York Sun,* June 19, Aug. 3, 1874. *National Republican,* June 5, 1874. New York *Daily Tribune,* July 16, 1874.

70. CR:43-2 (Feb. 12, 1875), pp. 1207–8.

71. *Evening Star,* May 1, 1880. Washington *Critic,* Sept. 28, 1881. Clipping dated Jan. 2, 1898, in the Alexander Shepherd file, Washingtoniana Room, District of Columbia Public Library.

72. Alexander and Mary Shepherd to Richard and Vinnie Ream Hoxie, June 28, 1879, July 10, Aug. 19, 1880, Apr. 9, Nov. 14, 1893, Jan. 6, 13, 1898, Apr. 4, May 23, 1899, Jan. 23, 1900. Grace Shepherd Merchant to Vinnie Ream Hoxie, Oct. 12, 1902, boxes 2–3, Vinnie Ream and Richard L. Hoxie Papers, Library of Congress. Shepherd's own papers in the Library of Congress contain similar correspondence, as well as volumes of scrapbooks of newspapers accounts from around the country concerning his years in Washington.

73. John Addison Porter, *The City of Washington: Its Origin and Administration* (Studies in Historical and Political Science series) (Baltimore: Johns Hopkins P, 1885), pp. 43–44. Charles Moore, *Washington, Past and Present* (New York: Century, 1929), pp. 53–58. Charles Moore, *Daniel Burnham: Architect, Planner of Cities* (New York: Houghton, Mifflin, 1916), vol. 1, p. 133.

74. Joint Invest. (1874), arguments, p. 14.

75. Baltimore *Sun,* June 27, 1874.

76. Max Weber, *The City,* trans. Don Martindale and Gertrud Neuwirth (New York: Free Press, 1958), pp. 80–89. Stuart M. Blumin, "When Villages Become Towns: The Historical Contexts of Town Formation," in Derek Fraser and Anthony Sutcliffe, eds., *The Pursuit of Urban History* (London: Edward Arnold, 1983), esp. pp. 64–66.

Chapter 4 The Origins of the District Commission

Epigraph: RecSen, 44A-E4.

1. Baltimore *Sun,* June 23–24, 1874. *New York Sun,* June 24, 1874, New York *Daily Tribune,* June 22–26, 1874. *National Republican,* June 23–24, 1874. *Executive Journal of the Senate,* 43rd Cong., 1st sess. (June 23, 1874), pp. 371–72. James H. Whyte, *The Uncivil War: Washington during the Reconstruction* (New York: Twayne, 1958), pp. 234–36.

2. *Democratic Campaign Textbook: The Republican Party Reviewed* (New York, 1876), pp. 205–7. Rep. Aylett H. Buckner, "District of Columbia Affairs," speech to Congress

on July 1, 1876, reprinted in history pamphlets, Johns Hopkins U library, p. 17. CR:44-1 (Feb. 3, 1876), p. 855. *New York Sun,* Aug. 17, 1874. A. M. Scott to William B. Allison, Aug. 21, 1874, William B. Allison Papers, Iowa State Historical Department, new list, box 4.

3. Morton Keller argues: "The postwar expansion of government was constrained by powerful countervalues: localism, cultural diversity, a widespread belief in laissez-faire. During the 1870s these facts of American life overcame the governmental inheritance of the war" (*Affairs of State: Public Life in Late Nineteenth-Century America* [Cambridge: Harvard UP, 1977], pp. 85, 121). Others note that while the wartime vision of "a powerful national state protecting the fundamental rights of American citizens" suffered a "decisive" setback, other state-building initiatives from this time endured and continued to unfold. Eric Foner, *Reconstruction: America's Unfinished Revolution* (New York: Harper and Row, 1988), pp. 29–30, 582–87; also Richard F. Bensel, *Yankee Leviathan: The Origins of Central State Authority in America* (Cambridge: Cambridge UP, 1990).

4. Henry Blow to President Grant, June 26, 1874, Grant Papers, ser. 1B, reel 2, Library of Congress. Joint Invest. (1874), report, pp. xxvii–xxxix. *Biographical Dictionary of the American Congress,* pp. 606, 1250. *National Cyclopedia of American Biography,* vol. 4, p. 291; vol. 8, p. 310. *National Republican,* June 24, 1874. *New York Sun,* July 6, 1874. In 1877, Ketcham returned to Congress. As a member of the Appropriations Committee, he managed the annual District bills in the early 1880s. This made him the only person ever to vote on a District budget under the 1878 act who had once been a Washington city official.

5. DCComsRLR, vol. 1, July 3–6, 1874. DCTComsMins, July 3–7, 1874. Board of Audit Invest., pt. 2, pp. 10–13, 135–37. CR:44-1 (Feb. 1, 1876), pp. 792–95. Dennison to Allison, July 17, 1874, Allison Papers, new list, box 4. *New York Sun,* July 6, 1874.

6. Joint Invest. (1874), report, p. xxix. Shepherd to Allison, June 6, 1874, Allison Papers, new list, box 3. CR:44-1 (Feb. 1, 1876), pp. 793–95. DCComsAR, 1874, pp. 14–19; 1875, pp. 20–22; 1876, p. 14. Board of Audit Invest., pt. 2, pp. 115–23.

7. W. T. Sherman to Vinnie Ream Hoxie, May 9, 1885, Feb. 21, Mar. 31, Apr. 25, 1886; D. W. Voorhees to Vinnie Hoxie, May 9, 1885, Hoxie Papers, Library of Congress, box 2. Bioessays, Historical Division, Army Corps of Engineers, Fort Belvoir, Va. Albert E. Cowdrey, *A City for the Nation: The Army Engineers and the Building of Washington, D.C., 1790–1967* (Washington, D.C.: Army Corps Historical Division, 1978), p. 26. Roland M. Brennan, "Brigadier General Richard L. Hoxie, United States Army, 1861–1930," RCHS, vols. 57–59, pp. 87–95.

8. H. L. Davis to President Hayes, enclosed with Hoxie to Secretary of War McCrary, June 26, 1878, Hayes Papers, ser. 4, reel 81, Hayes Memorial Library, Fremont, Ohio. CR:45-2 (Apr. 15, 1878), p. 2533. Taylor to Allison, July 18, 1874, A. M. Scott to Allison, Aug. 21, 1874, Allison Papers, new list, boxes 3–4.

9. Hoxie outlined his position in communications with the commissioners, DCComsRLR, vol. 1, July 30–Aug. 19, 1874. He and the commissioners defended themselves publicly in reports cited in subsequent notes, as well as in Board of Audit Invest., pt. 1, pp. 167–99; pt. 2, pp. 10–13, 133–41.

10. CR:44-1 (Jan 27–28, 1876), pp. 679 ff. DCComsAR, 1874, pp. 162–65; 1875, pp. 239–45.

11. Board of Audit Invest., pt. 1, pp. 167–99. DCComsAR, 1874, pp. 160–61; 1875, pp. 232–39.

12. DCComsAR, 1875, pp. 247–48. Board of Audit Invest., pt. 1, pp. 178, 181–84, 252–58, 427–28. Albert Gleason to commissioners, Aug. 10, 1874, DCComsRLR. *New York Sun,* Aug. 3, 17, 1874. CR:44-1 (Jan. 31, 1876), pp. 760–61.

13. Bowen to commissioners, and Alexander to commissioners, both received, Aug. 5, 1874; Cluss to commissioners, received Aug. 11, 1874, DCComsRLR, vol. 1.

14. DCTComsMins, Jan. 8, 1875. DCComsAR, 1874, pp. 264–65.

15. DCComsAR, 1875, pp. 237–38, 254–55. *Evening Star,* Oct. 15, 1875.

16. Washington *Critic,* Jan. 1, 27, 1875.

17. Washington *Critic,* Jan. 27, Feb. 5, 1875. DCTComMins, July 6, 1874.

18. Board of Audit Invest., pt. 1, pp. 199–200; pt. 2, pp. 1–17. Board of Audit, "Certain Reports Relating to Street Improvements," 43rd Cong., 2nd sess. (Mar. 3, 1875), H. Misc. Doc. 96. Board of Audit, *1875 Annual Report,* 44th Cong., 1st sess., H. Exec. Doc. 1. "Investigation of Charges against the Commissioners of the District of Columbia," 44th Cong., 1st sess., H. Rept. 702.

19. Board of Audit Invest., esp. pt. 1, p. 1; pt. 2, pp. 1–16. Buckner, "District of Columbia Affairs," pp. 22–24. DCComsAR, 1875, p. 33; 1877, pp. 5–6.

20. DCTComsMins, June 9, Oct. 22, 1875.

21. CR:44-1 (Feb. 1, 1876), p. 596.

22. CR:44-1 (Jan. 27–28, 31, 1876), pp. 679–711, 759–62. *Evening Star,* Jan. 27, 1876.

23. DCComsAR, 1874, p. 84. A flurry of communications and meetings with the New York bankers during the interim government's first weeks are listed in DCComsRLR, vol. 1, July 9–11, and in DCTComsMins, July 7–14, 1874. DCTComsMins, Jan. 15, 21, 29, 1875. House Appropriations Committee Papers, RecHRep, 43A-F3.15. "Certain Reports relating to Street Improvements," 43rd Cong., 2nd sess., H. Misc. Doc. 96. "Amount of Certificates of Indebtedness," 44th Cong., 1st sess. (May 18, 1876), S. Misc. Doc. 101. "Letter from the Commissioners of the District of Columbia, on Interest on Bonds of the District of Columbia," 43rd Cong., 2nd sess. (Jan. 12, 18, 1875), H. Misc. Doc. 35. *Evening Star,* Oct. 25–27, 1875.

24. House Invest. (1872), pp. 378 ff., 406 ff., 481–82.

25. Joint Invest. (1874), report pp. xi–xii. Shepherd to Allison, June 6, 1874, Allison Papers, new list, box 3. "Message of the President on payment of debts of the District of Columbia," 43rd Cong., 1st sess. (June 20, 1874), H. Exec. Doc. 288. "Message of the President on one feature of the act for government of the District of Columbia," 43rd Cong., 1st sess. (June 20, 1874), S. Rept. 473.

26. Commissioners to the Speaker, Jan. 10, 1876; commissioners to Rep. Buckner, Feb. 8, 1876, DCComsLS, vol. 3. F. Winston to Randall, June 2, 1876, House Appropriations Committee Papers, RecHRep, 44A-F3.3.

27. CR:44-1, esp. Feb. 23, 1876, pp. 1232 ff.; Feb. 25, 1876, pp. 1295 ff.; Mar. 13, 1876, pp. 1684–87. Commissioners to Randall, Jan. 19, 1876, DCComsLS, vol. 3.

28. Board of Audit Invest., pt. 1, pp. 2–167 *passim,* p. 181; pt. 2, pp. 10–12, 140. "Investigation of Charges against the Commissioners," 44th Cong., 1st sess., H. Rept. 702. "Concerning certain matters . . . in the administration of the provisional government . . . ," 44th Cong., 2nd sess., H. Exec. Doc. 26. Board of Audit, *1875 Annual Report,* 44th Cong., 1st sess., H. Exec. Doc. 1, p. 8. Washington *Daily Chronicle,* Feb. 13, 1876. *Evening Star,* Feb. 17, 1876.

29. Buckner, "District of Columbia Affairs," p. 17. *Democratic Campaign Textbook,* pp. 206–11. CR:44-1 (Feb. 2, 1876), pp. 824–25.

30. Keller, *Affairs of State,* pp. 68–69, 252–53.

31. Michael McGerr, *The Decline of Popular Politics, 1865–1928* (New York: Oxford UP, 1986). Mark Kornbluh, "From Participatory to Administrative Politics: A Social History of American Political Behavior, 1880–1910" (Ph.D. diss., Johns Hopkins U, 1987). Richard L. McCormick, *The Party Period and Public Policy* (New York: Oxford UP, 1986), chap. 5.

32. Leonard D. White, *The Republican Era, 1864–1901: A Study in Administrative History* (New York: Macmillan, 1958). William E. Nelson, *The Roots of American Bureaucracy, 1830–1900* (Cambridge: Harvard UP, 1982), pp. 77–78. George L. Robinson,

"The Development of the Senate Committee System" (Ph.D. diss., New York U, 1954), pp. 241 ff.

33. A similar problem occurred in British provincial cities, where "improvement commissions," "highway boards," and so forth emerged to manage modern public services and became entrenched prior to the creation or reform of municipal corporations. Derek Fraser, *Power and Authority in the Victorian City* (New York: St. Martin's, 1979).

34. W. B. Bryan, "Sketches of Various Forms of Local Government in the District of Columbia," in William V. Cox, ed., *The Centennial Celebration of the Establishment of the Seat of Government in the District of Columbia* (Washington, D.C.: GPO, 1901), pp. 281–97. Walter F. Dodd, *The Government of the District of Columbia* (Washington, D.C.: John F. Byrne, 1909), pp. 11–37. Constance M. Green, *Washington: Village and Capital* (Princeton: Princeton UP, 1962), pp. 23–32. *The Federalist* (New York: Modern Library, 1941), pp. 279–80.

35. Wilhelmus B. Bryan, *A History of the National Capital* (New York: Macmillan, 1916), vol. 2, pp. 274, 459–60.

36. *Evening Star,* Jan. 20–23, 1871. House Invest. (1872), pp. 586–87.

37. BPW-AR, 1872, pp. 14–32.

38. Joint Invest. (1874), report, p. xxii, answers of Governor Shepherd, pp. 460–61. Harry James Brown and Frederick D. Williams, eds., *The Diary of James A. Garfield* (East Lansing: Michigan State UP, 1967), vol. 2, pp. 121–23. Shepherd to Garfield, Nov. 9, 1872, Garfield Papers, Library of Congress, reel 24. CG:42-3 (Dec. 16, 1872), pp. 230–32. "Legal Relations of the District of Columbia and the United States," 43rd Cong., 1st sess. (June 1, 1874), H. Rept. 627.

39. House Judiciary Committee, "Legal Relations of the District of Columbia and the United States," 43rd Cong., 1st sess., H. Rept. 627. Bryan, *History of the National Capital,* vol. 2, pp. 625–26.

40. *New York Sun,* July 31, 1874. New York *Daily Tribune,* Nov. 27, 1874.

41. *New National Era,* Oct. 26, 1871. New York *Daily Tribune,* Nov. 27, 1874. Constance M. Green, *The Secret City* (Princeton: Princeton UP, 1967), pp. 103–14. Bryan, *History of the National Capital,* vol. 2, pp. 592–93. Whyte, *Uncivil War,* pp. 243–47.

42. *Daily Patriot,* Apr. 20–21, 1871. *Georgetown Courier,* June 20, 1874; also quoted in Green, *Village and Capital,* p. 361.

43. CR:43-2 (Dec. 16–21, 1874, Feb. 10–15, 1875), pp. 121–27, 165, 1103 ff., 1165 ff., 1245 ff., 1275. "On the bill for the government of the District of Columbia," 43rd Cong., 2nd sess. (Dec. 7, 1874), S. Rept. 479. Washington *Critic,* Feb. 5, 11, 13, 1875.

44. RecSen, 43A-J5. Washington *Critic,* Jan. 27–Feb. 13, 1875.

45. *Evening Star,* Jan. 22, 25, 1876, Mar. 2, 4, Apr. 1, May 9–14, 27–29, 1878.

46. "Views of the minority of the joint select committee . . . ," 44th Cong., 2nd sess. (Jan. 11, 1877), S. Rept. 572. Petition of Hugh Coyle, May 13, 1878, RecSen, 45A-H5. *Washington Post,* May 15, 1878. CR:45-2 (Apr. 15, 1878), p. 2528.

47. Baltimore *Sun,* Dec. 4, 1877.

48. CR:45-2 (Mar. 20, 1878), pp. 1922 ff. "Form of Government for the District of Columbia," 44th Cong., 2nd sess. (Dec. 27, 1876), H. Rept. 64.

49. An explication of principal House roll calls on the 1878 District bill, broken down by party and region, appears in my thesis, "The Federal Government and the National Capital: Washington, 1861–1902" (Ph.D. diss., Johns Hopkins U, 1990), pp. 222–30. On the House roll call that dealt most directly with the half-and-half plan [CR:45-2, (May 7, 1878), pp. 3242–46], Democrats from the Northeast and Midwest voted 41-12 to weaken the funding provision. Blackburn's fellow Southern Democrats gave him only a 32-23 majority. Northeastern and Midwestern Republicans voted 68-23 to keep the half-and-half. The chi square [X^2] for the Democrats' regional pattern is

23.441, which yields a confidence level of 99 percent and a Pearson's contingency coefficient [C] of .396. Corresponding figures for Republicans are 7.116, 90 percent, and .258. This vote's regional pattern would make sense to C. Vann Woodward, who believes that the first post-Reconstruction Congress consisted of an unstable alliance between Southern conservatives and pro-business Northern Republicans. C. Vann Woodward, *Reunion and Reaction: The Compromise of 1877 and the End of Reconstruction* (Boston: Little, Brown, 1951).

50. CR:45-2 (Apr. 15, 16, 1878), pp. 2528 ff., 2579. *Evening Star,* Apr. 16, 1878.

51. CR:45-2 (May 21, 25, 1878), pp. 3607, 3779–80. *Evening Star,* May 18, 27–28.

52. CR:45-2 (June 8, 1878), pp. 4320–21. *Evening Star,* May 29, 1878. I elaborate on this in "Federal Government and National Capital."

53. This tendency to downplay the legacy of history in shaping twentieth-century political and governmental patterns appears strongly in the influential "organizational synthesis," which, with its roots in modernization theory and structural/functional sociology, must favor analyses that treat political change as a manifestation of social and economic forces. Louis Galambos explains and reviews the organizational approach in "The Emerging Organizational Synthesis in Modern American History," *Business History Review* 44 (1970): 279–90; and "Technology, Political Culture, and Professionalization: Central Themes of the Organizational Synthesis, *Business History Review* 57 (1983): 471–93. In "Parsonian Sociology and Post-Progressive History," *Social Science Quarterly* 50 (1969): 25–45, Galambos discusses theoretical underpinnings of this approach. Even admirably historical explanations of the shift from "popular" to "administrative" politics succumb to making political transformation a product of socioeconomic forces. For example, Richard L. McCormick, *From Realignment to Reform: Political Change in New York State, 1893–1910* (Ithaca: Cornell UP, 1981); and McCormick, *The Party Period,* pp. 213, 227.

54. DCComsAR, 1875, p. 225–32; 1876, pp. 34–38. Commissioners to Senator Dorsey, Mar. 5, 1878, Seth Phelps to Senator Rollins, Mar. 11, 1878, RecSen, 45A-E5. *Evening Star,* Mar. 6, Apr. 11, 1878. Clifton K. Yearley, *The Money Machines: The Breakdown and Reform of Governmental and Party Finance in the North, 1860–1920* (Albany: State U of New York P, 1970), pp. 66–74. Bryan, *History of the National Capital,* vol. 2, p. 617.

55. DCComsAR, 1874, p. 7; 1875, p. 253. Sinking Fund Invest. (1880), pp. 91–95. "Certain Reports Relating to Street Improvements . . . ," 43rd Cong., 2nd sess., H. Misc. Doc. 96, pp. 2–5.

56. Washington *Critic,* Jan. 1, 1875. DCComsAR, 1877, pp. 77–78, 142–47, 182–84. Sinking Fund Invest. (1880), pp. 6–13. "Report of the Commissioners of the Sinking Fund on Certificates of Indebtedness," 44th Cong., 1st sess. (May 18, 1876), S. Misc. Doc. 101. "Assessment for Special Improvements in the District of Columbia," 45th Cong., 2nd sess. (Feb. 14, 1878), S. Misc. Doc. 47.

57. George Hendee to Hayes, June 17, 1878, Hayes Papers, series 4, reel 81. *Washington Post,* June 18, July 1, 1878. *Evening Star,* June 17, 1878. *Washington Sentinel,* June 15, 22, 1878.

58. Sinking Fund Invest. (1880), pp. 6–13. "Letter of the District Commissioners on the Sinking Fund of the District of Columbia," 46th Cong., 2nd sess. (Mar. 30, 1880), S. Misc. Doc. 68. "Memorial of Robert Christy on Assessments in the District of Columbia," 45th Cong., 3rd sess. (Jan. 16, 1879), H. Misc. Doc. 15.

59. U.S. Treasurer, "Sinking Fund of the District of Columbia," 46th Cong., 2nd sess. (Feb. 3, 1880), H. Exec. Doc. 35, pp. 6–10, 19.

60. "Sinking Fund of the District of Columbia," 46th Cong., 2nd sess., H. Exec. Doc. 35, p. 17. Commissioners' Letter on the Sinking Fund, 46th Cong., 2nd sess., S. Misc. Doc. 68. Sinking Fund Invest. (1880), p. 19.

61. RecHRep, petitions on Sinking Fund investigation, 46A-H7.1; District Committee Minutes, Jan. 29, Feb 26–Apr. 3, 1880, 46A-F8.3. Sinking Fund Invest. (1880),

pp. 115 ff., 265–66. Gilfillan to Aldrich, Feb. 28, Apr. 10, 1880, reel 3, Aldrich Papers, Library of Congress. DCComsMins, vol. 1B, Oct. 10, 1879, Mar. 31, 1880. *Washington Post,* Mar. 27, 31, 1880. *Evening Star,* Apr. 19, 1880.

62. E. O. Graves to Aldrich, Aug. 5, 1880, Mar. 8, 1881, Gilfillan to Aldrich, Oct. 6, 1880, Feb. 27, 1881, Aldrich Papers, reels 3–4. District Committee Minutes, Dec. 3, 1880, Feb. 14, 21, 1881, RecHRep, 46A-F8.3.

63. DCComsAR, 1881, pp. 207–9. "Revision of Special Assessments," 46th Cong., 1st sess. (Feb. 14, 1881), S. Misc. Doc. 11.

64. "Appropriations for the District of Columbia for 1896," 53rd Cong., 3rd sess., H. Rept. 1546.

Chapter 5 The District Commissioners and Congress

Epigraph: DCComsLS, vol. 22.

1. CR:45-2 (May 25, 1878), pp. 3780 ff.

2. DCComsMins, July 6, 1878. DCComsRLR, vol. 12, July 16, 1878. DCComsAR, 1878, pp. 83 ff.; 1879, p. 20.

3. "Defining the quorum of the Commissioners . . . ," 51st Cong., 2nd sess. (Dec. 6, 1890), H. Rept. 3250. DCComsAR, 1879, pp. 20, 43.

4. DCComsAR, 1879, pp. 18–19, 44.

5. DCComsMins, vol. 1B, Aug. 14, 1882; vol. 11, May 8, 1897; vol. 16, Nov. 24, 1899. Walter F. Dodd, *The Government of the District of Columbia* (Washington, D.C.: John Byrne, 1909), pp. 76–79.

6. DCComsAR, 1878, p. 272; 1879, pp. 20–23, 43–48. DCComsMins, vol. 11, May 14, 1897; vol. 12, July 1, 1897.

7. *Washington Post,* June 12, 1878. Washington *Critic,* Mar. 8, 1886. *Evening Star,* Mar. 2–24, 1897.

8. *Evening Star,* Mar. 8, 1886. DCComsMins, vol. 11, May 8, 1897; vol. 13, June 1, 1898. Moore to McMillan, Aug, 2. 1902, political collection, McMillan Papers, Detroit Public Library.

9. *Evening Star,* Mar. 3, July 14, 1883; May 16–17, 1889.

10. *National Cyclopedia of American Biography,* vol. 2, p. 230. *Evening Star,* Mar. 8, 1886, May 15, 1897. Allen B. Slauson, ed., *A History of the City of Washington: Its Men and Institutions,* (Washington, D.C.: Washington Post, 1903), pp. 377–79.

11. *National Cyclopedia of American Biography,* vol. 12, p. 230, *Evening Star,* May 15, 1897.

12. *Evening Star,* Feb. 16, 1897.

13. RecHRep, 53A-F7.2. "Argument on bill to incorporate National Gas and Electric Light, Heat and Power Company," 53rd Cong., 2nd sess. (July 27, 1894), S. Misc. Doc. 248. "Incorporation of the National Gaslight, Heat, and Power Company," 54th Cong., 1st sess. (Feb. 28, 1896), S. doc. 138, p. 3. CR:54-1, (May 16–18, 1896), pp. 5329 ff., 5345 ff.

14. *Evening Star,* Feb. 16–26, 1897.

15. For this paragraph and the next, *Evening Star,* Mar. 24, 1897, Oct. 14, 15, 25, 1902. Moore to McMillan, Aug. 1, 1902, political collection, McMillan Papers. For Moore's background, see H. Paul Caemerer, "Charles Moore and the Plan of Washington," RCHS, vols. 46–47, pp. 237–58.

16. Moore to Richard Rice, Aug. 2, 1902, personal collection; West to McMillan, Aug. 2, 1902; and Lodge to McMillan, Aug. 2, 1902, political collection, McMillan Papers. McMillan to Moore, Aug. 4, 1902, Moore Papers, Library of Congress, box 1. *Evening Star,* Oct. 25, 1902.

17. DCComsAR, 1890, pp. 8–9; 1892, pp. 6–7.

18. "Letter of the Commissioners . . . on officers and employees who have been

changed since March 4, 1885," 50th Cong., 2nd sess. (Feb. 1889), S. Misc. Doc. 86. *Washington Post,* Dec. 16, 1896.

19. Moore to McMillan, Apr. 25, 1893; Truesdell to McMillan, Sept. 1, 1894; Harry McLean to McMillan, Sept. 4, Nov. 11, 1894, political collection, McMillan Papers. Captain Powell to William Forsyth, Mar. 11, 1896, Records of the Surveyor, entry 100, box 9, RG 351.

20. DCComsAR, 1895, p. 8. HRApproHrgs, 1903, p. 15. Civil Service Commissioner Proctor to the commissioners, Apr. 2, 1896, DCComsRLR.

21. DCComsAR, 1879, p. 502–8. "Contingent Expenses of the District of Columbia," 1886, 49th Cong., 2nd sess. (Dec. 17, 1886), H. Misc. Doc. 50.

22. CR:47-2 (Feb. 23, 1883), pp. 3167. "Bookkeeping, Books, and Accounts in the Financial Departments of the District of Columbia," 48th Cong., 1st sess. (Apr. 30, 1884), H. Rept. 1434. HRApproHrgs, 1895, p. 12. DCComsAR, 1894, pp. 52–53.

23. HRApproHrgs, 1895, p. 5; 1896, pp. 9–12; 1899, pp. 4–5; 1902, p. 12. DCComsAR, 1886, pp. 160–61; 1887, p. 580; 1893, p. 92; 1894, pp. 361–63. For Senate hearings on the Ford's Theater disaster: 53rd Cong., 3rd sess. (Feb. 14, 1895), S. Rept. 933.

24. Request for Additional Assistant Attorney, RecHRep, 57A-F1.2.

25. DCComsAR, 1890, p. 22.

26. DCComsAR, 1890, p. 22; 1894, pp. 19–20.

27. HRApproHrgs, 1896, pp. 5–7; 1897, pp. 3–4. SenApproHrgs, 1904, p. 39. "To revive the office of Secretary of the District of Columbia," 57th Cong., 1st sess. (June 17, 1902), S. Rept. 1938. Enoch A. Chase, "Doctor William Tindall," RCHS, vols. 35–37, pp. 183–91.

28. William Tindall, "Homes of the Local Government," RCHS, vol. 3, pp. 279–302. Frederick Gutheim, consultant, *Worthy of the Nation* (Washington, D.C.: Smithsonian Institution P, 1977), pp. 46–47. C. E. H., "The Triumvirs of Four-and-a-Half Street," pamphlet, Nov. 1881, National Museum of American History.

29. DCComsAR, 1882, pp. 158–59; 1884, pp. 188–89.

30. "Municipal Building in the District of Columbia," 53rd Cong., 2nd sess. (July 6, 1894), H. Rept. 1205. DCComsAR, 1895, p. 7. HRApproHrgs, 1895, pp. 3–4; 1901, p. 25. SenApproHrgs, 1901, p. 40. Tindall, "Homes of the District Government," RCHS.

31. Jon C. Teaford, *The Unheralded Triumph: City Government in America, 1870–1900* (Baltimore: Johns Hopkins UP, 1984), pp. 285–86, 293. Terrence J. McDonald, *The Parameters of Urban Fiscal Policy* (Berkeley: U of California P, 1986), examines no-growth sentiment among taxpayers in post-panic San Francisco. Clifton K. Yearley, *The Money Machines: The Breakdown and Reform of Governmental and Party Finance in the North, 1860–1920* (Albany: State U of New York P, 1970), chap. 1.

32. DCComsAR, 1884, pp. 5–6.

33. Eric Monkkonen, *America Becomes Urban* (Berkeley: U of California P, 1988), p. 144.

34. For the financing route taken by Boston in its Back Bay reclamation, see Walter M. Whitehall, *Boston: A Topographical History,* 2nd ed. (Cambridge: Harvard UP, 1968), pp. 141–73.

35. DCComsAR, 1884, pp. 5–6.

36. DCComsMins, vols. 7–8, June 24–Aug. 29, 1895. Quotes are from June 25 and July 18. Martin V. Melosi, *Garbage in the Cities* (College Station: Texas A&M UP, 1981).

37. DCComsMins, vol. 8, Sept. 5–Oct. 1, 1895; vol. 9, Dec. 23, 1895, Apr. 18–21, 1896; vol. 13, Mar. 1, 1898.

38. Dodd, *Government of the District of Columbia,* pp. 81–90.

39. DCComsMins, vol. 7, June 18, 1895.

40. George L. Robinson, "The Development of the Senate Committee System" (Ph.D. diss., New York U, 1954), p. 304.

41. "Resolution that last Friday and Saturday of month be assigned . . . to the District of Columbia," 41st Cong., 2nd sess. (May 17, 1870), S. Misc. Doc. 137. CG:41-2 (May 18, 1870), p. 3555.

42. CG:41-2 (Mar. 9, 1870), p. 1804. "Amendments to the Rules," 49th Cong., 1st sess. (Mar.–Apr., 1886), H. Rept. 1452 and H. Misc. Doc. 162.

43. Minutes of the District of Columbia Committee, Jan. 9, Dec. 3, 1880, RecHRep, 46A-F8.3. Washington *Critic,* May 12, 1884. *Evening Star,* Aug. 6, 1886, Jan. 23, 1893.

44. Margaret Thompson, *The "Spider Web": Congress and Lobbying in the Age of Grant* (Ithaca: Cornell UP, 1985), pp. 71–86. Morton Keller, *Affairs of State: Public Life in Late Nineteenth-Century America* (Cambridge: Harvard UP, 1977), p. 305.

45. The Senate abolished the District Committee in 1977 and turned its work over to the Governmental Affairs Committee. The House District Committee still exists.

46. Moore to McMillan, Mar. 11, 1891, political collection, McMillan Papers. Charles Moore, *Autobiography* (photostat manuscript in Fine Arts Commission Papers, RG 66), pp. 46 ff. David J. Rothman, *Politics and Power: The United States Senate, 1869–1901* (Cambridge: Harvard UP, 1966).

47. Redfield Proctor to Allison, Dec. 5, 1901, Allison Papers, Iowa State Historical Department, old list, box 344. James to William McMillan, Feb. 11, 1901, personal collection, McMillan Papers.

48. Docket and Minutes of the District Committee, RecHRep, 41A-F7.5–7.6, 49A-F8.1–8.3, and 50A-F8.1

49. CR:49-1 (June 14, July 15, 1886), pp. 5683–90, 6893–6992. CR:49-2 (Jan. 27, 1887), p. 1095. RecSen, 49A-E7; 49A-H6; 49A-J12. *Evening Star,* July 16, Aug. 6–7, 1886.

50. "Appropriations for the District of Columbia," 46th Cong., 2nd sess., H. Rept. 1125. CR:46-2 (May 5, 1880), p. 3005.

51. *Evening Star,* Dec. 26, 1891, Jan. 2, 1902. Robinson, "Development of the Senate Committee System," pp. 285–98.

52. *Evening Star,* Jan. 30, 1892.

53. "Appropriations for the District of Columbia," 46th Cong., 2nd sess. (Apr. 20, 1880), H. Rept. 1125. CR:47-1 (May 10, June 7–8, 1882), pp. 3801–6, 4629–30, 4666–67. Washington *Critic,* Feb. 17, 1886. Charles H. Stewart, *Budget Reform Politics: The Design of the Appropriations Process in the House of Representatives, 1865–1921* (Cambridge: Cambridge UP, 1989), pp. 84–89.

54. Stewart, *Budget Reform Politics,* pp. 119–28. Leonard D. White, *The Republican Era, 1864–1901: A Study in Administrative History* (New York: Macmillan, 1958), chaps. 3–4.

55. Robinson, "Development of the Senate Committee System," pp. 272, 291. Keller, *Affairs of State,* p. 304.

56. CR:46-2 (May 5, 1880), p. 3005. CR:46-3 (Feb. 18, 1881), p. 1790. CR:47-2 (Feb. 23, 1883), p. 3159. CR:48-1 (May 29, 1884), p. 4660. CR:49-1 (May 24, 1886), pp. 4849–50. CR:50-1 (June 29, 1888), p. 5735. *Washington Post,* May 11, 1890.

57. *Evening Star,* July 29, 1886.

58. *Washington Post,* Feb. 25, Mar. 2–5, 1887. CR:49-2 (Mar. 2, 1887), p. 2568.

59. CR:51-1 (Jan. 7–8, 1890), pp. 438–43, 460–74. CR:51-2 (Jan. 16, 1891), pp. 1471–87. CR:52-1 (Mar. 2–3, 1892), pp. 1640–43, 1684–99. "Appropriations for the District of Columbia," 52nd Cong., 1st sess. (Mar. 1, 1892), H. Rept. 495.

60. CR:52-1 (Apr. 7–8, June 30, July 12, 1892), pp. 3048–89, 5681–94, 6058–60. "Message of the President . . . on appropriation for reception of the Grand Army of the Republic," 52nd Cong., 1st sess., H. Exec. Doc. 173. "Appropriations for the District of Columbia," 52nd Cong., 1st sess., S. Rept. 492.

61. *Evening Star,* Aug. 7, 1886. CR:51-1 (Mar. 24, Apr. 28, Sept. 25–26, 1890), pp. 2578–90, 3938–45, 10418–19, 10441–44, 10457–58. "Conference Report on Bill

to Establish a Park in the District of Columbia," 51st Cong., 1st sess. (Sept. 25, 1890), S. Misc. Doc. 242.

62. CR:51-2 (Apr. 22, 1890), pp. 3667–68. "Memorial to Congress of the Joint Executive Committees of the Citizens' Associations," Jan. 1894, pamphlet in Suter/Noyes Papers, Historical Society of Washington, pp. 17–20.

63. Moore, *Autobiography*, pp. 65. Robinson, "Development of the Senate Committee System," p. 290.

64. James to William McMillan, Apr. 22, 26, May 25, 1899; McMillan to George M. Black, May 31, 1899, personal collection, McMillan Papers. Mary Patten to Allison, June 22, 1901; Macfarland to Allison, June 27, 29, 1901; John Ross to Allison, June 28, 1901, Allison Papers, old list, boxes 343–44. Leland Sage, *William Boyd Allison: A Study in Practical Politics* (Iowa City: State Historical Society of Iowa, 1956). Rothman, *Politics and Power*, pp. 44–45.

65. McMillan to commissioners, Apr. 29, 1896, DCComsRLR, vol. 51. *In Memory of Hon. James McMillan* (Lansing: Michigan State Legislature, 1903), pp. 86–87. Melvin Holli, *Reform in Detroit: Hazen S. Pingree and Urban Politics* (New York: Oxford UP, 1969), p. 104.

66. Sherman to Thomas King, Apr. 8, 1890, copy in political collection, McMillan Papers. Sherman to Allison, Feb. 5, 1898, Allison Papers, new list, box 43. Charles Moore, *Washington, Past and Present* (New York: Century, 1929), pp. 51–52. Moore, *Autobiography*, p. 66. *Washington Post*, Mar. 1, 1887, Feb. 3, 1889. H. Wayne Morgan, *From Hayes to McKinley* (Syracuse: Syracuse UP, 1966), pp. 40–43.

67. Moore, *Autobiography*, p. 66. Roderick French, "Chevy Chase Village in the Context of the National Suburban Movement, 1870–1900," RCHS, 1973–74, 319–20.

68. Russell R. Elliot, *Servant of Power: A Political Biography of Senator William M. Stewart* (Reno: U of Nevada P, 1983), esp. chap. 5. Wilhelmus B. Bryan, *A History of the National Capital* (New York: MacMillan, 1916), vol. 2, p. 620. James H. Whyte, *The Uncivil War: Washington during the Reconstruction* (New York: Twayne, 1958), p. 208. James Goode, *Capital Losses: A Cultural History of Washington's Destroyed Buildings* (Washington, D.C.: Smithsonian Institution P, 1979), p. 78.

69. William Lilley III, "The Early Career of Francis G. Newlands, 1848–1897" (Ph.D. diss., Yale U, 1965).

70. Newlands to James H. Dobinson, Apr. 21, 1887; W. B. Bryan, interview with Francis Newlands, Jan. 15, 1891, box 1, Francis G. Newlands Papers, Manuscripts and Archives, Yale U Library. *History of the Chevy Chase Land Company*, typescript dated 1936, box 75, Newlands Papers, esp. pp. 12–14. Minutes of the Rock Creek and Capital Traction Railways, Capital Traction Papers, Historical Society of Washington; see esp. lists of shareholders and of property owned by Chevy Chase Company, Jan. 1894. French, "Chevy Chase Village," RCHS. Albert W. Atwood, "The Romance of Senator Francis G. Newlands and Chevy Chase," RCHS, 1966–68, 294–310. Albert W. Atwood, *Francis G. Newlands: A Builder of the Nation* (Washington, D.C.: Newlands Co., 1969).

71. *History of the Chevy Chase Company*, box 75, Newlands Papers. French, "Chevy Chase Village," RCHS. Olmsted to Newlands, Nov. 15–16, 1891, in "Community Design—Washington '91" file, Olmsted Papers, Library of Congress, reel 25. The Chevy Chase Company also certainly used its power as landholder, realtor, and underwriter to maintain racial homogeneity in its development. The author has personally seen no references to outright racial covenants dating from Newlands's life. This is unsurprising, as such agreements, although later common practice in Washington and elsewhere in the nation, did not become widespread until after the First World War. Davis McEntire, *Residence and Race* (Berkeley: U of California P, 1960), pp. 73–78, 258.

72. Rock Creek Minute Books for July–Sept. 1895 and Capital Traction Books for Sept. 1895–Jan. 1896, Capital Traction Papers. *Laws Relating to Street Railway Franchises*

in the District of Columbia (Washington, D.C.: GPO, 1896), p. 66. Leroy O. King, Jr., *One Hundred Years of Capital Traction* (n.p.: Taylor Publishing, 1972), pp. 28–31. John W. Boettjer, "Street Railways in the District of Columbia" (Master's thesis, George Washington U, 1963), pp. 79 ff.

73. *History of the Chevy Chase Company,* p. 46. French, "Chevy Chase Village," RCHS. Atwood, "The Romance of Senator Francis G. Newlands and Chevy Chase," RCHS.

74. Newlands to Joseph Cannon, [date unknown], box 1; Newlands to Samuel Stratton, July 19–27, 1901, box 3; Newlands to McMillan, May 26, 1900, box 56, Newlands Papers. Newlands to the House and Senate District committees, June 21, 1894, RecSen, 53A-F7, box 26. HRApproHrgs, 1897, p. 133; 1898, p. 147.

75. Newlands to the San Franciso *Chronicle,* Feb. 16, 1892, copy in Newlands Papers, box 1.

Chapter 6 The Army Corps and Gilded Age Washington

Epigraph: *Report of the Committee on Water and Sewers of the Citizens' Committee,* pamphlet dated Sept. 10, 1887, in the Historical Society of Washington, p. 7.

1. CR:45-2 (Mar. 28, 1878), pp. 2112–15.

2. David F. Noble, *American by Design* (New York: Oxford UP, 1977), pp. 20–36.

3. Todd A. Shallat, "Structures in the Stream: A History of Water, Science, and the Civil Activities of the United States Army Corps of Engineers, 1700–1861" (Ph.D. diss., Carnegie-Mellon U, 1986), chaps. 5–6. Martin Reuss, "Andrew A. Humphreys and the Development of Hydraulic Engineering: Politics and Technology in the Army Corps of Engineers, 1850–1950," *Technology and Culture* 24, no. 1 (1985): 1–33.

4. John H. Walker, ed. *Purification of the Washington City Water Supply,* 3rd ed., (Washington, D.C.: GPO, 1909), p. 10. Wilhelmus B. Bryan, *A History of the National Capital* (New York: Macmillan, 1916), vol. 2, p. 305.

5. Russell F. Weigley, *Quartermaster General of the Union Army: A Biography of M.C. Meigs* (New York: Columbia UP, 1959), pp. 13–61. Quotes are from p. 29.

6. Montgomery Meigs to R. M. Hunter, also to Mayor Maury and Senators Cass, Hale, and Pearce, Feb. 1853, reel add. 11, box add. 29, Meigs Papers, Library of Congress.

7. Meigs to Sen. Pearce, Feb. 26, 1853, Meigs Papers, reel add. 11, box add. 29. Drawings, maps, and specifications in Meigs Papers, reel add. 22, box add. 36; also in William Hutton Papers, box 12, Museum of American History. Walker, *Purification of the Washington Water Supply,* pp. 11–13. Interior Department, *Annual Report,* 1863, pp. 677–89. "Supplemental Report of the Chief Engineer of the Washington Aqueduct," 38th Cong., 1st sess., (Feb. 22, 1864). S. Misc. Doc. 83. William Curtis, "The Cabin John Bridge," RCHS, 2 (1899), 293–307. Donald B. Myer, *Bridges and the City of Washington,* (Washington, D.C.: U.S. Commission of Fine Arts, 1974), pp. 80–81. Weigley, *Quartermaster General,* pp. 57 ff. Nelson M. Blake, *Water for the Cities* (Syracuse: Syracuse UP, 1956), p. 266.

8. Weigley, *Quartermaster General,* p. 35, also, p. 61. See Meigs Papers, reel add. 11, box add. 29, especially Meigs to Lewis Cass, Mar. 1, 1853; Jefferson Davis to Meigs, Mar. 23, 1853; General Totten to Meigs, Mar. 29, 1853; Meigs to Horace Greeley, Feb. 8, 1854; Washington City Council to Meigs, June 9, 1854. "Supplemental Report of the Chief Engineer," 38th Cong., 1st sess., S. Misc. Doc. 83, pp. 24–25. Albert E. Cowdrey, *A City for the Nation: The Army Engineers and the Building of Washington, D.C., 1790–1967* (Washington, D.C.: Army Corps Historical Division, 1978), pp. 18–19.

9. Meigs to Lewis Cass, Mar. 1, 1853, reel add. 11, box add. 29, Meigs Papers. Also, correspondence between Floyd and Meigs and Thomas Walter and Meigs, reels add.

11–12, box add. 29; and Attorney General Black to President Buchanan, July 31, 1860, copy in reel add. 12, box add. 29. "Supplemental Report of the Chief Engineer," 38th Cong., 1st sess., S. Misc. Doc. 83, pp. 22–23. Myer, *Bridges and the City of Washington,* pp. 80–81. Weigley, *Quartermaster General,* chaps. 4, 5.

10. For Meigs's dispute with Babcock: CEngsAR, 1877, app. KK, pp. 1093–1104. Meigs to Sen. Spencer, Dec. 29, 1876, RecSen, 44A-E4. Meigs to Gen. Wright, July 18, 1883, reel add. 16, Meigs Papers. Myer, *Bridges and the City of Washington,* p. 58.

11. CG:39-2 (Mar. 2, 1867), p. 1983.

12. CR:45-2 (Apr. 15, 1878) p. 2534. For contemporary discussions of Babcock's activities, see clippings in Babcock Papers, Newberry Library, box 5. Also, Bioessays, Historical Division, Army Corps of Engineers, Fort Belvoir, Va.

13. CEngsAR, 1873, app. AA, pp. 1151–54; 1874, vol. 2, app. BB, pp. 385–90.

14. Gleason to Babcock, Mar. 21, 1873, PBO, entry 87, box 2.

15. "Government Property in and around Washington," 42nd Cong., 2nd sess. (May 27, 1872), H. Misc. Doc. 224. Professor Henry to Babcock, Feb. 6, 1873, PBO, entry 87, box 2. CEngsAR, 1867, pp. 523 ff.; 1871, app. 10, pp. 967–70; 1875, app. HH, pp. 803–4. Cowdrey, *A City for the Nation,* pp. 24–26. Frederick Gutheim, consultant, *Worthy of the Nation* (Washington, D.C.: Smithsonian Institution P, 1977), pp. 78–84.

16. CEngsAR, 1872, app. Y, pp. 1015–26; 1874, app. BB, pp. 385–94; 1875, app. HH, pp. 807–12; 1877, app. KK, pp. 1061–71. Cowdrey, *A City for the Nation,* p. 25.

17. CEngsAR, 1872, app. Y, pp. 1015–17; 1874, app. BB, pp. 392–93; 1875, app. HH, p. 807–12. Letters on sparrows in PBO, entry 87, boxes 2–3, including Speaker Kerr to Babcock, Apr. 10, 1876. Also, receipts from Charles Reiche and Bros., Charles Jefferson to Thomas Casey, Mar. 14, 1877, and Casey to Jefferson, Mar. 15, 1877, PBO, entry 87, box 3. *Evening Star,* Jan. 20, 1882. John Ross to Representative Heard, Jan. 31, 1895, RecHRep, 53A-F7.7.

18. CEngsAR, 1877, app. KK, p. 1069.

19. Cowdrey, *A City for the Nation,* pp. 26–29.

20. The main source for officers' biographies is the Bioessays at the Army Corps Historical Division, Fort Belvoir, Va.

21. Olmsted Papers, reel 40, and Olmsted Associates' Papers, box 134, files 2820–21, for documents on the Capitol grounds. Gutheim, *Worthy of the Nation,* pp. 95–96.

22. Correspondence concerning the Thornett method, Mar.–May, 1877, PBO, entry 87, box 3. The extermination contest, with State Department summaries, is in PBO, entry 87, box 17, and C. J. Uhler of Sweden to "His Highness Cleveland," Apr. 4, 1888, in box 18.

23. "Improvement of the Harbors of Washington and Georgetown," 42nd Cong., 3rd sess. (Dec. 17, 1872), S. Misc. Doc. 15. DCComsAR, 1879, pp. 7–11. Minutes of the District of Columbia Committee, June 3–7, Dec. 3, 1880, RecHRep, 46A-F8.3. "Improvement of the Sanitary Condition of Washington . . ." 45th Cong., 3rd sess., S. Exec. Doc. 32. "Reclamation of Marshes in the Harbors . . ." 46th Cong., 2nd sess. (Dec. 19, 1879), S. Exec. Doc. 23. "Testimony . . . as to the Condition of the Potomac River Front at Washington" 47th Cong., 1st sess., S. Misc. Doc. 133. "Reclamation of the Marshes of the Cities of Washington and Georgetown," 47th Cong., 1st sess. (Jan. 26, 1882), H. Rept. 83. "Survey of the Potomac River in the Vicinity of Washington," 47th Cong., 1st sess. (Mar. 8, 1882), S. Exec. Doc. 126. Gutheim, *Worthy of the Nation,* pp. 92–95.

24. "Testimony . . . as to the Condition of the Potomac River," 47th Cong., 1st sess., S. Misc. Doc. 133, pp. 33–34. *Evening Star,* Mar. 4, 1882. Washington *Critic,* July 5, 1882.

25. Washington *Critic,* Nov. 13–15, 1882. The progress of the Potomac Flats recla-

mation is best followed in the Potomac River sections of the Chief of Engineer's annual reports. The project's status as it entered its final stages is summarized in CEngsAR, 1897, app. J, p. 1318.

26. For this paragraph and the next: CEngsAR, 1895, app. 1, p. 1209; 1896, app. 1, pp. 1017–31; 1897, app. J, pp. 1315–1319. Ross to Harris, Apr. 3, 1894; Ross to John Heard, Apr. 9, 1894, with copy to Henry Blount of the Board of Trade Parks Committee, DCComsLS, vol. 41. WBT-AR, 1894, p. 27; 1896, p. 40. R. B. Haynes to Allison, Apr. 4, 1896?, Allison Papers, Iowa State Historical Department, old list, box 304. CR:54-2 (Feb. 15, 24, 1897), pp. 1837, 2214. Gutheim, *Worthy of the Nation,* p. 94. Jessica I. Elfenbein, *Civics, Commerce, and Community: The History of the Greater Washington Board of Trade* (Dubuque, Iowa: Kendall-Hunt, 1989), pp. 13–14.

27. Joint Invest. (1874), report, p. xxviii.

28. CR:45-2 (Mar. 20, Apr. 15, 1878), pp. 1925, 2534.

29. CR:45-2 (Mar. 28, 1878), pp. 2112–15.

30. Ibid. Also CR:45-2 (Apr. 15, 1878), pp. 2533–35. D. W. Voorhees to Vinnie Ream Hoxie, June 11, 1878; William T. Sherman to Vinnie Hoxie, June 16, 24, 1878; John Morgan to Vinnie Hoxie, June 10, 1878, Hoxie Papers, Library of Congress, box 2.

31. Robert's classic was inspired by the unruly citizens of San Francisco, not Washington. See introduction to Henry M. Robert, *Robert's Rules of Order,* newly revised (Glenview, Ill.: Scott, Foresman, 1981), pp. xxxvii–xxxix. Eugene V. McAndrews, "William Ludlow: Engineer, Governor, Soldier" (Ph.D. diss., Kansas State U, 1973), esp. pp. 100–108.

32. Resolution on Commissioner Beach, RecHRep, 55A-F6.3. *Evening Star,* July 25, 1901. Beach to Allison, Aug. 7, 1901, Allison Papers, old list, box 341.

33. DCComsAR, 1883, p. 281.

34. *Evening Star,* July 14, 1883. *National Republican,* July 10, 1883.

35. Information on the organization of the Engineer Department comes from the commissioners' *Annual Reports.*

36. "Plans for the Improvement of the Sewerage and the Sanitary Condition of the District of Columbia," 45th Cong., 3rd sess., S. Misc. Doc. 19. "Estimates for Relieving Defects in the Main System of Sewerage in Washington City," 45th Cong, 3rd sess. (Dec. 10, 1878), S. Misc. Doc. 17. CEngsAR, 1889, app. K, p. 985. "Completing the sewerage system in the District of Columbia," 48th Cong., 1st sess., H. Rept. 1115. DCComsAR, 1884, pp. 174–78. Martin K. Gordon, "The Origins of the Anacostia River Improvement Project," *Soundings,* Spring 1987.

37. DCComsAR, 1882, p. 129; 1889, p. 233; 1890, p. 16; 1893, pp. 406–7. Commissioner Webb to Representative Clements, Mar. 3, 1888, DCComsLS, vol. 23. HRApproHrgs, 1894, pp. 37–41; 1896, p. 26; 1897, pp. 40–42. SenApproHrgs, 1903, p. 67.

38. Clay McShane, "Transforming the Use of Urban Space: A Look at the Revolution in Street Pavements, 1880–1924," *Journal of Urban History* 5, no. 3 (1979): 279–307.

39. "Report of the Commissioners on Repaving Pennsylvania Avenue," 44th Cong., 2nd sess. (Dec. 20, 1876), S. Exec. Doc. 8. "Repavement of Pennsylvania Avenue," 45th Cong., 1st sess., H. Exec. Doc. 11. DCComsAR, 1880, p. 206; 1882, p. 90; 1884, p. 166; 1887, p. 531; 1899, p. 25. George W. Tillson, "Asphalt and Asphalt Pavements," *Transactions of the American Society of Civil Engineers* 38 (Dec. 1897): 214–45.

40. DCComsAR, 1880, pp. 206–8; 1883, p. 283; 1899, vol. 1, pp. 25–28. HRApproHrgs, 1903, p. 115. SenApproHrgs, 1904, pp. 63–64. *Evening Star,* May 14, 1900. McShane, "Transforming Urban Space."

41. James R. Severance, "Amzi Lorenzo Barber," *Oberlin Alumni Magazine* 5, no. 9 (1909): 341–46.

42. DCComsAR, 1878, p. 241. "Pavements in the District of Columbia,"

45th Cong., 2nd sess. (Apr. 30, 1878), H. Misc. Doc. 53. "Repair and Improvement of Streets in the District of Columbia," 45th Cong., 2nd sess. (Jan. 19, 1878), S. Misc. Doc. 22.

43. Severance, "Amzi Lorenzo Barber," p. 343. *Evening Star,* Apr. 30, 1891.

44. DCComsAR, 1887, pp. 23–24, 528–32; 1888, p. 29; 1899, vol. 1, pp. 25–28. CR:49-2 (Mar. 2, 1887), p. 2566.

45. DCComsAR, 1890, p. 397; 1893, pp. 403–6; 1895, pp. 14–16, 575–91; 1899, vol. 1, pp. 25–28. HRApproHrgs, 1898, p. 37; 1901, pp. 30–31. "Municipal Matters in the District of Columbia," 55th Cong., 3rd sess. (Dec. 19, 1898), S. Doc. 38, pp. 50–53. Severance, "Amzi Lorenzo Barber" 344–45. Tillson, "Asphalt," 227–28. McShane, "Transforming Urban Space," 282.

46. Jon C. Teaford, *The Unheralded Triumph: City Government in America, 1870–1900* (Baltimore: Johns Hopkins UP, 1984), pp. 133–41.

47. *United States Statutes at Large,* vol. 11, (35th Cong., 2nd sess., Mar. 3, 1859), pp. 435–37.

48. CR:46-2 (May 10, 1880), pp. 3168–73.

49. DCComsAR, 1878, pp. 260–61; 1882, pp. 125–28; 1894, pp. 1016–17. "Additional Water Supply on Capitol Hill," 46th Cong., 2nd sess. (Mar. 6, 1880), S. Misc. Doc. 51. "Memorial of the Citizens of East Washington praying for equal distribution . . . ," 45th Cong., 1st sess. (Jan. 20, 1879), S. Misc. Doc. 37, p. 5. *Report of the Committee on Water and Sewers,* pp. 3–7.

50. "Water Supply to Elevated Portions of Washington," 45th Cong., 3rd sess. (Jan. 22, 1879), S. Misc. Doc. 43. "Defects in the Water Supply . . . ," 45th Cong., 3rd sess. (Jan. 24, 1879), S. Misc. Doc. 48. "Appropriations to Secure Proper Water Supply . . . ," 45th Cong., 3rd sess., S. Misc. Doc. 58.

51. "Water Supply to Residents of Capitol Hill," 45th Cong., 3rd sess. (Jan. 21, 1879), S. Misc. Doc. 41. "Plans and Estimates for Additional Supply of Water," 45th Cong., 3rd sess. (Feb. 25, 1879), S. Misc. Doc. 76. "Supply of Pure Water for the District of Columbia," 46th Cong., 2nd sess. (Dec. 8, 1879), S. Rept. 39. "Waste of Water in the District of Columbia," 46th Cong., 2nd sess. (Mar. 5, 1880), S. Misc. Doc. 52. "Completion of the Dam at Great Falls . . . ," 47th Cong., 1st sess. (Mar. 9, 1882), S. Rept. 242. "Statements before District of Columbia Committee," RecSen, 46A-E6. Aqueduct Tunnel Invest., testimony, pp. 448–49. *Evening Star,* Jan. 14, 1882.

52. Aqueduct Tunnel Invest., report, p. 3; testimony, pp. 2–5.

53. Lydecker to General Wright, Oct. 5, 1882, WashAque, vol. 3.

54. Lydecker to Gen. Wright, July 12, 14, 1883, as well as monthly reports for Nov. 1882–June 1883, in WashAque, vol. 3. Aqueduct Tunnel Invest., esp. testimony, pp. 465–67.

55. Monthly reports for July–September, 1883, WashAque, vol. 3. CEngsAR, 1883, app. QQ, pp. 2080–86. Aqueduct Tunnel Invest., report, pp. 3–5; testimony, pp. 5–18, 459–66.

56. William T. Sherman to Vinnie Hoxie, Nov. 21, 1884, June 9, 1885, Feb. 21, Mar. 31, Apr. 25, 1886; Daniel Voorhees to Vinnie Hoxie, May 9, 1885, box 2, Hoxie Papers. Roland M. Brennan, "Brigadier General Richard L. Hoxie," RCHS, vols. 57–59, pp. 87–95.

57. Symons to Lydecker, Jan. 19, 1885; Minutes of the Board of Engineers, June 24, July 15, 1885, WashAque, vols. 3–4. CEngsAR, 1885, app. UU, pp. 2478–90. "Resolutions on Construction of a New Reservoir in the District of Columbia," 48th Cong., 2nd sess. (Dec. 16, 1884, Jan., 15, 1885), S. Misc. Docs. 17, 28. *Washington Post,* Jan. 28, 1886.

58. Statement of Meigs to Senate District Committee, Jan. 31, 1879, in RecSen, 46A-E6. Lydecker to Wright, Oct. 5, 1882; Report for Jan. 1884, WashAque, vol. 3. CEngsAR, 1885, app. UU, pp. 2483–84. "Report on completion of the tunnel between two res-

ervoirs in the District of Columbia," 51st Cong., 1st sess. (June 12, 1890), S. Exec. Doc. 151.

59. Report for April 1884 and May 1885; Symons to Beckwith and Quackenbush, May 15, July 2, 10, Dec. 12, 15, 22, 1884, Jan. 10, 15, 1885; Symons to Lydecker, Jan. 7, 1885; Lydecker to General Newton, June 29, 1885; Lydecker to the chief of engineers, Sept. 7, 1886, July 13, 1887; Lydecker to George Coryell, Feb. 3, 1887, WashAque, vols. 3–5. Aqueduct Tunnel Invest., testimony, pp. 55–64, 123–95 *passim,* 374–75. "Liabilities of Certain Contractors . . . ," 51st Cong., 1st sess. (Mar. 18, 1890), H. Exec. Doc. 286. *Washington Post,* Oct. 2, 1888. Washington *Critic,* Sept. 29, 1888.

60. CEngsAR, 1885, app. UU, pp. 2470–73. Aqueduct Tunnel Invest., testimony, pp. 44–54, 367–70. Crosby Noyes to Vinnie Ream Hoxie, May 30, 1885, Apr. 13, 1886, Nov. 24, 1888, Hoxie Papers, box 2. Lydecker to General Newton, with attached memos, July 9, 1885, Apr. 21, 1886; Lydecker to Representative W. L. Wilson, May 11, 1886, WashAque, vol. 4. *Evening Star,* July 26, 1886. *Washington Post,* Jan. 28–29, 1886.

61. Lydecker to Newton, Apr. 21, 1886, WashAque, vol. 4; "Memorandum," Feb. 1887, p. 22; Lydecker to the chief of engineers, Mar. 29, 1888, WashAque, vol. 5. *Washington Post,* Jan. 29, 1886. CEngsAR, 1887, app. VV, pp. 2537–40. "Appropriation for the District of Columbia Water Supply," 49th Cong., 1st sess. (Jan. 4, 1886), H. Exec. Doc. 39. "Estimate of Appropriation for Increasing the Water Supply of Washington, D.C.," 49th Cong., 2nd sess. (Feb. 1, 1887), H. Exec. Doc. 123.

62. Townsend to Beckwith and Quackenbush, July 2, 12, 1888; Townsend to Lydecker, July 20, 1888; Lydecker to the chief of engineers, Oct. 2, 15, 1888, WashAque, vol. 5. *Washington Post,* Oct. 2–4, 1888. Washington *Critic,* Sept. 25-Oct. 2, 1888.

63. Aqueduct Tunnel Invest., esp. report, pp. 10–11. Aqueduct Tunnel Investigation papers, RecSen, 50A-F5. "Report on completion of the tunnel between two reservoirs in the District of Columbia," 51st Cong., 1st sess., S. Exec. Doc. 151. *Evening Star,* Jan. 11, 1892.

64. *Evening Star,* Jan. 29, 30, 1892.

65. HRApproHrgs, 1896, pp. 106 ff.; 1899, pp. 134, 156. CEngsAR, 1898, app. BBB, pp. 3658–59. WBT-AR, 1898, pp. 11, 109–12. "Resolution on Construction of the Washington Aqueduct," 52nd Cong., 1st sess. (Mar. 4, 1892), S. Rept. 313. "Increasing the Water Supply of Washington, D.C.," 54th Cong., 1st sess., H. Doc. 166. W. Thompson to Hoxie, Dec. 6, 1901, Hoxie Papers, box 11, with accompanying clippings. *Washington Post,* Feb. 3, 5, 1898. *Evening Star,* Jan. 4, 1902.

66. *Washington Post,* Oct. 2–4, 1888, Dec. 12, 1891. Washington *Critic,* Oct. 2, 1888.

67. Washington *Critic,* Mar. 8, 1886. *Sunday Chronicle,* Dec. 25, 1887. *National Republican,* Dec. 13, 1886. *Washington Sentinel,* Dec. 31, 1887. *Report of the Committee on Water and Sewers,* pp. 8–9. Todd Shallat quotes a snide contemporary about dandyism in the Corps in "Structures in the Stream," p. 306.

68. *Sunday Chronicle,* Dec. 25, 1887. *Washington Sentinel,* Dec. 31, 1887, Feb. 4, Mar. 10, 1888. Washington *Critic,* Feb. 3, 1888.

69. Washington *Critic,* Jan. 26–27, 1888. *Washington Sentinel,* Feb. 4, 23, 1888. McAndrews, "William Ludlow," pp. 107–8.

70. OpinCorpCoun, vol. 3, pp. 712–25. Commissioner Douglass to Sen. Ingalls, July 22, 1890, RecSen, 51A-F8. Washington *Critic,* Jan. 17, 31, Feb. 1, Sept. 7, 1888.

71. Commissioner Wheatley to Representative Hemphill, Jan. 16, 1888; Commissioner Webb to Sen. Ingalls, Feb. 3, 1888; Webb to Representative Hemphill, Feb. 15, Mar. 5, 1888, DCComsLS, vols. 22–23.

72. CR:51-1 (Sept. 25, 1890), p. 10419.

73. Shallat, "Structures in the Stream," pp. 296–98.

74. "Report of the Engineer Commissioner on removing electric wires from the air or surface . . . ," 50th Cong., 2nd sess. (Dec. 6, 1888), S. Misc. Doc. 15. "Report of the

Electrical Commission to consider the location, arrangement, and operation of electrical wires," 52nd Cong., 1st sess. (Oct. 26, 1891), H. Exec. Doc. 15.

75. The Hering plan is *Report on the System of Sewerage in the District of Columbia,* 51st Cong., 2nd sess., H. Exec. Doc. 445. Also, "Continuing the system of trunk sewers . . . ," 53rd Cong., 2nd sess. (July 20, 1894), S. Rept. 623. DCComsAR, 1893, p. 328; 1896, pp. 22–23, 659–61; 1897, vol. 1, p. 24.

76. DCComsAR, 1895, pp. 10–12, 1306–52; 1896, pp. 12–13; 1901, vol. 3, p. 8. WBT-AR, 1898, pp. 60 ff.; 1901, pp. 24, 76–78. HRApproHrgs, 1902, Supplemental Rept. "Bacteriological Examination of the Water Supply of the District of Columbia," 55th Cong., 2nd sess. (Mar. 28, 1898), S. Doc. 211. Washington Medical Society, "Water Supply and Sewerage Disposal in the District of Columbia," 55th Cong., 2nd sess. (Mar. 10, 1898), S. Doc. 183. "Filtration of the Water Supply . . . ," 55th Cong., 2nd sess. (Jan. 28, 1898), S. Doc. 94. Walker, ed., *Purification of the Washington Water Supply,* p. 54. John S. Billings, "Municipal Sanitation in Washington and Baltimore," *Forum* 15 (Aug. 1893), 727–37. *Evening Star,* Feb. 13, 1897.

77. CEngsAR, 1886, app. SS, pp. 2021–43; 1894, app. BBB, pp. 3203–11; 1896, app. BBB, p. 3917; 1898, app. BBB, p. 3642. DCComsAR, 1897, vol. 2, pp. 183–94. Walker, *Purification,* pp. 3–5, 59.

78. WBT-AR, 1898, pp. 60 ff. HRApproHrgs, 1902, Supplemental Rept. Walker, *Purification of the Washington Water Supply,* esp. pp. 24–51, 71–72.

79. BWT-AR, 1898, pp. 60 ff. Walker, *Purification of the Washington Water Supply,* pp. 24–51. HRApproHrgs, 1902, Supplemental Rept.

80. HRApproHrgs, 1902, pp. 155–57. CEngsAR, 1898, app. BBB, pp. 3642–50. Walker, *Purification of the Washington Water Supply,* p. 6.

81. Walker, *Purification of the Washington Water Supply,* pp. 6, 58–69.

82. Ibid., pp. 48, 157–58, 195. WBT-AR, 1897, pp. 65–68; 1900, pp. 8–11; 1901, pp. 19–20. Charles Moore, *Autobiography* (photostat manuscript in Moore Collection, Fine Arts Commission Papers, RG 66), pp. 58–59.

83. CEngsAR, 1901, app. CCC, p. 3681. HRApproHrgs, 1903, p. 310.

84. See Commissioner Truesdell's remarks to the Board of Trade Shad Bake, *Evening Star,* May 13, 1895.

Chapter 7 An Unsectional Public

1. CR:51-1 (Sept. 17, 1890), pp. 10119–23. Constance M. Green, *Washington: Capital City, 1879–1950* (Princeton: Princeton UP, 1963), pp. 25–28. James H. Keeley, *Democracy or Despotism in the American Capital* (Riverdale, Md.: privately printed, 1939), pp. 214–16.

2. CR:53-2 (Mar. 9, 1894), pp. 2792–93. "To establish a representative form of government for the District of Columbia," 57th Cong., 1st sess., S. Rept. 1951.

3. Ross to Representative Heard, RecHRep, 53A-F7.7. CR:51-1 (Sept. 17, 1890), pp. 10123. Green also quotes this passage in *Capital City,* p. 26.

4. CR:53-3 (Feb. 2, 1895), p. 1671.

5. *Washington Bee,* Jan. 13, Mar. 10, 1883.

6. Raymond Mohl, *The New City* (Arlington Heights, Ill.: Harlan Davidson, 1985), p. 20.

7. DCComsMins, vol. 11, Jan. 19, 1897. *Washington Bee,* June 4, 1887. *Evening Star,* Dec. 18, 19, 22, 1888. "Prohibiting building along certain alleys," 52nd Cong., 1st sess., H. Rept. 523. CR:52-1 (July 16, 18, 1892), pp. 6274, 6347–48. Petition of Bankers and Real Estate Men to Senator Allison, Feb. 6, 1893, RecSen, 52A-F7. James Borchert, *Alley Life in Washington* (Urbana: U of Illinois P, 1980), pp. 40–42. James Borchert, "Builders and Owners of Alley Dwellings in Washington, D.C., 1877–1892," RCHS, 50

(1980), 345–58. Constance M. Green, *The Secret City* (Princeton: Princeton UP, 1967), chap. 7.

8. *Washington Bee,* June 21, 1884, Mar. 28, 1891, Feb. 4, 1893, Dec. 11, 1897, Jan. 29, May 7, 1898. *People's Advocate,* July 21, 1883.

9. *Evening Star,* May 13, 1895. Jessica I. Elfenbein, *Civics, Commerce, and Community: The History of the Greater Washington Board of Trade* (Dubuque, Iowa: Kendall-Hunt, 1989), p. 6.

10. *Evening Star,* July 14, 1883.

11. Ibid. *National Republican,* July 16–17, 1883.

12. *Evening Star,* Oct. 23, 1893, Feb. 11, 1902. *Washington Post,* Feb. 24, 1902. William V. Cox, ed., *The Centennial Celebration of the Establishment of the Seat of Government in the District of Columbia* (Washington, D.C.: GPO, 1901). pp. 69–70.

13. WBT-AR, 1897, p. 18; 1899, p. 31; 1900, p. 41. Theodore W. Noyes, "Speech to the Board of Trade," Feb. 24, 1898, typescript in Suter/Noyes papers, Historical Society of Washington. Green, *Capital City,* pp. 25–28.

14. Citizens' Representative Committee, *Proposal to Improve the Present Form of Government for the District of Columbia,* pamphlet dated Feb. 14, 1888, in Suter/Noyes Papers. Jesse B. Wilson, *Minority Report of the Special Committee of Thirteen* (Washington, D.C.: Gibson Brothers, 1888). *Evening Star,* Dec. 13, 19, 1888; Jan. 1, 1889. "Memorial to Congress of the Joint Executive Committees of the Citizens Associations," 53rd Cong., 2nd sess., S. Misc. Doc. 67, pp. 1, 9.

15. Samuel P. Hays, *American Political History as Social Analysis: Essays by Samuel P. Hays* (Knoxville: U of Tennessee P, 1980), p. 343. Jon C. Teaford, *The Unheralded Triumph: City Government in America, 1870–1900* (Baltimore: Johns Hopkins UP, 1984), chap. 2. Martin J. Schiesl, *The Politics of Efficiency: Municipal Administration and Reform in America, 1800–1920* (Berkeley: U of California P, 1977).

16. *Evening Star,* July 14, 1883.

17. "Memorial to Congress of the Joint Executive Committees of the Citizens Associations," 53rd Cong., 2nd sess. (Feb. 1 1894), S. Misc. Doc. 67, p. 9.

18. *Suburban Citizen,* Apr. 1, 1893. Memorial of the South Washington Improvement and Protective Association, Feb. 12, 1881, RecHRep, 46A-H7.1.

19. "Memorial of the Brightwood Avenue Citizens Association relative to Sewers," 54th Cong., 1st sess., S. Doc. 234. "Memorial to Congress of the Joint Executive Committees of the Citizens Associations," 53rd Cong., 2nd sess. (Feb. 1 1894), S. Misc. Doc. 67. DCComsAR, 1886, p. 29; 1888, pp. 8, 12; 1891, p. 313.

20. For example, RecSen, 49A-H6 and J12, or RecHRep, 50A-H2.8. DCComsAR, 1886, p. 28; 1887, p. 21.

21. "Proper Site for a Union Station in the City of Washington," 47th Cong., 1st sess. (Dec. 13, 1881), S. Misc. Doc. 15. South Washington Improvement Association, pamphlet concerning railroad routes, c. 1882, in RecSen, 47A-E6. Hearings and pamphlets on the Baltimore and Ohio Railroad, Apr.–June, 1894, in RecHRep, 53A-F7.4. *National Republican,* Nov. 19, 1886. *Washington Post,* Mar. 8, 1887. Washington *Critic,* Feb. 9, 1888.

22. *Suburban Citizen,* Jan. 25, Feb. 15, 1902. *Evening Star,* Jan. 14, 1902. DCComsMins, vol. 20, Jan. 23, 1902. Walter F. Dodd, *The Government of the District of Columbia* (Washington, D.C.: John Byrne, 1909), p. 267.

23. Commissioner Edmonds to S. C. Clarke, Mar. 1884, DCComsLS, vol. 15, no. 21950. "Tax Collections, Receipts, and Disbursements in Various Departments of the District of Columbia, 1875–1884," 48th Cong., 2nd sess., S. Misc. Doc. 104. DCComsAR, 1885, pp. 165–69; 1886, p. 29.

24. *Washington Post,* Mar. 2–4, 1887. DCComsAR, 1887, pp. 22–23; 1888, p. 237.

25. RecHRep, 51A-F3.2, esp. Parker to Representative McComas, May 7, 1890; Evan Tucker to McComas, Oct. 31, 1890; and Warner et al. to McComas, Dec. 13, 1890.

26. For examples, see RecSen, 49A-H6, 49A-J12, and 54A-F8, box 26. "Memorial of owners of property on L Street . . . ," 53rd Cong., 2nd sess. (Apr. 23, 1894), S. Misc. Doc. 161. DCComsMins, vol. 1B, Feb. 8–12, 1892.

27. Washington *Critic,* Jan. 4, 1888. *Evening Star,* Dec. 13, 19, 1888, Jan. 1, 1889, Jan. 10, 1902.

28. *Evening Star,* Dec. 19, 1888.

29. *Washington Post,* Apr. 18, 1890. WBT-AR, 1890, p. 7. Also quoted in Elfenbein, *Civics, Commerce, and Community,* pp. 2–3.

30. This paragraph owes much to comments in a personal letter from Jessica I. Elfenbein. Blaine Brownell, *The Urban Ethos in the South, 1920–1930* (Baton Rouge: Louisiana State UP, 1975), pp. xvi-xvii. Carl V. Harris, *Political Power in Birmingham, 1871–1921* (Knoxville: U of Tennessee P, 1977), chap. 3. Carl Abbott, "Dimensions of Regional Change in Washington, D.C." *American Historical Review* 95, no. 5 (1990): 1378–80.

31. *Washington Post,* Dec. 17. 1896. Dodd, *Government of the District of Columbia,* pp. 268–70. James B. Crooks, *Politics and Progress: The Rise of Urban Progressivism in Baltimore, 1895–1911* (Baton Rouge: Louisiana State UP, 1968).

32. WBT-AR, 1899, p. 31. *Washington Post,* Apr. 18, 1890. Elfenbein, *Civics, Commerce, and Community,* p. 1. Benjamin McKelvey, "Seventy-Fifth Anniversary Speech," mimeograph in the Board of Trade Papers, George Washington University. Green, *Capital City,* pp. 29–31. On Wilkins, see *National Cyclopedia of American Biography,* vol. 6, p. 133.

33. WBT-AR, 1891, pp. 16–17; 1894, p. 61; 1898, secretary's report; 1899, pp. 6, 33–34. Minutes of the Board of Directors, esp. Nov. 17, 1899, Feb. 28, 1900, Board of Trade Papers. Elfenbein, *Civics, Commerce, and Community,* p. 5.

34. WBT-AT, 1894, pp. 5–7; 1895, p. 6; 1897, p. 44; 1898, pp. 6–7; 1900, p. 41.

35. Parker quoted in Elfenbein, *Civics, Commerce, and Community,* p. 2, also pp. 4–5. WBT-AR, 1893, pp. 31–35; 1894, pp. 54–58; 1898, pp. 6–7; 1900, p. 61. "Investigation of Tax Assessments in the District of Columbia," 52nd Cong., 1st sess. (May 24, 1892), H. Rept. 1469. DCComsAR, 1893, pp. 15–17; 1894, pp. 35–36. DCComsMins, vol. 8, Nov. 9, 1895.

36. "Supplement to act authorizing construction of the Baltimore and Potomac Railroad in the District of Columbia," 51st Cong., 1st sess. (July 10, 1890), S. Rept. 1480. "Conference Committee on the Baltimore and Potomac Railroad Company," 51st Cong., 1st sess., S. Misc. Doc. 31. CR:51-2 (Jan. 5, 1891), pp. 907–11. Charles Moore, *Autobiography* (photostat manuscript in Moore Collection, Fine Arts Commission Papers, RG 66), p. 41. Charles Moore, ed., "Federal and Local Legislation on Canals and Steam Railroads, 1802–1903," 57th Cong., 2nd sess., S. Doc. 220, pp. 114–15.

37. Moore, *Autobiography,* p. 41. Board of Trade report on railroad routes, submitted, Mar. 10, 1890, in RecSen, 51A-F8. WBT-AR, 1890, pp. 10–11; 1891, p. 19. *Evening Star,* Apr. 11, 18, 22, May 3, 1890. *Washington Post,* May 11, 1890.

38. WBT-AR, 1899, pp. 99–101.

39. WBT-AR, 1894, p. 15; 1900, pp. 44–45. Washington Board of Trade, *A Handbook of Useful Information Concerning the City of Washington and the Relations Existing between the General Government and the District of Columbia* (Washington, D.C., 1895). *Evening Star,* May 4, 1895; Jan. 23, 1902.

40. *The Nation,* Mar. 30, 1871. WBT-AR, 1900, p. 37.

41. WBT-AR, 1890, p. 27; 1894, p. 62; 1897, pp. 38–41. Elfenbein, *Civics, Commerce, and Community,* pp. 2, 7. Green, *Capital City,* p. 31.

42. WBT-AR, 1891, p. 27; 1893, p. 6; 1896, pp. 19, 37; 1897, pp. 38–41; 1900, p. 63. Elfenbein, *Civics, Commerce, and Community,* pp. 7–11.

43. Harris, *Political Power in Birmingham,* p. 41. Brownell, *Urban Ethos,* pp. 47–60.

44. Such a conclusion seems to be the present state of the academic debate over the relation between municipal structure and urban power. Hays, *American Political History*, pp. 214–20, 337–43. James Weinstein, *The Corporate Ideal in the Liberal State* (Boston: Beacon, 1968), chap. 4. Schiesl, *Politics of Efficiency*, chap. 7. Kenneth Fox, *Better City Government* (Philadelphia: Temple UP, 1977), pp. 86–89. Bradley Rice, *Progressive Cities: The Commission Government Movement in America, 1901–1920* (Austin: U of Texas P, 1977). David C. Hammack, *Power and Society: Greater New York at the Turn of the Century* (New York: Columbia UP, 1987). Christine M. Rosen, "Business, Democracy, and Progressive Reform in the Redevelopment of Baltimore after the Great Fire of 1904," *Business History Review* 63 (Summer 1989): 283–328.

45. WBT-AR, 1898, pp. 6–7; 1899, p. 7.

46. *Evening Star*, Oct. 17–18, 1894; Jan. 10–11, 1902; Jan. 26, 1907. Allen B. Slauson, ed., *A History of the City of Washington: Its Men and Institutions,* (Washington, D.C.: Washington Post, 1903), pp. 266–67, 303–4, 423–24.

47. Information on officers, directors, and committee chairmen of the Board of Trade is from Board of Trade, *Annual Report*, Jan. 10, 1894. Participants in the Citizens Joint Executive are listed at the end of "Memorial of the Joint Executive Committees of the Citizens Associations," 53rd Cong., 2nd sess. (Feb. 1, 1894), S. Misc. Doc. 67. I managed to trace seventy of the seventy-one signers of this document. Apparently, no official index of District assessments for this period survives, so I had to rely on information contained in lists of large property holders published by the *Evening Star*, Oct. 27–Nov. 4, 1893. The paper listed only holders of property worth more than $10,000, which means that table 7.2 compares only the large property holders in each group. Biographical information was compiled from city directories, contemporary accounts, memoirs, profiles in the *Records of the Columbia Historical Society*, the local histories and biographical dictionaries cited in the Note on Sources, and newspaper obituaries. Some members could be traced with confidence in the 1880 and especially the 1900 censuses, the latter being the first with a detailed index.

48. Abbott, "Dimensions of Change," 1378–80.

49. *National Cyclopedia of American Biography*, vol. 13, p. 364; vol. 28, p. 213. Slauson, *History of Washington*, pp. 193–94.

50. *National Cyclopedia of American Biography*, vol. 1, p. 267; vol. 11, p. 570; vol. 14, p. 319; vol. 25, p. 44. Slauson, *History of Washington*, pp. 229–30, 256, 295–96, 424. Green, *Capital City*, pp. 31–32.

51. *National Cyclopedia of American Biography*, vol. 21, p. 33; vol. 32, p. 338. Slauson, *History of Washington*, pp. 192–93.

52. *Washington Post*, Sept. 24–25, 1901. DCComsMins, vol. 10, Aug. 26, Sept. 18, 1896. HRApproHrgs, 1898, p. 37.

53. As long as the federal government continued to cover a substantial portion of municipal expenses, that is. If District taxpayers had suddenly faced the full cost of municipal works and services, the "growth"/"no-growth" split discerned by Terrence J. McDonald in San Francisco might quickly have emerged. Still, even in "no-growth" San Francisco, neighborhood-based "improvement clubs" formed to pressure the Board of Supervisors for new services. Significantly, these clubs were strongest in outlying areas that benefited least from the wave of capital expenditures undertaken by that city in the decade after the Civil War. Terrence J. McDonald, *The Parameters of Urban Fiscal Policy* (Berkeley: U of California P, 1986), pp. 177 ff.

54. Mohl, *New City*, p. 20.

55. WBT-AR, 1899, p. 31.

56. WBT-AR, 1897, pp. 38–41. Minutes of the general meeting of June 10, 1902, Board of Trade Papers.

57. WBT-AR, 1899, p. 31.

58. WBT-AR, 1894, p. 7; 1896, p. 34. Warner also quoted in Elfenbein, *Civics, Commerce, and Community*, p. 8.

59. WBT-AR, 1900, p. 64.

60. WBT-AR, 1894, pp. 22–24; 1896, pp. 15, 33–36; 1898, pp. 44–47. Elfenbein, *Civics, Commerce, and Community*, p. 9.

61. Roger D. Simon, *The City-Building Process: Housing and Services in New Milwaukee Neighborhoods, 1880–1910* (Philadelphia: American Philosophical Society, 1978), p. 12. For a comparison of the employment structure and the manufacturing sector in Washington and cities of similar size in 1880, see Alan Lessoff, "The Federal Government and the National Capital: Washington, 1861–1902" (Ph.D. diss., Johns Hopkins U, 1990), p. 509.

62. Louis Galambos and Joseph Pratt, *The Rise of the Corporate Commonwealth: United States Business and Public Policy in the Twentieth Century* (New York: Basic Books, 1988), pp. 53–56. Crooks, *Politics and Progress*, pp. 108–21. Dodd, *Government of the District of Columbia*, pp. 254–55.

63. Mary Dudley McLean, "The Gas Company and Congress" (Master's thesis, George Washington U, 1985), p. 50. Wilhelmus Bogart Bryan, *A History of the National Capital* (Washington, D.C.: Macmillan, 1916), vol. 2, pp. 294–302. Kathryn A. Jacob, "High Society in Washington during the Gilded Age" (Ph.D. diss., Johns Hopkins U, 1987), pp. 235–39.

64. *Evening Star,* June 6, 1883. "Inquiry into the expediency of . . . $1 per 1,000 cubic feet," 49th Cong., 1st sess. (July 7, 1886), S. Rept. 1460, esp. final report, and testimony, pp. 73–81. R. G. Havens to the Senate District Committee, Apr. 6, 1894, RecHRep, 53A-F7.2. "Fixing the maximum price . . . for gas sold by the Washington Gaslight Company . . . ," 53rd Cong., 3rd sess. (Mar. 2, 1895), S. Rept. 1038, p. 13.

65. "Inquiry into the expediency of . . ." 49th Cong., 1st sess., S. Rept. 1460, testimony, p. 13. Board of Trade Special Committee report, "Gas and Electric Light Rates," Oct. 25, 1895, RecSen, 54A-F8, box 27. East Washington Citizens Association, "Argument in Favor of Purchase by the Government . . . ," 53rd Cong., 2nd sess., S. Misc. Doc. 91. "Fixing the maximum price to be charged for gas," 53rd Cong., 3rd sess. (Mar. 2, 1895), S. Rept. 1038, minority report by Gallinger et al. Ross to Senator Harris, Apr. 30, 1894, RecSen, 53A-F7, box 25. Ross to Senator Harris, Jan. 16, 1895, RecHRep, 53A-F7.2. Crooks, *Politics and Progress*, p. 112.

66. Commissioner Truesdell's comments in "National Gas and Electric Light, Heat, and Power Company," minority report, 53rd Cong., 3rd sess. (Feb. 21, 1895), H. Rept. 1904.

67. "National Gas and Electric Light, Heat, and Power Company," minority report, 53rd Cong., 3rd sess. (Feb. 21, 1895), H. Rept. 1904. Board of Trade Special Committee report, RecSen, 54A-F8, box 27. "Incorporation of Gas Light Companies in the District of Columbia," 46th Cong., 2nd sess. (Apr. 9, 1880), H. Rept. 1108. "Incorporation of the United States Gas and Fuel Company," 47th Cong., 2nd sess. (Feb. 3, 1883), H. Rept. 1928.

68. For the Sands dispute, see chapter 5, this volume. CR:54-1 (May 18, 1896), pp. 5348–55.

69. *Evening Star,* Aug. 3, 1886, Apr. 22–23, 1896. *Sunday Chronicle,* Jan. 22, 1888. S. B. Elkins to McMillan, Apr. 20, 1894, political collection, McMillan Papers. Charles Moore, *Makers of Washington* (manuscript in Moore papers, Library of Congress, box 22), p. 105. McLean, "The Gas Company and Congress," chaps. 2, 3.

70. Thomas P. Hughes, *Networks of Power: Electrification in Western Society, 1880–1930* (Baltimore: Johns Hopkins UP, 1983), chap. 8. Frederic Howe, *Confessions of a Reformer* (Chicago: Quadrangle, 1967), chap. 12.

71. "Electricity as a Motive Power for Streetcars," 50th Cong., 1st sess., S. Misc.

Doc. 84. "Removing Electric Wires from the Air or the Surface of Streets . . . ," 50th Cong., 2nd sess., S. Misc. Doc. 15. "Report of the Electrical Commission . . . ," 52nd Cong., 1st sess., H. Exec. Doc. 15.

72. "Overhead and Underground Wires in the District of Columbia," 54th Cong., 1st sess. (Mar. 4, 1896), S. Doc. 14. "Hearings on Electric Lighting in the District of Columbia," 54th Cong., 2nd sess., S. Doc. 96. Statements of O. T. Crosby for the Potomac Electric Power Company and Col. A. T. Britton for the United States Electric Lighting Company, Jan. 1897, pamphlets in Public Utilities Folder, Historical Society of Washington. Commissioner Ross to Representative Babcock, Mar. 3, 1896, with accompanying letters and documents, RecHRep, 54A-F7.1. O. T. Crosby to District commissioners, Feb. 19, 1896, RecSen, 54A-F8, box 27. O. T. Crosby to Representative Grout, Jan. 16, 1897, RecHRep, 54A-F3.2. *Washington Post,* Apr. 3, 4, 15, 1896. *Evening Star,* Feb. 16, 18, Mar. 12, 1897.

73. Newlands to the District commissioners, etc., June 21, 1894, RecSen, 53A-F7, box 26. Documents regarding reciprocal transfer agreements, RecHRep, 53A-F7.1. Pamphlet of the Metropolitan Railroad Company, dated May 11, 1896, in RecHRep, 54A-F3.2. "Answer of the Rock Creek Railway to the Inquiry of the Commissioners," pamphlet dated Jan. 23, 1895, esp. p. 5. Copy in minutes of the Capital Traction Company, Capital Traction Papers. "Authorizing the Metropolitan Railroad Company to change its motive power," 53rd Cong., 2nd sess. (June 15 1894), S. Rept. 1199. On public opposition to overhead wires, John P. McKay, *Tramways and Trolleys: The Rise of Urban Mass Transport in Europe* (Princeton: Princeton UP, 1976), chap. 3.

74. Washington *Critic,* Feb. 11, 1888. David M. Newbold to Representative Babcock, Feb. 24, 1896, RecHRep, 54A-F7.1. Leroy O. King, Jr., *One Hundred Years of Capital Traction* (n.p.: Taylor Publishing, 1972), pp. 13–47. John W. Boettjer, "Street Railways in the District of Columbia" (Master's thesis, George Washington U, 1963), pp. 55–66. Clay McShane, *Technology and Reform: Street Railways and the Growth of Milwaukee* (Madison: State Historical Society of Wisconsin, 1974), p. 20. Kenneth T. Jackson, *Crabgrass Frontier: The Suburbanization of the United States* (New York: Oxford UP, 1985), pp. 118–24.

75. HRApproHrgs, 1896, p. 47. Commissioner Truesdell to Senator Harris, June 8, 1894, RecHRep, 53A-F7.4. Commissioner Ross to Senator Harris, June 4, 1894, DCComsLS, vol. 41. *Evening Star,* Oct. 26, 1893.

76. HRApproHrgs, 1902, esp. pp. 144–48. DCComsMins, vol. 10, Oct. 30, Nov. 2, 1896.

77. "Incorporating the District of Columbia Suburban Railway," 52nd Cong., 1st sess., S. Rept. 637.

78. George Harries to Representative Cannon, June 24, 1902, RecHRep, HR 57A-F1.2. SenApproHrgs, 1901, pp. 19, 124–27. Harries to Captain Beach, Oct. 16, 1900, DCComsLS, vol. 59; Tindall to Harries, May 20, 1902, DCComsLS, vol. 62. "To amend charters . . . ," 55th Cong., 2nd Ses, H. Repts. 705, 708. "Consolidation of Certain Street Railways," 56th Cong., 1st sess., S. Rept. 1398. James to William McMillan, Apr. 7, 1900, McMillan Papers, personal collection. *Evening Star,* May 8, 1899, May 18, 22, 1900. *Washington Post,* Jan. 23, 1902. Boettjer, "Street Railways," chap. 4. John H. White, Jr. "Public Transport in Washington before the Great Consolidation of 1902," RCHS, 1966–68, pp. 216–30.

79. Frederic Howe, *The City: The Hope of Democracy* (1905; Seattle: U of Washington P, 1967).

Chapter 8 Promotional Government and Urban Planning

Epigraph: Frederick Law Olmsted, Jr., to E. D. Shaw, managing editor, *Washington Times,* Mar. 16, 1906. Copy in box 7, Charles Moore Papers, Library of Congress.

1. Olmsted quoted in Thomas Bender, *Toward an Urban Vision* (Baltimore: Johns Hopkins UP, 1982), p. 176. *Evening Star,* Apr. 29, 1890.

2. "Public Park in the District of Columbia," 51st Cong., 1st sess., H. Rept. 870. "Assessed Valuation of Property within the Bounds of Rock Creek Park," 51st Cong., 1st sess., H. Misc. Doc. 184. CR:51-1 (Mar. 24, 1890), pp. 2582–83. Stewart quoted in William Lilley, III, "The Early Career of Francis G. Newlands, 1848–1897" (Ph.D. diss., Yale U, 1965), p. 209. Eugene P. Moehring, *Public Works and the Patterns of Urban Real Estate Growth in Manhattan, 1835–1894* (New York: Arno, 1981), chap. 9.

3. "Conference Report on Bill to Establish a Park . . . ," 51st Cong., 1st sess., S. Misc. Doc. 242.

4. *Evening Star,* Jan. 12, 1892. Papers of the Rock Creek Park Commission and Board of Control, RG42, entries 238–40, esp. General Wilson to Representative Babcock, June 29, 1898; and R. Ross Perry to President McKinley, June 27, 1898. *History of the Chevy Chase Company,* p. 50, typescript in Francis G. Newlands Papers, Manuscripts and Archives, Yale U library, box 75.

5. *National Republican,* July 20, 1883. *Sunday Chronicle,* May 31, 1885. "Memorial of the Brightwood Avenue Citizens' Association . . . ," 54th Cong., 1st sess., S. Doc. 234, p. 4.

6. Andrew F. Hilyer to Representative Grout, in papers on Sherman Avenue Extension, RecHRep, 51A-F3.2. "Incorporating the District of Columbia Suburban Railway," 52nd Cong., 1st sess., S. Rept. 637.

7. *History of the Chevy Chase Company,* pp. 1–4, Newlands Papers.

8. Wilhelmus B. Bryan, *A History of the National Capital* (New York: Macmillan, 1916), vol. 2., pp. 370–71. Thomas J. Cantwell, "Anacostia: Strength in Adversity," RCHS, 1973–74, pp. 330–70. WBT-AR, 1898, pp. 60–69. Constance M. Green, *The Secret City* (Princeton: Princeton UP, 1967), p. 83. Frederick Gutheim, consultant, *Worthy of the Nation: The History of Planning for the National Capital* (Washington, D.C.: Smithsonian Institution P, 1977), p. 108. Edwin S. Mills and Bruce W. Hamilton, *Urban Economics,* 2nd ed. (Glenview, Ill.: Scott, Foresman, 1984), pp. 206–7.

9. Bryan, *History of the National Capital,* vol. 2, p. 370. George W. McDaniel and John N. Pearce, ed., *Images of Brookland: History and Architecture of a Washington Suburb* (Washington, D.C.: George Washington U Center for Washington Area Studies, 1982). Gutheim, *Worthy of the Nation,* pp. 57, 106–8.

10. *History of the Chevy Chase Company,* box 75, Newlands Papers, pp. 50–57. DCComsAR, 1887, pp. 39–46. "Plans for bridge on Connecticut Avenue Extended across Rock Creek," 55th Cong., 2nd sess. (Jan. 25, 1898), S. Doc. 96; "Designs and estimates for bridge across Rock Creek," 55th Cong., 2nd sess., H. Doc. 163. Donald B. Myer, *Bridges and the City of Washington* (Washington, D.C.: U.S. Commission of Fine Arts, 1974), pp. 65–69. Sara White Hamilton, Louise M. Madden, et al., *Historic Preservation Study of Cleveland Park,* rev. ed. (Washington, D.C.: American U Seminar in Historic Preservation, 1977). Roderick French, "Chevy Chase Village in the Context of the National Suburban Movement, 1870–1900" RCHS, 1973–74, pp. 300–329.

11. DCComsAR, 1889, p. 258. Gutheim, *Worthy of the Nation,* p. 106.

12. DCComsAR, 1889, p. 39. French, "Chevy Chase Village," 311. Gutheim, *Worthy of the Nation,* p. 106.

13. "Widening the extension of Fourteenth Street," 47th Cong., 1st sess. (Apr. 26, 1882), S. Misc. Doc. 87. Petitions of Chapin Brown and A. L. Barber Co., in documents on Senate amendments to District appropriations bill for fiscal 1892, RecHRep, 51A-F3.2. *Evening Star,* May 19, 1883. Ronald M. Johnson, "LeDroit Park: Premier Black Community," in Kathryn Schneider Smith, ed., *Washington at Home: An Illustrated History of Neighborhoods in the Nation's Capital* (Northridge, Calif.: Windsor, 1988), 139–47.

14. Melissa McLoud, "Craftsmen and Entrepreneurs: Washington, D.C.'s Late

Nineteenth-Century Builders" (Ph.D. diss., George Washington U, 1988), perceives a trend from craft to industrial organization in Washington's building industry and attributes it to the opening of the suburbs. The practices of subdividers and speculative builders are described in Roger D. Simon, *The City-Building Process: Housing and Services in New Milwaukee Neighborhoods, 1880–1910* (Philadelphia: American Philosophical Society, 1978). Michael J. Doucet, "Urban Land Development in Nineteenth-Century North America: Themes in the Literature," *Journal of Urban History* 8, no. 3 (1982): 299–342. Sam Bass Warner, Jr. *Streetcar Suburbs: The Process of Growth in Boston, 1870–1900,* 2nd ed. (Cambridge: Harvard UP, 1978), pp. 121–22, 138–39. Ann D. Keating, *Building Chicago: Suburban Developers and the Creation of a Divided Metropolis* (Columbus: Ohio State UP, 1988), pp. 70–78.

15. DCComsAR, 1885, pp. 173–74, 325–27; 1886, p. 25; 1889, pp. 26, 260.

16. DCComsAR, 1891, p. 279–90; 1893, pp. 320–22; 1894, p. 444–46; 1896, pp. 19, 38. HRApproHrgs, 1898, p. 124; 1899, pp. 41–42. SenApproHrgs, 1903, p. 3. John H. Walker, ed., *Purification of the Washington Water Supply,* 3rd ed. (Washington, D.C.: GPO, 1909), p. 15.

17. DCComsAR,. 1887, p. 113–16. "Cost of converting Rock Creek into a closed sewer," 52nd Cong., 2nd sess. (Jan. 10, 1893), S. Misc. Doc. 21, p. 1. *Evening Star,* Jan. 7, 1893. SenApproHrgs, 1903, p. 78; 1904, pp. 12–16. HRApproHrgs, 1901, p. 130.

18. SenApproHrgs, 1903, pp. 207–12.

19. HRApproHrgs, 1894, pp. 38–41; 1896, p. 26; 1899, p. 8.

20. *National Republican,* July 20, 1883. Washington *Critic,* Mar. 1, 1888.

21. DCComsAR, 1879, p. 386; 1889, p. 258. *National Republican,* July 20, 1883. *Sunday Chronicle,* May 31, 1885.

22. OpinCorpCoun, vol. 3, May 19, 1884, Sept. 6, 1886.

23. William Tindall to A. L. Barber, Jan. 6, 1886, DCComsLS, vol. 19. Washington *Critic,* Jan. 6, 1886. *Washington Post,* Jan. 7, 1886. Commissioner Webb to Representative Hemphill, Mar. 5, 1888, DCComsLS, vol. 23. DCComsAR, 1887, p. 51; 1888, p. 266; 1889, p. 258. CR:50-1 (June 25, 1888), p. 5541. Gutheim, *Worthy of the Nation,* p. 109.

24. DCComsAR, 1889, p. 258. OpinCorpCoun, vol. 5, Nov. 14, 1893. *Evening Star,* Jan. 5, 1889. "Report from Commissioners on certain subdivisions," 52nd Cong., 1st sess. (June 17, 1892), S. Misc. Doc. 180. "Preventing recording of subdivisions . . . in office of recorder of deeds," 53rd Cong., 2nd sess., S. Rept. 88. CR:53-2 (Aug. 23, 1894), pp. 8635–36.

25. DCComsAR, 1889, pp. 258–59. "Extension of streets and avenues in the District of Columbia," 49th Cong., 2nd sess. (Jan. 22, 1887), S. Misc. Doc. 44. "Establishing streets and avenues in the District of Columbia," 49th Cong., 2nd sess. (Feb. 11, 1887), H. Rept. 4019. Washington *Critic,* Mar. 1, 1888. *Evening Star,* Dec. 22, 1888. *Washington Post,* Feb. 18, 1889.

26. Mel Scott, *American City Planning since 1890* (Berkeley: U of California P, 1969), pp. 2–6. Brian Ladd, *Urban Planning and Civic Order in Germany, 1860–1914* (Cambridge: Harvard UP, 1990), chap. 3. Anthony Sutcliffe, *Towards the Planned City* (New York: St. Martin's, 1981), pp. 16–27.

27. WBT-AR, 1890, p. 13; 1891, pp. 29–33. "Permanent System of Highways in the District of Columbia," 51st Cong., 1st sess. (May 22, 1890), H. Rept. 2074. "Highways in the District of Columbia," 52nd Cong., 1st sess. (Feb. 10, 1892), S. Rept. 207. Pamphlet on "Board of Trade Amendment, Highway Act, 1897," in Records of the District Surveyor, entry 99, box 1, file 11, RG 351. *Washington Post,* Nov. 29, 1891. *Evening Star,* Jan. 26, 1892.

28. CR:52-1 (Feb. 19, Mar. 23, Apr. 12, May 23, 1892), pp. 1318–27, 2388–89, 3208, 4568–82. Commissioner Ross to Representative Babcock, Apr. 9, 1898, with commissioners' history of 1893 Highway Act, RecHRep, 55A-F6.2.

29. CR:52-1 (June 30, 1892), pp. 5665–73. CR:52-2 (Feb. 28, 1893), pp. 2249, 2264.

30. Ross to President Harrison, Mar. 2, 1893, DCComsLS, vol. 37. Report of the Streets and Avenues Committee, WBT-AR, 1894, pp. 48–53. Wight to Representative Heard, July 7, 1894, RecHRep, 53A-F7.5. Ross to Representative Babcock, Apr. 9, 1898, RecHRep, 55A-F6.2. *Washington Post,* Nov. 27, 1897. HRApproHrgs, 1902, p. 169.

31. HRApproHrgs, 1899, p. 7.

32. Olmsted to Newlands, Nov. 15, 1891, Olmsted Papers, Library of Congress, reel 25; also, Olmsted's 1887 report on the National Zoo, reel 37. Olmsted to Stewart, Jan. 12, 1892, Olmsted Associates Papers, Library of Congress, box 134, file 2821. Also in Olmsted Associates Papers: Chevy Chase Land Company, box 89, file 1341; National Zoo, box 134, file 2822. References for Olmsted correspondence cited in this and the next two notes were found in Hamilton, Madden, et al., *Historic Preservation Study of Cleveland Park,* pp. 25–32.

33. Moore to McMillan, Apr. 25, 1893, political collection, McMillan Papers, Detroit Public Library. Newlands to Olmsted, July 17, 1894; Charles Powell to Olmsted Assoc., Oct. 17, 1894, Olmsted Associates Papers, box 134, file 2821. CR:53-2 (July 10, Aug. 2, 1894), pp. 7531, 8133. Scott, *American City Planning,* p. 50.

34. DCComsAR, 1886, pp. 40–44; 1890, p. 424; 1894, p. 15; 1895, p. 833. Powell to Olmsted, Feb. 9, 1895, Olmsted Assoc. Papers, box 134, file 2821. DCComsMins, vol. 11, May 12, 1897.

35. "To repeal the Highway Extension Act," 55th Cong., 2nd sess. (May 5, 1898), H. Rept. 1274, p. 7. "Board of Trade Amendment, Highway Act, 1897," p. 11, in District Surveyor's Records, entry 99, box 1, file 11, RG 351. OpinCorpCoun, vol. 8, Aug. 21, 1897. Wyman Cole to District Commissioners, Feb. 23, 1898, RecSen, 55A-F7, box 50. DCComsAR, 1895, p. 832–33. DCComsMins, vol. 14, Aug. 10, 1898.

36. DCComsAR, 1896, pp. 23–24; 1901, vol. 1, pp. 110–12, 118–19. OpinCorpCoun, vol. 8, Jan. 8, 1898. Wyman Cole to Cannon, May 22, 1896, RecHRep, 54A-F3.2. *Evening Star,* Apr. 24, 1896. "To repeal the Highway Extension Act," 55th Cong., 2nd sess. H. Rept. 1274.

37. "Continuing the system of trunk sewers in the District of Columbia," 53rd Cong., 2nd sess. (July 20, 1894), S. Rept. 623. CR:53-3 (Feb. 21, 1895), pp. 2480–82. WBT-AR, 1896, pp. 12–14. *Washington Post,* Jan. 17–23, 1895. "Memorial to Congress of the Joint Executive Committee of the Citizens Associations," 53rd Cong., 2nd sess. (Feb. 1, 1894), S. Misc. Doc. 67, p. 12. Emily E. Briggs to House District Committee, June 24, 1894; and report of W. C. Dodge, June 16, 1894, in papers on the "Trunk Sewer Bond Bill," RecHRep, 53A-F7.5.

38. Ellis Spear to B. H. Warner, June 13, 1894, RecHRep, 53A-F7.5. Brightwood Avenue Citizens Association to the House District Committee, Apr. 21, 1896, RecHRep, 54A-F7.1.

39. WBT-AR, 1895, p. 18. Clipping from A. T. Britton's *Financial Review,* Jan. 24, 1896, RecHRep, 54A-F7.1.

40. DCComsAR, 1896, pp. 23–24. Board of Trade pamphlet and newspaper clippings in surveyor's records, entry 99, box 1, file 11, RG 351. *Washington Post,* Feb. 24, 1898.

41. Documents on Highway Act repeal, Jan. 1898, RecHRep, 55A-F6.2. Also, RecSen, 55A-F7, box 50. "Board of Trade Amendment, Highway Act, 1897," pp. 14–15, surveyor's records, entry 99, box 1, file 11, RG 351; also draft letter on suburban parcels in entry 99, box 2, misc. file 357; and legislation and orders relating to subdivisions in entry 100, box 9. "To repeal the Highway Extension Act," 55th Cong., 2nd sess., H. Rept. 1274. CR:55-2 (May 9, June 9, 1898), pp. 4729–30, 5691. DCComsAR, 1899, vol. 2, p. 146; 1900, p. 31. *Evening Star,* May 7, 10, June 1, 16, 1898. Gutheim, *Worthy of the Nation,* p. 110.

42. Street extension reports include 55th Cong., 2nd sess., H. Rept. 1620; and 55th Cong., 3rd sess., S. Rept. 1605, 1606. HRApproHrgs, 1902, p. 169.

43. Commissioner Wight to Representative Babcock, Jan. 3, 1900, RecHRep, 56A-F6.2. "Relief of Taxpayers from Assessments for Extension of Rhode Island Avenue," 57th Cong., 1st sess. (Jan. 31, 1902), S. Rept. 270.

44. SenApproHrgs, 1903, pp. 9–10. DCComsAR, 1901, vol. 1, p. 112, and vol. 2, p. 161; 1902, vol. 1, pp. 120–21. Macfarland to Allison, June 2, 1902, DCComsLS, vol. 62. "Appropriations for the District of Columbia, 1903," 57th Cong., 1st sess., S. Rept. 1919. Thomas Hensey to House Appropriations Committee, June 20, 1902, RecHRep, 57A-F1.2. *Evening Star,* Jan. 16, 30, 1902. *Washington Post,* Jan. 16, Feb. 12, 1902.

45. DCComsAR, 1901, vol. 1, p. 80; 1902, vol. 1, p. 86. SenApproHrgs, 1903, p. 35. HRApproHrgs, 1902, p. 10; 1903, p. 3. "Advances from the United States Treasury," 56th Cong., 2nd sess. (Jan. 25, 1901), S. Rept. 2031. "Appropriations for the District of Columbia, 1903," 57th Cong., 1st sess., S. Rept. 1919. *Evening Star,* Mar. 6–7, 1901, May 24, 1902. *Washington Post,* Jan. 17, 1902.

46. SenApproHrgs, 1903, p. 9. HRApproHrgs, 1901, pp. 10–11. See 57th Cong., 1st sess., S. Repts. 564, 565, 566, 1062, 1366, 1669.

47. DCComsAR, 1902, p. 7–8, 10–14. "Appropriations for the District of Columbia, 1903," 57th Cong., 1st sess., S. Rept. 1919. Macfarland to Representative Cannon, Nov. 26, 1902, RecHRep, 57A-F1.2. "For a municipal building in Washington," 56th Cong., 2nd sess., H. Rept. 2706. HRApproHrgs, 1903, p. 4. Minutes of the Board of Directors, Jan. 20, 1902, Board of Trade Papers, George Washington U.

48. "Advances from the Treasury," 57th Cong., 2nd sess. (Feb. 5, 1903), H. Rept. 3548. "Appropriations for the District of Columbia, 1903," 57th Cong., 1st sess., H. Rept. 1790, S. Rept. 1919; 1904, 57th Cong., 2nd sess., H. Rept. 3160, S. Rept. 2896. E. W. Whitaker to Speaker Henderson, June 20, 1902, RecHRep, 57A-F1.2. HRApproHrgs, 1902, pp. 8–10. *Evening Star,* Feb. 21, 1902.

49. "Assessment and collection of taxes on personal property," 57th Cong., 1st sess. (Apr. 9, 1902), S. Rept. 1035. "Conference report on 1903 District Appropriations Bill," 57th Cong., 1st sess., H. Rept. 2723, p. 19. SenApproHrgs, 1903, p. 41; 1904, p. 4. DCComsMins, vol. 16, Mar. 9, 1900. DCComsAR, 1902, pp. 17–18. *Evening Star,* Jan. 11, 17, May 23, 1902.

50. John W. Reps, *Monumental Washington* (Princeton: Princeton UP), p. 134. Scott, *American City Planning,* p. 47.

51. Richard E. Foglesong, *Planning the Capitalist City* (Princeton: Princeton UP, 1986), pp. 152, 163.

52. Paul Boyer, *Urban Masses and Moral Order in America, 1820–1920* (Cambridge: Harvard UP, 1978), pp. 266–76.

53. DCComsAR, 1901, p. 8. *Evening Star,* Jan. 16, 18, 1902.
For more detailed accounts see: Jon A. Peterson, "The Nation's First Comprehensive Plan: A Political Analysis of the McMillan Plan for Washington, D.C., 1900–1902," *APA Journal* (Spring 1985): 134–50; and "Hidden Origins of the McMillan Plan for Washington, D.C., 1900–1902," in Antoinette Lee, *Historical Perspectives on Urban Design, Washington, D.C., 1890–1910* (Washington, D.C.: George Washington U Center for Washington Area Studies, 1983), pp. 3–18. Also, Gutheim, *Worthy of the Nation,* chap. 5.

54. William V. Cox, ed., *The Centennial Celebration of the Establishment of the Seat of Government in the District of Columbia* (Washington, D.C.: GPO, 1901), pp. 19–21, 169–76. WBT-AR, 1899, pp. 27–31. Minutes of the general meeting, Jan. 19, 1900, Board of Trade Papers. CEngsAR, 1886, pp. 892–97. Myer, *Bridges and the City of Washington,* p. 18.

55. WBT-AR, 1899, p. 25–27; 1900, pp. 108–9. *Evening Star,* Apr. 29, 1899. "To eliminate grade crossings on the Baltimore and Potomac Railroad," 56th Cong., 1st sess. (Apr. 10, 1900), S. Rept. 928, pp. 3–7. "To eliminate grade crossings of the

Baltimore and Ohio Railroad," 56th Cong., 1st sess. (May 14, 1900), S. Rept. 1303. DCComsMins, vol. 16, Nov. 27, Dec. 27, 1899. Dian Olson Belanger, "The Railroad in the Park: Progress, Politics, and the Pastoral Ideal in Washington" (Master's thesis, George Washington U, 1982), chaps. 3–4. Constance M. Green, *Washington: Capital City* (Princeton: Princeton UP, 1962), pp. 52–55.

56. Bingham to Captain Beach, Dec. 13, 1899, PBO, entry 91, box 31. Bingham to General Wilson, Dec. 17, 1899, with accompanying documents; Bingham to Francis Newlands, Jan. 17, 1900, PBO, entry 91, box 37. "To eliminate grade crossing on the Baltimore and Potomac Railroad," 56th Cong., 1st sess. (Apr. 10, 1900), S. Rept. 928, pp. 20–21. CEngsAR, 1901, p. 3719. "To remove grade crossings of the Baltimore and Potomac Railroad," minority report, 56th Cong., 2nd sess., H. Rept. 2026. Bingham also quoted in Peterson, "Nation's First Comprehensive Plan," pp. 135–41. Reps, *Monumental Washington*, pp. 70–82.

57. Major Bingham to George Harries, May 3, 1899, PBO, entry 91, box 31. Bingham to Warren Manning, June 19, 1899, PBO, entry 91, box 32.

58. Glenn Brown, *Memories, 1860–1930: A Winning Crusade to Revive George Washington's Vision of a Capital City* (Washington, D.C.: W. F. Roberts, 1931), pp. 32–33, 37 ff., 110–12, 205 ff., 259–62. Glenn Brown, ed. *Papers Relating to the Improvement of the City of Washington,* 56th Cong., 2nd sess., S. Doc. 94, pp. 59–69. Peterson, "Nation's First Comprehensive Plan," 141–42. Reps, *Monumental Washington*, 83–92. Gutheim, *Worthy of the Nation*, pp. 77, 115–17. Scott, *American City Planning*, pp. 48–49. William Brian Bushong, "Glenn Brown, the American Institute of Architects, and the Development of the Civic Core of Washington, D.C." (Ph.D. diss., George Washington U, 1988), pp. 18–20, 52–55, 83, 119.

59. Brown, *Memories*, pp. 259–62. Also, Brown, *Papers Relating to Improvement,* pp. 11, 19, 23–34, 83–86. Charles Moore, ed., *Improvement of the Park System of the District of Columbia,* 57th Cong., 1st sess., S. Rept. 166, pp. 43–44.

60. Minutes of the general meeting, Dec. 14, 1900, Board of Trade Papers. Peterson, "Nation's First Comprehensive Plan," 142.

61. Macfarland to McMillan, Jan. 15, 1901, RecSen, 56A-F7, box 46.

62. Moore, *Improvement of the Park System,* pp. 7–8. *Evening Star,* Mar. 9, 1901.

63. Moore, *Improvement of the Park System,* pp. 8–9. Charles Moore, *Autobiography* (photostat manuscript in Moore Collection, Fine Arts Commission Papers, RG 66), chap. 6. Charles Moore, autobiographical letter to "Wheeler," Sept. 21, 1925, Moore Papers, Library of Congress, box 19. Charles Moore, *Daniel Burnham: Architect, Planner of Cities* (New York: Houghton Mifflin, 1916), vol. 1, pp. 136–40. *Evening Star,* Mar. 15, 19, 1901. Brown, *Memories*, pp. 262–67. Reps, *Monumental Washington*, pp. 92–93.

64. Moore, *Improvement of the Park System,* p. 15 and photographs. Moore, *Autobiography*, pp. 89–97. Reps, *Monumental Washington*, chap. 4. Scott, *American City Planning*, pp. 51–52.

65. Moore, *Autobiography*, p. 110. Brown, *Memories*, pp. 206–7, 269–71. McKim to Burnham, Aug. 28, 1901, copy in McKim book, box 2, Moore Papers. Charles Moore, *Daniel Burnham,* vol. 1, chap. 11. Reps, *Monumental Washington*, pp. 99–108, 139–44. Jon A. Peterson, "The Origins of the Comprehensive City Planning Ideal in the United States, 1840–1911" (Ph.D. diss., Harvard U, 1967), pp. 257–58.

66. William H. Wilson, *The City Beautiful Movement* (Baltimore: Johns Hopkins UP, 1989), chap. 3. Judd Kahn, *Imperial San Francisco: Politics and Planning in an American City* (Lincoln: U of Nebraska P, 1979).

67. Minutes of the general meeting, May 2, June 10, 1902, Board of Trade Papers. DCComsMins, vol. 20, Jan. 23, 1902. "Union railroad station at Washington, D.C.," 57th Cong., 1st sess. (Apr. 3, 1902), S. Rept. 982. "Location of union railroad station," 57th Cong., 2nd sess., (Dec. 9, 1902), H. Rept. 2788. "Bridge across the Potomac River," 57th Cong., 1st sess. (Dec. 17, 1901), H. Doc. 138. Moore, *Improvement of*

the Park System, p. 15. *Evening Star,* Mar. 13, June 8, 13, 1901, Jan. 15, Feb. 25, 26, May 16, 1902.

68. See Moore's manuscript review of the McMillan Plan after twenty years, in Moore folder, box 4, Moore Collection, Fine Arts Commission Papers, RG 66.

69. Peterson, "Origins of the City Planning Ideal," pp. 134–35.

70. Stanley K. Schultz, *Constructing Urban Culture: American Cities and City Planning, 1800–1920* (Philadelphia: Temple UP, 1989), pp. 209–17. Stanley K. Schultz and Clay McShane, "To Engineer the Metropolis: Sewers, Sanitation, and City Planning in Late-Nineteenth Century America," *Journal of American History* 65, no. 2 (1978): 389–411. Jon A. Peterson, "The Impact of Sanitary Reform upon American Urban Planning, 1840–1890," *Journal of Social History* 13, no. 1 (1979): 83–104.

71. Sutcliffe, *Towards the Planned City,* pp. 134–38. Donald J. Olsen, *The Growth of Victorian London* (New York: Holmes and Meier, 1976). Anthony Sutcliffe, *The Autumn of Central Paris: The Defeat of Town Planning* (London: Edward Arnold, 1970). Ladd, *Urban Planning and Civic Order,* chap. 4.

72. Sutcliffe, *Towards the Planned City,* p. 198.

73. Wilson, *City Beautiful Movement,* chap. 4. Boyer, *Urban Masses,* chaps. 15–18.

74. *Improvement of the Park System,* pp. 23–24, 38–40, 43–44, 63–65. *Evening Star,* June 6, 1901, Feb. 22, 1902. The aesthetic critique comes from the *Star,* Jan. 14, 1908, clipping in Fine Arts Commission Papers, RG 66, box 77. Also cited in Reps, *Monumental Washington,* pp. 152–53.

75. McKim to Burnham, Aug. 28, 1901, copy in McKim book, box 2, Moore Papers. Brown, *Memories,* pp. 56–59, 96–102, 283–301. Charles Moore, *Makers of Washington* (manuscript in Moore Papers, box 22), pp. 114 ff. Moore, *Autobiography,* pp. 113 ff. Moore, *Burnham,* vol. 1, pp. 184–85, 197, 212–18. Reps, *Monumental Washington,* pp. 74, 92, 144, 155–59.

76. *Evening Star,* Jan. 23, Apr. 1, 2, 1902. Olmsted, Jr., to Olmsted Associates, Mar. 19, 22, 1901, Olmsted Associates Papers, box 134, file 2820. Moore, *Improvement of the Park System,* p. 18.

77. McKim to P. N. Butler, Apr. 11, 1901, box 4, McKim Papers, Library of Congress. Moore's review of McMillan Plan, Moore folder, box 4, Moore Collection, RG 66. McKim to Moore, July 29, 1902, McKim book, box 2, Moore Papers. Root to McMillan, Apr. 11, 1902, box 1, Moore Papers. Moore, *Burnham,* vol. 1, pp. 205–29. Brown, *Memories,* pp. 272, 305–7. See letters from Moore, Burnham, Nicholas Murray Butler, Frank Miles Day, and others to Gallinger and Newlands, Mar. 1904, in Newlands Papers, box 6.

78. See speeches by Newlands on the McMillan Plan, Newlands Papers, box 76, folder 782. Moore to Gallinger, Mar. 12, 1904, in Newlands Papers, box 6. Moore, *Autobiography,* chap. 10. Moore, *Burnham,* vol. 1, p. 213. Gutheim, *Worthy of the Nation,* pp. 131–32. Reps, *Monumental Washington,* pp. 144–49.

79. McKim to Mrs. Frelinghuysen, 1902?, McKim Papers, box 8. Burnham et al., to Taft, Nov. 15, 1906, PBO, Ent. 91, box 30.

80. Cox, *Centennial Celebration,* pp. 61–64. Moore, *Autobiography,* pp. 74–75. Brown, *Memories,* pp. 108–9. CEngsAR, 1901, pp. 3754–56. Charles Moore, *The Life and Times of Charles Follen McKim* (New York: Houghton Mifflin, 1929), pp. 204–22.

81. McMillan to Root, Apr. 9, 1902; Root to McMillan, Apr. 11, 1902; McMillan to Bingham, Apr. 17, 1902: Bingham to General Gillespie, July 5, 1902; General Mackenzie's reply to Burnham, et al., Nov. 1906, with accompanying letters and documents, PBO, entry 91, box 30.

82. Moore's review of McMillan Plan, Moore folder, box 4, Moore Collection, Fine Arts Commission Papers, RG 66. Gutheim, *Worthy of the Nation,* pp. 125, 135, 144, 195–96. Gail Karesh Kassan, "The Old Post Office Building in Washington, D.C.," *RCHS,* 1971–1972, pp. 570–95. Scott, *American City Planning,* pp. 51–54. Nearly every

book on American planning history critiques the McMillan Plan. Sympathetic discussions include Reps, *Monumental Washington,* which labels the 1902 report the century's "first and greatest essay in civic design" (p. 134), and Thomas M. Walton, "The 1901 McMillan Commission: Beaux-Arts Plan for the Nation's Capital" (Ph.D. diss., Catholic U, 1980), p. 33. Lewis Mumford, *The City in History* (New York: Harcourt, Brace, and World, 1961), p. 406, argues that instead of highlighting L'Enfant's "fire barrier," planners should have tried to offset its alienating effects.

83. DCComsAR, 1902, p. 11. Moore, *Autobiography,* p. 156. Reps, *Monumental Washington,* pp. 152–54. Gutheim, *Worthy of the Nation,* p. 152.

84. Frederic Howe, *The City: The Hope of Democracy* (1905; Seattle: U of Washington P, 1967), pp. 239–42. Wilson, *City Beautiful Movement,* chaps. 4, 13.

85. Moore, *Burnham,* vol. 1, pp. 168–69. Moore's review of McMillan Plan, Moore folder, box 4, Moore Collection, Fine Arts Commission Papers, RG 66. Moore, *Improvement of the Park System,* pp. 75 ff. Olmsted, Jr., to E. D. Shaw, Mar. 16, 1906, copy in box 7, Moore Papers. Foglesong, *Planning the Capitalist City,* p. 150.

86. Olmsted, Jr., to E. D. Shaw, Mar. 16, 1906, copy in box 7, Moore Papers.

87. McMillan to Moore, Aug. 7, 1901, box 1, Moore Papers.

88. Howe, *The City,* pp. 239–42.

89. Elbert Peets, "Current Town Planning in Washington," *Town Planning Review* 14, no. 4 (1931): 231–32.

Conclusion

1. Bradley R. Rice, *Progressive Cities: The Commission Government Movement in America, 1901–1920* (Austin: U of Texas P, 1977), pp. 3–18.

2. Rice, *Progressive Cities,* p. 41.

3. Horace E. Deming and Knowlton Mixer, "Is the Commission Form Applicable to Large Cities," in Clinton R. Woodruff, ed., *City Government by Commission* (New York: Appleton, 1911), p. 184. Edwin C. Robbins, ed., *Selected Articles on the Commission Plan of Municipal Government* (Minneapolis: H. W. Wilson, 1912), p. 170. Rice, *Progressive Cities,* pp. 9, 42.

4. Beard quoted in Martin J. Schiesl, *The Politics of Efficiency* (Berkeley: U of California P, 1977), p. 143. Rice, *Progressive Cities,* pp. 78–81, 101–4.

5. Ernest R. Bradford, *Commission Government in American Cities* (New York: Macmillan, 1911), pp. 282–83. Rice, *Progressive Cities,* p. 69. Melvin Holli, *Reform in Detroit: Hazen S. Pingree and Urban Politics* (New York: Oxford UP, 1969), p. 180.

6. Robbins, *Selected Articles,* pp. 89–97. Lincoln Steffens, *The Autobiography of Lincoln Steffens* (New York: Literary Guild, 1931), p. 450.

7. F. E. Chadwick, "The Newport Plan," in Woodruff, *City Government by Commission,* p. 191. Frederic Howe, *The City: The Hope of Democracy* (1905; Seattle: U of Washington P, 1967), pp. 7, 47–48.

8. Howe, *The City,* pp. 1, 9–10.

9. Jon C. Teaford, *The Unheralded Triumph: City Government in America, 1870–1900* (Baltimore: Johns Hopkins UP, 1984). Stanley K. Schultz, *Constructing Urban Culture: American Cities and City Planning, 1800–1920* (Philadelphia: Temple UP, 1989).

10. Richard L. McCormick, *Party Period and Public Policy* (New York: Oxford UP, 1986), p. 14. Christine M. Rosen, *The Limits of Power: Great Fires and the Process of City Growth in America* (Cambridge: Cambridge UP, 1986), pp. 12–35, 334–37. Jon C. Teaford, "Finis for Tweed and Steffens: Rewriting the History of Urban Rule," in Stanley I. Kutler and Stanley N. Katz, eds., *The Promise of American History* (Baltimore: Johns Hopkins UP, 1982), p. 139.

11. Stephen Skowronek, *Building a New American State* (Cambridge: Cambridge UP, 1982), p. viii.

12. Brian Ladd, *Urban Planning and Civic Order in Germany, 1860–1914* (Cambridge: Harvard UP, 1990), chap. 7.

13. Howe, *The City,* p. 48.

14. CR:51-1 (Sept. 17, 1890), p. 10121.

15. *New York Daily Tribune,* Dec. 4, 1863.

Index

Abbott, Carl, 70
Adams, Henry, 17, 51
Aldrich, Nelson, 127–28, 151
Alexander, Columbus, 59, 60, 96, 107–8, 120–21, 125
Alexandria, Va., 6, 59, 238
Alexandria and Washington Railroad, 21, 74
Allison, William B.: as Appropriations Committee chair, 151, 153–55, 249; influence of, 128, 158, 179, 180; and interim commissioners, 106, 110; investigation of Territory by, 77, 98, 160
American Institute of Architects (AIA), 51; and McMillan Plan, 255–57, 262, 263–64
Anacostia, 15–16, 238
Aqueduct tunnel, 165, 245; completed, 192, 196, troubles of, 185–92. See also Washington Aqueduct; Water
Architects, landscape, 173, 246–47; and McMillan Plan, 255, 257
Army Corps of Engineers, 10, 116, 165–66; assistant engineer commissioners, 180–81, 193; and the Comprehensive Plan, 84–85, 88–89, 169, 178; criticisms of, 39, 164–65, 192, 199, 236, 246; and electricity, 194, 228; engineer commissioner, 121, 164, 177–81, 192–93; and extension planning, 241, 243, 246–47; institutional culture of, 11, 166, 178–80, 188, 194, 199, 273; and McMillan Plan, 256, 258, 262–63; and pavements, 9, 34, 37, 86–88, 182–84; personnel assignments in, 172, 179–80; politics of, 164, 166, 177, 196–97; and Potomac Flats, 146, 172, 173–76; and Public Buildings Office, 82, 169; and residents, 165, 177–78, 180–81, 183–84, 191–94, 198, 205, 206–7, 212, 237; and sewerage, 89, 195, 240–41
Asphalt. See Pavements
Asphalt Trust, 183–84

Babcock, Joseph, 151
Babcock, Maj. Orville E., 63, 76, 94; accusations against, 51, 96, 170; and Board of Public Works, 56, 72, 80, 82, 86, 90, 95, 97, 117, 170, 172; as public buildings officer, 169–72
Baker, George F., 76
Baltimore and Ohio Railroad (B&O), 258; antagonism towards, 31–32; and city streets, 211, 250; and northeast Washington, 159, 205, 207
Baltimore and Potomac Railroad, 21. See also Pennsylvania Railroad
Baltimore Sun, 73, 81, 99, 119
Barber, Amzi Lorenzo, 183–84, 239, 242
Barry Farm, 16, 238
Bayard, Thomas, 74, 120
Beach, Capt. Lansing, 179, 180, 198
Beard, Charles, 269–70
Beck, James, 155
Beckwith and Quackenbush (building contractors), 189–91
Bell, Charles J., 217
Berret, James G., 40, 52, 83
Biddle, Col. John, 180, 241
Bingham, Maj. Theodore, 255–56, 262
Birney, William, 216, 221
Black, Capt. William, 132, 179–80
Blackburn, Joseph, 121–22, 128, 150, 151, 178–79
Blacks: and Board of Trade, 213; during Civil War, 18, 40; under the commissioners, 12, 103, 201–2, 274; emancipation of, 40, 60; and home rule, 52, 119–20, 138; housing conditions of, 22, 195, 202; during Reconstruction, 40–42; and suburban expansion, 236, 238, 239; under Territory, 74, 118–19
Blair, Henry W., 199–201, 276
Blake, John B., 36, 59, 60, 61
Blow, Henry T., 104
Board of Health, 86, 91, 119, 131

Board of Public Works, 10, 54, 72–73; contractors and, 63–64, 78–79; finances of,
107–9, 117; procedures of, 56–57, 81–
82, 112, 125; and residents, 73–74; Shepherd's role in, 44, 55, 80
Board of Trade, 44, 177; and commercial-
civic movement, 162, 209; and commissioner appointments, 136, 137, 245–
46; and Highway Act (1893), 234, 236,
243–49; and home rule, 203, 273; influence of, 10, 148, 199, 201, 205, 208–12,
214–15, 221–23; leadership of, 216–21;
and McMillan, 151–52, 197, 211; and
McMillan Plan, 253–60; membership of,
213–22; publicity activities of, 202, 210,
212, 223; and·residents, 215, 222, 234,
248–49; and urban professionals, 165,
235, 273–74; and utilities, 226–27, 229;
and water filtration, 195–98
Borrowing, public, 56, 64, 107, 108–12. *See
also* Finances; Taxes
Bowen, Sayles J., 107; as radical mayor,
33–34, 41–42, 90, 119
Brentano, Lorenzo, 164
Briggs, Emily E., 74
Brightwood, 205, 239, 248
Britton, Alexander T., 217, 248
Brodhead, J. M., 109
Brookland, 205, 238
Brooks, Noah, 4
Brown, Austin, 239, 242
Brown, Chapin, 239
Brown, Glenn, 255, 257, 261–62
Brown, Samuel P., 48, 53, 55, 238–39
Brownell, Blaine, 209
Buchanan, James, 41, 168
Buckner, Aylett, 112
Building inspection, 139–40
Burnham, Daniel H., 206, 257–64
Business, Washington, 7, 231; and Board of
Trade, 213, 216–21; and commissioners,
136–37, 181; enterprises stressed by, 88,
223–25; and home rule, 10, 202–4;
and the improvers, 43, 46, 66–68; and
neighborhood groups, 207–8, 217, 221;
"Northern" spirit in, 31, 47, 71, 216;
practices of, 50, 63, 66–68, 78–79; and
radicals, 41–43; retail trade, 23, 183, 217,
221, 223; "Southernized" image of, 30–
31; Territory's legacy for, 94, 99–100.
See also Economic structure; Real estate
developers

Cabin John Bridge, 26, 167
California Syndicate, 7, 159–60, 246
Cameron, Simon, 45, 98
Canal. *See* Washington Canal
Cannon, Joseph, 7; and District finances,
153, 154, 183, 251; and McMillan Plan,
260, 262, 263
Capital Traction Co., 161, 229, 250
Capitol, extension of, 4, 15, 168
Capitol Hill, 15; neighborhood groups in,
207, 215; perceived neglect of, 74, 183,
205; water shortages on, 185, 191, 240
Casey, Col. Thomas L., 172, 173, 185, 191
Cassatt, Alexander, 258
Centennial celebration (1900), 8, 137, 254,
262
Center Market, 50, 221
Chandler, William E., 50–51, 72
Chesapeake and Ohio Canal, 22, 158
Chesbrough, Ellis, 27, 187
Chevy Chase, 161–62, 238. *See also* Newlands, Francis G.; Suburbs
Chipman, Norton P., 55, 61, 75, 98
Cities: capital, 1–3, 27–29; civic identity
of, 100, 223; commercial-civic movements in, 209, 214–15; condition of,
26–30; finances of, 64, 79–80, 142–46;
governance of, 114–15, 205, 268–70;
methods for analyzing, 13–14, 272; municipal engineering in, 184; public health
in, 131; subdivision of, 239–40, 242–43;
utilities in, 226–28, 231–32; water filtration in, 196–97. *See also* Planning, urban
Citizens Association (1871), 56, 57, 59, 61
Citizens associations. *See* Neighborhood
groups
Civil War, effects on Washington of, 18–
20, 39–40, 70–71
Clephane, Lewis, 59, 62, 98; and the improvers, 48, 50, 53, 67, 96
Cleveland, Grover, 136, 193
Cluss, Adolph, 48–49, 51, 62, 107, 160;
in District improvement controversy,
80–81, 86–87, 89, 105, 117, 170, 217
Columbia Institution for the Deaf, Dumb,
and Blind, 32, 159, 217, 238
Commercial-civic movements: Board of
Trade as example of, 10, 201, 209, 221; in
city politics, 213–15, 232, 268–69
Commissioners, interim board of (1874–
78), 102, 104–11, 125–26
Commissioners of the District of Columbia

(1878–1967), 94, 273; appointment of, 133, 135–38; and Army Corps of Engineers, 177–79, 193; and Board of Trade, 211, 222; and Congress, 128–29, 138–39, 152–53, 250; and engineer commissioner, 121, 164, 177–81, 192–93; and McMillan Plan, 253–54, 256, 258; origins of, 52–53, 102–3, 114–23; out-of-town views of, 10, 201, 204, 268–71, 275–76; procedures of, 130–33, 139–41, 147–48; and residents, 10, 129, 148, 200, 205–7; and suburban services, 234, 242–43, 248–50; and taxation, 124–28; and utilities, 227–29

Commission format: and Gilded Age government, 103, 114–15, 123–24, 200, 204; in Progressive era, 268–70

Comprehensive Plan of Improvements, 44, 72, 205; analysis of, 83–94; and Army Corps of Engineers, 84–85, 88, 169, 178; finances of, 55–56, 64, 76–77, 107–11; as nationalist enterprise, 70–71; within promotional tradition, 10–11, 46, 65–66, 273; Shepherd's departure from, 56, 77–78

Conflict of interest: in Territory, 46, 52, 63–64, 67–68, 78–79, 162. *See also* Corruption

Congress, 149–58; and Army Corps of Engineers, 164, 166, 178–79, 187, 191–94, 197; and blacks, 40–41, 202; and Board of Trade, 221–22, 248–49; and commissioners, 130, 138–39; and commission proposal, 52–53, 114–15, 118, 120–23, 131, 276; disputes between houses of, over Washington, 130, 154–57, 197, 207, 233–34, 245, 248–52, 260; and District finances, 8, 54, 107–13, 145–47, 153–57; and federal-local relations, 34–35, 102, 128–29; and half-and-half principle, 212, 233; and the Mall, 21; members of, personal interests in Washington, 158–62; and Public Buildings Office, 38–39, 169, 172; and residents, 152–53, 205–6, 208; and sewerage, 181–82; and street extensions, 242, 249–50; and taxation, 125–28; and Territory, 49–50, 53–54, 76–81, 83, 97–98, 117; and utilities, 29, 136–37, 226–29; and Washington Canal, 22, 90. *See also* District Committee, House; District Committee, Senate; House of Representatives; Senate

Cooke, Henry D., 29, 52–53, 62, 94, 120; accusations against, 49, 63, 68, 96; as territorial governor, 55–56, 72–73, 75, 76, 111; and Washington Market Company, 50–51; in Washington social life, 50, 63

Corcoran, William W., 39–40, 50, 52, 57, 59, 63, 87

Corruption, 38, 203; Army Corps of Engineers accused of, 191–93; Babcock accused of, 51, 96, 170, 178; in territorial period, 45–46, 95–97. *See also* Conflict of interest

Cox, Jacob D., 164, 178–79, 180

Cox, Walter S., 59, 61

Cox, William V., 137

Cranford Paving Co., 217

Crawford, Thomas, 15

Dana, Charles A., 51, 75, 118

Davis, Jefferson, 168–69

Dawes, Henry L., 110

DeGolyer and McClelland (paving firm), 78

Delafield, Gen. Richard, 22, 89

Democratic party: and the commission proposal, 119–20, 121–22; and District finances, 109–12; in District improvement controversy, 76, 101; stance of, towards Washington, 102, 113, 149–50, 154

Dennison, William O., 104, 110

Dent, Josiah, 126–29, 132, 134

De Smedt, E. J., 184

Dickens, Charles, 6–7

District bill, 154, 155

District Building, 141–42, 250, 264

District Committee, House, 37, 139, 158; and Appropriations Committee, 153–54; compared to Senate District Committee, 150–52; and Highway Act (1893), 248, 249; investigations by, 72, 77–78, 90–91, 112, 127–28; procedures of, 149, 152–53

District Committee, Senate, 138, 153, 158, 211, 253; and Board of Trade, 201, 212; and commissioner appointments, 136; compared to House District Committee, 150–52; and expert consultants, 197, 235; and street extensions, 234, 244, 248–50; and utilities regulation, 227–28

"District Day," 149

District improvement controversy. *See* Board of Public Works; Corruption; Shepherd, Alexander R.; Territory of the District of Columbia

District of Columbia: Alexandria, retro-
cession of, 6; consolidation of, 31, 52–
54; population of and federal employ-
ment in, 18–19; proposal to move capital
from, 30, 95
Douglass, Frederick, 55, 57, 60, 73, 119, 138
Douglass, John W., 134, 136, 193, 202
Downing, Andrew Jackson: work on Mall
of, 20–21, 171, 255, 260, 263
Drainage. *See* Sewerage
Dunnell, Mark, 123
Dupont Circle, 160
Durant, Thomas J., 60

Eastern Market, 49
Eaton, D. L., 97
Eckington, 229–30, 238
Economic structure of Washington, 6, 213,
223–25; effect of Comprehensive Plan
on, 88, 99–100
Edmonds, James B., 134, 135
Edmonston, Charles E., 59, 61, 73
Edmunds, George, 26, 54, 74, 131, 169
Edson, John Joy, 212, 217
Electricity: underground conduits for, 154,
194–95, 228–29, 231
Ellicott, Andrew, 5
Emery, Matthew G., 34, 42, 51, 137
Employees, federal, 18–19
Employees, municipal, 105, 132–33, 138–
42, 252
Engineering, municipal, 184, 259; under
Army Corps of Engineers, 172, 181–84,
193; practices of, 67, 82
Evans, John O., 49, 57, 62, 68, 96; as con-
tractor, 87, 90

Federal-local relations: Board of Trade
and, 222–25; and commission proposal,
102–3; and half-and-half principle, 145–
47, 199–200, 203; and public works,
36–37, 172; strains in, 157, 234–36, 245,
250–52; and utilities, 225–28; views on,
8–9, 34–35, 52–53, 115–16. *See also* Finances, District of Columbia
Federal Triangle, 265; Murder Bay slum in,
22, 90, 258
Fessenden, W. P., 33
Finances, District of Columbia, 22–23, 33,
142–47, 153–57, 245, 250–52; and half-
and-half principle, 54, 102–3, 117–18,

145–47, 150, 157, 192, 212, 245; under
the Territory, 75–77, 109, 111; and U.S.
Treasury, 126–28. *See also* Borrowing,
public; Federal-local relations
Fine Arts, Commission of, 262, 264
Flooding: central Washington subject to,
24–25, 91–93, 174, 182. *See also* Potomac
River; Sewerage
Floyd, John, 168–69
Foggy Bottom, 20, 148, 240
Foglesong, Richard, 253
Ford's Theater, 140, 141–42
Freedman's Bank (Freedman's Savings and
Trust Co.), 49, 96–97
Freedmen's Bureau, 16, 97, 238
French, Benjamin B., 41, 50; comments of,
4, 25, 39, 54; as Commissioner of Public
Buildings and Grounds, 35–38, 169, 171,
172

Gallinger, Jacob, 201, 227–28
Garbage disposal, 148
Garfield, James A., 78–79, 138, 175; com-
ments of, 21, 73, 117
Garrett, John Work, 32
Gallaudet College. *See* Columbia Institution
for the Deaf, Dumb, and Blind
Georgetown, 17, 31, 205–6, 216
Gilfillan, James, 126–28
Gleason, Albert, 170
Glover, Charles, 210, 217, 221, 240–41
Godkin, E. L., 25, 81–83, 99
Goodrich, Carter, 70
Gorman, Arthur P., 151, 157–58, 193–94
Government, Gilded Age: methods for ana-
lyzing, 13–14, 103, 123–24
Grand Army of the Republic (G.A.R.), 55,
138, 157
Grant, Albert, 61, 86
Grant, Ulysses S., 105; and Babcock, 51,
170; and Shepherd, 45, 52, 101, 103; and
the Territory, 34, 55, 81
Great Falls: dam at, 4, 166, 196
Greeley, Horace, 17, 30, 75, 276
Green, Constance M., 94
Greene, Lt. Francis V., 184

Half-and-half principle. *See under:* Con-
gress; Federal-local relations; Finances
Hamlin, Hannibal, 48, 53–54
Harper's Monthly, 3, 4, 6

Harries, George H., 199, 212, 217, 220, 231
Harrington, Richard, 95–96
Harris, Carl, 213
Harris, Isham, 138, 151, 177, 245
Haussmann, Baron Georges-Eugène, 259;
    nationalism in public works of, 2–3, 5,
    68–69; politics in public works of, 27–
    29, 82–83
Hayes, Rutherford B., 121, 126, 133
Hays, Samuel P., 204, 205
Health, public, 131, 148, 195–97, 259. *See
    also* Board of Health
Hemphill, John, 245, 249
Henderson, David, 156–57
Hendricks, Thomas, 53
Henry, Joseph, 72, 89, 90
Hering, Rudolph, 91, 195, 197
Herriot, F. I., 269
Highway Act (1893), 242–50. *See also*
    Streets, extension of; Suburbs, service
    extensions to
Hildreth, Richard, 42
Hine, Lemon G., 134, 136
Home rule: abolition of, 10, 114, 121–23;
    absence of, 221–22, 228, 231–32, 272–
    76; Congress and, 104–5, 199–201; resi-
    dents' attitudes towards, 52, 103, 115–16,
    200, 201, 203–4, 276
House of Representatives: Appropriations
    Committee of, 117, 139, 153–57, 199–
    200, 207, 241, 250; and commission pro-
    posal, 117–18, 121–23; and Highway Act
    (1893), 245, 246–47; and McMillan Plan,
    255–56; stance of, towards Washington,
    149–51, 212, 233–34; and territorial bill
    (1871), 54, 116
Howe, Frederic: on urban planning, 264,
    265; on utilities, 228, 232; on Washing-
    ton government, 268, 271, 276
Hoxie, Capt. Richard L., 105; and aqueduct
    tunnel, 187–89; as assistant engineer
    commissioner, 179, 182, 185; under in-
    terim commissioners, 106–7, 112, 125–
    26, 178; and pavements, 86–87, 183; and
    sewerage, 93, 180, 181
Hoxie, Vinnie Ream, 105, 188
Humphreys, Gen. A. A., 56, 86–87

Improvement, municipal, 9
Improvers, the, 52, 95, 198, 273; character-
    istics of, 57–62; and federal-local rela-
tions, 116–17, 120; Shepherd faction de-
    fined as, 46; and suburban expansion,
    237, 239; in territorial politics, 54–56
Ingalls, John J., 122, 150, 151, 193
Interior Department, 34, 35, 168
"Island, the," 21

Jacksonian movement: nationalism in,
    69–70
Jefferson, Thomas, 5, 25, 117
Johnson, Andrew, 38, 40–41
Joint Executive Committees of the Citizens
    Associations (1894), 204, 205, 208, 215–
    21, 248. *See also* Neighborhood groups

Keller, Morton, 70
Kelly, Moses, 49, 96
Kendall, Amos, 36, 238
Ketcham, John H., 104
Kilbourn, Hallett, 53, 57, 62–63, 68, 176;
    and Freedman's Bank scandal, 49, 96;
    paving "ring" of, 49–50, 87, 107
Knott, J. Proctor, 34

Lafayette Square, 36, 59, 87, 170, 260
Langston, John M., 119
Latta, James M., 65
LeDroit Park, 239, 242
L'Enfant, Pierre Charles, 4–5, 17, 19–21,
    117, 257
L'Enfant Plan, 255, 256; ambitiousness of,
    4–5, 19; criticisms of, 24, 86, 117; exten-
    sion of, 236, 237, 242, 249; and McMillan
    Plan, 258, 267
Lenôtre, André, 257, 260
Library of Congress, 166, 172, 260, 263
Lincoln, Abraham, 4, 15, 35, 38, 48
Lincoln Memorial, 260–61, 263
Lincoln Square, 37, 171
List, Friedrich, 69, 71
Lodge, Henry Cabot, 137–38
Logan, John A., 30, 76
Long Bridge, 176, 205, 258
Ludlow, Col. William, 179, 192–93
Lydecker, Maj. Garret J., 180–81, 187–92,
    202

McDonald, Terrence J., 64
Macfarland, Henry B. F.: as commissioner,
    135, 137, 158, 250–52, 256; views of, 45,
    203

McKim, Charles F., 257, 261–62
McKim, Mead, and White (architectural firm), 261, 264
McKinley, William, 8, 133, 137, 180, 217, 254
McKnight, John W., 63
McLean, John R., 226, 228
McMillan, James, 258; and Board of Trade, 151–52, 201, 211, 212; and District appointments, 135, 136–38; and McMillan Plan, 254–56, 260–62, 265; outlook and politics of, 158–59, 162, 232; and railroads, 211, 254–55; as Senate District Committee chair, 151, 153–54; and street extensions, 237, 245, 246–47, 249–50; and utilities, 228–31; and urban professionals, 165, 273–74; and water filtration, 197
McMillan Plan, 20, 162, 206; and Army Corps of Engineers, 173, 258, 262–63; critiques of, 235, 260, 263, 265, 267, 274; politics of, 12, 137, 235–36, 258, 260–65; reception of, 257–60; results of, 263–67; as urban planning, 252–53, 255–60
Madison, James, 5, 116
Magruder, James A., 53, 55, 59, 79, 109, 120
Mall, the, 20–21, 28, 170–71; railroads and, 74, 89, 206, 211, 254–55, 258. See also McMillan Plan
Massachusetts Avenue, 193, 238
Meigs, Gen. Montgomery C., 56; and sewerage, 90, 91; and streets, 84–87, 169; and Washington Aqueduct, 166–69, 185–91
Memorial Bridge, 254, 258, 261
Meridian Hill, 239, 247
Merrick, Richard T., 52, 55, 57, 63, 99
Metropolis (sometimes Metropolitan) Paving Co., 49, 50, 56, 67, 96
Metropolitan Railroad (streetcar company), 29, 48, 239
Michler, Maj. Nathaniel, 39, 84–85, 87, 90, 171
Miller, Lt. Col. A. M., 197–98
Moore, Charles, 7, 99; and Army Corps of Engineers, 197, 246, 262; and McMillan Plan, 256–60, 263, 264–65; as McMillan's political secretary, 135, 137–38, 151, 158, 159
Morgan, Thomas P., 134
Morrill, Lot: and commission proposal, 41, 52–53, 115–16, 118, 120–22, 132
Morton, Oliver P., 54, 76, 120–22

Mount Pleasant, 205, 239, 240
Mullett, Alfred B., 51, 57, 62, 120; and Board of Public Works, 55, 72, 78, 80, 82, 90, 95
Murder Bay. See Federal Triangle

Napoleon III, 2–3, 11, 69, 83
Nation, 25, 81
Nationalism: and capital cities, 2–3; Democrats and, 113; in efforts to improve Washington, 3–4, 7–9, 47; in post-Reconstruction United States, 103, 150; and promotional tradition, 10, 69–71, 273
National Zoo, 157, 245
Neighborhood groups, 204–8, 221, 237, 248; and home rule, 204, 273; leadership of, 207, 215–21
Newlands, Francis G., 237–38, 256, 261–62; and Capital Traction Co., 161, 229, 231; and Chevy Chase, 160–61, 233
New National Era, 55, 60, 73, 119
New York Sun, 51, 75, 96, 118
New York Tribune, 15, 276; in District improvement controversy, 52, 75, 78, 118, 119
Nicolson, Samuel, 37
Northeast Washington, 32, 206–8, 238
North East Washington Citizens Association, 205, 206, 207–8
Northern Liberty Market: demolition of, 74
Northwest Washington, 17, 238–39; alleged favoritism towards, 148, 156, 182–83, 205–7, 216, 233, 241
Noyes, Crosby S., 41, 189, 203, 217–18
Noyes, Theodore, 203, 211, 215, 217, 222, 254

"Old citizens": characteristics of, 57–62; outlook of, 46–47, 54, 63–64, 83, 85–86, 119, 120, 273. See also Territory of the District of Columbia, opposition to
Olmsted, Frederick Law, Jr., 247; and McMillan Plan, 233, 236, 255, 257, 264–65
Olmsted, Frederick Law, Sr., 28, 233, 263; Washington work of, 20–21, 56, 161, 173, 246

Parker, Myron M., 207–8; and Board of Trade, 208–9, 210, 213, 220–21, 243; as commissioner, 135, 245–46
Parks, 28, 146, 170–71, 173. See also McMil-

lan Plan; Mall, the; Potomac Park; Rock Creek Park
Parsons, Richard, 78
Partisanship: in commissioner appointments, 133, 135; and District finances, 156–57; in District improvement controversy, 57, 60–61, 113, 170; and federal-local relations, 149–50
Pavements, 9, 23–24, 27, 156, 240; asphalt, 27, 86–88, 182–84; Board of Public Works and, 49–50, 77–78, 86–88; wood block, 27, 37, 77–78, 86–87, 108, 183, 207. *See also* Streets
Peets, Elbert, 267
Pennsylvania Avenue, 4, 17, 22–24; paving of, 23, 37, 86–88, 182
Pennsylvania Railroad, 176, 211, 250; and the Mall, 21, 89, 206, 254–55, 258
Phelps, Seth L., 126–27, 132, 134
Planning, urban, 12, 242–43, 252–53, 259, 271–72; Comprehensive Plan as, 84; McMillan Plan as, 235, 255–60
Poland, Luke, 117–18
Police, Metropolitan, 39, 116
Post Office tower, 255, 263
Potomac Electric Power Co., 229, 231
Potomac Park, 176–77, 258, 262
Potomac River: docks, 17, 223; flats, 6, 20, 91; pollution in, 26, 89, 91, 195–96; reclamation of, 94, 146, 173–76, 181–82, 205
Powell, Capt. Charles F., 247
Press, the, 137, 236; and Army Corps of Engineers, 181, 189–93; and Board of Trade, 209–10, 217; and commission format, 268, 270; in District improvement controversy, 47, 56, 75; and home rule, 121, 203. *See also publications by name*
Professionals, urban: and Army Corps of Engineers, 165, 173, 194–98, 236, 255–56, 262–63; and sewerage, 91–94; and urban governance, 204, 214–15, 269–72; in Washington's governance, 11–12, 162–63, 232, 235–36, 256, 263–65, 273–74. *See also* Engineering, municipal; Planning, urban
Progress, notions of, 42–43, 46–47, 235–36
Promotional tradition: and Board of Trade, 215, 232; and Comprehensive Plan, 46, 65–66, 83, 99–100; and nineteenth-century governance, 10–12, 69–71; persistence of, in Gilded Age Washington, 10, 162, 222, 253, 273–75; and public works, 234–36
Property owners, 201, 207, 243, 247–49
Public Buildings and Grounds, Office of: before 1867, 35–39, 116; under Army Corps of Engineers, 39, 80, 82, 84, 146, 169, 172–73, 262
Public works: financing of, 33, 250–51; techniques and practices, under Shepherd, 83–94. *See also* Engineering, municipal

Railroads, 31; on city streets, 159, 205, 206, 208, 211, 254; and the Mall, 21, 28. *See also* Baltimore & Ohio Railroad; Pennsylvania Railroad; Union Station
Randall, Samuel J., 110, 112, 153, 154
Raymond, Maj. Charles, 193
Reagan, John, 122, 157
Real estate developers: and Comprehensive Plan, 65–66, 73; and Rock Creek Park, 157, 233; and service extensions, 182, 241–42; and suburban expansion, 161–62, 225, 236–41; and transit, 229–31
Reid, Whitelaw, 75
Reps, John W., 252–53
Republican party: blacks and, 40–41, 103, 119–20; and commission proposal, 120, 122; in District improvement controversy, 10–11, 46, 48, 53–54, 60–61, 66, 68, 76–77, 98, 101, 170; and interim commissioners, 110, 113; and patronage, 105, 138; stance of, towards Washington, 113, 150; and Washington radicals, 9–10, 41–42
Richards, Maj. A. C., 22, 95
Riddle, Albert G., 61
Riggs, George W., 52–53, 59–61, 63, 87
Robert, Col. Henry, 179
Rock Creek, 26, 240
Rock Creek Park, 28; politics of, 157, 193–94, 233–34, 236, 245
Rock Creek Railway, 161
Roosevelt, Robert, 68, 72
Roosevelt, Theodore, 257, 262
Root, Elihu, 261
Ross, John W.: as commissioner, 132, 134, 136, 177, 200, 227, 231, 245

Safe-burglary affair, 95–96
St. Elizabeths Hospital, 15–16, 238

Saint-Gaudens, Augustus, 257
Saks, Isadore, 213, 221, 223
Sands, F. P. B., 136–37, 227
Sargent, Aaron A., 120–21
Schenck, Robert C., 38
Scott, Mel, 263
Searle, Henry R., 68
Senate, 149–51, 168, 207–8; Appropri-
ations Committee of, 139, 153–56, 241;
and commission proposal, 120, 122; and
Highway Act (1893), 244–45; rejection
of Shepherd by, 45, 101–2. *See also* Congress; District Committee, Senate
Senate Parks Commission. *See* McMillan
Plan
Sewerage, 24–27; Army Corps of Engineers
and, 175, 181–82; Board of Public Works
and, 89–94, 106–7; B Street system of,
91, 94, 174, 181–82; combined system
of, 93, 180; Hering plan for, 91–92, 94,
195, 240, 248; in suburbs, 240–41
Sharon, William, 160
Shepherd, Alexander R., 53, 96, 120, 237;
accomplishments of, 72–74; arrogance
of, 63, 72, 73–75, 81; assessments of, 10,
44–46, 66, 68–69, 88, 94–95, 97–100;
and Babcock, 172; blacks and, 74, 119;
and Bowen's mayoralty, 41–43; business
activities of, 49–51; conflict of interest
and, 63, 68; contractors and, 78–79, 97;
and District finances, 65, 76–77, 111;
domination of Board of Public Works by,
55–56, 80; early career of, 31, 33, 47–
48, 57, 59; and federal-local relations,
116–17; Ulysses S. Grant and, 52, 101–3;
and interim commissioners, 105–6, 108;
later life of, 45, 98–99; sewerage and,
89–94, 181; streets and, 85–87, 182. *See
also* Board of Public Works; Comprehensive Plan of Improvements; Improvers,
the; Territory of the District of Columbia
Shepherd, Arthur, 112
Shepherd, Mary, 99
Shepherd Row, 49
Sherman, John, 50, 54, 110–11, 159, 179,
239
Sherman, Gen. William T., 105, 159, 179,
188
Sixteenth Street: extension of, 249–50
Slavery. *See* Blacks
Smith, Thomas W., 215, 221
Smithsonian grounds. *See* Mall, the

Smithsonian Institution, 62, 89, 157, 255,
260, 263
Southard, Samuel, 34, 117
South Washington, 21; as industrial re-
gion, 148, 215; neighborhood groups in,
205–7, 215; railroads in, 205–6, 211
Spear, Ellis, 216, 221, 248
Staples, O. G., 217
State, War, and Navy Building, 30, 51, 91,
171, 172
Steffens, Lincoln, 270–71
Stellwagen, E. J., 234
Stevens, Thaddeus, 29, 37, 217
Stewart, William M., 7, 41, 120, 256; in District improvement controversy, 80, 160;
and real estate, 159–61, 233, 246
Streetcars. *See* Transit
Streets, 4–5, 31, 73–74; extension of, 240,
242–50; neighborhood rivalries over,
182, 205–7; "parking" of, 34, 84–86. *See
also* Pavements
Suburbs: growth patterns of, 205, 237–39;
neighborhood groups in, 205–6, 207; service extensions to, 225, 234, 236–37,
240–42; subdivision of, 242–43, 249;
and transit, 229–31
Supervising Architect of the Treasury, Office of, 51, 264
Symons, Maj. Thomas W., 188–89, 195–
96, 240, 242–43

Taxes, 124–25, 139, 211, 251–52. *See also*
Taxes, improvement
Taxes, improvement, 27–28; 182, 234,
244–45, 247, 249–50; resistance to, 33,
73, 77, 125–28
Tayler, R. W., 109–10
Teaford, Jon C., 142
Territory of the District of Columbia (1871–
74), 52–54, 66–68, 81–83; finances of,
75–77, 124–25; investigations of, 49–50,
72, 76–82, 109; legislature of, 53, 55, 56,
63, 66, 119; opposition to, 45–46, 54–57,
60–61, 64, 72, 75, 79, 107. *See also* Board
of Public Works; Comprehensive Plan of
Improvements
Thompson, Jacob, 34, 116
Thompson, John W., 47–48
Thurman, Allen G., 97–98, 105, 106
Tiber Creek, 21–22, 91
Tidal Basin: origins of, 173–74
Tindall, William, 141

Todd, Charles Burr, 4, 7
Townsend, Lt. Curtis, 189–91
Townshend, Smith, 131
Transit, 29–30, 148, 208; cable, 153; and suburbs, 161, 221, 237, 240; underground conduits for, 229–31
Treasury Department, 96; and commissioners, 126–28, 140; and interim commissioners, 107–10; and Territory, 79, 107, 109, 125
Trollope, Frances, 6
Truesdell, George, 220–21; as commissioner, 135, 141, 202; as developer, 229–31, 238; and Highway Act (1893), 243–44, 246
Twain, Mark, 17, 18–19, 67
Tweed, William M. ("Boss"), 26, 56; Shepherd compared to, 45, 47, 54, 80, 113
Twining, Maj. William, 132, 173–75, 187, 206

Union Station, 206, 255, 258, 261
Uniontown, 16, 238
United States Electric Co., 229, 231
Usher, John P., 34, 38
Utilities: regulation of, 136–37, 225–32; and suburbs, 240

Vandenburg, J. V. W., 97

Wallach, Richard, 25, 40, 42, 90
Waring, Col. George, 26, 175, 180
Warner, Brainard, 207, 234; and Board of Trade, 210, 216–17, 221, 243, 248
Washington, George, 5–6, 19, 44, 100, 117
Washington and Georgetown Railroad, 29, 161
Washington Aqueduct, 4, 25, 26, 113; construction of, 82, 166–68; finances of, 145, 185. *See also* Aqueduct tunnel; Water
Washington Bee, 201–2
Washington Canal, 6, 21–23, 89–91
Washington Chronicle, 42, 56, 90
Washington City (municipality, 1802–71), 31, 33, 40, 115–16
Washington Club, 52, 74, 96
Washington County, 31, 225, 236–37

Washington Critic, 62, 121
Washington *Daily Patriot*, 55–57, 59–60, 66, 119
Washington *Evening Star*, 41, 133, 189, 192; on Congress, 153, 154; in District improvement controversy, 44, 56, 62, 65, 76; and home rule, 121, 135–36, 202–3; and McMillan Plan, 254, 260
Washington Gas-Light Co., 136, 226–28
Washington Market Co., 50–51, 141
Washington Medical Society, 195–98
Washington Monument, 4, 17, 172
Washington *National Intelligencer*, 1, 3, 24, 25, 32, 56
Washington *National Republican*, 48, 56, 203
Washington Post, 62, 156, 191, 208, 226, 243; and commissioners, 121, 133, 137
Washington Railway and Electric Co. ("Werco"), 231
Water, 26, 160, 240; filtration of, 195–98; finances of, 146, 185; shortages of, 166, 185, 196. *See also* Aqueduct tunnel; Washington Aqueduct
Webb, William B., 130, 134, 136
Weber, Max, 100, 223
Weigley, Russell, 166–67
Weller, Michael, 217, 221
West, Henry L., 135, 137–38
West, Joseph R., 134, 135, 202
Wheatley, Samuel E., 133, 134, 136, 210, 217
White House, 17, 35, 63, 173; remodeling of, 255, 261–62
Wight, John B., 132, 135, 217
Wilkins, Beriah, 209–10, 217
Willard, Henry, 59, 105, 120, 210, 217
Willard Hotel, 59, 217, 275
Wilson, Jeremiah, 217
Wilson, Col. John M., 172, 234
Winston, Frederick, 112
Wood blocks. *See* Pavements
Woodward, Samuel W., 203, 217, 221
Woodward and Lothrop (department store), 23, 217
Wright, Carroll D., 6, 8, 45–46
Wright, Gen. Horatio, 187–88